Data Structures and their Implementation

Robert J. Baron
The University of Iowa

Linda G. Shapiro
Virginia Polytechnic Institute
Formerly at Kansas State University

Van Nostrand Reinhold/University Computer Science Series

VAN NOSTRAND REINHOLD COMPANY
NEW YORK   CINCINNATI   TORONTO   LONDON   MELBOURNE

QA
76.9
D35
B37

Van Nostrand Reinhold Company Regional Offices:
New York Cincinnati

Van Nostrand Reinhold Company International Offices:
London Toronto Melbourne

Copyright © 1980 by Van Nostrand Reinhold Company Inc.

Library of Congress Catalog Card Number: 79-18643
ISBN: 0-442-20586-4

All rights reserved. No part of this work covered by the copyright hereon may
be reproduced or used in any form or by any means—graphic, electronic, or
mechanical, including photocopying, recording, taping, or information storage
and retrieval systems—without permission of the publisher.

Manufactured in the United States of America

Published by Van Nostrand Reinhold Company Inc.
135 West 50th Street, New York, N.Y. 10020

Published simultaneously in Canada by Van Nostrand Reinhold Ltd.

15 14 13 12 11 10 9 8 7 6 5 4 3

Library of Congress Cataloging in Publication Data
Baron, Robert J
    Data structures and their implementation.

    Includes index.
    1. Data structures (Computer science)
I. Shapiro, Linda G., joint author. II. Title.
QA76.9.D35B37   001.6'42   79-18643
ISBN 0-442-20586-4

To our parents

Van Nostrand Reinhold
University Computer Science Series

DATA STRUCTURES AND THEIR IMPLEMENTATION, by Robert J. Baron and Linda G. Shapiro

Preface

Data structures are used in all areas of computer science. Compilers use stacks, symbol tables, and parse trees; operating systems maintain lists of processes and files and employ memory management schemes that use lists or tables of available space; programs in artificial intelligence use stacks, queues, sets, search trees, tables, and graphs; and database systems use strings, lists, trees, rings, and tables. The purpose of this book is to introduce the computer science student to the most commonly used data structures and their implementation. Algorithms are presented for operations on all major data structures, and examples show the use of data structures in various areas of computer science. Particular emphasis is placed on memory management.

This book is organized around implementation techniques. We believe that examples of standard, efficient, or novel implementations will be more helpful to the student than techniques or algorithms without mentioning programming details. The exercises encourage the reader to analyze and improve given algorithms, to develop new algorithms, and particularly to practice implementing them; the projects given at the end of each chapter challenge the student to incorporate the data structures and algorithms in major programming projects. The importance of actually coding as many of the structures as time permits cannot be overemphasized; running programs is the one sure way to master the concepts and techniques presented in this text.

This book is intended as an undergraduate text. We assume the reader has a working knowledge of some general purpose programming language, such as FORTRAN IV, PL/I, PASCAL, or ALGOL, and knowledge of SNOBOL4 and LISP would be helpful but not essential. The algorithms are presented in a structured algorithmic notation which is defined in Chapter 1; this notation can easily be converted into code in almost any high-level programming language.

Robert J. Baron
Linda G. Shapiro

v

Contents

1
Preliminaries

OVERVIEW

The first section of this chapter discusses those aspects of a computer's main memory system that are directly relevant to data structure implementation techniques. The second section gives a brief overview of software, with emphasis on procedures and memory allocation disciplines, and the third section presents the algorithmic notation used throughout the remainder of the text.

1.1 INTRODUCTION

A *structure* is: "1) a manner of building, constructing or organizing; 2) something built or constructed, as a building or dam; 3) the arrangement or interrelation of all of the parts of a whole."[1] A *data structure* is a structure whose elements are items of data, and whose organization is determined both by the *relationships* between the data items and by the *access functions* that are used to store and retrieve them. For example, a vector array is a data structure where the elements are linearly ordered and its access function maps subscripts into the machine addresses of the elements. Data structures are used extensively in virtually all areas of computer science, from applications programming to theory, from microprocessors to large-scale computer systems, and from hardware to operating systems. This text is about data structures, how they are used, and how they are implemented.

Data structures are created and manipulated by programs executing on computers, and they are stored in the computer's memory system. The *memory representation* of a data structure is the way that the data structure is stored and organized in the computer's memory. The memory representation of a data structure is generally influenced by the hardware capabilities of the computer on

---

[1]*Webster's New World Dictionary of the American Language,* New York: The World Publishing Company, 1957.

which the structure will be used, and the efficiency of a particular representation is directly influenced by the way in which the elements of the structure must be accessed by the memory hardware. For these reasons, we begin with a discussion of memory hardware. The reader who has studied memory hardware may wish to omit this section.

After a brief overview of memory hardware, we shift our attention to computer software. We assume that the reader already has a working knowledge of some general purpose computer language, such as FORTRAN, PL/I, ALGOL, PASCAL, or COBOL, and we begin our discussion by reviewing some fundamental concepts, including variables, constants, program identifiers, and designational expressions. We conclude with a discussion of procedures and parameter passage techniques. The reader who is familiar with these software topics may also omit reading this section.

In the third and final section of this introduction, we present the algorithmic notation used throughout the remainder of the text. This notation was chosen not only to enable a precise statement of each algorithm, but also to describe exactly how the data structures will be represented in memory. The third section of this chapter must be understood before the remainder of the text is read.

1.2 Memory hardware

The way that data is passed between main memory and the central processing unit of a computer has a direct bearing on the efficiency of various representations of data structures in memory. For this reason, we begin by reviewing memory hardware and addressing. The reader is directed to any standard text on computer architecture for a description of other hardware topics.

1.2.1 General considerations

The smallest unit of data that can be manipulated by hardware is the *binary digit* or *bit*. A bit can take on the value 0 or the value 1, and may be stored by any hardware device that has two states: an 'on' state representing the value 1 and an 'off' state representing the value 0. A device having two states is called *bi-stable,* the flip-flop being the most common bi-stable device in a computer. In this text we will use '0' to represent the 0 bit and '1' to represent the 1 bit.

A *register* is a collection of bistable devices that are processed as a single unit. An 8-bit register, for example, has 8 bistable devices and related circuitry. Registers are used within the central processor for holding data, for holding inputs to the arithmetic and logical processing circuitry, for holding the results of computations, for holding program instructions, and so forth. Registers are generally very fast and are used for temporary storage of data. The *size* of a register is the number of bits it can hold. The bit pattern in an N-bit register may represent a character string, an integer, a floating-point number, a machine instruction, or anything else that can be represented by N bits.

The number and sizes of registers in any given computer are fixed. This implies that any unit of data that is longer than the length of a register cannot be held in a single register. Similarly, if a data structure is very large, it cannot be held in the CPU at one time. Instead, when working with large data structures, portions of the structure are brought into the CPU and processed. This clearly places constraints on the organization of data in a structure for efficient processing. The following section describes in somewhat more detail how the memory and CPU exchange data. The reader should try to recognize the restrictions placed on data structures because of the way that data is stored in memory and passed between memory and the CPU. A poor choice of memory representation for a data structure is often a major cause of program inefficiency, the inefficiency resulting either because of unnecessary memory accesses or wasted memory.

1.2.2 The main memory system

The main memory system of a computer is an ordered collection of registers, one register for each unit of data that the memory can hold. When referring to main memory, however, the registers are called *memory locations*. In older computers, the memory locations were constructed from magnetic 'cores' and the memory systems are called core memories. In newer machines, the memory locations are generally comprised of solid state flip-flops. The *word* size of a memory is the number of bits in each memory location, and the *word size* of a computer is the number of bits treated as a unit by the CPU. The word size of a computer is generally the same as the word size of its memory and memory locations.

The smallest unit of data that most memories process is the word, and in some machines words are numbered from 0 to N−1 for a memory that can hold N words. These numbers are the *word addresses* of the words in memory, and such a memory is said to be *word addressed*. A *byte* is either 6 or 8 bits and is the number of bits required to encode one character on a particular machine. Words are generally an integral number of bytes. For example, a 32-bit word may consist of four 8-bit bytes (IBM), whereas a 60-bit word may consist of ten 6-bit bytes (CDC). Many computers number the bytes in memory rather than words, and the memory systems of these machines are said to be *byte addressed*. For an N word memory having four bytes per word, the bytes would be numbered from 0 to 4N−1. In general, however, even when the memories are byte addressed, words are the smallest unit of data processed by the memory systems.

The main memory system of a computer has two distinguished registers that do not hold data like the rest of the memory: a *memory address register* (MAR), and a *memory buffer register* (MBR) also called the *memory data register* (MDR). A 4096 (4K) word memory that is word addressed is shown below.

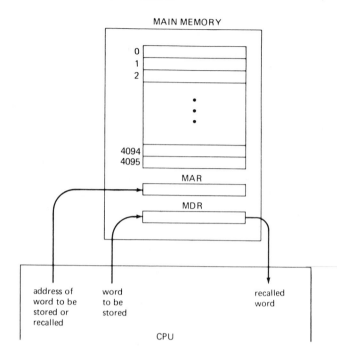

With few exceptions, the memory address register holds the word address of the unit in memory that can be accessed by a read or write operation. Even for byte-addressed machines, the memory address register holds the address of a word in memory, which is simply the address in byte units of the first byte of a word. When the memory address register holds the address of a word in memory, only that word can be accessed. During a *read operation,* the value in the word whose address is in the memory address register is copied into the memory data register where it can be directly accessed by the central processor. During a *write operation,* the contents of the memory data register are copied into the word whose address is in the memory address register. Prior to a read or write operation, the CPU must place the address of the desired word in the memory address register, and, in addition, prior to a write operation, the CPU must place the value to be stored in the memory data register. These operations are performed directly by the hardware and are generally invisible to the programmer. Since all words in a memory system of this type can be accessed in the same way and since the access time is independent of the address of the word in memory, the memory system is called a *random access memory.*

Although words are the smallest unit of data recognized and processed by the memory system, some computers provide special hardware so that smaller units of memory can be accessed by the CPU. For example, the IBM systems 360 and

370 computers use *byte* (8-bit) addresses rather than word addresses to reference memory: The first word in memory has address 0; the second word has address 4; the third word has address 8, and so forth. The first word in memory consists of bytes 0-3, the second word consists of bytes 4-7, the third word consists of bytes 8-11, and so on. The byte address of each word is evenly divisible by four. Because memory systems process words, bytes 2-5 are not accessible as a word, even though they form a word-sized field of memory. Accordingly, the imaginary lines between consecutive words are *word boundaries*. Similarly, the imaginary lines between the middle two bytes of each word are *halfword boundaries*, the imaginary lines between two bytes are *byte boundaries*, and the imaginary lines between odd and even-numbered words (starting at word 0) are *doubleword boundaries*. Bytes cannot cross byte boundaries; halfwords cannot cross halfword boundaries; words cannot cross word boundaries; and doublewords cannot cross doubleword boundaries. Only character manipulation instructions can access individual bytes of memory, halfword instructions can access halfwords of memory, fullword instructions can access words of memory, and doubleword instructions can access doublewords of memory. In general, even when character or halfword instructions are used, the memory system processes words of data, and special hardware is used to extract and insert the values in the designated characters or halfwords of memory.

Designers of computer architectures choose word sizes and data formats depending on the intended application of the machine (business, scientific, interactive) and upon economic considerations. Large words involve the use of more costly hardware in order to retrieve more bits at one time, but large words are also able to encode higher precision numbers. Many word sizes are used today as the following list suggests:

word size	example computer
64 bits	CRAY—I
60 bits	CDC cyber
48 bits	B 5500
36 bits	Univac 1100
32 bits	IBM series 360 and 370
24 bits	XDS 930
18 bits	PDP-15
16 bits	PDP-11
12 bits	PDP-8
8 bits	Intel 8080
4 bits	Intel 4040

Words are the units of data most efficiently and conveniently manipulated by computers. The implications that memory addressability has for the creation and manipulation of a data structure should now be clear. If a data object is smaller than the size of a memory word, the additional bits of memory within a word are generally wasted; otherwise, consecutive data objects would cross word boundaries and require inefficient code for their access and manipulation. As a corollary to word addressability, great care should be taken to design algorithms that execute efficiently yet require the least amount of memory for their implementation. Each additional bit required for implementing an algorithm reduces the amount of memory available for the data, and sometimes the addition of a single bit in a structure element makes it necessary to use an entire extra word of storage for that element. If the structure has thousands of elements, the additional memory requirements may become prohibitive.

Programming languages also utilize the word sizes of machines. An INTEGER in FORTRAN is generally the same size as one word on the host computer. As a result, a program that uses a very large integer may execute perfectly well on a machine having a 60-bit word but not at all on a machine having a 32-bit word. It is the programmer's responsibility to be aware of the word size of the machine, and the limitations imposed on the creation and use of data structures by the word size.

A second limitation imposed by word addressability concerns the way identifiers can be used to designate variables. Suppose, for example, that a character string is represented as a sequence of contiguous characters in adjacent words of memory and also suppose that the address of a string is the address of its first character. If the first character of a string is aligned on a word boundary, then the address of the string is a hardware address and a simple program identifier can be used to designate the string. If, however, the machine uses word addresses and each word can hold ten characters, then the substring that consists of the second through fourth characters of a given string has no hardware address and cannot be designated by a simple identifier. Because of this general type of restriction, most implementations of programming languages restrict the use of identifiers to designate units of memory that can be accessed by the hardware. A LOGICAL variable in FORTRAN, for example, generally uses a full word of memory even though a single bit would do.

Some programming languages provide data structure facilities that enable a programmer to define a structure whose data fields are packed into words of memory. Special designational expressions are used to designate the subfields of a defined structure, and, even though the designated fields can be referenced within a given program, there is no hardware address associated with them. As a result, restrictions are placed on the use of such designational expressions. In particular, if such a designational expression is used as an actual parameter to a procedure, the result may be an error, or it may be unanticipated.

1.2.3 Indexing hardware

The ability to efficiently implement a data structure, even a structure as simple as a one-dimensional array, often depends on the presence of certain hardware for addressing main memory. In this section, we will briefly discuss indexing, a memory addressing technique available on most computers that can often substantially reduce the time required to compute the address of an array element in a one-dimensional array. Several of the techniques described in Chapter 5 for representing sparse matrices are designed to utilize index registers and therefore reduce execution time to a minimum.

A *memory access* occurs each time that a main memory read or write operation is initiated. The value sent to the memory address register is the *effective address* of that memory reference and is generally expressed as an absolute binary number. Depending on the computer, the effective address may or may not be the address that appears in an instruction. When the address in an instruction is the same as the effective address, the address is called an *absolute binary address.*

Most computers provide addressing schemes in addition to absolute binary; the most common addressing scheme is *indexed addressing* or *indexing.* For indexed addressing, the computer either has special *index registers,* or it has general purpose registers which can be used as index registers. In either case, several bits of each instruction are used to indicate which index register is to be used, if any. When an index register is indicated, the effective address of the memory reference is obtained by adding the contents of the selected index register to the address given in the instruction. This is illustrated in Figure 1.1.

In indexing, the instructions contain the address of the first word of the referenced structure, and the index register contains the index (or subscript) of the desired element within the structure; the first word has index 0; the second word index 1, and so forth. When the elements in a one-dimensional array are stored in sequence in main memory, then an index register can be used to hold the subscript of the desired element, where subscript 0 refers to the first array element, subscript 1 to the second, and so on. The address in the instruction is the address of the first element of the array, which is also called the *base address* of the array.

The utility of index registers stems from two facts. First, special instructions are usually provided for incrementing and decrementing index register contents. In fact, some computers automatically increment or decrement the contents of index registers when they are used in an address computation. This means that when the words in a structure are to be sequentially processed, program loops can be written that increment or decrement the appropriate index registers, thereby automatically changing the memory reference from one structure element to the next during successive loop executions. When the hardware

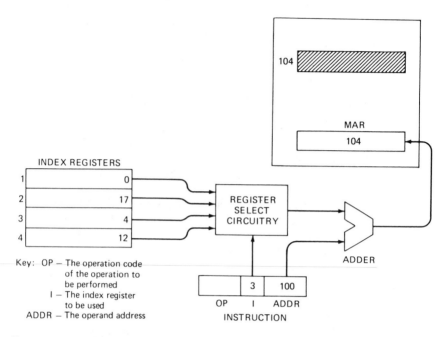

Figure 1.1. Index register hardware. Index register 3 is selected. Since index register 3 holds the value 4, and the instruction address is 100, the effective address of the operand is 104.

supports these incrementing and decrementing operations, execution time can be sharply reduced and therefore program efficiency increased. Second, array subscripts can be computed using the special index register hardware which is extremely fast. This greatly speeds up the time it takes to compute an address when accessing array elements.

Most compilers take advantage of a computer's special addressing hardware when generating code, so the programmer need not be directly concerned with index registers. As a result, when adequate data structure facilities are provided, the programmer should use them rather than creating his or her own memory representations and access functions. Compilers are generally better able to generate code that efficiently utilizes the computer's hardware than the programmer coding in a high-level language.

1.2.4 Virtual memory

Many modern computers use special addressing hardware which enables them to execute programs in a relatively small main memory that would otherwise require a large amount of storage. These computers are said to have *virtual memory*, since the computer's main memory is often smaller than the program's memory. The two most common types of virtual memory systems are *paging* and *segmentation*. Paging and segmentation are supported by a combination of computer hardware and software. When a computer uses a virtual memory system, it is of primary importance when implementing algorithms and data structures to choose memory representations that will localize memory references; that is, keep consecutive memory accesses in nearby memory locations. For example, sequential memory management techniques (see Chapter 6) tend to localize references, whereas available-space-list techniques (see Chapter 7) do not. As a second example, when multi-dimensional arrays are stored by rows (see Chapter 5) but are accessed by columns, the memory references tend to be distributed; when the same arrays are accessed by rows, the references are localized. We will briefly describe paging and segmentation in this section and indicate the reasons for desiring locality of references. The reader should consult a standard text on operating systems for a more comprehensive discussion of virtual memory systems. A good introduction can be found in Denning (1970).

Paging and *segmentation* are very flexible addressing techniques that isolate *physical addresses* in main memory from the addresses that the program uses, called *logical addresses*. The program's (logical) memory is contained on a large, external storage device, such as magnetic disk or magnetic drum, and addresses of program words are sequential on the external storage device, just as they would be if the program and data were placed directly in main memory. At any given time during program execution, a copy of only part of the program's memory may be found in the computer's main memory; this is the *active* part of the program. Whenever a memory access is to occur, the addressing hardware determines if the referenced word is currently in an active part of the program's memory, and if it is, the addressing hardware converts the logical (program) address to the correct physical (main memory) address and the memory access is completed. If, however, the addressed word is not active, then a *page* or *segment fault* occurs that indicates that the desired word is not in main memory. Special hardware and software are then used to copy the *demanded page* or *segment* containing the desired word from external storage into main memory. This may require that one of the currently active pages or segments be copied back into external storage. In either case, once the demanded page or segment is in main memory, the addressing hardware determines the correct physical address for the memory access, and the memory access is completed.

Paging and segmentation are similar, although paging is more closely related to memory hardware than segmentation. Furthermore, paging and segmentation are not exclusive concepts: a system that uses segmentation can also use paging. Paging is hardware oriented. The logical addresses are partitioned into identically sized *pages,* one or more of which can be active at any time. Main memory is divided into physical *blocks* that have the same number of words as do the pages. The number of words in each page (and therefore block) is generally a power of 2, such as 512, 1024 or 2048 words. When a page is copied into memory, it can be placed in any desired block; pages, however, may not cross block boundaries. In segmentation, the program's memory is not divided into identically sized pages but rather into arbitrarily sized *segments*. These segments generally reflect the logic of the program rather than the physical block size of main memory; for example, a segment might contain one array or it might contain one procedure. The second difference between paging and segmentation is that segments can be placed anywhere in main memory; they need not be aligned on any particular block boundary. Paging and segmentation are illustrated in Figures 1.2 and 1.3.

Whenever a page or segment fault ocurs during program execution, an entire page or segment of data must be copied from external storage into main memory, and often an entire page or segment must be copied from main memory back into external storage. As with all main memory operations, this must be done one word at a time and requires a substantial amount of execution time. Great effort should clearly be exercised to see that memory references do not result in unnecessary page or segment faults. In particular, when implementing algorithms that use data structures, the memory representations for the data structures and the order in which elements of the data structures are accessed can strongly influence program efficiency. Under some circumstances, frequent memory accesses do occur that result in frequent page or segment faults. This happens, for example, when consecutive elements of a structure are stored on different pages or segments and are processed in sequence. *Segment thrashing* and *page thrashing* refer to the frequent replacement of segments or pages, due to frequent segment or page faults. Thrashing can be reduced by insuring that sequential memory references are all made to the same page or segment, but this is often not possible. List processing systems that use linked lists (Chapters 2 and 7), for example, tend to create structures whose elements are located in different regions of memory and, therefore, often on different pages or segments. The result is that such systems run inefficiently in a virtual memory environment. Special software techniques must be used in order to reduce thrashing, and although many of the problems are beyond the scope of this text, several issues will be discussed in the relevant chapters.

1.3 SOFTWARE

In this section we discuss several, fundamental software topics and lay the conceptual foundation for the remainder of the text.

A *programming language* is any language designed for use by programmers to write computer programs. An *assembly language* is a programming language whose statements translate directly, in a one-to-one manner, into machine language instructions. For this reason, assembly languages are called low-level languages. Each computer has its own assembly language, and programs written

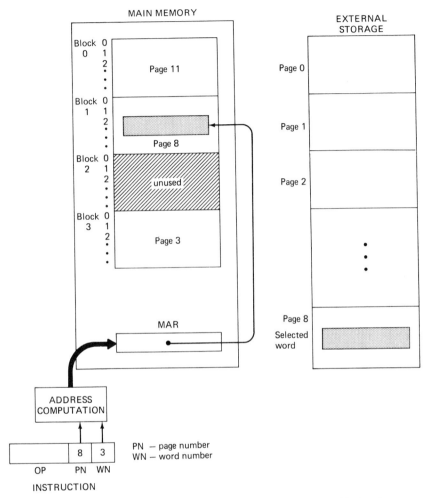

Figure 1.2. Addressing on a computer with paging. The computer has 4 blocks of memory. At the current time block 0 holds page 11, block 1 holds page 8, and block 3 holds page 3. The current instruction is To access word 3 of page 8. The address computation hardware determines an effective address of word 3, block 1.

in the assembly language of one computer can not be used on any other machine. An *assembler* is a program that operates on assembly language programs to produce machine language programs, and *assembly* is the process of translating an assembly language program into a machine language program.

In contrast, a *high-level language* is a programming language designed for

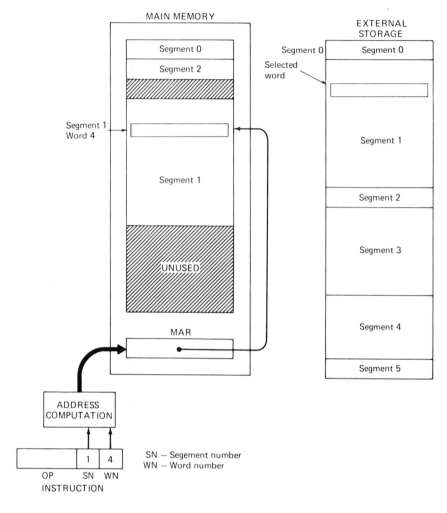

Figure 1.3. Addressing on a computer with segmentation. The computer currently has these active segments: 0, 1, and 2. The current instruction is to access word 4 of segment 1. The address computation hardware determines the correct effective address for the memory access.

conciseness and programming ease. A *compiler* is a program that, like an assembler, operates on symbolic input data to produce machine language programs. The input data for compilers are programs written in high-level languages, and each compiler is designed to translate statements of one high-level language into machine instructions for a particular computer. *Compilation* is the process of translating a high-level language program into a machine language program. Depending on the computer and the compiler, one statement in a high-level language may compile into several, and sometimes hundreds, of machine language statements. FORTRAN and COBOL are high-level languages for which there are compilers available on most computers.

1.3.1 Statement labels and program control

Both assembly languages and high-level languages allow statements to be labelled. A *statement label* is a symbolic name (or number) that is used to designate the *logical* or *program address* of the labelled statement. In an assembly language, a statement label may be used to designate a target address in a branch statement (a statement that alters the flow of control in a program). In IBM 360 assembly language, for example, the statement BR LOOP would assemble into a unconditional branch statement whose target address is the address of the statement labelled LOOP. Execution of this statement would pass control to the instruction at that address. In high-level languages, the typical unconditional branch statement would be written GO TO LOOP, and the branch would generally be to the first instruction generated by the compiler when the statement labelled LOOP is compiled.

Recent trends in programming language design have moved away from using the *goto* statement in favor of structured control constructs. Common control structures now include *if-then* and *if-then-else* statements, *do* loops, *do while* and *do until* statements, and *case* statements. These control structures differ for different programming languages, and it is beyond the scope of this text to delve into the peculiarities of the various control structures of different languages. In general, however, statement labels are not required when using these control structures, and may be eliminated entirely.

1.3.2 Constants and variables

A *constant* is a value in memory that cannot be changed during program execution; a *variable* is a value in memory that can be modified by a program during execution. Program references to constants and variables are made using symbolic names called program identifiers. A *program identifier* is a symbolic name used to designate an item or body of data, and generally identifiers refer to program variables. Some programming languages such as PASCAL allow identifiers to be designated as constants, in which case the referenced values cannot be changed during program execution. Some identifiers refer to single values that can be modified; these values are *simple variables*. Arrays, lists, graphs or other structures that contain more than one item of data are not simple variables. Simple variables are most frequently values that are processed directly by the computer's hardware: integers, floating-point numbers, memory addresses, and characters.

The *data type* of an identifier is the data type of the values that may be designated by the identifier, and the *value* of an identifier is the value of the quantity for which the identifier stands. In most programming languages, including FORTRAN, PL/I, PASCAL, and ALGOL, the type of an identifier is fixed by the compiler during compilation and can not be changed during program execution; this is called *static type setting*. However, in some programming languages, such as SNOBOL4 and LISP, the type of an identifier is determined during program execution: a program variable may at one time designate an integer, while at a later time a list, array, or floating-point number; this is called *dynamic type setting*.

1.3.3 Declarations, data types and referencing variables

As a general rule, assembly languages do not have statements for manipulating data structures other than simple variables. In contrast, high-level programming languages such as PL/I and FORTRAN allow identifiers to designate more than one variable. These variables are called arrays, and each identifier used as an array identifier must be declared in a declaration statement. The declaration statement INTEGER ARRAY(100) in FORTRAN and DECLARE ARRAY (100) FIXED; in PL/I notify the compilers that ARRAY is to designate a collection of 100 variables denoted ARRAY(1), ARRAY(2), and so on up to ARRAY(100). The single statement VALUE = ARRAY(10) in either language notifies the compilers to generate all the necessary machine language statements to cause the indicated data transfer.

Several questions may be asked:
1. What kinds of data structures are available in high-level languages?
2. How does the programmer notify the compiler that a particular identifier is to designate a particular type of data or data structure?
3. How are the elements of the data structures designated?
4. What types of data can the elements hold?
5. Who reserves the memory for the elements of the structure?
6. When is the memory reserved for the elements of the structure?

Question 1 will be answered in part in the remainder of this book; the other questions will be answered in the following paragraphs.

A *designational expression* is an expression that specifies or designates an item or body of data. Simple program variables are designational expressions, and array identifiers, with their subscript lists, are also designational expressions. The particular item or body of data that a designational expression designates may depend on the placement of the expression in a program and also on when the designational expression is evaluated; this will be discussed shortly.

A *declaration statement* is a statement that specifies the data type of an identifier. Once the data type of an identifier is specified, the types of designational expressions involving that identifier are also specified. For example, if the FORTRAN variable A is declared INTEGER A(100), then the symbol A has data type "integer array," and a designational expression is the identifier A followed by a subscript list having a single subscript entry. The designational expressions A(1), A(2), and so forth refer to the elements of the array A.

A *structure definition statement* is a statement that names a structure and also indicates how variables or constants within the structure are to be designated. Arrays are structures that need no structure definition statements in most high-level languages. This is because the appearance of subscript lists in declaration statements notifies the compiler that the designated object is an array. Now consider the following PL/I structure definition:

DECLARE 1 CELL,
           2 DATA FIXED,
           2 LINK POINTER;

This statement specifies that the identifier CELL is to designate a structure named CELL having two variables, one having data typed FIXED and the other data type POINTER. These variables are referenced by the designational expressions CELL.DATA and CELL.LINK. The identifier CELL, when used alone, is a designational expression that designates the entire structure, a body of data having two values, CELL.DATA, and CELL.LINK. The PASCAL **type** statement and the SNOBOL4 DATA definition statement are two other examples of structure defining statements.

When programming in a high-level language, memory may be reserved for variables by the compiler, or it may be reserved during program execution by code generated by the compiler. A *memory allocation discipline* determines how and when memory will be allocated for a variable. We will discuss three memory allocation disciplines that are commonly used in modern programming languages.

The simplest memory allocation discipline is *static memory allocation*. The compiler reserves memory locations for program variables which always reside in the same logical memory locations and are always designated by the same identifiers; standard FORTRAN is a programming language that uses static memory allocation. Within the body of a program, each identifier designates one and only one variable, and the designated variables do not change during program execution. (The values of variables may, of course, change.)

Automatic memory allocation is a second standard memory allocation discipline. Automatic memory allocation is used by block-structured progamming languages such as ALGOL or PASCAL. In this discipline, consecutive program statements are organized into *blocks;* each procedure is a block. In ALGOL, blocks can also be formed within procedures and within other blocks. For block structured languages, memory for all variables declared within a block is allocated upon *block entry.* When control transfers from within a block to a statement that is outside the block, memory that was allocated for declared variables is reclaimed. Memory is liberated at *block exit,* and the values of variables established within the block are lost. Memory allocation is not under program control, and the programming language does not provide statements for the explicit allocation or liberation of memory. Memory is automatically allocated for variables in the programming language ALGOL, for variables that are declared in a **var** statement in PASCAL, and for variables having the AUTOMATIC attribute in PL/I. (In PL/I, AUTOMATIC is assumed unless otherwise stated.)

Some programming languages such as PL/I and PASCAL provide statements that cause memory for variables to be allocated during program execution under program control. This is called *dynamic memory allocation* and is the last memory allocation discipline to be discussed. In PL/I the variables of this type are called BASED, and in PASCAL they are *dynamic variables.*

When using dynamically allocated variables, one or more static or automatic variables must be declared **pointer,** a data type that contains the logical address of a variable. When a dynamic variable is allocated, the allocation procedure places in a pointer variable the logical address of the allocated variable. Other statements can then reference the dynamic variable by using designational expressions that name the pointer variable and specify the desired fields within the object. For example, if P is a pointer variable that points to a CELL, and CELL has two fields, LINK and DATA, then:

P → LINK	(PL/I)
P → DATA	(PL/I)
P ↑.LINK	(PASCAL)
P ↑.DATA	(PASCAL)
[P].LINK	(this text)
[P].DATA	(this text)

designate the link and data fields of the cell referenced by P. This will be discussed in more detail in the third part of this introduction.

Dynamic allocation gives the programmer the greatest control over the data structures of any of the disciplines already described; however, it also leaves the programmer with greater responsibilities: the programmer must guarantee that the pointers to structures are properly maintained, that references to structures are valid, and that all unwanted structures are liberated.

1.3.4. Procedures

Probably the most important facility of a programming language is the facility for defining and executing procedures. A *procedure* is a body of code that performs a specific function, such as the evaluation of an arithmetic expression, an input or output operation, a data structure modification, and so forth. Internal and external procedures in PL/I, procedures in ALGOL, and PASCAL, and SUBROUTINEs and FUNCTIONs in FORTRAN are examples. In this section, we describe how procedures are defined, how they are invoked, and what the effect of their execution is.

A *procedure definition* generally consists of a sequence of four types of statements: a *procedure header, declaration statements,* the *procedure body,* and a *procedure terminator.* The procedure header consists of the *procedure name* and a *formal parameter list.* When the procedure name appears in a *procedure invocation statement,* program control is given to the procedure. When the procedure finishes execution, control is transferred to the statement that invoked the procedure. The formal parameter list that appears in a procedure definition indicates that the named identifiers are to refer to specific variables during procedure execution. The variables that the formal parameters designate depend on the *parameter passage discipline* as described shortly.

The declaration statements that appear within a procedure are generally of two types: declaration statements that describe the formal parameters of the procedure and declaration statements that describe how other program identifiers are to be used within the procedure. Any identifiers other than formal parameters that designate variables that are declared within a procedure are *local* to the procedure; they cannot be referenced outside of the block defined by the procedure itself. If a procedure declaration is nested within a larger block, then all identifiers that are declared within the outer block and not redeclared within the procedure are *global* identifiers. Global variables are the same within the called procedure as they are in the block surrounding the called procedure. Declaration statements that describe the formal parameters to a procedure indicate the data type of the variables that will be designated by the identifiers and, in some cases (e.g. **value** in ALGOL), the parameter passage discipline. The variables designated by formal parameters will be described shortly (c.f. Section 1.3.6).

We illustrate these concepts by showing an ALGOL 60 main program with a single procedure and a FORTRAN IV program with a single SUBROUTINE; both programs do essentially the same thing. As illustrated, ALGOL 60 is block structured and the procedure is defined within the main program; in contrast, FORTRAN is not block structured, and the SUBROUTINE is coded as an independent procedure.

A procedure body consists of all executable statements that comprise the

```
comment        MAIN ALGOL 60 PROCEDURE;
begin

    integer array A [10] ;
    integer SUM;
    integer procedure  ADDA (AR);

            comment nested procedure block;
            integer array AR;
            begin
                integer    I, SUM;
                SUM       := 0;
                for        I:= 1      step 1 until 10 do
                                SUM:= SUM + AR [I] ;
                ADDA      := SUM;
            end

    <read values of A>
    SUM:= ADDA (A);
    <print value of SUM>
end;
```

```
C    MAIN FORTRAN IV PROGRAM
     INTEGER A(10), SUM
     <read values of A>
     SUM = ADDA (A, 10)
     <print value of SUM>
     END

C    SEPARATE FUNCTION
     INTEGER FUNCTION ADDA (AR, N)
     INTEGER AR (N), SUM, I
     SUM = 0
     DO 10 I = 1, 10
10   SUM = SUM + AR (I)
     ADDA = SUM
     RETURN
     END
```

procedure, and a procedure terminator is generally an *end* statement. In addition there are two types of statements that are special to procedures: *return* statements and assignment statements that assign a value to the procedure name. A *return* statement specifies that procedure execution is to be terminated and program control is to be returned to the statement that invoked the procedure in the first place; we will elaborate on this shortly. If a value is assigned to the procedure name, then that value is the value designated by the procedure name in the statement that invoked the procedure.

1.3.5 Procedure invocation

A procedure is invoked by one of several different types of program statements. Most programming languages provide a *call statement*, which consists of the procedure name followed by an *actual parameter list;* this is an *explicit* procedure invocation. In many programming languages (e.g. FORTRAN and PL/I), the keyword CALL precedes the procedure name; in other languages (e.g. ALGOL and SNOBOL) it does not. The *call* statement indicates which procedure is to be given control, and it also indicates which variables are to be *bound* to the formal parameters of the procedure. Procedure names and actual parameter lists can also appear within expressions in the calling program. When this occurs, the procedure is invoked *implicitly*. As an example, if F is a procedure having a single formal parameter, then the statement Z := F(3) invokes F implicitly with actual parameter 3. The value to be assigned to Z is the value assigned to the procedure name by the procedure during its execution.

1.3.6. Parameter passage

When a procedure is invoked, either explicitly or implicitly, the procedure that is making the call is the *calling procedure,* and the procedure being called is the *called procedure*. The parameters that appear in the statement causing the invocation are called *actual parameters*. Upon entry to the procedure, the actual parameters are *bound* to the formal parameters of the procedure. In most programming languages, the binding is *positional:* the first actual parameter is bound to the first formal parameter; the second actual parameter is bound to the second formal parameter; and so forth. In some programming languages the binding is by *keyword*. Each actual parameter is an expression of the form <identifier> = <argument>, where <identifier> is the name of one of the formal parameters of the procedure, and <argument> is the argument that is to be bound to the named formal parameter. For this type of parameter passage, the order in which the actual parameters appear is not important. As an example, suppose that F is a procedure having two formal parameters, A and B, in that order. If parameter passage is positional, then the statement **call** F (10, 20) would bind A to the value 10 and B to the value 20; if parameter passage is by keyword, the statement **call** F (B = 7, A = 14) would bind A to the value 14 and B to the value 7.

When a procedure is invoked, the formal parameters refer to specific variables depending on the parameter passage discipline. We will now describe three parameter passage disciplines: parameter passage by value; parameter passage by reference; and parameter passage by value-result. The reader should consult a standard text on programming languages for a description of other parameter passage disciplines. When parameter passage is by value, the value of each actual parameter is copied into a temporary memory location (or locations) prior to entry to the called procedure. The corresponding formal parameters designate the values in these temporary memory locations; thus the called procedure has access to the values of the actual parameters at the time of procedure invocation. However, the variables designated by the formal parameters are temporary, and their values are lost upon exit from the procedure. Any changes made to the values of the formal parameters during procedure execution are not known to the calling program. The corresponding actual parameters are not modified. This kind of parameter passage is used by SNOBOL and may be specified in ALGOL and PASCAL.

Parameter passage by reference is somewhat more complicated, and two cases must be considered: 1) the actual parameter is a designational expression; and 2) the actual parameter is an expression but not a designational expression. If the actual parameter is not a designational expression, then the expression is evaluated prior to entry to the called procedure, the value of the expression is placed in a temporary memory location, and the corresponding formal parameter designates that temporary variable. This is completely equivalent to parameter passage by value. As a general rule, the actual parameters are evaluated in a left-to-right order in the parameter list; however, there are exceptions to this left-to-right evaluation rule. When a designational expression appears as an actual parameter, the corresponding formal parameter in the called procedure designates the same variable; i.e. the same memory location, as the actual parameter. The value of the variable upon entry to the called procedure is the last value it had in the calling procedure, and the value of the variable upon exit from the called procedure is the last value it had in the called procedure. This type of parameter passage is used by FORTRAN and PL/I and may be specified in PASCAL.

Parameter passage by value-result is as follows: Upon entry to the procedure, the values of the actual parameters are placed in temporary memory locations that are referenced by the formal parameters of the procedure; this is like parameter passage by value. However there is one difference: If an actual parameter is a designational expression, then upon exit from the called procedure, the value of the designated variable is changed to the final value of the corresponding temporary memory location in the called procedure. Thus, any intermediate changes to the value of a formal parameter that occur during execution of the called procedure do not change the corresponding variable in the calling procedure; only the final value is reflected in the calling procedure. This kind of parameter passage is used by some versions of FORTRAN, and, under most circumstances, is equivalent to parameter passage by reference.

1.3.7 Functions and subroutines

In some programming languages, restrictions are placed on formal parameters of procedures, and different names are given to the resulting procedures. For example, in FORTRAN, a SUBROUTINE is a procedure than can be invoked explicitly with a CALL statement; however, a SUBROUTINE cannot be invoked implicitly. A FUNCTION is a procedure that can be invoked either implicitly or explicitly in a CALL statement; however, a FUNCTION is not allowed to modify its formal parameters. A function returns a value through its name, not by modifying a formal parameter. These restrictions are somewhat arbitrary, and many compilers allow FUNCTIONs to change their formal parameters.

1.4 AN ALGORITHMIC LANGUAGE

In this section, we introduce the notation, conventions, and algorithmic style used throughout the remainder of the text. This algorithmic notation was selected so that the algorithms can easily be translated into other programming languages for execution. The structure definition statements, in particular, were designed so that structures could be specified in a way that reflects the underlying computer hardware. We assume that the reader has writing knowledge of at least one high-level programming language, such as FORTRAN, ALGOL, PASCAL, PL/I or SNOBOL4.

1.4.1 Symbols

We will use several standard symbols throughout this text. The boolean connectives (*and* or &, *or* or |, and *not* or ¬) will be used, as will the standard arithmetic operators (unary plus $'+'$, unary minus $'-'$, plus $'+'$, minus $'-'$, times $'*'$, divided by $'/'$, and exponentiation $'**'$) and the relational operators $(=, \neq, <, \leq, >, \geq)$. Parentheses can be used to group terms for evaluation. The symbol $'|x|'$ denotes the absolute value of x and also acts like parentheses in grouping terms. The symbols $'\lfloor x \rfloor'$ and $'\lceil x \rceil'$ denote the floor of x and ceiling of x, and also act like parentheses in grouping terms. The floor of x is the largest integer whose value is less than or equal to x, and the ceiling of x is the smallest integer whose value is greater than or equal to x. The symbol $' := '$ is the assignment operator, and the symbols $'\bullet'$, $'[x]'$, and $'@'$ denote the variable field length specifier, indirect reference, and address extraction. They will be described later in this section.

1.4.2 Evaluation of expressions

Arithmetic and boolean expressions are evaluated as follows. Identifiers and functions are evaluated from left to right in an expression. The values are temporarily held for the final evaluation of the expression as described below. If an identifier designates a function or procedure, that function or procedure is evaluated and may affect the values of identifiers and functions appearing to the right in the expression; however, it does not affect the values already determined. Expressions appearing as actual parameters to functions are evaluated from left to right, applying these rules recursively if necessary. The value of a procedure identifier is the last value assigned to the procedure name during its execution. After the evaluation of all identifiers and functions, the final value of the expression is determined as follows:

1. Expressions within parentheses, absolute value symbols, and floor and ceiling symbols are evaluated by applying the following rules, recursively if necessary.
2. Unary $'+'$ and $'-'$ are applied first.
3. Exponentiation operators are next applied in right-to-left order. Thus A**B**C would be evaluated as follows: First A, then B, and finally C would be evaluated, and suppose A', B', and C' are their values. The expression evaluates to $A'**X$, where X is the value of $B'**C'$.
4. Multiplications and divisions are next carried out in left-to-right order.
5. Additions and subtractions are carried out in left-to-right order. Using the notation of 3 above, A*B/C + D evaluates to Y + D', where $Y = X/C'$, and $X = A'*B'$.
6. Relational expressions are evaluated.
7. The boolean operator *not* is applied.
8. Boolean quantities are *and*ed together in left-to-right order.
9. Boolean quantities are *or*ed together in left-to-right order.

1.4.3 Executable Statements

Statements are either *executable* or *non-executable*. A *program* is a sequence of statements, separated by semicolons. Comments may appear anywhere. Other executable statements follow the non-executable statements. We will first describe the executable statements. Executable statements are either *simple statements* or *compound* statements. Simple statements are of the following types: *if-then* statements, *if-then-else* statements, *while-do* statements, *case* statements, *assignment* statements, *call* statements, and *return* statements. Each of these will be defined shortly. A compound statement is a sequence of statements delimited by *begin-end* brackets. The statements between the *begin-end* brackets in a compound statement may be simple or compound, and they are separated by semicolon (:) delimiters. A semicolon preceding the *end* delimiter is optional. Example simple statements are:

```
A := 10
if (A = 0) then call f(A) endif
while (I ≠ 0) do call g(I,A)
```

Example compound statements are:

```
begin
    A := A + 1;
    B := B + 1;
    C := C + 1
end
```

```
begin
    I := 1;
    while (I ≤ 10) do
        begin
            A(I) := 0;
            I := I + 1
        end;
end
```

If-then

An *if-then* statement appears as:

if (<boolean>) **then** <statement> **endif**

An *if-then* statement is evaluated as follows: The <boolean> is first evaluated; if its value is **true**, then the <statement> is executed; if the boolean evaluates to **false**, then the statement following the *if-then* statement is executed. Example *if-then* statements follow:

```
if (X = 0) then X := 1 endif
if (X = 0 and Y = 0)
then begin
        X := 10;
        Y := 10;
        return
    end endif
```

If-then-else

An *if-then-else* statement appears as:

if (<boolean>) **then** <statement 1> **else** <statement 2> **endif**

The boolean is first evaluated. If it evaluates to **true** then <statement 1> is executed, and after <statement 1> is executed, control transfers to the statement following the *if-then-else* statement. If the boolean evaluates to **false**, then <statement 2> is executed after which control transfers to the statement following the *if-then-else* statement.

Example *if-then-else* statements follow:

```
if (N = 0) then f := 1 else f := 100 endif
if (B (10) = true)
then begin
```

              call f(I);
               I : = 0
          end
          else return endif

The flow of control of an if then else statement is:

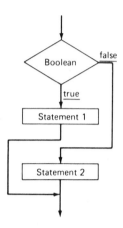

Case

The *case* statement allows control to be transferred to one of a group of statements and appears this way:

    case
        (<boolean 1>) : <statement 1>;
        (<boolean 2>) : <statement 2>;
                    •
                    •
        (<boolean k>) : <statement k>;
    end case

Each boolean is evaluated, in order, until a boolean evaluates to **true**. The statement following that boolean is then executed, after which control transfers to the statement following the *case* statement. When a boolean evaluates to **true**, subsequent booleans are not evaluated. If none of the booleans evaluate to true, then control transfers to the statement following the *case* statement. This is illustrated below.

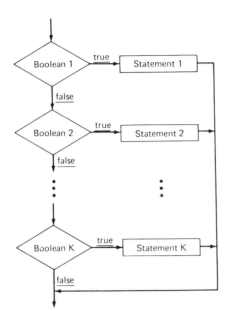

An example *case* statement is given below:

```
case
   (LENGTH < 0) :
      begin
         call ERROR;
         return
      end;
   (LENGTH < 10) :
      begin
         A (LENGTH) := 0;
         LENGTH := LENGTH + 1
      end;
   (LENGTH ≥ 10) :
      A (LENGTH) := LENGTH;
end case
```

While-do

The *while-do* statement has the form:

$$\textbf{while } (<\text{boolean}>) \textbf{ do } <\text{statement}>$$

The boolean is first evaluated; if it evaluates to **true** then the <statement> is executed. This process is repeated until the boolean evaluates to **false**. At that time, control is transferred to the statement following the *while-do* statement. This is illustrated below.

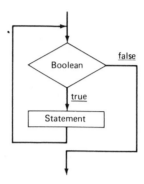

Examples of *while-do* statements follow:

    while (I ≠ 0) **do** A(I) := F(I)

    while (J < 20) **do**
      begin
        B (J) : = B (J) + 20;
        J := J + 1
      end

Call

A *call* statement appears as:

$$\text{call fname } (\text{<actual parameter list>})$$

In a call statement, fname is the name of a procedure, and <actual parameter list> is a list of expressions, or designational expressions, separated by commas. The form of a designational expression is described shortly. The number of designational expressions in the actual parameter list must be the same as the number of formal parameters in the procedure definition (c.f. procedure definitions). The *call* statement invokes the procedure. Any expressions appearing as actual parameters are evaluated from left to right, and the values are placed in temporary memory locations. These become temporary variables used by the called procedure. Upon procedure entry, the formal parameters of the procedure are bound to the temporary variables or variables designated by the corresponding designational expressions; parameter passage is positional and by reference. Bit addresses are assumed, so that any field in a structure may be designated as an actual parameter to a procedure. When the procedure executes a *return* statement, control is transferred to the statement following the *call* statement.

Return

A *return* statement consists of the keyword **return**; a *return* statement may only appear within a procedure. When a *return* statement is executed, control is transferred either to the statement following the *call* statement that invoked the procedure or to the statement that invoked the procedure implicitly by having the procedure name appear within an expression. If the procedure was invoked implicitly, the value of the procedure name in the calling procedure is the last value assigned to the procedure name within the called procedure. If the procedure name was not assigned a value, then an error condition results.

Assignment

An assignment statement is of the form:

$$<\text{designational expression}> := <\text{expression}>$$

The data type of the item or body of data designated by the designational expression must be the same as the data type of the expression. The value obtained by evaluating the expression becomes the new value of the variable designated by the designational expression.

1.4.4 Non-executable statements

There are four statements that are not executable: *comments, template* statements, *declare* statements, and *procedure* statements; each of these is described below.

Comment

A comment consists of the keyword **comment** followed by any sequence of characters not containing a semicolon; for example,

> **comment** This is a valid comment statement.

is a comment.

Procedure

A *procedure* statement appears as follows:

procedure <name> (<formal parameter list>);
<declarations>;
<procedure body>;
end name

The first statement of the definition declares <name> to be a procedure identifier. The procedure can then be invoked by a *call* statement or invoked implicitly when the procedure identifier and an actual parameter list appear within an expression.

The <declarations> are *declare, template,* and *procedure* statements that describe the data type and structures referenced by formal parameters to the procedure identifiers that are local to the procedure and any nested procedure definitions. These will be defined shortly. Any number of *declare, template,* and *procedure* statements may appear, separated by semicolons.

The <procedure body> is a sequence of executable statements that defines the action of the procedure; these statements are separated by semicolons. If the procedure is to be invoked implicitly, then the procedure name must be appropriately declared, and it must be assigned a value within the procedure. Parameter passage to a procedure is by reference. Each formal parameter must be declared within the procedure, but this declaration only assigns a data type to the formal parameter; memory is not allocated at procedure entry for the associated variable. The way that the designated field is used by a procedure depends only on the way that the formal parameters are declared within the procedure, not on the way the actual parameter is declared in the calling procedure. Two procedures can therefore process the same block of memory in different ways. Identifiers appearing in a *procedure* definition that are not declared within the procedure must be declared in either an outer block (i.e. outer procedure) and are global to the procedure, or they must be declared *global* (c.f. Section 1.4.5, Allocation of memory). The declaration statements describe the data type of the corresponding variables. The following procedure definition illustrates some of these points:

procedure FACTORIAL(N);
declare (N, FACTORIAL) INTEGER;
if (N = 0)
then FACTORIAL := 1
else FACTORIAL := N * FACTORIAL (N − 1) **endif**;
return;
end FACTORIAL

In this definition, N and FACTORIAL are of type INTEGER. The actual parameter N−1 is evaluated and the value placed in a temporary memory location before the procedure is entered recursively. (See Chapter 8.)

Template Statements

We will be primarily concerned with two data organizations: *blocks* and *linked structures*. Blocks are contiguous units of memory that are processed as structural entities. Linked structures are structures comprised of several blocks having some logical interconnection. *Pointers,* also called *links,* form these logical connections and are logical addresses of other fields or blocks. A pointer within one block logically connects that block to another block. This is shown below.

Blocks may be divided into fields, which may be further divided into subfields; fields (or subfields) are the smallest units of blocks that can be designated by a designational expression.

Whenever a data structure is to be implemented, the implementer must select a memory representation for the blocks of the structure. For example, the first two bits of the block may be used to indicate the organization of information in the block; some bits may be wasted so that the following field falls on a word boundary; the next four characters may be the print image of the block's data type, and so forth. The purpose of the *template* statement is to provide a precise definitional framework for mapping a block's internal structure onto the computer's hardware. This enables a precise discussion of efficient memory representations and data structure implementation techniques.

A *template* statement is a statement that names a block, names its subfields, and specifies how the block and its subfields are designated. Each *template* statement consists of the keyword **template** followed by a sequence of *number-name* pairs separated by commas. Each number is a *level number,* and a name following level number K is called a *level-K name* which names a subfield in a block. The first number-name pair must begin with level number 1, and the name following the number 1 is the *block name.* Each block so named defines a new data type. As an example:

template	1	CELL,	
	2	DATA	INTEGER,
	2	LINK	POINTER **to** CELL

defines a block of data type CELL having two level-2 subfields named DATA and LINK; the level-2 fields in this structure have data types INTEGER and POINTER, respectively.

The level-2 names identify the major subfields of the block; level-3 names define subfields of level-2 fields, and so forth. This may be done to any desired level of nesting. A level-K field that has no subfields must be given a basic data type (c.f. *declare*). Such fields will hold the variables of the structure.

Each field name, except the block name, may be followed by a single positive integer, enclosed in parentheses. This number is similar to an array dimension and indicates the number of contiguous fields of the named type in the structure; for example:

template 1   A,
2   B(10) INTEGER

specifies that a block of data type A has 10 level-2 subfields, B(1), B(2), and so on up to B(10). As another example:

template 1   STRING,
2   CURRENTLENGTH   INTEGER,
2   MAXIMUMLENGTH   INTEGER,
2   CHAR(10)   CHARACTER

defines STRING to be a block having 12 fields, two INTEGER fields named CURRENTLENGTH and MAXIMUMLENGTH, and 10 CHARACTER fields named CHAR(1), CHAR(2) thru CHAR(10).

Each level-K field can be divided into any number of level-(K + 1) fields. As an example:

template 1   A,
2   B   8 BITS,
2   C,
3   D   4 BITS,
3   E   4 BITS,
2   F   8 BITS

defines a block having the structure shown below;

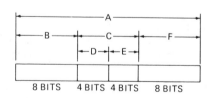

and

template	1	F,	
	2	G(3)	8 BITS,
	2	H(2),	
	3	I	4 BITS,
	3	J(3)	2 BITS

describes the structure shown below.

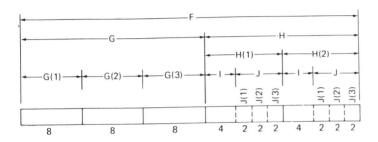

When illustrating the structure of a block, a *block diagram* may be used. A block diagram shows the fields of the block with the field names given either above or below the fields in the diagram. Where appropriate, actual data may be specified within a field. The order in which the fields are shown in a block diagram is the order in which the fields occur in memory as specified by the template statement. For clarity, blocks are sometimes drawn vertically, each row in the diagram representing some convenient unit of storage.

A second aspect of a block diagram is that for linked structures, pointers from one block to another are represented as arrows. Arrows are used because the actual addresses are generally not known and are usually not relevant. If a pointer field does not point anywhere, it contains a *null POINTER* and is indicated in a diagram by a slash (/) through the indicated field. The value of a null pointer is **null**, although the value 0 is used in many implementations.

It is sometimes either necessary or useful for implementation purposes to align subfields of blocks on particular types of physical memory boundaries. The *filler* field specification allows this type of boundary alignment. Consider the following block definition:

template	1	A,	
	2	LENGTH	WORD,
	2	MARK	BIT,
	2	**filler**	CHARACTER,
	2	TYPE1	CHARACTER,
	2	TYPE2	CHARACTER,
	2	TYPE3	CHARACTER

The **filler** keyword specifies that the following field is to begin on a memory boundary of the type specified in the *filler* statement, relative to the beginning of the block. In the above example, **filler** specifies that 0 or more bits are to be inserted into the block just after the MARK bit so that the TYPE1 field begins on a CHARACTER boundary. The structure would appear as follows, assuming four CHARACTERS per word and eight bits per CHARACTER.

A

LENGTH	MARK		TYPE 1	TYPE 2	TYPE 3
32	1	7	8	8	8

Sometimes the number of fields within a structure depends on the value in one of the fields of the structure. When this is the case, the subscript bound following the field name in the number-name pair may be a variable name preceded by a bullet ('•'), which is a variable field length specifier. The bullet indicates that the variable is contained within the block itself. As an example,

template	1	STRING,	
	2	LENGTH	INTEGER,
	2	DATA (•LENGTH)	CHARACTER

specifies that STRING is a block whose first word contains an INTEGER value, LENGTH. The remainder of the block consists of LENGTH DATA fields, each containing one CHARACTER variable.

Declare

A *declare* statement describes how an identifier will be used within a procedure. A declare statement appears as follows:

declare <list of identifiers> <data type>

The list of identifiers is either a single identifier, possibly subscripted, or a list of identifiers separated by commas and enclosed in parentheses; if subscripted, a list of subscript bounds must appear within parentheses following the identifier. The <data type> may be one of the *basic data types:* INTEGER, REAL, WORD, CHARACTER, POINTER, BOOLEAN, BIT, or it may be any block name described in a *template* statement. However, unless a declared variable is a formal procedure parameter, it must not be defined using the variable field length specifier '•'. When an identifier is declared POINTER, it is generally followed by the qualification **to** <data types>, where <data types> is either a single data type or a list of data types enclosed in parentheses and separated by commas. Restrictions on the data types, and exceptions to this general rule, are described in Section 1.4.6. When so qualified, the pointer can only point to an object of the specified data type. This is illustrated below:

> **declare** I INTEGER
> **declare** (P1, P2) POINTER **to** BLOCK
> **declare** (A(100), X) REAL
> **declare** B (10, 10) CHARACTER
> **declare** W WORD
> **declare** (R, S(10)) CELL
> **declare** C (1:7, − 3:6) STRING

In the above declarations, I is a fullword integer; P1 and P2 are fullword addresses that point to blocks containing data objects of data type BLOCK; A(1) thru A(100) and X are fullword floating point variables; and B(1,1) thru B(10,10) are single character variables. The variable W is one word long. (This declaration is useful for reserving memory in a procedure that does not modify the value of the variable.) The last two examples declare R and S(1) thru S(10) to be CELLs and C(1, −3) thru C(7,6) to be STRINGs. *Template* statements for CELL, BLOCK, and STRING must be given for these to be valid *declare* statements, and the data types CELL, BLOCK, and STRING must not have any fields defined using the bullet ('•').

Within a procedure, the special symbol star ('*') may be used instead of a subscript bound when declaring a formal parameter of the procedure. The star may be used only for singly subscripted variables and notifies the procedure that some indeterminate number of fields are present. It is up to the program to keep track of the exact number. For example,

> **procedure** P(A);
> **declare** A(*) INTEGER;

declares A to be vector array of integers; the exact number of integers may vary.

A formal parameter may also be declared as a structure defined using the bullet ('•'). Designational expressions involving the fields are formed as described in section 1.4.6.

1.4.5 Allocation of variables

Procedure blocks are the only blocks in the language, and memory for variables declared within a procedure, except formal parameters or as noted in the following paragraph, is allocated automatically upon initial invocation of the procedure. Memory is deallocated upon procedure exit. Procedure definitions may, but need not, be nested; when nested, procedures are block structured.

Any declared variable that is not a formal parameter for the procedure may be declared **global.** This designation causes memory to be allocated statically in an area external to any procedure. All procedures that designate variables that are declared **global** and have the same name designate the same variables. Global variables having the same name in different procedures must have identical declaration statements.

1.4.6 Designational expressions

A *designational expression* is an expression that designates a single variable or a block of data. Simple identifiers designate variables and are designational expressions. A subscripted variable followed by a subscript list designates a variable and is a designational expression. We now describe how blocks and fields of blocks are designated.

There are two ways to designate variables and fields in structures. If STR is an identifier that is declared to be a structure data type, then STR is itself a designational expression that designates the corresponding structure. The individual fields of the structure are designated by expressions involving the *field qualification operator* '.' *(dot).* The structure identifier is followed by a dot, then a level-2 field name, then another dot, then the level-3 field name, and so forth, until the desired field is completely specified. If a level name is subscripted, then a subscript may follow that name in the designational expression. If no subscript follows a subscripted level name, then further level qualifications may not appear, and the designational expression designates the field consisting of all subfields and all subscripts of the qualified field. The following examples illustrate the formation of designational expressions:

template	1	CELL,	
	2	DATA	INTEGER,
	2	LINK	POINTER;
declare		VAR1	CELL;

In the above statements, CELL is a data type, and VAR1 is a variable of type CELL. When the block containing these statements is entered, memory is allocated for VAR1. The identifier VAR1 designates the entire block, and VAR1.DATA and VAR1.LINK designate the INTEGER and POINTER variables within the block. As a second example, consider the following:

template	1	STRING,	
	2	MAXLEN	INTEGER,
	2	CURLEN	INTEGER,
	2	CHAR(100)	CHARACTER;
declare		(STR1, STR2)	STRING;

Upon entry to the block containing these statements, STR1.MAXLEN, STR1.CURLEN, STR2.MAXLEN, and STR2.CURLEN designate INTEGER variables, and STR1.CHAR(1) through STR1.CHAR(100) and STR2.CHAR(1) through STR2.CHAR(100) designate CHARACTER variables. As a third example, consider the following:

template	1	A,	
	2	B(3)	8 BITS,
	2	C(2),	
	3	D	4 BITS,
	3	E(3)	2 BITS;
declare	X(10)	A;	

In this example, X is an identifier of type A and designates ten blocks of 44 BITS. Moreover,

X(1).B(1)	designates the first 8 bits of X(1)
X(1).B(2)	designates the second 8 bits of X(1)
X(1).B(3)	designates the third 8 bits of X(1)
X(1).C(1)	designates bits 25 thru 34 of X(1)
X(1).C(2)	designates bits 35 thru 44 of X(1)
X(2)	designates all 44 bits of X(2)
X(3).B	designates bits 1 thru 24 of X(3)
X(3).C	designates bits 25 thru 44 of X(3)

X(5).C(1).D	designates bits 25 thru 28 of X(5)
X(5).C(2).E (1)	designates bits 39 and 40 of X(5)
X(8).C(2).E	designates bits 39 thru 44 of X(8)
X	designates all 440 bits of X

There is a second way that variables in structures can be designated. A variable or data type POINTER may contain the address of a block, and the variables in the referenced block may be designated using field qualification in much the same way that was described above. The POINTER variable is enclosed in square brackets ([ ]), and the field qualifications follow the right bracket. As a first example, consider the following:

template	1	STRING,	
	2	MAXLEN	INTEGER,
	2	CURLEN	INTEGER,
	2	CHAR(●MAXLEN)	CHARACTER;
declare	(STR1, STR2)	POINTER **to** STRING;	

Now suppose that STR1 and STR2 already contain the addresses of two blocks of type STRING as defined above. Then [STR1].MAXLEN, [STR1].CURLEN, [STR2].MAXLEN, and [STR2].CURLEN are INTEGER designational expressions that designate the MAXLEN and CURLEN fields of the two blocks, and [STR1].CHAR(1) through [STR1].CHAR(K) designate the characters of STR1 (where K is equal to [STR1].MAXLEN, and similarly for STR2).

As a second example, consider the following:

template	1	CELL,	
	2	DATA	INTEGER,
	2	LINK	POINTER **to** CELL;
declare	LIST	POINTER **to** CELL;	

Suppose also that LIST already points to an object of data type CELL, the LINK field of that cell points to another CELL, and so forth. Then the DATA fields of the first three cells in the statement are designated by:

[LIST].DATA
[[LIST].LINK].DATA
[[[LIST].LINK].LINK].DATA

Pointers To Multiple Data Types

It is often convenient to allow one pointer to point to more than one data type. For example, in some list processing applications, the fields of a cell may either contain numeric data, or they may contain pointers to other cells; this is illustrated below:

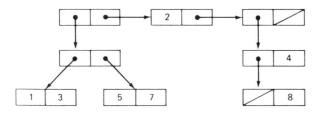

In the illustration are four types of cells: pointer-pointer, pointer-integer, integer-pointer, and integer-integer. Assuming that integers and pointers require the same amount of memory, we can create a data type CELLPOINTER that can point to any of the four types of cells. This is done as follows:

template 1 CELLPOINTER POINTER to (CELL00, CELL01, CELL10,
                                                        CELL11);
where CELL00, CELL01, CELL10, and CELL11 are defined by:

template	1	CELL00,	
	2	DATA1	INTEGER,
	2	DATA2	INTEGER;
template	1	CELL01,	
	2	DATA1	INTEGER,
	2	LINK2	CELLPOINTER;
template	1	CELL10,	
	2	LINK1	CELLPOINTER,
	2	DATA2	INTEGER;
template	1	CELL11,	
	2	LINK1	CELLPOINTER,
	2	LINK2	CELLPOINTER;

If P is a CELLPOINTER, then [P].DATA1 always refers to the first field of the cell, is an integer, and is correct if P is either a pointer to a cell of type CELL00 or CELL01; [P].LINK1 always refers to the first field of the cell, is a CELLPOINTER, and is correct if P is a pointer to a cell of type CELL10 or CELL11; and [P].DATA2 and [P].LINK2 are used analogously. (In this example, only the template statements for CELL00 AND CELL11 are required, since both INTEGER and CELLPOINTER data types can be designated for either field.)

The following restriction is placed on the data types that pointers can point to when more than one is specified: *If the same field name appears in more than one data type, then that field name must occupy the same bit positions in each of the data types in which it appears.* There may also be situations where it is either inappropriate to specify the data type to which a pointer points, or where the field name restriction stated above is inappropriate. In that case, the pointer is not restricted by a **to** <data types> qualification, and the designational expression where the pointer variable is used must indicate the data type of the object pointed to. As an example, suppose PTR is a pointer declared as:

declare PTR POINTER;

and suppose that PTR points to an object of data type CELL01 as defined above. Then [PTR]CELL01.DATA1 and [PTR]CELL01.LINK2 designate the two fields of the referenced cell.

As a general rule, when a data object is created whose fields may be used in different ways, a type field is placed within the object that indicates how the fields of the object are used. In this way, the procedures that reference the object can test the type field and determine the proper way to access its other fields. For example, consider cells whose fields are defined by the following two template statements:

template 1 CELLPOINTER POINTER **to** (CELL1, CELL2);			
template	1	CELL1,	
	2	TYPE	2 BITS,
	2	DATA1	INTEGER,
	2	DATA2	INTEGER;
template	1	CELL2,	
	2	TYPE	2 BITS,
	2	LINK1	CELLPOINTER,
	2	LINK2	CELLPOINTER;

Further suppose that if TYPE is '00'B, then the two fields are INTEGER; if TYPE is '01'B, then the first field is INTEGER and the second CELLPOINTER; if TYPE is '10'B, then the first field is CELLPOINTER and the second INTEGER; and if TYPE is '11'B, then both fields are CELLPOINTER. The following statements illustrate the use of the TYPE field:

declare   (D1,D2) INTEGER;
declare   (L1,L2,PTR) CELLPOINTER;
comment Assume PTR already points to a cell;
case
  ([PTR].TYPE = '00' B):

```
        begin
                D1 := [PTR].DATA1;
                D2 := [PTR].DATA2
        end;
    ([PTR].TYPE = '01' B):
        begin
                D1 := [PTR].DATA1;
                L2 := [PTR].LINK2
        end;
    ([PTR].TYPE = '10' B):
        begin
                L1 := [PTR].LINK1;
                D2 := [PTR].DATA2
        end;
    ([PTR].TYPE = '11' B):
        begin
                L1 := [PTR].LINK1;
                L2 := [PTR].LINK2
        end;
end case;
```

1.4.7 Address extraction

One operation that is frequently needed when working with linked data structures is obtaining the address of a block in order to create a pointer to it. This occurs most frequently when working at the assembler language level but may occur in high-level languages as well. As an example, suppose we have blocks A and B as shown below:

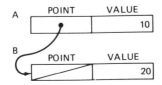

and we wish to create the structure:

To do this, we must place the address of block B in the POINT field of block A. The statement A.POINT := B is incorrect, because it specifies that a copy of the entire contents of block B should be placed in the POINT field of BLOCK A. In order to specify the correct address, we introduce the *address operator* '@'. The address operator is a unary prefix operator that denotes the address of the field or block specified. Addresses may be machine addresses, array subscripts, or addresses relative to some base register, depending on the implementation. In particular, @A and @B denote the addresses of blocks A and B, respectively. The statement A. POINT := @B places in the POINT field of block A the address of block B and hence creates the desired linkage. The complete sequence of statements for creating the example structure shown above is:

template	1	CELL,	
	2	POINT	POINTER **to** CELL,
	2	VALUE	INTEGER;
declare	(A, B)	CELL;	

A.POINT := @B;
A.VALUE := 10;
[A.POINT].VALUE := 20;
[A.POINT].POINT := **null;**

The changes are illustrated below:

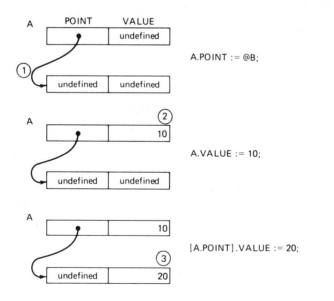

A

[A.POINT].POINT := null;

Note that the address operator cannot be used on the left-hand-side of an assignment statement. If A and B are points that point to the same data type, then A : = @[B] is equivalent to A : = B. If B is not a pointer, then [B] is undefined.

REFERENCES AND ADDITIONAL READINGS

Books

Elson, M. (1973) *Concepts of Programming Languages.* Chicago: Science Research Associates, Inc.

Foster, C. (1970) *Computer Architecture.* New York: Van Nostrand Reinhold Co.

Gries, D. (1971) *Compiler Construction for Digital Computers.* New York: John Wiley & Sons, Inc.

Hamacher, V.C.; Vranesic, Z.G.; and Zaky, S.G. (1978) *Computer Organization.* New York: McGraw-Hill Book Company, Inc.

Hayes, J.P. (1978) *Computer Architecture and Organization.* New York: McGraw-Hill Book Company.

Jensen, K., and Wirth, N. (1976) *PASCAL User Manual and Report.* New York: Springer-Verlag.

Mano, M.M. (1976) *Computer System Architecture.* Englewood Cliffs, New Jersey: Prentice-Hall, Inc.

Pratt, T.W. (1975) *Programming Languages: Design and Implementation.* Englewood Cliffs, New Jersey: Prentice-Hall, Inc.

Rosen, S. (1967) *Programming Systems and Languages.* New York: McGraw-Hill Book Co., Inc.

Sloan, M.E. (1976) *Computer Hardware Organization.* Chicago: Science Research Associates, Inc.

Stone, H.S. (Ed.) (1975) *Introduction to Computer Architecture.* Chicago: Science Research Associates, Inc.

Tanenbaum, A.S. (1976) *Structured Computer Organization.* Englewood Cliffs, New Jersey: Prentice-Hall, Inc.

van Wijngaarden, A.; Mailloux, B.J.; Peck, J.E.L.; Meertens, L.G.L.T.; and Fisker, R.G. (1976) *Revised Report on the Algorithmic Language ALGOL 68.* New York: Springer-Verlag.

Articles

Denning, P.J. Virtual Memory. *Computing Surveys* Vol 2., No. 3, Sept. 1970, 153-189.

Hansen, P.B. Concurrent programming concepts. *Computing Surveys* Vol. 5, No. 4, Dec. 1973, 223-245.

Lamport, L. Multiple byte processing with full-word instructions. *CACM* Vol. 18, No. 8, Aug. 1975, 471-475.

Presser, L. Multiprogramming coordination. *Computing Surveys,* Vol. 7, No. 1, Mar. 1975, 21-44.

Reddi, S.S., and Feustel, E.A. A conceptual framework for computer architecture. *Computing Surveys* Vol. 8, No. 2, June 1976, 277-300.

2
Linear Structures

OVERVIEW

In this chapter, we examine the implementation and use of linear structures. We cover sequential storage techniques, including storing lists in vector arrays, in multi-dimensional arrays, and in plex structures; and linked storage techniques, including singly linked, doubly linked, and circular lists. We also describe a string representation for linear lists. The operations of adding elements, deleting elements, and searching for elements are discussed for each structure. Implementations for the most common linear lists—sets, stacks, and queues—are described and sample applications given.

2.1 INTRODUCTION

Lists of names and sequences of numbers are *linear structures*—that is, structures consisting of a number of similar parts that are 'lined up' in the order in which they are to be processed. The vector arrays provided by most programming languages are linear structures. Stacks used by translators, queues used by operating systems, sets used by database systems, and display files used by graphics systems are also linear structures. Because of their prominence in virtually all areas of programming, linear structures will be the first data structures covered in this text.

There are several operations on linear structures that are frequently performed: searching for elements, inserting elements, deleting elements, and changing the ordering of elements. Sorting a list of names, for example, involves searching for an element to be moved, finding its new location, inserting the element in its new location, and deleting the element from its old location. We will discuss techniques for implementing linear structures, algorithms for implementing the above operations, and the relationship between efficiency and implementation techniques.

There are two different techniques used for implementing linear structures:

sequential techniques, where consecutive elements are stored in contiguous memory locations, and linked techniques, where each element contains a pointer to its successor element. We will discuss both techniques and their relationship to the various operations on linear structures.

A *linear list* is a finite, linearly ordered set of *elements*. Each element contains one or more items of information, and although for an arbitrary list, each element may have a different structure, we will examine lists whose elements all have the same structure. As an example, a file consisting of records that contain the names, social security numbers, and addresses of all the students at a university is a linear list. See Figure 2.1a. Each element has three fields: the name field (NAME), the social security number field (SSN), and the address field (ADDRESS). As a second example, the set of all identifiers used in a FORTRAN program is a list which can be arranged in alphabetical order. Lists of identifiers are created and used by compilers while translating programs into object code. Such lists commonly contain elements with four fields as follows: The NAME field contains the print image of the identifier; The TYPE field contains a code that indicates whether the value will be INTEGER, REAL, LOGICAL, or COMPLEX; the LENGTH field contains an integer that specifies the number of storage locations needed to hold the value of the identifier; and the ADDRESS field contains the relative location of the storage for the identifier with respect to the beginning of the program. See Figure 2.1b.

NAME	SSN	ADDRESS
LARRY CZISCHKI	123456789	CHICAGO, IL
IRA GOLDSCHMIDT	987654321	NEW YORK, NY
MARIA DE STEPHANO	854263719	SAN FRANCISCO, CA
JOHN DOE	555444333	ANYWHERE, USA

a.

NAME	TYPE	LENGTH	ADDRESS
A	2	4	0
B1D	2	40	4
NUM	1	4	44
SPEC	2	4	48

b.

Figure 2.1. Two examples of linear lists. (a) A list of students in a university. (b) A list of identifiers as maintained by a compiler.

2.2 SEQUENTIAL MEMORY REPRESENTATIONS

At the assembly language level, a sequentially stored linear list would be kept, in element order, in a contiguous block of memory. In high-level languages, however, multi-element structures are provided and can be conveniently used for implementing linear lists. The most common such structure, the array, is a data type in almost all programming languages. Arrays range from simple one-dimensional vector arrays to more complex multi-dimensional arrays. (See Chapter 5.) A more versatile data structure that can be used for implementing linear structures is the plex structure, which can be created using either the PL/I structure facility or the PASCAL type facility and record data type. In Section 2.2.1, we will examine the use of each of these structures for implementing linear lists; in Section 2.2.2, we will discuss the manipulation of data in lists implemented as arrays; in Section 2.2.3, we will describe three commonly used lists: stacks, queues, and sets. We will define operations on these structures, discuss their implementation in arrays and give examples of their use. In Section 2.2.4, we will discuss the problem of storing more than one list in a single array.

2.2.1 Implementing sequential lists in data structures provided by high-level languages

Storing sequential lists in vector arrays

Vector arrays are ideally suited for storing lists when 1) each element has only one field, and 2) the value of that field is one of the data types supported by the programming language used; for example, a list of integers or real numbers is easy to store in a FORTRAN array. A list of character strings of up to 50 characters each is more difficult to implement in standard FORTRAN, which does not support string processing, but simple to implement in PL/I, PASCAL, and SNOBOL, which do.

When a list element has several fields which together are longer than an array element, then vector arrays are more difficult to use. One technique that can often be used is to let several array elements represent one list element. If the list elements have several fields and each field can be stored in a single array element, then the field extraction operations are relatively simple. For example, suppose that a list with the following structure is to be implemented in a vector array:

```
template   1  LIST,
              2  HEADER,
                 3  MAXELS                    INTEGER,
                 3  NUMELS                    INTEGER,
                 3  NUMFLD                    INTEGER,
              2  ELEMENT (• MAXELS),
                 3  FIELD (• NUMFLD)          INTEGER;
```

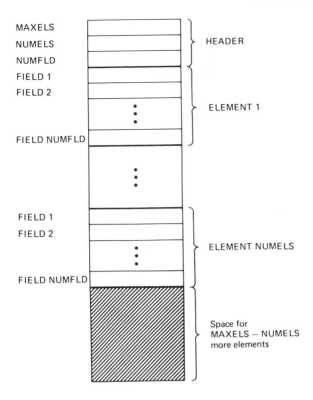

Figure 2.2. A method of storing a linear list in a vector array.

The first three words in this storage representation of a list are its header and contain integers indicating the maximum number of elements in the list (MAXELS), the current number of elements in the list (NUMELS), and the number of fields in each element of the list (NUMFLD), respectively. The remainder of the structure consists of up to MAXELS elements, each having NUMFLD fields of INTEGER values. This structure is shown in Figure 2.2.

A vector array can be used to store both the header and the elements of the list. The size of the array is 3 + MAXELS * NUMFLD words. A set of simple routines are required to manipulate the data. The following routines are typical of those that can be written. In each function, LIST designates an array containing the list.

EXTRAK (LIST,I,J)   An INTEGER function that returns the value in field J of element I of list LIST. That is, EXTRAK returns LIST.ELEMENT(I).FIELD (J). An error message is printed and the program aborted in case an illegal element reference is attempted.

NEWELM (LIST,J,VALUE) — An INTEGER function that inserts a new element at the end of LIST, places the value VALUE in the J'th field of the new element, and places zeros in the remaining fields. The value returned is the element number of the new element. If the list already has MAXELS elements, NEWELM prints an error message and aborts the program.

RPLVAL (LIST,I,J,VALUE) — A function that returns the old value of field J of element I of LIST and replaces that value with VALUE. In case an illegal element reference is made, RPLVAL prints an error message and aborts the program.

MAXELS (LIST) — A function that returns LIST.HEADER.MAXELS.

NUMELS (LIST) — A function that returns LIST.HEADER.NUMELS.

NUMFLD (LIST) — A function that returns LIST.HEADER.NUMFLD.

NEWELS (LIST,I) — A function that places the value I in LIST.HEADER.NUMELS and returns the old value of LIST.HEADER.NUMELS.

NEWFLD (LIST,I) — A function that places the value I in LIST.HEADER.NUMFLD and returns the old value of LIST.HEADER.NUMFLD.

The procedures EXTRAK and MAXELS are given below. The procedure ABORT called by EXTRAK prints the error message that is its argument and terminates program execution; ABORT will be used as an error procedure throughout the remainder of this text.

```
procedure EXTRAK (LIST,I,J);
comment EXTRAK returns LIST.ELEMENT(I).FIELD(J);
declare LIST(*) INTEGER;
declare (I,J) INTEGER;
if (I > NUMELS(LIST) )
then call ABORT ('ILLEGAL ELEMENT REFERENCE IN EXTRAK') endif;
if (J > NUMFLD(LIST) )
then call ABORT ('ILLEGAL FIELD REFERENCE IN EXTRAK') endif;
```

EXTRAK := LIST(3 + (I - 1) * NUMFLD(LIST) + J);
return;
end EXTRAK;

procedure MAXELS (LIST);
comment MAXELS returns LIST.HEADER.MAXELS;
declare (LIST(*), MAXELS) INTEGER; MAXELS := LIST(1)
return;
end MAXELS;

Exercise 2.1. Write the functions NEWELM, RPLVAL, NUMELS, NUMFLD, NEWELS, and NEWFLD.

It sometimes happens that a list consists of elements containing values that are much smaller than the data types supported by the programming language. In this case, it can be very wasteful of memory to store each field in a different array element as done in the previous example. If the programming language does not provide facilities for packing data in memory, the programmer is left with that responsibility. PASCAL provides such facilities with its 'pack' and 'unpack' instructions; however, standard FORTRAN does not. If a list of LOGICAL values is to be implemented in standard FORTRAN on a machine with 60-bit words and no bit manipulation instructions, a whole word is needed to store each 1-bit LOGICAL value. One solution is to use numeric operations to pack several fields into one word. To see how this can be done, suppose the elements of a list each have three fields as described below:

template	1	ELEMENT,	
	2	IFLAG	1 BIT,
	2	ITYPE	5 BITS,
	2	IVAL	9 BITS;

All three fields of one element can be packed into one word for storage for any computer that has words of 18 bits or more. The FORTRAN statement:

$$IPKCEL = IVAL + 1000 * ITYPE + 100000 * IFLAG$$

packs the three values IVAL, ITYPE, and IFLAG into the variable IPKCEL in the form of an integer. For example, if IVAL has value 502, ITYPE has value 16, and IFLAG has value 1, then IPKCEL will get the value 116502 (decimal) which fits in an 18 bit word. The field values can be extracted by using the following FORTRAN statements:

$$IVAL = IPKCEL - (IPKCEL / 1000) * 1000$$
$$ITYPE = IPKCEL / 1000 - (IPKCEL / 100000) * 100$$
$$IFLAG = IPKCEL / 100000$$

Although the data is not encoded into actual binary fields as the template suggests, the same information is properly encoded in the word. The multiplication and division operations are, however, computationally expensive. If packing and extraction are performed often, an assembly language routine that uses shifting operations instead of multiplication and division should be written.

Storing sequential lists in multi-dimensional arrays

In the previous example, the address (subscript) of a list element could be computed by using the formula:

length of header + (#words per element) * (element number − 1)

This computation can often be eliminated by storing the list in a multi-dimensional array. This technique works well for lists where:

1. all the fields of each element are of the same data type, and
2. that data type is supported by the programming language used.

As an example, suppose each element of a list has N fields and no subfields. Then the list can be stored in a two-dimensional array having MAXELS + three rows and N columns, where MAXELS is the maximum number of list elements the array can store. The first three rows are again used as a header which contains

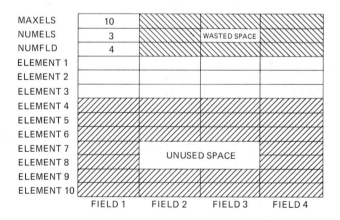

Figure 2.3. The memory representation for storing a linear list in a two-dimensional array.

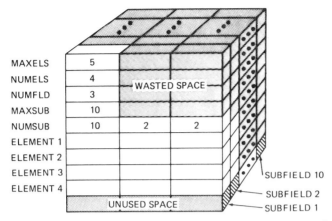

Figure 2.4. The memory representation for storing a linear list in a three-dimensional array.

MAXELS, NUMELS (the current number of elements), and NUMFLD (the number of fields (columns) being used). Figure 2.3 illustrates the memory representation for a list which has four fields per element, a maximum capacity of ten elements, and three elements currently in use.

If the fields of the list have subfields, the list can be stored in a three-dimensional array. The first subscript would represent the element number; the second subscript would represent the field number; and the third subscript would represent the subfield number. The header must now contain MAXELS, NUMELS, NUMFLD, MAXSUB (the maximum number of subfields allowed for each field), and NUMSUB(J) (the actual number of subfields being used in field J) for each J between 1 and NUMFLD. Figure 2.4 illustrates the memory representation for a list which can hold a maximum of five elements. Each element has three fields, and each field may have ten subfields; field 1 uses all ten subfields, but fields 2 and 3 use only two subfields each. Clearly this scheme can use storage very inefficiently!

Exercise 2.2. Write the function EXTRAK(LIST,I,J) which extracts and returns the J'th field of the I'th element of the list stored in two-dimensional array LIST. Assume the list is stored as in Figure 2.3.

Exercise 2.3. Write the function EXTRAK(LIST,I,J,K) which extracts and returns the K'th subfield of the J'th field of the I'th element of the list stored in three-dimensional array LIST. Assume the list is stored as in Figure 2.4.

Storing sequential lists in PL/I structures and PASCAL records

A list can be implemented in PL/I as an array whose elements are *structures;* a structure is a PL/I data type. When a programmer declares an item to be a structure, he or she also specifies how the variables in that structure will be designated. This is done in a way that resembles the template statement used in this text. Fields in the structure are assigned level numbers, names, and basic data types. The basic data types in PL/I include FIXED BINARY (integer), FLOAT BINARY (real), and CHARACTER, among others. There is only one level 1 name per structure. Level 1 can contain an item of data, or it can be further divided into level 2 fields. Each level 2 field can contain an item of data, or it can be further divided in the same way. In general, any level can contain an item of data, or the next higher level can be used to divide it into subfields. Data items in a structure are designated using the field qualification operator '.' just as in this text.

When implementing a list in a PL/I structure, the programmer gives each level a name that corresponds to one field or subfield of a list element. The following is an example of a PL/I declaration for an array of structures:

```
DCL  1  ELEMENT (100),
        2  NAME          CHARACTER (20),
        2  SSN           CHARACTER (9),
        2  PERSONAL,
           3  HEIGHT     FIXED BINARY,
           3  WEIGHT     FIXED BINARY,
           3  AGE        FIXED BINARY,
        2  GRADES (10)   FLOAT BINARY;
```

In this example, ELEMENT is an array having 100 elements; each element of ELEMENT has four fields: NAME, SSN, PERSONAL, and GRADES. The NAME field holds a character string of twenty characters; the SSN field holds a character string of nine characters; the PERSONAL field has three subfields: HEIGHT, WEIGHT, and AGE; each contains a fixed point binary integer. The GRADES field is itself an array of ten floating point binary numbers. We can also think of the GRADES field as having ten nameless subfields. The expression ELEMENT(5).PERSONAL.AGE refers to the AGE subfield of the PERSONAL field of the fifth element; the expression ELEMENT-(5).GRADES(3) refers to the third element of the grade array of the fifth element of the list. PL/I also allows a statement of the form "ELEMENT(10) = ELEMENT(5)" which copies each data field of ELEMENT(5) into ELE-MENT(10).

The PASCAL programming language has a similar facility in the *record* data type. A record, like a PL/I structure, can have multiple levels of data items; unlike PL/I, however, the data items are not assigned level numbers. Records are composed of a set of parts. Each part can be any data type including record. The following PASCAL code creates a structure which is similar to the PL/I structure declared above:

```
type people = record
                name:      packed array [1..20] of char;
                ssn:       packed array [1..9] of char;
                personal: record
                              height : integer;
                              weight : integer;
                              age :     integer
                              end;
                grades:    array [1..10] of real
                end;
var element = array [1..100] of people
```

In PASCAL, a new data type is defined by using the *type* statement, and variables are associated with data types by using the *var* statement. In the above code, the *type* statement defines the data type "people," which is then used in the *var* statement to declare the variable "element" to be of type "people."

The PL/I structure and the PASCAL record are very versatile data types and take much of the work out of implementing sequential lists. The main advantage of using these structures is their ability to store many different data types in one structure; a second advantage is the ability to copy all the fields of one element into another element using just one statement. Finally, the compiler will utilize any special hardware to optimize the access functions for the field designations.

Exercise 2.4. Describe a suitable implementation for the above ELEMENT array (PL/I) or "element" array (PASCAL) in FORTRAN. Describe all primitive functions required for operations on fields.

2.2.2. Manipulating data in sequentially stored lists

The three main operations performed on data in a linear list are:

1. inserting an element,
2. deleting an element, and
3. finding and possibly changing the value of an element.

Inserting and deleting elements of sequentially stored lists are simple and efficient operations when the data is always inserted or removed at one end of the list. As soon as arbitrary elements are to be inserted or deleted from the list, however, sequential storage becomes inefficient and therefore less desirable. For example, when removing any element other than the last element of the list in Figure 2.2, all elements below the one being removed must be shifted up by NUMFLD words. Similarly, when adding an element anywhere but after the last element, all the elements below the one being added must be shifted down by

NUMFLD words. This takes on the average (NUMFLD * NUMELS)/2 data moves.

Inserting and deleting elements in a list stored sequentially in an array

Suppose we have a list with the structure:

```
template   1   LIST,
               2   HEADER,
                   3   MAXELS                              INTEGER,
                   3   NUMELS                              INTEGER,
                   3   NUMFLD                              INTEGER,
               2   ELEMENT (● MAXELS),
                   3   FIELD (● NUMFLD)                    INTEGER;
```

stored sequentially in a vector array as in Section 2.2.1. In order to allow insertion of a new element at an arbitrary position in the list, we must define a procedure ADD whose arguments are: 1) LIST: the array containing the list; 2) I: an integer between 0 and LIST.HEADER.NUMELS, specifying after which element on the list the new element should be inserted; 3) J: an integer between 1 and LIST.HEADER.NUMFLD, specifying which field of the new element is to be initialized; and 4) VALUE: the integer value to be placed in the J'th field of the new element. The procedure ADD is given below:

```
procedure ADD(LIST,I,J,VALUE);
comment ADD adds a new element with VALUE in its J'th field directly after the I'th
        element in the list;
declare LIST(*) INTEGER;
declare (I,J,VALUE) INTEGER;
declare (NUMEL,NUMFL,MAX,PREVADDR,LASTADDR,ADDR,COUNT)  INTE-
        GER;
NUMEL := NUMELS(LIST);
NUMFL := NUMFLD(LIST);
MAX := MAXELS(LIST);
if (I < 0 or I > NUMEL)
then call ABORT('ILLEGAL ELEMENT REFERENCE IN ADD') endif;
if (J < 1 or J > NUMFL)
then call ABORT('ILLEGAL FIELD REFERENCE IN ADD') endif;
if (NUMEL = MAX)
then call ABORT ('NO MORE SPACE IN ADD') endif;
comment PREVADDR is the subscript of the array element just prior to the new list
        element;
PREVADDR := 3 + I * NUMFL;
```

comment LASTADDR is the subscript of the array element containing the last field of
         the last list element;
LASTADDR := 3 + NUMEL * NUMFL;
comment Move each element after the I'th down NUMFL array elements starting at the
         bottom;
ADDR := LASTADDR;
while (ADDR > PREVADDR) **do**
    begin
        LIST(ADDR + NUMFL) := LIST(ADDR);
        ADDR := ADDR − 1
    end;
comment Zero out all the fields of the new element;
COUNT := 1;
while (COUNT ⩽ NUMFL) **do**
    begin
        LIST(PREVADDR + COUNT) := 0;
        COUNT := COUNT + 1
    end;
comment Set the J'th field to VALUE;
LIST(PREVADDR + J) := VALUE;
comment update NUMELS;
call NEWELS(LIST,NUMEL + 1);
return;
end ADD;

Exercise 2.5. Write the procedure DELETE (LIST,I) that deletes the I'th element of a
list having the above list structure.

Searching a sequentially stored list

Suppose a university keeps a list of students where each element of the list has
the following form:

NAME	SSN	STREET	CITY	STATE	GPA

Such a list can be used to obtain information about a student or group of students.
For example, it might be necessary to look up a student by name, in order to find
his GPA; or an honor society might wish to obtain a list of all students with high
GPA's. A sociology researcher might want a list of all students from cities with
population over one million. In all of these cases, searching procedures must be
used to search the list and return the desired information.

   Searching procedures generally consist of finding either one or all of the
elements on a list whose specified field satisfies a given condition; for example,

finding all the people whose AGE field contains the value 65 is such a procedure. We will examine the simple case of searching for a single element whose specified field contains a given value (for example, finding the name of a student given his social security number). If the list is not ordered according to the values in the specified field, then searching is done sequentially, since there is no advantage in doing anything else. On the average, searching takes NUMELS/2 comparisons, where NUMELS is the number of elements in the list; this is because the desired element is just as likely to be found in the first half as the second half of the list. For a list having 100 elements, 50 comparisons would be the expected number. If the list is ordered according to the specified field, a *binary search* can be performed; in a binary search, the middle element of the list is first checked. If the specified field has the desired value, the process terminates. If not, the value in the specified field must either be higher or lower than the given value. If it is higher, the desired element must be in the top half of the list, and if it is lower, the desired element must be in the bottom half of the list. In either case, half the elements in the list can be eliminated from the search at each step, and the remaining half of the list can be searched using the same technique; this process takes at most $\log_2$ (NUMELS) comparisons. For a list having 100 elements, seven comparisons at most would be made.

The following procedure illustrates a binary search of a linear list sequentially stored in a vector array as in Section 2.2.1. The elements are ordered according to the values in the J'th fields. The algorithm searches for an element whose J'th field contains the value VALUE, and if such an element is found, it returns the element number. The parameter LIST is the array containing the list.

```
procedure  BINARY_SEARCH(LIST,J,VALUE);
comment This procedure returns the element number of the list element whose J'th field
        has value VALUE. It returns 0 if no such element exists.;
declare LIST(*) INTEGER;
declare (J,VALUE) INTEGER;
declare (NUM,FIRST,MID_ELEMENT_NUMBER) INTEGER;
declare (MID_ELEMENT_VAL,BINARY_SEARCH) INTEGER;
NUM := NUMELS (LIST);
FIRST := 1;
comment If there are no more elements to search, then quit;
while (NUM > 0) do
    begin
        MID_ELEMENT_NUMBER := FIRST + [NUM/2] ;
        MID_ELEMENT_VAL :=
            EXTRAK(LIST,MID_ELEMENT_NUMBER,J);
        case
            (MID_ELEMENT_VAL = VALUE):
                begin
                    BINARY_SEARCH := MID_ELEMENT_NUMBER;
```

```
            return
         end;
      (MID _ ELEMENT _ VAL > VALUE):
         NUM := ⌊NUM / 2⌋;
      (MID _ ELEMENT _ VAL < VALUE):
         begin
            FIRST := FIRST + ⌊NUM / 2⌋ + 1;
            NUM := ⌊ (NUM - 1) / 2⌋
         end;
      end case;
   end;
BINARY_SEARCH := 0;
return;
end BINARY_SEARCH;
```

Exercise 2.6. Give an implementation of BINARY _ SEARCH in a high-level language.

2.2.3. Sets, stacks, and queues

Sets

A *set* is a well-defined collection of distinct objects or entities. A set can be represented as a linear list having no duplicate elements. For example, the list of all identifiers in a FORTRAN program is a set; the list of all active processes maintained by an operating system is a set; and the list of all attributes of an object in a scene analysis system is a set.

The most common operations on sets are union, intersection, and complementation; they are defined as follows. Let A and B be sets. The *union* of A and B (A ∪ B) is the set C obtained by adding to the elements of A all the elements of B not already in A. The *intersection* of A and B (A ∩ B) is the set C consisting of all the elements that are in both A and B. The *complement* of A with respect to B (B − A) is the set C obtained from the set B by removing from B those elements that are also in the set A. For example, if A = {1,3,4,5,6,8} and B = {1,2,3,6}, then A ∪ B is the set {1,2,3,4,5,6,8}, A ∩ B is the set {1,3,6}, and A − B is the set {4,5,8}.

Implementing sets using arrays

The memory representations and access procedures described in Section 2.2.1 are suitable for implementing sets. Using this implementation, the procedure COMPLEMENT is given below. The procedure COMPLEMENT has two arguments, A and B, which are sets (arrays), and it creates a third set (array) C, defined by C = B − A. The function EQUAL (B,I,A,J) returns *true* if every field of the I'th element of B is equal to the corresponding field of the J'th element of A. The procedure COPYEL (B,I,A,J) copies the entire I'th element of set B into the J'th element of set A. Alternative implementations using recursion are given in Chapter 8.

```
procedure COMPLEMENT (A,B,C);
comment COMPLEMENT stores in set C the complement of set A with respect to set B;
comment Set C is assumed to have MAXELS and NUMFLD set and NUMELS
        initialized to zero before COMPLEMENT is called;
declare (A(*), B(*), C(*)) INTEGER;
declare FLAG BOOLEAN;
declare (I,J,LA,LB,LC,NFIELD) INTEGER;
NFIELD := NUMFLD(C);
LA := NUMELS(A);
LB :=NUMELS(B);
I := 1;
while (I ≤ LB) do
    begin
        J := 1;
        FLAG := true;
        while (J ≤ LA) do
            begin
                if (EQUAL(B,I,A,J)) then FLAG := false endif;
                J := J + 1
            end;
        if (FLAG = true)
        then begin
                comment move the first field;
                LC := NEWELM(C,1, EXTRAK (B,I,1));
                comment move the remainder of the fields;
                if (NFIELD > 1) then call COPYEL (B,I,C,LC) endif
            end endif;
        I := I + 1
    end;
end COMPLEMENT;
```

Exercise 2.7. Why is COMPLEMENT inefficient? Rewrite it to be more efficient.
Exercise 2.8. Give an efficient algorithm for INTERSECTION.
Exercise 2.9. Give an efficient algorithm for UNION for the case where NUMFLD=1 and the elements of both A and B are stored in increasing order. That is, if I2 > I1, then A(I2) > A(I1) and B(I2) > B(I1).
Exercise 2.10. Give an algorithm for EQUAL and one for COPYEL.

Stacks

A *stack* is a storage device or data structure with the storage policy that the last data item to be stored is the first item that can be removed. A common example is a stack of trays on a spring-loaded platform in a cafeteria line. When a customer removes the top tray, the rest of the trays move upward. An attendant adding clean trays piles them on the top of the stack. The last tray placed on the stack is the next tray to be used.

A stack can be empty or contain a collection of elements. Let S be a stack. The first accessible element in S is its *top element* (denoted *top (S)*). The element that can be accessed if the top element is removed is the *second element*, and the element that can only be accessed if all the other elements are removed is the *bottom element*. Of course, if S is empty, no elements may be accessed. For stack S and value VAL, we define the insertion and deletion operators PUSH and POP, the retrieval function TOP, and the query function EMPTY as follows:

EMPTY (S) returns **true** if stack S is empty and **false** otherwise.

PUSH (S, VAL) adds one element with value VAL to stack S. The new element becomes the top of S, the previous top element becomes the second element, and so on. If S was initially empty, then the new element also becomes the bottom element.

POP (S) removes the top element from S and returns the value of that element. The second element becomes the top of S. If the top element was the only element in S, then S becomes empty. If S was initially empty, then an error condition results.

TOP (S) returns the value of the top element of S. The stack remains unchanged. If S was initially empty, then an error condition results.

For example, if SB is the stack pictured below, then EMPTY(SB) returns **false**. TOP(SB) returns the value 2, and POP(SB) returns the value 2 and also removes that element from SB. PUSH(SB,6) would add an element with value 6 to the top of SB.

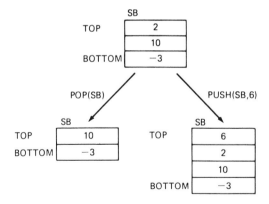

Exercise 2.11. The function BOT(S) would return the value of the bottom element of stack S, leaving S unchanged. Given a stack S and an auxilliary stack A, give an algorithm for BOT(S) using the operations PUSH and POP and the function EMPTY.

Stacks are used in most areas of computer science. The use of stacks in implementing recursion is described in Chapter 8. The following example illustrates one use of a stack during compilation.

Example. Conversion of an infix expression to Polish postfix

Arithmetic expressions such as those allowed in the FORTRAN language are in infix notation. For example, the expression $'A*B+(C-D/E)'$ is an infix expression. Such expressions are usually converted by a compiler to an intermediate form before object code is generated. One such intermediate form is the Polish postfix representation (also known as reverse Polish notation). In this representation, an operator appears directly after its operand(s). For example, the expression $'A+B'$ in Polish postfix becomes $'AB+'$, signifying the addition of the two operands A and B. The expression $'A*(B+C)'$ becomes $'ABC+*'$, signifying the multiplication of two operands. The first operand is A and the second is the result of adding B and C. The expression $'A*B+(C-D/E)'$ becomes $'AB*CDE/-+'$. The Polish postfix notation shows the order in which the operations are to be performed. Parentheses do not appear, since the order of evaluation of the intermediate results is encoded in the expression. Moreover, code for the expression can be generated directly from the Polish postfix notation.

The following algorithm converts an infix expression into its equivalent postfix form. To simplify the algorithm for this presentation, the infix expressions are restricted to contain the binary operators $*$, $/$, $+$, and $-$; left and right parentheses; single letter variables; and no blanks. The unary minus (e.g. -16) will not be considered. Finally it is assumed that each infix string ends with the delimiter $'\#'$. The stack OP_STK will be used to store operators during the conversion process. Since we have not yet shown how to implement a stack, the algorithms will deal with OP_STK abstractly, using the operations PUSH and POP and the functions TOP and EMPTY. Each operator is assigned an input priority and stack priority as follows:

OPERATOR	$*$	$/$	$+$	$-$	(	)	#
INPUT PRIORITY (IP)	2	2	1	1	3	0	0
STACK PRIORITY (SP)	2	2	1	1	0	$-$	0

The infix string is processed one character at a time. Variables are moved directly from the infix string to the postfix string. The input priority of each new operator is compared with the stack priority of the operator on the top of the stack. If the new operator has higher priority, it is pushed in the stack. If not, operators with priority greater than or equal to the new operator are popped from the stack and added to the postfix string until one of lower priority is reached. Then the new operator is pushed in the stack. The ')' operator is never pushed in the stack but causes everything up to and including the matching '(' to be popped out of the stack. The symbol '#' is initially pushed on the bottom of the stack. Its low stack priority (0) is used to force the processing of the entire infix expression.

```
Procedure CONVERT (INFIX_STRING, POSTFIX_STRING);
comment Convert INFIX_STRING to Polish postfix notation and return the result in
        POSTFIX_STRING;
comment I is a pointer to the current character in INFIX_STRING and J is a pointer to
        the current character in POSTFIX_STRING;
declare INFIX_STRING(*) CHARACTER;
declare POSTFIX_STRING(*) CHARACTER;
declare OP_STK STACK;
declare (I,J) INTEGER;
declare (SYM, OSYM, OP) CHARACTER;
I := 1;
J := 1;
comment Initialize the stack;
call PUSH(OP_STK, '#');
while (true) do
    begin
        SYM := INFIX_STRING(I);
        I := I + 1;
        case
          (SYM is an operand):
            begin
                POSTFIX_STRING(J) := SYM;
                J := J + 1
            end;
          (SYM is an operator or '('):
            begin
                while (IP(SYM) ≤ SP(TOP(OP_STK)))
                    do
                        begin
                            OSYM := POP(OP_STK);
                            POSTFIX_STRING(J) := OSYM;
                            J := J + 1;
                            if (OSYM = '#') then return endif
                        end;
                call PUSH(OP_STK, SYM)
            end;
          (SYM is ')'):
```

```
            begin
              while (TOP(OP_STK) ≠ '(') do
                  begin
                    if (EMPTY(OP_STK))
                    then call ABORT(
                    'UNBALANCED PARENS IN CONVERT') endif;
                    OP := POP(OP_STK);
                    POSTFIX_STRING(J) := OP;
                    J := J + 1
                  end;
              call POP(OP_STK)
            end;
        end case
    end;
end CONVERT;
```

Sample execution

CONVERT('A*B+(C−D/E)#',POSTFIX_STRING)

Input Symbol SYM	OP_STK (top . . . bottom)	POSTFIX_STRING
	#	
A	#	A
*	*#	A
B	*#	AB
+	+#	AB*
(	(+#	AB*
C	(+#	AB*C
−	−(+#	AB*C
D	−(+#	AB*CD
/	/−(+#	AB*CD
E	/−(+#	AB*CDE
)	+#	AB*CDE/−
#		AB*CDE/−+#

Exercise 2.12. Trace the execution of CONVERT('T*((R+S)−U/V+W)#', PSTRING).

Exercise 2.13. Modify the CONVERT algorithm to include exponentiation (**) and unary negation.

Queues

A *queue* is a storage device or data structure with the storage policy that the first element to be inserted is the first element to be removed. Cars passing through an automatic car wash form a queue, since the first car to enter the car wash is the first car to be washed and the first car to leave. Another example is a queue of jobs waiting to be executed by a computer.

Like a stack, a queue can be empty or contain a collection of elements. Let Q be a queue. The first element in Q is its *front element*, the next is its *second element*, and the last is its *rear element*. Only the current front element can be removed from the queue, and an element that is added to the queue becomes the rear element. The operations ENTER and LEAVE and the functions FRONT, REAR, and EMPTY are defined for queue Q and value VAL as follows:

EMPTY(Q) returns **true** if the queue Q is empty and **false** otherwise.

ENTER(Q,VAL) adds an element with value VAL to Q. The new element becomes the rear element of Q. If Q was initially empty, then VAL also becomes the front element.

LEAVE(Q) removes the front element from the queue and returns its value. The second element becomes the front element, the next element becomes the second element, and so on. If Q was initially empty, then an error condition results.

FRONT(Q) returns the value of the front element of Q. Q is unchanged. If Q was initially empty, then an error condition results.

REAR(Q) returns the value of the rear element of Q. Q is unchanged. If Q was initially empty, then an error condition results.

For example, if QB is the queue shown below, then EMPTY(QB) returns **false**, FRONT(QB) returns the value 'A1', REAR(QB) returns the value 'D4', and LEAVE(QB) returns the value 'A1' and removes that element from QB. ENTER(QB,'E5') would add an element with value 'E5' to the rear of QB.

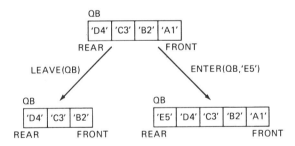

Exercise 2.14. A *deque* (double-ended queue, pronounced 'deck') is a data structure with the storage policy that elements can be added or removed from either end. If the two ends of a deque are called the LEFT and RIGHT, what operations and functions will be needed to work with a deque?

Example. Job queues in a computer system

Suppose all the jobs that enter a computer system can be classified as CLASS A (0-50K bytes), CLASS B (51-200K bytes), or CLASS C (more than 200K bytes), according to the maximum core requirement MAXECORE specified on the job card. The system provides a multiprogramming environment with three fixed size partitions (see Chapter 7). Partition A is for CLASS A jobs, partition B is for CLASS A or B jobs, and partition C is for CLASS A, B, or C jobs. When partition A becomes free, the CLASS A job that has waited longest is run. When partition B becomes free, the CLASS B job that has waited longest is run. If there are no CLASS B jobs waiting, the next CLASS A job is run. When partition C becomes free, the CLASS C job that has waited longest is run. If there are no CLASS C jobs, the next CLASS B job is run; if there are also no CLASS B jobs, the next CLASS A job is run.

The following procedure, FINDJOB, implements the scheduling algorithm and returns (a pointer to) the next job to be run. FINDJOB uses three queues QUEUE_A, QUEUE_B, and QUEUE_C to hold jobs waiting for memory in CLASS A, CLASS B and CLASS C, respectively. If there are no waiting jobs that can be run, FINDJOB returns the value 0, indicating that there are no jobs of the desired class or smaller classes to be run. Again, the algorithm treats the queues as abstract objects, using the operations ENTER and LEAVE and the function EMPTY.

```
procedure FINDJOB(CLASS);
comment This procedure is executed when the job in partition CLASS has finished
        executing and has been purged from the system. It returns the next job to run in
        partition CLASS;
declare CLASS CHARACTER;
declare FINDJOB INTEGER;
case
      ( ¬EMPTY(QUEUE_A) and CLASS = 'A'):
        FINDJOB := LEAVE(QUEUE_A);
      ( ¬EMPTY(QUEUE_B) and CLASS ≠ 'C'):
        FINDJOB := LEAVE(QUEUE_B);
      ( ¬EMPTY(QUEUE_C)):
        FINDJOB := LEAVE(QUEUE_C);
      (true):
        FINDJOB := 0;
end case;
return;
end FINDJOB;
```

Sequential allocation of stacks and queues

Stacks and queues can be efficiently implemented using sequential allocation techniques, because they are only altered at their ends. Sequential allocation of a stack or queue requires a large block of memory in which the elements are stored contiguously. This can be implemented using a one-dimensional array whose elements become the elements of the stack or queue. The following sections describe the array implementation of stacks and queues. For simplicity, the implementation assumes one field per element. The algorithms can be modified for elements with many fields by using the method described in Section 2.2.1.

Implementing a stack using an array

A one-field-per-element stack has the following structure:

template	1 STACK,	
	2 HEADER,	
	3 TOPEL	INTEGER,
	3 MAXELS	INTEGER,
	2 ELEMENTS(• MAXELS)	INTEGER;

A stack can be stored sequentially in a one-dimensional array. The first two elements of the array hold the header information. The first array element (TOPEL) contains the subscript of the array element containing the top element of the stack. The second array element (MAXELS) contains the value of the maximum number of elements that the stack can hold. The array must have MAXELS + 2 elements to hold the header plus the stack elements. The algorithms for EMPTY, PUSH, and POP using this implementation are given below. In these algorithms, STACK is a one-dimensional array with subscripts 1 to MAXELS + 2; TOPEL ranges between 2 and MAXELS + 2. If TOPEL has the value 2, the stack is empty. If TOPEL equals I, where I is between 3 and MAXELS + 2, then the stack contains I − 2 elements, and the top element is STACK(I). If TOPEL equals MAXELS + 2, the stack is full. The function FULL(STACK) called by PUSH returns **true** if the stack is full and **false** otherwise. VAL is a variable containing the value to be inserted in the stack.

```
procedure EMPTY(STACK);
declare EMPTY BOOLEAN;
declare (STACK(*),TOPEL) INTEGER;
TOPEL := STACK(1);
if (TOPEL = 2)
then EMPTY := true
else EMPTY := false endif;
return;
end EMPTY;

procedure PUSH(STACK,VAL);
declare (STACK(*),TOPEL, VAL) INTEGER;
```

```
if (FULL(STACK))
then call ABORT('OVERFLOW IN PUSH') endif;
TOPEL := STACK(1) + 1;
STACK(1) := TOPEL;
STACK(TOPEL) := VAL;
return;
end PUSH;


procedure POP(STACK);
declare (STACK(*),TOPEL,POP) INTEGER;
if (EMPTY(STACK))
then call ABORT ('UNDERFLOW IN POP') endif;
TOPEL := STACK(1);
STACK(1) := TOPEL - 1;
POP := STACK(TOPEL);
return;
end POP;
```

To show variations in coding, PUSH and POP are coded in FORTRAN and SNOBOL4 below. PL/I code is similar to the FORTRAN code and is therefore omitted. In the FORTRAN main program, STACK1 is the array used to hold the stack. The first two words of the array are used as a header; they contain the value of TOPEL and the value of MAXELS, respectively. The stacks are of type INTEGER, but there is no reason why they could not be of some other data type. In the functions PUSH, POP, FULL, and EMPTY, the formal parameter S is the array used to hold the stack. In each of these functions, the statement "INTEGER S(1)" is used to declare S an integer array. The dimension 1 is used because the size of the array is not known. The use of dimension 1 is a common FORTRAN coding practice that works with most FORTRAN compilers.

```
C        SAMPLE MAIN PROGRAM
         INTEGER STACK1(102)
         EQUIVALENCE (STACK1(1),TOP1)
         (STACK1(2),MAX1)
         INTEGER TOP1
         TOP1 = 2
         MAX1 = 100
            .
            .
            .
         CALL PUSH(STACK1,XINF)
            .
            .
            .
         YINF = POP(STACK1)
            .
            .
            .
```

```
          END
      SUBROUTINE PUSH(S,VAL)
          INTEGER S(1),TOPEL,VAL,FULL
          TOPEL = S(1)
          IF(FULL(S).NE.0) CALL OVERR('PUSH')
          TOPEL = TOPEL + 1
          S(TOPEL) = VAL
          S(1) = TOPEL
          RETURN
          END
      INTEGER FUNCTION POP(S)
          INTEGER S(1),TOPEL,EMPTY
          TOPEL = S(1)
          IF (EMPTY(S).NE.0) CALL UNDERR('POP ')
          POP = S(TOPEL)
          TOPEL = TOPEL - 1
          S(1) = TOPEL
          RETURN
          END
      INTEGER FUNCTION FULL(S)
          INTEGER S(1)
          FULL = 0
          IF(S(1).GE.S(2) + 2) FULL = 1
          RETURN
          END
      INTEGER FUNCTION EMPTY(S)
          INTEGER S(1)
          EMPTY = 0
          IF(S(1).LE.2) EMPTY = 1
          RETURN
          END
      SUBROUTINE OVERR(NAME)
          WRITE(6,100) NAME
100       FORMAT('   *** OVERFLOW ENCOUNTERED '
     +    'DURING A ', A4, ' OPERATION')
          STOP
          ENTRY UNDERR(NAME)
          WRITE(6,101) NAME
101       FORMAT('   *** UNDERFLOW ENCOUNTERED '
     +    'DURING A ', A4, ' OPERATION')
          STOP
          END
```

In the SNOBOL4 program given below, a STK is a data type representing a stack that consists of a LIST (the array) and a TOP. The function STACK creates a stack using an N-element array. STACK1 is the stack created.

```
                    DATA('STK(LIST,TOP)')
*
STACKDEF        DEFINE ('STACK(N)')                      :(PUSHDEF)
STACK           STACK = STK(ARRAY(N), 0)                 :(RETURN)
*
PUSHDEF         DEFINE('PUSH(S,VAL)')                    :(POPDEF)
PUSH            ITEM(LIST(S), TOP(S) + 1) = VAL          :F(FRETURN)
                TOP(S) = TOP(S) + 1                      :(RETURN)
*
POPDEF          DEFINE('POP(S)')                         :(CONTINUE)
POP             POP = ITEM(LIST(S), TOP(S))              :F(FRETURN)
                TOP(S) = TOP(S) - 1                      :(RETURN)
*
CONTINUE
*
*               MAIN PROGRAM
*
                STACK1 = STACK(100)
*
                PUSH(STACK1, 'AN ELEMENT')               :F(OVERFLOW)
*
                INFO = POP(STACK1)
*
END
```

The technique used in this program is due to Griswold (1975).

Exercise 2.15. Give the corresponding SNOBOL4 procedure for TOP.

Implementing a queue using an array

A one-field-per-element queue has the following structure:

template	1 QUEUE,	
	2 HEADER,	
	3 FRONTEL	INTEGER,
	3 REAREL	INTEGER,
	3 MAXELS	INTEGER,
	2 ELEMENTS(• MAXELS)	INTEGER;

Sequential allocation of a queue is more complicated than sequential allocation of a stack, since the queue changes at both ends. One satisfactory method is a *circular implementation*. In this implementation, the first element of the array that holds a queue element can be thought of as directly following the last element of the array. In the following algorithms for ENTER and LEAVE, QUEUE is a one-dimensional array with subscripts ranging from 1 to MAXELS + 3. QUEUE(1) contains FRONTEL, the subscript of the array element just before the front element of the queue; QUEUE(2) contains REAREL, the subscript of the rear element of the queue; and QUEUE(3) contains MAXELS, the maximum number of elements that can be stored in the queue. FRONTEL and REAREL have values between 3 and MAXELS + 3 and initially are both 3, indicating an empty queue. After QUEUE(MAXELS + 3) is used, the next element is placed in QUEUE(4) if that cell is not being used. This structure is illustrated below:

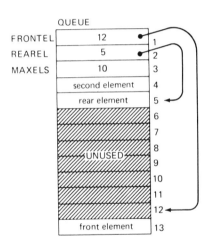

```
procedure ENTER(QUEUE,VAL);
declare (QUEUE(*),REAREL, MAXELS,VAL) INTEGER;
if (FULL(QUEUE))
then call ABORT('OVERFLOW IN ENTER') endif;
REAREL := QUEUE(2);
MAXELS := QUEUE(3);
if (REAREL < MAXELS + 3)
then REAREL := REAREL + 1
else REAREL := 4 endif;
QUEUE(REAREL) := VAL;
QUEUE(2) := REAREL;
return;
end ENTER;
```

```
procedure LEAVE(QUEUE);
declare (QUEUE(*),REAREL,FRONTEL,MAXELS) INTEGER;
if (EMPTY(QUEUE))
  then call ABORT('UNDERFLOW IN LEAVE') endif;
FRONTEL := QUEUE(1);
REAREL := QUEUE(2);
MAXELS := QUEUE(3);
if (FRONTEL < MAXELS + 3)
  then FRONTEL := FRONTEL + 1
  else FRONTEL := 4 endif;
LEAVE := QUEUE(FRONTEL);
QUEUE(1) := FRONTEL;
if (REAREL = FRONTEL)
  then begin
       QUEUE(1) := 3;
       QUEUE(2) := 3
       end endif;
return;
end LEAVE;
```

Exercise 2.16. Give algorithms for the functions FULL and EMPTY.

Exercise 2.17. Give the corresponding algorithms for FRONT and REAR.

Exercise 2.18. Describe a non-circular sequential implementation for a queue and give the algorithms for ENTER and LEAVE. HINT: Assume you have a large amount of storage reserved for the queue.

2.2.4 Sequential allocation with more than one list

In the above discussion, each stack or queue is stored in a different array. If overflow occurs, there is no chance for recovery. Another possibility is to store all the stacks and/or queues used by a program in one large array. Each stack or queue has its own bounded area in the large array. If one stack or queue overflows its area, some of the other stacks and queues can be moved around to make room for the element that needs to be added but does not fit. This process is called *memory reallocation*. The special case where two stacks are stored in a single array is left as an exercise. (Exercise 2.21.)

Suppose one array called STACK of dimension SIZE is used to sequentially store N separate stacks. Two more arrays BOT and LENGTH are used to locate each stack in STACK. BOT(I) contains the subscript of the bottom element of the I'th stack. LENGTH(I) contains the current number of elements in the I'th STACK. Initially, if there is no prior knowledge of the potential sizes of the stacks, we can allocate [SIZE/N] locations in STACK to each stack. Such a scheme, with four stacks stored in an array of 40 elements, is illustrated below. Stack 1 has its bottom element in STACK(1) and is eight elements long; Stack 2 has bottom element in STACK(11) and is five elements long; Stack 3 has no elements. BOT(3) contains the value 21, so the first element added to Stack 3 will be placed in STACK(21). Stack 4 has bottom element in STACK(31) and is three elements long.

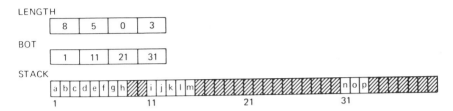

The procedure PUSH to add an element to the top of the I'th stack is given below. In this procedure, STACK, BOT, LENGTH, N, and SIZE are as described above, and I is the index of the stack to which an element with value VAL is to be added. PUSH calls the routine REALLOCATE (described below) if there is no more room in the I'th stack.

```
procedure PUSH(STACK,I,BOT,LENGTH,N,SIZE,VAL)
declare (I,N,SIZE,MAX,VAL) INTEGER;
declare STACK(SIZE) INTEGER;
declare BOT(N) INTEGER;
declare LENGTH(N) INTEGER;
declare (BOT_OF_STACK_I,TOP_OF_STACK_I) INTEGER;
BOT_OF_STACK_I := BOT(I);
TOP_OF_STACK_I := BOT_OF_STACK_I + LENGTH(I) − 1;
if (I = N)
then MAX := SIZE
else MAX := BOT (I + 1) − 1 endif;
if (TOP_OF_STACK_I = MAX) then call REALLOCATE
    (STACK,I,BOT,LENGTH,N,SIZE) endif;
STACK(TOP_OF_STACK_I + 1) := VAL;
LENGTH(I) := LENGTH(I) + 1;
return;
end PUSH;
```

The job of REALLOCATE is to reallocate memory so that another element can be added to stack I. There are several suitable reallocation methods (Knuth, 1973). We will describe one very simple reallocation algorithm.

There are I−1 stacks to the left of stack I and N−I stacks to its right in the array STACK. If any of these stacks is not full, say stack K, where K is greater than I, then we can shift all the data from stack I+1 to stack K one location right and end up with an extra location for stack I. If K is smaller than I, then stacks

K+1 through I are shifted left by 1, making an extra location for stack I. The following procedure implements the algorithm for moving the stacks to the right.

```
procedure REALLOCATE(STACK,I,BOT,LENGTH,N,SIZE);
declare (I,N,SIZE,K,TOP,MAX,MIN,ASTACK,POSITION) INTEGER;
declare STACK(SIZE) INTEGER;
declare BOT(N) INTEGER;
declare LENGTH(N) INTEGER;
comment First search to the right;
K := I + 1;
while (K ≤ N) do
      begin
          if (K = N)
          then MAX := SIZE
          else MAX := BOT(K + 1) - 1 endif;
          TOP := BOT(K) + LENGTH(K) - 1;
          if (TOP = MAX)
          then K := K + 1
          else begin
              comment Move all the elements of stack K thru stack I + 1 one location
                      right;
              POSITION := TOP;
              MIN := BOT(I + 1);
              while (POSITION ≥ MIN) do
                  begin
                      STACK(POSITION + 1) := STACK (POSITION);
                      POSITION := POSITION - 1
                  end;
              comment Change all the BOT pointers to the stacks that were moved;
              ASTACK := I + 1;
              while (ASTACK ≤ K) do
                  begin
                      BOT(ASTACK) := BOT(ASTACK) + 1;
                      ASTACK := ASTACK + 1
                  end;
              return
          end endif
      end;
comment There were no free positions to the right. Now search to the left;
          .
          .
          .

          .

end REALLOCATE;
```

Exercise 2.19. Write the missing second half of procedure REALLOCATE. If no free positions are found in the left part of the array, an error routine should be called.

Exercise 2.20. If a stack overflows, perhaps it is being used more often than the other stacks and may soon overflow again. Suggest a modification to REALLOCATE to keep this from happening.

Exercise 2.21. Show how two sequentially implemented stacks may be stored in one area of memory so that if either stack overflows, the whole area of memory has been used up.

2.3 LINKED MEMORY REPRESENTATIONS

When a list other than a stack or queue must be altered frequently, sequential storage techniques become inefficient. In order to insert an element in the middle of a sequentially stored list, all the elements above the position where the element is to be inserted must be moved up in memory. When an element is deleted, all elements following the deleted element position must be moved down in memory. The changes to a sequentially stored list during insertion and deletion are shown below. In general, there is also a large amount of wasted memory. Either the maximum amount of memory required by the list must be allocated (which is a poor use of memory), or lists must be reallocated when one list uses up the amount of memory provided. This requires a large amount of execution time.

```
   ORIGINAL        INSERT X,Y,Z      DELETE Y
     LIST           AFTER A

    ┌───┐           ┌───┐           ┌───┐
    │ A │           │ A │           │ A │
    ├───┤           ├───┤           ├───┤
    │ B │           │ X │           │ X │
    ├───┤           ├───┤           ├───┤
    │ C │           │ Y │           │ Z │
    └───┘           ├───┤           ├───┤
                    │ Z │           │ B │
                    ├───┤           ├───┤
                    │ B │           │ C │
                    ├───┤           └───┘
                    │ C │
                    └───┘
```

Many of the difficulties that arise in sequentially implemented lists do not pertain to linked lists. A *linked list* is a linear list where each element has, in addition to its information fields, one or more *link fields* that point to other elements of the list. This section will describe how to implement linked lists and give algorithms that use linked implementations. Section 2.3.1 discusses an implementation with a single link field in each element. Section 2.3.2 describes the storage of stacks and queues in singly linked lists, and section 2.3.3 discusses multi-linked linear structures.

2.3.1 Singly linked lists

A *singly linked list* is a linked list where each element has only one link field which contains a pointer to the next element of the list. As an example, a singly linked list of integers is illustrated below. For each cell, the NUM field contains an integer and the LINK field contains the address of the next element of the list. A program variable, FIRST, points to the first element of the list. The last element of the list has a null LINK field indicating no more elements. If the list is empty, then FIRST has value **null**. The values of the three elements of this list can be accessed as follows:

template 1 CELL,
    2 NUM INTEGER,
    2 LINK POINTER to CELL;
declare (FIRST, POINTER1, POINTER2, POINTER3) POINTER **to** CELL;
POINTER1 := FIRST;
NUM1 := [POINTER1].NUM;
POINTER2 := [POINTER1].LINK;
NUM2 := [POINTER2].NUM;
POINTER3 := [POINTER2].LINK;
NUM3 := [POINTER3].NUM;

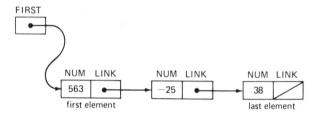

In general, a routine that processes the elements of a singly linked list in order starts at the first element, processes it, then uses its link field to find the next element, and continues in this way until a link field contains the null pointer. The following procedure illustrates this process for finding the sum of the values in the NUM fields of a singly linked list of unknown length:

procedure SUM(FIRST);
comment FIRST is a pointer to the first element of the list;
declare (FIRST, ELEMENT) POINTER **to** CELL;
declare SUM INTEGER;
declare DONE BOOLEAN;
template 1 CELL,
    2 NUM INTEGER,
    2 LINK POINTER **to** CELL;
SUM := 0;
ELEMENT := FIRST;
DONE := **false**;
while (DONE = **false**) **do**

begin
    SUM := SUM + [ELEMENT].NUM;
    if ([ELEMENT]. LINK ≠ **null**)
    then ELEMENT := [ELEMENT].LINK
    else DONE := **true endif**
  end;
return;
end SUM;

Inserting and Locating Elements

Adding an already created element to a singly linked list is done by altering pointers. For example, the following two statements add the element pointed to by E to the beginning of the list pointed to by FIRST:

$$[E].LINK := FIRST;$$
$$FIRST := E;$$

The first statement sets the LINK field of E to point to the current first (and soon

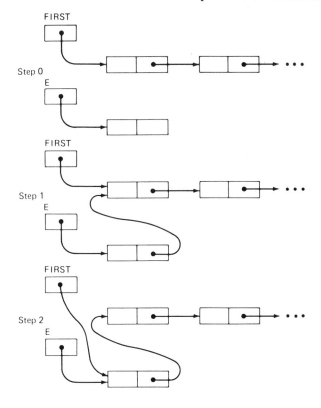

to be second) element of the list. The pointer FIRST is then changed to point to E, the new first element. The addition of a new first element to a singly linked list is illustrated on the preceding page.

Exercise 2.22. Write algorithms to add the element pointed to by E to a singly linked list pointed to by FIRST
  a. at the end of the list.
  b. after the element pointed to by variable E1.
  c. after the first element whose NUM field contains 82, if one exists, otherwise at the end of the list.
  d. before the first element whose NUM field contains 82, if one exists, otherwise at the end of the list.

Exercise 2.23. Write algorithms to delete
  a. the first element of the list.
  b. the last element of the list.
  c. the first element whose NUM field contains 82, if one exists.

2.3.2 Linked stacks and queues

Linked allocation is well suited for systems that require many stacks or queues whose lengths are unpredictable. A linked stack is illustrated below. STACK is a

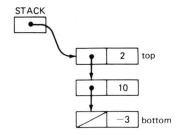

variable that contains a pointer to the top cell of the stack. The bottom cell is distinguished by having a null pointer in its link field. When the stack is empty, STACK has a null or zero value. Two extra functions, GETCELL and RCELL, may be needed to implement PUSH and POP in a linked allocation scheme. The function GETCELL returns a pointer to a new cell allocated from the pool of available storage, and, in languages without garbage collection, the routine RCELL returns a cell to the storage pool when it is no longer being used. GETCELL and RCELL are similar to the memory management routines described in Chapter 7. Algorithms for PUSH and POP for a linked implementation system are given below. ACELL is a temporary variable that contains a pointer to the cell being added or removed, and VAL is the value to be inserted.

```
procedure PUSH (STACK, VAL);
declare (STACK, ACELL) POINTER to CELL;
declare VAL INTEGER;
template 1 CELL,
           2 INFO INTEGER,
           2 LINK POINTER to CELL;
ACELL := GETCELL( );
[ACELL].INFO := VAL;
[ACELL].LINK := STACK;
STACK := ACELL;
return;
end PUSH;

procedure POP (STACK);
declare (STACK, ACELL) POINTER to CELL;
declare POP INTEGER;
template 1 CELL,
           2 INFO INTEGER,
           2 LINK POINTER to CELL;
if (STACK = null)
then call ABORT ('UNDERFLOW IN POP') endif;
ACELL := STACK;
STACK := [ACELL].LINK;
POP := [ACELL].INFO;
call RCELL(ACELL);
return;
end POP;
```

Exercise 2.24. Give a PL/I implementation of PUSH and POP using the BASED variable CELL defined by:

```
DCL 1 CELL      BASED (ACELL),
      2 INFO     FIXED BINARY,
      2 LINK     POINTER;
```

Exercise 2.25. Give a SNOBOL4 implementation of PUSH and POP using linked structures and the user defined data type:

```
DATA ('CELL (INFO, LINK)')
```

Linked allocation for queues is similar to linked allocation for stacks. A linked queue is shown below. FRONTEL is a pointer to the first cell of the queue and REAREL a pointer to its last cell. The last cell of a queue has a **null** link field. When the queue is empty, FRONTEL and REAREL are both **null**. The algorithms ENTER and LEAVE for a linked queue are left as an exercise for the reader.

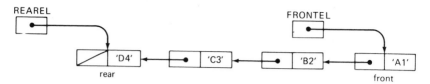

Exercise 2.26. Give algorithms for ENTER and LEAVE for a linked queue. The parameters for both routines should be FRONTEL, a pointer to the first element of the queue and REAREL, a pointer to the last element of the queue.

2.3.3 Multi-linked linear structures

Suppose we have a singly linked list pointed to by variable L, and that variable E2 points to element ELEMENT2 of L. Further suppose that we wish to insert an element ELEMENT1 pointed to by variable E1 just prior to the element ELEMENT2. This situation is illustrated below. We can easily change the LINK field of ELEMENT1 to point to ELEMENT2, but we do not know the address of the cell which precedes ELEMENT2, so we cannot change its LINK field to point to ELEMENT1. This problem can be solved by searching the entire list for element ELEMENT2. Unfortunately, the search takes time proportional (on the average) to half the length of the list.

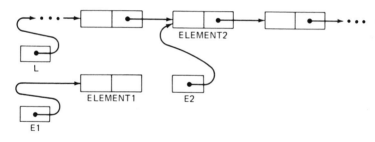

A *doubly linked* list is a linked list where each element has two pointer fields: the *forward link field* contains a pointer to the next element of the list, and the *backward link field* contains a pointer to the previous element. A doubly linked list is illustrated below. The variable FIRST points to the first element of the list,

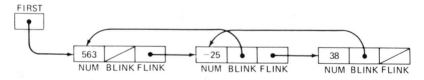

and the NUM field contains an integer value. The FLINK field is the forward link and the BLINK field is the backward link. The BLINK field of the first element and the FLINK field of the last element are **null**. Now suppose we wish to insert the element pointed to by E1 just prior to the element pointed to by E2. The following procedure will accomplish the insertion:

```
procedure INSERT(E1, E2, FIRST);
comment Insert an element whose address is E1 just prior to the element whose address is
       E2 in the list pointed to by FIRST;
declare (FIRST, E1, E2, PREVADR) POINTER to CELL;
template  1 CELL,
          2 NUM INTEGER,
          2 FLINK POINTER to CELL,
          2 BLINK POINTER to CELL;
PREVADR := [E2].BLINK;
[E2].BLINK := E1;
comment If E2 is the first element in the list, set FIRST to point to the new element;
if (PREVADR = null)
then FIRST := E1
else [PREVADR].FLINK := E1 endif;
comment Set up the double linkage to the cell before the cell pointed to by E2;
[E1].FLINK := E2;
[E1].BLINK := PREVADR;
end INSERT;
```

The **null** links at the end of a singly linked list or at the beginning and end of a doubly linked list are suitable for algorithms where the list is processed from beginning to end (or end to beginning). They are not as useful for algorithms that start processing the list at an arbitrary element in its middle, and need to process every element in the list. For such algorithms, circular structures are better suited. A *singly linked circular list* is a singly linked list where the link field of the last element contains a pointer to the first element. A *doubly linked circular list* is a doubly linked list where the forward link field of the last element contains a pointer to the first element, and the backward link field of the first element contains a pointer to the last element. Figure 2.5 shows a singly linked circular list and a doubly linked circular list.

In Figure 2.5, each cell of the list contains an item of data (a number), but there is no place to store data about the structure of the list (such as its length). A *header cell* is a special cell that marks the beginning of a list and contains information about the list as a whole. Shown below are two possible memory representations for a doubly linked circular list with header cell. In both organizations, the variable FIRST points to the header cell, and the NAME field of the header cell contains or points to a character string name for the list (which may be used for output purposes). In the first organization, the LENGTH field of the header contains an integer specifying the number of elements in the list, and the FLINK field points to the last element of the list. The remainder of the list is identical to the doubly linked circular list of Figure 2.5. The header can be used to identify the end of the list, since if E is a pointer to the last element and H is a

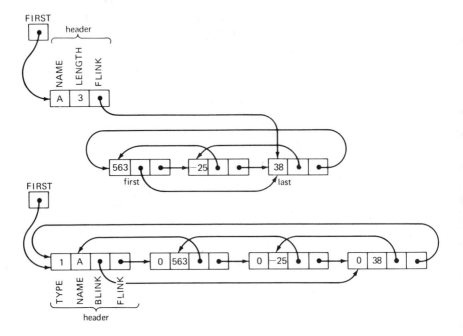

pointer to the header, then [H].FLINK equals E. Given the header and a pointer to any element of the list, the LENGTH field may be used to implement traversal of the entire list with the equivalent of a DO-loop.

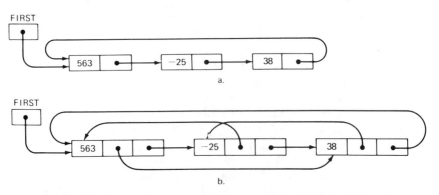

Figure 2.5. a. A singly linked circular list. b. A doubly linked circular list.

In the second organization, the header is linked into the list with BLINK and FLINK fields just like any other element. The header can be distinguished from the data elements by the TYPE field, a one bit field in both header and data cells which has value B'1' in header cells and B'0' in data cells. Here the last element of the list is that element E where [E.FLINK].TYPE equals B'1'. This organization is useful in algorithms that have to process the header cell immediately after processing the last cell of the list.

Exercise 2.27. Given a list having the first organization, give an algorithm to increment by 1 the value in the NUM field of each element in the list. Assume that FIRST is a pointer to the header. Do the same for the second organization.

Exercise 2.28. Give the singly linked form of organization 1. Why is it more efficient for the FLINK field of the header to point to the last element instead of the first element of the list?

List headers solve another important problem. Suppose the number of elements of a list varies with time, and in particular, suppose that the list can sometimes by empty. Suppose further that there can be more than one pointer to the list, for instance, in the cells of other structures. If the list becomes empty and if there is no header cell, all the pointers to the list must be changed to **null**. With a header cell present, none of the pointers to the list need be changed. They all point to the header which indicates that the list is empty.

Example. Keeping a dictionary using lists with headers

We will use the above concepts to create and maintain a dictionary. The structure will be as follows: For each letter of the alphabet, there is a doubly linked list with a header. The list is used to store the words starting with that letter; each list is in alphabetical order. The header cells have the form:

LETTER	COUNT	BLINK	FLINK

where the LETTER field contains a pointer to a character string consisting of one of the letters 'A'-'Z', and all the words in that list begin with that letter. The COUNT field contains an integer indicating the current number of words in the list and is initially set to zero. The FLINK field contains a pointer to the first element of the list, and the BLINK field contains a pointer to the last element; They are initially null. The information cells are of the form:

WORD	DEF	BLINK	FLINK

where the WORD field contains a pointer to a character string representing the word being defined, the DEF field contains a pointer to a character string representing the definition, and the BLINK and FLINK fields contain pointers to the preceding and following cells.

The 26 headers are accessed in the following manner: DICTIONARY is an array of pointers to the 26 headers of the lists. For example, DICTIONARY(1) is a pointer to the header of the list of 'A' words. A string ALPHABET is composed of the 26 letters of the alphabet.

$$\text{ALPHABET} := \text{'ABCDEFGHIJKLMNOPQRSTUVWXYZ'}$$

When given a letter of the alphabet, the function INDEX returns the position of that letter in the string. For example,

$$\text{INDEX(ALPHABET, 'B')}$$

returns the integer 2, and INDEX (ALPHABET, 'Z') returns the integer 26. (See Chapter 3.) The first letter of a word can be extracted by using the function SUBSTR. The function call:

$$\text{SUBSTR(WORD, 1, 1)}$$

returns the first character of the word WORD. Thus for a given word WORD, a pointer to the header of the only list that can contain that word is given by:

$$\text{HEADER} := \text{DICTIONARY(INDEX(ALPHABET, SUBSTR(WORD, 1,1)))}$$

In particular, after the above statement is executed, the variable HEADER will point to the header of the correct list. The memory representation of the dictionary is shown below. Given such a representation, the routine ENTER may be used to enter words in the dictionary. The routine ACCESS is a utility routine that uses the DICTIONARY as described above to return a pointer to the correct header. The routine GETCELL returns a pointer to an empty (unused) cell, and the routine FILLCELL sets the values in the WORD and DEF fields of a new cell and returns a pointer to the new cell. The routine INSERT2 (ACELL, CELL) inserts the cell pointed to by ACELL into one of the word lists. The cell is inserted in the list just prior to the cell pointed to be CELL.

```
procedure ACCESS(WORD);
comment ACCESS returns a pointer to the header of the list where WORD belongs;
declare ACCESS POINTER to HEADER _ CELL;
declare DICTIONARY (26) POINTER to HEADER _ CELL global;
declare ALPHABET STRING global;
        ACCESS :=DICTIONARY(INDEX(ALPHABET, SUBSTR(WORD, 1, 1)));
return;
end ACCESS;
```

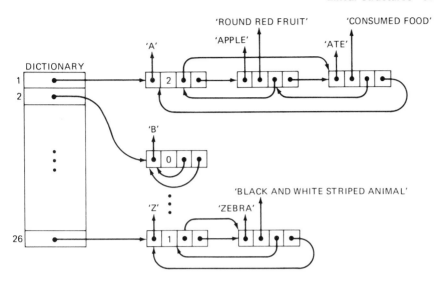

```
procedure ENTER(WORD,DEFINITION);
comment ENTER enters the word WORD and its definition
        DEFINITION in the dictionary. If WORD is already in the dictionary, the old
        definition is replaced by DEFINITION;
comment The data type STRING is a pointer to a character string. We assume that the
        data types STRING and INTEGER are the same length;
declare (WORD,DEFINITION) STRING;
declare I INTEGER;
declare HEADER POINTER to HEADER _ CELL;
template 1 HEADER _ CELL,
        2 LETTER    STRING,
        2 COUNT     INTEGER,
        2 BLINK     POINTER to (HEADER _ CELL,WORD _ CELL),
        2 FLINK     POINTER to (HEADER _ CELL,WORD _ CELL);
declare (ACELL,CELL) POINTER to WORD _ CELL;
template 1 WORD_CELL,
        2 WORD      STRING,
        2 DEF       STRING,
        2 BLINK     POINTER to (HEADER _ CELL,WORD _ CELL),
        2 FLINK     POINTER to (HEADER _ CELL,WORD _ CELL);
HEADER := ACCESS(WORD);
comment If the list is empty, WORD becomes the first entry;
if ([HEADER].COUNT = 0)
then begin
    [HEADER].COUNT := 1;
    ACELL := FILLCELL(WORD,DEFINITION);
    [ACELL].FLINK := HEADER;
```

```
            [ACELL].BLINK := HEADER;
            [HEADER].FLINK := ACELL;
            [HEADER].BLINK := ACELL;
            return
            end
else begin
        comment If the list is not empty, search for the place where WORD should be
                entered;
        CELL := [HEADER].FLINK;
        I := 1;
            while (I ≤ [HEADER].COUNT) do
            begin
                case
                  ([CELL].WORD = WORD):
                      begin
                        [CELL].DEF := DEFINITION;
                        return
                      end;
                  ([CELL].WORD is lexically greater than WORD):
                      begin
                        ACELL := FILLCELL(WORD,DEFINITION);
                        call INSERT2(ACELL,CELL);
                        [HEADER].COUNT := [HEADER].COUNT + 1;
                        return
                      end;
                  ([CELL].WORD is lexically less than WORD):
                      CELL := [CELL].FLINK;
                end case;
              I := I + 1
            end;
        comment insert a new cell at the end of the list;
        ACELL := FILLCELL(WORD,DEFINITION);
        call INSERT2(ACELL,HEADER);
        [HEADER].COUNT := [HEADER].COUNT + 1
    end endif;
end ENTER;


procedure FILLCELL(WORD,DEFINITION);
comment FILLCELL allocates a new WORD_CELL and inserts WORD and DEFINI-
        TION into its WORD and DEF fields;
declare FILLCELL POINTER to WORD_CELL;
template 1 WORD_CELL,
            2 WORD      STRING,
            2 DEF       STRING,
            2 BLINK     POINTER to WORD_CELL,
            2 FLINK     POINTER to WORD_CELL;
```

```
FILLCELL := GETCELL();
[FILLCELL].WORD := WORD;
[FILLCELL].DEF := DEFINITION;
return;
end FILLCELL;
```

Exercise 2.29.
  a. Give the algorithm for INSERT2.
  b. Write a procedure called DELETE that deletes a word from the dictionary.
  c. Write a procedure called LOOKUP which looks up a word and either returns a pointer to its definition or **null** if the word is not in the dictionary.

2.4 STRING REPRESENTATION OF LINEAR LISTS

In the above implementations, the information fields could potentially contain any kind of data. When the information is limited to character strings, and the language to be used enables string processing, a string representation of a list is possible. Some character, such as ';', that does not appear in any of the data strings, is chosen as a delimiter. The list is represented as a character string consisting of substrings that represent the element values separated by the delimiter character.

Example. A string that represents a stack:

ABC;A STRING;***;THE LAST ELEMENT;

This representation may be easily implemented in languages like SNOBOL4 or PL/I which have string handling operations. The code below is a sample implementation of PUSH and POP in SNOBOL4. The routine PUSH concatenates the new string V and a delimiter to the beginning of the stack. Overflow occurs only if all of memory is exhausted, in which case the program terminates. POP removes and returns the string of characters up to the first delimiter and also removes the delimiter from the stack. Underflow is signalled by failure of the statement in which POP is invoked.

Example. The string implementation of a stack in SNOBOL4:

```
                DATA('STACK(SVAL)')
                DEFINE('PUSH(V,S)')
                DEFINE('POP(S)')
                PAT = BREAK(';') . POP ';'
*
PUSH SVAL(S) = V ';' SVAL(S)        :(RETURN)
*
POP SVAL(S) PAT =                   :S(RETURN)F(FRETURN)
```

Exercise 2.30. Give a string implementation of a stack in PL/I.
Exercise 2.31. Give a string implementation of a queue.

2.5 COMPARISON OF METHODS

There is no one implementation technique that is preferred for all applications of linear lists. The SNOBOL4 string representation just described, although interesting, is probably the least efficient of the techniques described. This is because the entire string representing the list is recreated whenever a PUSH or POP operation is performed. If a list is encoded as a string whose length is 1000 characters, then adding a new element consisting of a single letter will cause the creation of a brand new string of length 1002 (consisting of the old string, the new letter, and the delimiter). The simplicity of the representation and the shortness of the code should not be misinterpreted as an efficient implementation.

The sequential implementation technique is very fast for one or two stacks or for a single queue, but the user must provide an array whose size is equal to the maximum size of the lists. The sequential method can also be extended to multiple stacks or queues, but the execution time for element insertions may increase substantially if lists are relocated during the process. The sequential technique becomes much less efficient when arbitrary insertions and deletions are allowed. In this case, the insertion or deletion time is proportional to half the length of the list.

The linked implementation technique is well suited to arbitrary insertions and deletions and is almost as fast as the sequential technique for stacks and queues. However, the memory required to maintain the links is often very large, since each element requires at least one link field which can be as big as the datum itself. Furthermore, memory regeneration routines are required to maintain the pool of available cells, and if garbage collection is used, the time required to regenerate memory is proportional to the number of cells that are currently in use. (See Chapter 7.) This can be substantial. Thus the choice of technique must be influenced by the list sizes, as well as the frequency of insertion and deletion operations.

Another factor that must be considered when selecting an implementation technique is the frequency with which the structure is to be searched. For linked lists, the search time is proportional to the length of the list, whereas for a sorted sequential list, the search time using a binary search is proportional to the logarithm (base 2) of the length of the list. If a list, once created, will be frequently searched and infrequently modified, then sequential techniques should be used. If the list will be frequently modified and infrequently searched, then linked techniques should be employed. If the list will never be modified, then hashing techniques should be considered (see Chapters 4 and 5); if the list will be searched and modified frequently, then balanced tree-structures should be considered (see Chapter 4). The final decision must be based on the individual application.

2.6 SUMMARY

Linear lists are frequently used in programming. List elements can be stored sequentially, or they can be linked together using pointers. Sequential lists can be stored in vector arrays, multi-dimensional arrays, or plex structures. Linked lists require some type of dynamic memory management; they can be singly or doubly linked, they can be circular, and they can contain header cells. The choice of implementation technique should depend on the frequency and type of operation to be performed on the structure.

PROJECTS

Project 2.1. Write a program according to the following specifications: Input can be any infix expression involving integers, single letter identifiers, and the binary operators +, −, *, /, and =. If an expression consists of an identifier followed by the assignment operator '=', followed by an arbitrary infix expression, the program converts the infix expression to postfix notation and places in a table the identifier as an attribute, together with the postfix expression as a value. If the expression does not involve the assignment operator, it is converted to postfix notation and the postfix string returned. As an example, the result of inputting the following data cards is the creation of the following table:

$$A = (B + 10) * (C - 2 * D)$$
$$B = 7 * C$$
$$C = 7$$
$$D = 2$$

Resulting table:

A	B 10 + C 2 D * − *
B	7 C *
C	7
D	2

Also write a function called VALUE that takes as an argument a postfix string and returns the value of the string. If the string involves only integers, the value is obtained by evaluating the string. If the string contains identifiers, they are first evaluated and their values used in evaluating the string. The value of an identifier is the value of its associated expression in the table. This must be understood recursively. If an identifier does not appear in the table, its value is zero. As an example, the following would result:

VALUE ('D') would return 2
VALUE ('C') would return 7

VALUE ('B') would return 49
VALUE ('A') would return 590
VALUE ('B + C − D') would return 54

Project 2.2. Design a memory representation for sets. Give algorithms for the various set-theoretic operations using your memory representation, and implement them in a high-level language. Include at least the following procedures:

CREATE _ SET( )   returns a newly-created empty set.

ADD _ TO _ SET(S,V)   adds an element with value V to set S. The new set should be returned.

REMOVE _ FROM _ SET(S,V)   removes the value V from set S. The new set should be returned.

INTERSECTION(S1,S2)   returns a new set that is the intersection of sets S1 and S2.

UNION(S1,S2)   returns a new set which is the union of sets S1 and S2.

DIFFERENCE(S1,S2)   returns a new set which is the difference of sets S1 and S2.

INPUTS(S)   creates a new set S whose elements are given as input. The elements should be enclosed within parentheses and separated by blanks in the input file.

OUTPUTS(S)   lists the elements of set S, enclosed in parentheses and separated by blanks.

Project 2.3. Write a program that simulates the computer system described in this chapter. Your program should consist of a loop that does the following:

Generate a random number I. The value of I should be an integer between 0 and 100.

case 1.	$(0 \leq I \leq 49)$	A job has entered the system.
1.1	$(0 \leq I \leq 25)$	Class A job; enter in QUEUE _ A.
1.2	$(26 \leq I \leq 39)$	Class B job; enter in QUEUE _ B.
1.3	$(40 \leq I \leq 49)$	Class C job; enter in QUEUE _ C.
case 2.	$(50 \leq I \leq 100)$	A job has finished execution and another job can be run.
2.1	$(50 \leq I \leq 75)$	Partition A is now empty.
2.2	$(76 \leq I \leq 89)$	Partition B is now empty.
2.3	$(90 \leq I \leq 100)$	Partition C is now empty.

The three queues should be implemented as linked structures. If a partition becomes empty, and there is no job that can be run in it, generate the next random number and continue. Repeat the loop for 100 iterations, and, at every fifth iteration, print the following information:

a. Current state of each queue.
b. Current state of each partition.
c. How many jobs of each class have been run so far.

Project 2.4. There are several programming languages that are designed specifically for simulating discrete systems, systems in which events occur at fixed times between which nothing happens. Such a language might be used to simulate the computer system described in this chapter. The events are:

1. A new job arrives at the system. The job either begins execution, or it is placed in a queue awaiting execution. If it begins execution, an event is scheduled for its completion.
2. A job terminates execution. If another job can begin execution, it does so and an event is scheduled for its completion.

Whenever a new job enters the system, an event is scheduled for the next job to arrive. Arrival of a job causes three numbers to be generated: The first is a random integer from 1 to 3; the second is a random integer from 1 to 100; and the third is a random integer from 1 to 20. The first number gives the job class (1=A, 2=B, 3=C); the second gives the length of time the job will remain in core (execution time); and the third is the amount of time until the next job arrives at the system. The system begins at simulated time 0 and runs for 1000 simulated seconds. The following trace illustrates these concepts:

Simulated time 0:   Event ='job arrives'
                    Numbers generated: 2   60   6
                    This job is class B and runs for 60 simulated seconds.
                    An event 'job of class B terminates' is scheduled to occur at time 60.
                    Next job arrives at simulated time 6.
Simulated time 6:   Event = 'job arrives'
                    Numbers generated: 1   10   4
                    This job is class A and runs for ten simulated seconds.
                    This job begins execution.
                    An event 'job of class A terminates' is scheduled to occur at simulated time 16.
                    Next job arrives at simulated time 10.
Simulated time 10: Event = 'job arrives'
                    Numbers generated: 3   10   3
                    This job is class C and runs for ten simulated seconds.
                    This job begins execution.
                    An event 'job of class C terminates' is scheduled to occur at simulated time 20.
                    Next job arrives at simulated time 13.
Simulated time 13: Event = 'job arrives'
                    Numbers generated: 3   20   6

This job is class C and runs for 20 simulated seconds.

This job enters class C queue.

Next job arrives at simulated time 19.

Simulated time 16: Event = 'job of class A terminates'

Job leaves class A partition.

Since class A queue is now empty, no special action is taken. The simulation continues.

Simulated time 19: Event = 'job arrives'

etc.

Write general procedures for scheduling events and updating the simulated clock. Use an array for the events. Each array entry gives the event number, event time, and other parameters (i.e. class of job if terminating execution). Maintain the event list in order of next event. In the previous sequence, the event list would appear this way at simulated time 10:

array subscript	time	type	parms.	next event
1	0	ARRIVAL		2
2	6	ARRIVAL		4
3	70	FINISH	Class B	0
4	10	ARRIVAL		5
5	13	ARRIVAL		6
6	16	FINISH	Class A	3

The current event becomes garbage after its execution.

Maintain the following statistics:
   a. Average amount of time a class A, B, and C job awaits core.
   b. Core utilization—average amount of core in use at any time.
   c. Average and maximum length of the job queues.

Project 2.5. A topological sort program is given a sequence of pairs of objects, $\{(a,b) \mid a<b$ by some ordering $<\}$.

The output is a linear list of objects $O_1, O_2,...O_N$, such that if $j<k$, then $O_j<O_k$. An outline of the algorithm for producing a topological sort is given below.

There are N objects numbered 1 to N. There are M pairs of objects indicating the partial ordering $<$. The storage representation used consists of a sequential table of N headers pointing to N linked lists. Each header has the form:

```
COUNT    TOP
┌────────┬────────┐
│        │        │
└────────┴────────┘
```

where the COUNT field of the k'th header contains the number of objects that precede k in the ordering, and TOP contains a pointer to the linked list of objects that follow k in the ordering. Each element of the list has the form:

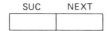

where SUC is an object that succeeds or follows object k, and NEXT is a pointer to the next element of the linked list of successors.

Your program must input N, M, and the M ordered pairs, create the memory representation just described, and then repeat the process of outputting an object whose COUNT field is zero and decrementing the COUNT fields of all successors of that object by 1. In order to avoid searching the table for headers whose COUNT field is equal to 0, the program should keep a queue of those headers with COUNT = 0. The links for this queue can be kept in the COUNT fields of the headers on the queue since all of their COUNT fields are known to be 0. A header is added to the queue whenever subtracting 1 from its COUNT field results in the value 0.

EXAMPLE
INPUT   N=5
        M=5
        (5,1) (2,3) (3,4) (1,3) (1,4)
MEMORY REPRESENTATION

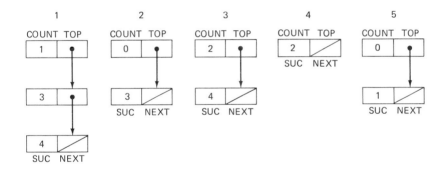

RESULTING LINEAR ORDERING   2, 5, 1, 3, 4.

REFERENCES AND ADDITIONAL READINGS

Books

Genuys, F. (1968) *Programming Languages*. New York: Academic Press.

Griswold, R.E. (1975) *String and List Processing in SNOBOL4: Techniques and Algorithms.* Englewood Cliffs, New Jersey: Prentice-Hall, Inc.

Jensen, K., and Wirth, N. (1976) *PASCAL User Manual and Report.* New York: Springer-Verlag.

Knuth, D.E. (1973) *The Art of Computer Programming, Volume 1/Fundamental Algorithms,* Second Edition. Reading, Massachusetts: Addison Wesley Publishing Co., Inc.

Articles

Baecker, H.D. Implementing a stack. *CACM* Vol. 5, No. 10, Oct. 1962, 505-507.

Chung-Phillips, A., and Rosen, R.W. A note on dynamic data storage in FORTRAN IV. *Computer J.* Vol. 18, No. 4, Nov. 1975, 342-343.

Comfort, W.T. Multiword list items. *CACM* Vol. 7, No. 6, June 1964, 357-362.

Dijkstra, E.W. Co-operating sequential processes. In Genuys (1968), 43-112.

Garwick, J. Data storage in compilers. *BIT* Vol. 4, No. 3, 1964, 137-140.

Scattley, K. Allocation of storage for arrays in ALGOL 60. *CACM* Vol. 4, No. 4, Jan. 1961, 60-65.

Wise, D.S., and Watson, D.C. Tuning Garwick's algorithm for repacking sequential storage. *BIT* Vol. 16, No. 4, 1976, 442-450.

3
String Processing

OVERVIEW

In this chapter, we will describe basic string processing operations, and we will describe in detail two different string implementation techniques. The first technique is employed by languages, such as PL/I, that allocate memory at compile time and provide only the simplest string handling operations. The second technique is more general and is used by languages, such as SNOBOL4, that allocate memory dynamically and provide a greater variety of string handling operations. We will briefly describe several different linked memory representations for character strings and conclude by discussing the efficiency of the various different implementation techniques.

3.1 INTRODUCTION

The earliest applications for computers were scientific: fixed-length integers and floating point numbers dominated the computations, and programs were primarily concerned with 'number crunching'. Even to this day, computer architectures with word-addressed memory and word-oriented central processing units reflect the requirements of numerical computations.

As the applications of the computer grow, so do the needs for non-numeric processing, principally with character string data. Assemblers and compilers process character strings (programs to be assembled or compiled); business programs process character data (names and addresses of clients, names of inventory items); information retrieval systems process character strings (bibliographic data, abstracts, dictionary entries); test formatting systems, report generators, question-answering systems, natural language translation programs, music analysis programs—all these and many more applications systems process character string data.

Depending on the application, and sometimes on the computer, the techniques used for implementing string processing operations differ. In some cases, such as inventory systems, the character strings are of limited length, and the primary emphasis of the programs is still numeric (keeping item counts, cost, location and availability of items, etc.). For these systems, only the most rudimentary character processing techniques are used. In contrast, for systems that process text (text editors, language translation programs, question-answering systems), the sizes and numbers of the strings vary greatly and are often not even known until execution time. Furthermore, for these systems, the operations performed on the strings are often very complex. Special string processing systems are used, and special string implementation techniques are required.

3.2 CHARACTER STRINGS

A *character string,* or *string* for short, is a sequence of zero or more characters. In this text, strings will always be delimited by single quotes. The unique string having zero characters is the *null string.* The *length* of a string is the number of characters in the string. A *substring* of a string is any consecutive subsequence of characters in the string. The *index* of a character in a string is an integer indicating its position in the string. The index of the first character in a string is 1. The *index* of a substring is the index of its first character. By convention, if a string is not a substring of another string, its index is 0. As an example, the sequence of characters 'A SIMPLE EXAMPLE' is a character string having length 16. The index of the letter 'S' in the string is 3, and the index of the substring 'SIMP' is also 3. Since the string 'TEST' is not a substring of the given string, its index is 0.

3.3 STRING PROCESSING OPERATIONS

In programming languages that support string processing, identifiers that designate strings are of data type STRING (SNOBOL4), CHARACTER (PL/I), CHAR (PASCAL), and so forth. The *value* of a string identifier is the character or sequence of characters designated by that identifier.

Strings are created and variables assigned values during the execution of certain types of statements. The simplest statement that can cause creation of a string is the assignment statement. In an assignment statement, the identifier named on the left-hand side of the assignment operator is given the value obtained by evaluating the string-valued expression appearing on the right-hand side. For example, the statement:

$$STR = \text{'AN EXAMPLE STRING'}$$

is a SNOBOL4 statement that assigns the value 'AN EXAMPLE STRING' to the identifier STR. Similar statements are used in other languages. When embedding string processing operations in a language that does not support string processing, string assignment statements appear as:

STR := STRING ('AN EXAMPLE STRING', 17)

or:

call STRING (STR, 'AN EXAMPLE STRING', 17)

depending on the particular implementation. In either case, the value of the identifier STR is the string 'AN EXAMPLE STRING'.

There are several restrictions that may be placed on the types and values of string variables. In PL/I, for example, an identifier may be declared to be a fixed-length string that always has the same number of characters. The declaration statement "DECLARE S CHARACTER (10);" declares S to be a fixed-length string having exactly ten characters. When a fixed-length string is assigned a value, characters are truncated from the right if the string in the expression is longer than the declared length of the string, or blanks are padded on the right if the expression yields a shorter string. For example, the statements:

DECLARE (S1, S2) CHARACTER (8);
S1 = 'A TEST STRING';
S2 = 'FAILS';

assign to S1 the string 'A TEST S' and to S2 the string 'FAILS

Strings can also be variable length. In PL/I, the statements:

DECLARE (ST1, ST2) CHARACTER (8) VARYING;
ST1 = 'A TEST STRING';
ST2 = 'FAILS';

declare ST1 and ST2 to be variable length strings having a maximum length of 8 characters. ST1 will be assigned the string 'A TEST S', which is the maximum length of ST1, but ST2 will be assigned the string 'FAILS', which is shorter than its maximum length. As illustrated above, when a variable length string is assigned a value that has more characters than its maximum length, characters are truncated from the right.

In SNOBOL4, all strings are variable length, and no maximum is imposed on their lengths. The statements:

STR1 = 'A TEST STRING'
STR2 = 'FAILS'

assign to STR1 the string 'A TEST STRING' and to STR2 the string 'FAILS'.

String-valued expressions are of various types: Constant expressions are one type of string-valued expression. A string identifier appearing alone is a second type. In the statements:

$$STR = 'THIS'$$
$$STR2 = STR$$

the string 'THIS' is a constant string expression, and, in the second statement, STR is an expression consisting of a string identifier. The statements assign 'THIS' both to STR and to STR2.

Another way of forming a string-valued expression is to concatenate two or more strings. *Concatenation* (also called *catenation*) consists of joining two strings together end-to-end. If A and B designate strings, "A $||$ B" denotes the concatenation of A with B and is the string consisting of the characters of A followed by the characters of B without intervening blanks. As an example, if the value of STR1 is 'TEST' and the value of STR2 is 'ABLE', then STR1 $||$ STR2 denotes the string 'TESTABLE'.

Programming languages that allow concatenation use statements of the form:

C = A $||$ B	(PL/I)
C = A B	(SNOBOL4)
C = CONCAT (A, B)	(typical statement if CONCAT is a function in a language)
call CONCAT (C, A, B)	(typical statement if CONCAT is a procedure in a language)

Each statement assigns to C the concatenation of A with B.

Another operation that has a string as its value is the extraction of a substring from a given string. If A is a string of length LA, then the operation of extracting the substring of A, whose index is INDX and whose length is LB, is achieved by statements of the following form:

B = SUBSTR(A, INDX, LB)	(PL/I)
A POS(INDX − 1) LEN(LB) . B	(SNOBOL4)
call SUBSTR(B, A, INDX, LB)	(typical statement if SUBSTR is a procedure)

As an example, if A = 'ABCDEF', INDX = 3, and LB = 3, then B will be assigned the value 'CDE' in each case. In the SNOBOL4 example, "POS (INDX − 1) LEN(LB) . B" is called a *pattern* which specifies that a substring should begin at position INDX − 1 and be followed by a substring of length LB. Furthermore, the substring of length LB should be assigned to the variable B. The position of the leftmost character is 0, the second character is 1, and so forth, and the dot ('.') is an assignment operator. Thus in this example, the string

'CDE' would be assigned to B. In either case, if INDX is less than 1 or LB is greater than LA − INDX + 1, then an error condition results.

There are other operations that are basic to string processing systems. Functions that return the length of a string, such as "LENGTH(STR)" (PL/I) or "SIZE(STR)" (SNOBOL), are usually provided. Testing of string equality is also a fundamental operation and is either specified by a predicate of the form "L = M" (PL/I) or by a function call of the form "IDENT(L, M)" (SNOBOL). The operation of locating a given substring in a second string is also fundamental to string processing systems. If L and M are strings, the location of L in M is determined when a statement of the form "I = INDEX(M, L)" (PL/I) or "M @I L" (SNOBOL4) is executed. The string being sought is the *pattern,* and the string being searched is the *subject.* I is either set to 0, if L is not a substring of M (PL/I), unchanged (SNOBOL4), or set to the index of the leftmost occurrence of L in M (both PL/I and SNOBOL4). Algorithms for INDEX are given later in this chapter.

One final operation that is allowed in PL/I is the modification of a substring of a string without otherwise changing the string. If L and M are strings, then the statement:

$$\text{SUBSTR(L, START, LEN)} = \text{M}$$

modifies the string L. The substring of L beginning at character position START and having length LEN is changed into the first LEN characters of M. If M is shorter than LEN, blanks are padded on the right in the substring. In PL/I an error condition results if the indicated substring is not in fact a substring of L; that is, if START<1 or START+LEN−1>LENGTH(L). Used in this way, SUBSTR is called a *pseudo-function* because it causes a change to take place rather than returning a value. As an example, suppose L = 'ABCDEFGHI' and M = 'WXYZ'. Then the statement "SUBSTR(L, 3, 5) = M" causes L to become 'ABWXYZ HI'. There are many other operations that can be performed on strings, and once a suitable memory representation for the string is selected, the methods of implementing the various operations are generally straightforward.

3.4 IMPLEMENTATION TECHNIQUES

Strings may be implemented using either contiguous memory locations for all of the characters of the string, or by using linked blocks or cells, where each block or cell contains one or more characters of the string. We will first discuss sequential string implementation techniques which are more common. The last section of this chapter will be devoted to a brief discussion of string implementation techniques using linked data structures.

3.4.1 Sequential string processing techniques

There are two different techniques used for implementing strings using sequential structures. First, an identifier that designates a string may refer directly to the block of memory containing the string and possibly additional information, such as its length. This is analagous to an array identifier that designates the block of memory containing the array elements. The program identifier is a *string identifier*. Second, the program identifier that designates a string may be either a pointer or contain a pointer to the characters of the string. Although the data type of the designated variable is string, the identifier is called a *string descriptor*. Descriptors may contain, in addition to the pointer, information such as the length of the string. In some systems, string descriptors refer to character strings by two levels of indirection rather than by one. In systems such as SNOBOL4 that have many different datatypes, string descriptors also contain a datatype specification flag indicating that the object pointed to is a string.

Figure 3.1 shows seven different memory representations used for implementing character strings. Question marks in the figure are used to indicate unused character positions. The first three memory representations use string identifier techniques. The first string, STR1, has a fixed length and is a *fixed-length string*. An amount of memory exactly equal to the length of the string must be allocated for the string, and the program or programming language that uses the string must keep track of its length. STR2 is a *variable-length string*, and its first field contains its current length. It is up to the program or programming language that uses strings of this type to keep track of their maximum lengths. (In Figure 3.1, STR2 has maximum length 20.) STR3 also has variable length. Its first two fields contain its current and maximum length, respectively, and it is therefore not necessary for the program to keep track of length information. Each routine that manipulates a string of this type has access to its length information.

The remaining four representations use string descriptors. The fourth representation has a descriptor, STR4, that points to the string, and the first field of the string contains its length. The fifth representation uses a descriptor, STR5, that contains the length of the string. Only the actual characters of the string are pointed to by this descriptor. Like string STR4, the length of string STR6 is contained in its header. In STR6, however, the header contains a field that has additional information (indicated by the '*') that is used during memory regeneration. (See Chapter 6.) String STR7 is referenced indirectly. The descriptor points to an intermediate pointer that points directly to the header of the string. The string contains a length field and a second field that points back to the intermediate string pointer. Multiple levels of indirection are useful for some memory management systems (c.f. Project 3.1).

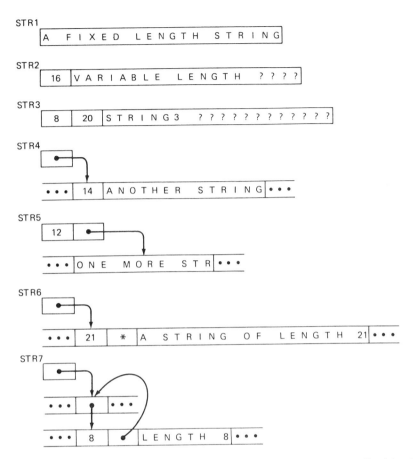

Figure 3.1. Seven representations of character strings: STR1 designates a fixed length string having 21 characters; STR2 and STR3 are variable length strings, each having a maximum length of 20; All other strings have variable length.

3.4.2 Moving characters from one field to another

The process of moving characters from one field to another occurs so frequently in string processing systems that special 'primitive' procedures are generally defined for that purpose. The procedure MOVCH (*MOV*e *CH*aracters) has three parameters: TO, FROM, and NUM. They are used as follows:

TO   is the address of the field into which characters are to be moved.

FROM   is the address of the field from which characters moved are taken.

NUM   is the number of characters to be moved.

The procedure MOVCH is given below:

```
procedure MOVCH (TO, FROM, NUM);
declare (TO(*), FROM(*)) CHARACTER;
declare (I,NUM) INTEGER;
I := 1;
while (I ≤ NUM) do
      begin
            TO(I) := FROM(I);
            I := I + 1
      end;
return;
end MOVCH;
```

As an example of how one might use this procedure, suppose L and M are strings having the following representation:

template	1 STRING,	
	2 CURLEN	INTEGER,
	2 MAXLEN	INTEGER,
	2 DATA (• MAXLEN)	CHARACTER;
declare	(M, L) STRING;	

The statement M := L if available in a programming language would compile into statements that copy the CURLEN of L into M (provided that M.MAXLEN ≥ L.CURLEN) and then move the characters from L.DATA into M.DATA. This would be done using MOVCH as follows:

```
NUMBER := L.CURLEN;
if (NUMBER ≥ M.MAXLEN) then NUMBER := M.MAXLEN
endif;
M.CURLEN := NUMBER;
call MOVCH (M.DATA (1), L.DATA (1), NUMBER);
```

It is sometimes necessary to move characters from one field to another where the two fields overlap in memory. If the source field is to the right of the destination field, the procedure MOVCH can be used. However, if the source field is to the left of the destination field (such as shifting the characters of a string one position to the right), then MOVCH cannot be used, because the characters moved first will destroy characters that have not yet been moved. (See Exercise 3.1.) Under such circumstances, the procedure MOVCHR given below should be used. MOVCHR moves characters from right to left in the string rather than from left to right:

```
procedure MOVCHR(TO, FROM, NUM);
declare (TO(*), FROM(*)) CHARACTER;
declare (NUM, I) INTEGER;
I := NUM;
while (I ≥ 1) do
    begin
        TO(I) := FROM(I);
        I := I - 1
    end;
return;
end MOVCHR;
```

Exercise 3.1. Consider the following code:

```
template 1 STRING,
         2 DATA(10) CHARACTER;
declare (STR1, STR2) STRING;
STR1 := 'ABCDEFGHIJ';
STR2 := STR1;
call MOVCH (STR1.DATA (2), STR1.DATA (1), 9);
call MOVCHR (STR2.DATA (2), STR1.DATA (2), 9);
```

What are the values of STR1 and STR2 after execution? Now assume that only single character assignment statements are allowed. That is, STR1.DATA (5) := 'E' would be allowed, but STR1 := 'ABCDEFGHIJ' would not be allowed. Give a two statement segment of code for clearing STR1; that is, code that sets all of its characters to blanks.

3.4.3 Implementing string processing routines using string identifiers

In this section, we will describe how variable-length strings are implemented using string identifiers. (See structure STR3 in Figure 3.1.) Algorithms for the operations of concatenation, substring, and index are presented here; algorithms for string assignment, testing of equality, and the pseudo-function SUBSTR are left as exercises.

The memory representation of a string is shown below. Each string has 3 fields: CURLEN, MAXLEN, and DATA. The CURLEN and MAXLEN fields contain the current and maximum lengths of the string and are each one word long. The DATA field contains the characters of the string and is MAXLEN characters long. The first CURLEN characters in the DATA field are in use; the remaining characters are undefined.

CURLEN	MAXLEN	DATA
←1 word→	←1 word→	←MAXLEN characters→

Two problems arise when concatenating strings. First, the result of the concatenation may be longer than the target string, in which case OVERFLOW occurs and characters must be truncated. Second, the target string may be the same string as the second argument of the concatenation (i.e. L := M || L), in which case the characters of L must be shifted to the right (using MOVCHR) to make room for the characters of M before the characters of M can be inserted. Figure 3.2 shows the three cases that must be considered when implementing concatenation. The algorithm for concatenation is given below:

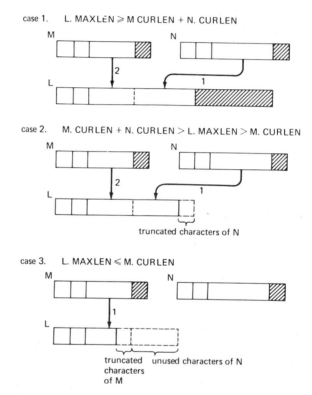

case 1. L. MAXLEN ⩾ M CURLEN + N. CURLEN

case 2. M. CURLEN + N. CURLEN > L. MAXLEN > M. CURLEN

truncated characters of N

case 3. L. MAXLEN ⩽ M. CURLEN

truncated characters of M   unused characters of N

Figure 3.2. The 3 cases for concatenation. Notice that case 3 cannot occur if M and L are the same string.

Concatenation

The procedure CONCAT given below creates the string M || N, and places it in L. A boolean variable OVERFLOW is set in case characters are lost due to truncation.

procedure CONCAT (L, M, N, OVERFLOW);
comment L := M || N;
template 1   STRING,
        2   CURLEN   INTEGER,
        2   MAXLEN   INTEGER,
        2   DATA (• MAXLEN)   CHARACTER;
declare (L, M, N) STRING;
declare OVERFLOW BOOLEAN;
OVERFLOW := **false**;
case
   (L.MAXLEN ≥ M.CURLEN + N.CURLEN):
     begin
       comment M || N fits in L.
              This is case 1 of Figure 3.2;
       call MOVCHR (L.DATA (M.CURLEN + 1), N.DATA(1), N.CURLEN);
       call MOVCH(L.DATA(1), M.DATA(1), M.CURLEN);
       L.CURLEN := M.CURLEN + N.CURLEN
     end;
   (L.MAXLEN > M.CURLEN):
     begin
       comment Only part of N will fit in L.
              This is case 2 of Figure 3.2;
       OVERFLOW := **true**;
       call MOVCHR(L.DATA (M.CURLEN + 1), N.DATA(1),
          L.MAXLEN − M.CURLEN);
       call MOVCH(L.DATA(1), M.DATA(1), M.CURLEN);
       L.CURLEN := L.MAXLEN
     end;
   (L.MAXLEN ≤ M.CURLEN):
     begin
       comment Only M or part of M will fit in L.
              This is case 3 of Figure 3.2;
       OVERFLOW := **true**;
       call MOVCH (L.DATA (1), M.DATA(1), L.MAXLEN);
       L.CURLEN := L.MAXLEN
     end;
end case;
return;
end CONCAT;

The use of this procedure is illustrated by the following example. Suppose that A and B are strings defined by:

$$A := \text{'A TEST'}$$
$$B := \text{' STRING'}$$

Then the statement:

call CONCAT(C,A,B,OVERFLOW)

would make C into the string 'A TEST STRING', provided that C.MAX-LEN≥13. If C.MAXLEN were 10, then C would become 'A TEST STR' and OVERFLOW would be set to **true**, and if C.MAXLEN were 4, then C would become 'A TE' and again OVERFLOW would be set to **true**.

Exercise 3.2. Some computers have a special hardware instruction that is equivalent to MOVCH but no instruction equivalent to MOVCHR. When CONCAT is implemented on such a machine, it should be coded so that character movement is from left to right, except when it is absolutely necessary to move characters from right to left. Rewrite the procedure CONCAT so that it is tailored for such a machine.

Substr

The procedure SUBSTR given below assigns to L that substring of M whose index is START and whose length is LENGTH. If the maximum length of L is shorter than LENGTH, characters are truncated on the right. An ABORT procedure is invoked if START<1 or START+LENGTH−1 exceeds the length of string M, and an OVERFLOW flag is set if characters are lost due to truncation.

```
procedure SUBSTR (L, M, START, LENGTH, OVERFLOW);
comment The substring of M beginning at index START and having length LENGTH is
        assigned to L. Characters are truncated from the right if necessary;
template 1    STRING,
          2    CURLEN              INTEGER,
          2    MAXLEN              INTEGER,
          2    DATA (• MAXLEN)     CHARACTER;
declare (M,L) STRING;
declare (START,LENGTH) INTEGER;
declare OVERFLOW BOOLEAN;
OVERFLOW := false;
if (START + LENGTH − 1 > M.CURLEN or START < 1)
then call ABORT ('IMPROPERLY SPECIFIED SUBSTRING IN SUBSTR') endif;
if (LENGTH > L.MAXLEN)
then begin
     L.CURLEN := L.MAXLEN;
     OVERFLOW := true
     end
else L.CURLEN := LENGTH endif;
call MOVCH (L.DATA(1), M.DATA(START), L.CURLEN);
return;
end SUBSTR;
```

As an example, suppose A is defined by:

$$A := \text{'A TEST STRING'}$$

and B denotes a string whose maximum length is at least 8. Then the statement:

call SUBSTR (B, A, 4, 8, OVERFLOW)

would make B into the string 'EST STRI'.

Index

One procedure for finding the index of a pattern string M in a subject string L is given below:

```
procedure INDEX (L, M);
comment Search L for M;
template 1     STRING,
          2    CURLEN         INTEGER,
          2    MAXLEN         INTEGER,
          2    DATA (• MAXLEN)  CHARACTER;
declare (M, L) STRING;
declare (START, LENGTH, NUMTOMOVE) INTEGER;
declare (J, K, INDEX) INTEGER;
INDEX := 0;
comment L is the subject string and M is the pattern.
          J is a pointer into the pattern string M.
          K is a pointer into the subject string L.
          K−J+1 is the index of the current substring being tested;
J := 1;
K := 1;
while (J ≤ M.CURLEN and K ≤ L.CURLEN) do
     begin
          if (M.DATA(J) ≠ L.DATA(K))
          then begin
               comment Characters did not match. Advance pattern to next trial
                    position in the subject string;
               K := K − J + 2;
               J := 1
          end
          else begin
               comment Characters matched. Try next character;
               K := K + 1;
               J := J + 1
          end endif;
```

    end;
if (J > M.CURLEN) **then** INDEX := K − J + 1 **endif**;
return;
end INDEX;

The illustration below shows the memory representations of two strings, L and M, just before a successful match. The values are shown just before incrementing J and K in the *else* clause. After J and K are incremented, the procedure will exit the *while-do* statement, since J will exceed M.CURLEN.

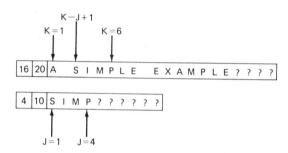

Just after exiting the *while-do* statement, J will have value 5 and K will have value 7, so that INDEX will return the value K−J+1=7−5+1=3.

Exercise 3.3. Give algorithms for string assignment, testing of string equality, and the pseudo-function SUBSTR.

3.4.4 An efficient implementation of INDEX

Under some conditions, the INDEX procedure described above is very inefficient. For example, if the subject string is 'AAAAAAAAAAAAB' and the pattern is 'AAAAAAB', then numerous partial matches occur, and K is backed up many times before the correct substring is located. In fact, for the above case, the algorithm requires time proportional to the square of the length of the pattern string.

Exercise 3.4. Trace through procedure INDEX with parameters L= 'AAAAAAAAB' and M= 'AAAAAB'.

Exercise 3.5. Show that for subject strings of the form 'A^K B' and pattern strings of the form 'A^{N}B', the algorithm requires time proportional to K*N.

The following algorithm, INDEX2, will give the index of a substring in a string in time proportional to the sum of lengths of the subject and pattern strings. (An even faster algorithm is left as an exercise for the reader.) The algorithm gains its efficiency by using the fact that once the first J characters of the pattern string have been successfully matched, the corresponding characters in the subject string are known. (Note that an unsuccessful match only tells us that the subject string character is not the same as the corresponding character in the pattern string; it does not tell us what the subject string character is.) Using that knowledge, it is never necessary to re-compare a character of the subject string that has already entered into a successful match; that is, the pointer K in the previous algorithm never has to be backed up. A character will enter into at most S comparisons even if unsuccessfully matched, where S is the size of the alphabet. If the pattern string is shorter than S, say length T, then T becomes the bound rather than S. Therefore, the algoritm requires time proportional to the length of the subject string for its execution, not counting the time necessary to compute the function NEXT(J) used in the algorithm. We will later show that NEXT(J) can be computed in time proportional to the length of the pattern string. This gives the time-bound for INDEX2 stated above.

To see why K never has to be backed up, consider the following example. The subject string is $L = $ 'ABCABCACAB' and the pattern string is $M = $ 'ABCAC'. In procedure INDEX, when $K=5$ and $J=5$, a mismatch (the first) occurs; this is shown below:

```
                    J=5
                     ↓
    A   B   C   A   C
    A   B   C   A   B   C   A   C   A   B
                     ↑
                    K=5
```

At this point, K would be set to 2 and J to 1 in INDEX, as shown below:

```
    J=1
     ↓
     A   B   C   A   C
 A   B   C   A   B   C   A   C   A   B
     ↑
    K=2
```

However, it is not necessary to consider matches for $J=1$, $K=2$; for $J=1$, $K=3$; or for $J=1$, $K=4$, since we know that the first two comparisons are bound to fail, while the last comparison is bound to succeed. (We know that the first four characters of the subject string are 'A', 'B', 'C', and 'A', in that order.) Hence the first necessary comparison, in this example, is for $J=2$ and $K=5$. This is shown below:

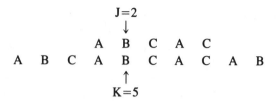

In general, depending on the pattern string, if a character comparison fails for some value of J, then we decrease J to some new value, NEXT(J), without changing K. For the example illustrated above, the first mismatch occurs when J has value 5 and K has value 5. In this case, K retains the value 5, while J is given the new value 2; hence NEXT(5) is 2 for the pattern 'ABCAC'. This is equivalent to advancing the position of the pattern in the subject string by an amount J − NEXT(J) characters, and starting the comparison with character NEXT(J) in the pattern string. If the comparison fails when J has value 1, then K is incremented by 1 and J is left at 1. At this point, we do not know what the subject string character is, but we know it is not the same as the first character in the pattern string.

In the following algorithms, the condition for advancing the pattern is easily determined. NEXT(1) always has value 0 (see COMPUTE_NEXT), and J is tested for value 0 in the procedure. The modified INDEX procedure is given below:

procedure INDEX2 (L, M);
comment L is the subject string and M is the pattern.
       J is a pointer into the pattern string M.
       K is a pointer into the subject string L.
       K−J+1 is the index of the current substring being tested;
template 1   STRING,
         2   CURLEN   INTEGER,
         2   MAXLEN   INTEGER,
         2   DATA (• MAXLEN)   CHARACTER;
declare (M, L) STRING;
declare NEXT(LENGTH(M))   INTEGER;
declare (INDEX2, J, K) INTEGER;
INDEX2 := 0;
J := 1;
K := 1;
comment Compute the table NEXT for pattern M;
call COMPUTE_NEXT(M, NEXT);
comment Now locate the substring M in L;
while (J ≤ M. CURLEN and K ≤ L. CURLEN) do
      begin
              if (M.DATA(J) ≠ L.DATA(K))

```
        then begin
                comment Character did not match;
                J := NEXT(J);
                if (J = 0)
                then begin
                        comment First character mismatch;
                        J := 1;
                        K := K + 1
                        end endif
                end
        else begin
                comment Characters matched. Try next one;
                J := J + 1;
                K := K + 1
                end endif
    end;
if (J > M.CURLEN) then INDEX2 := K - J + 1 endif;
return;
end INDEX2;
```

INDEX2 is faster than INDEX, provided that the procedure COMPUTE
NEXT is fast and that there are many partially successful matches, so that J is
frequently greater than 1. If J always fails at 2, then INDEX would be faster, and
if J fails at 3, then the cost of looking up NEXT(J) may be as time consuming as
re-comparing the one previous character. On the other hand, if the table
NEXT(J) is stored and the string search for a given pattern is used very
frequently, then considerable time can be saved by the INDEX2 procedure even
if failure occurs for J=3.

What remains to be shown is that COMPUTE_NEXT is an efficient
procedure. The procedure is given below:

```
procedure COMPUTE_NEXT (M, NEXT);
comment M should be thought of both as subject string and pattern.
            S is a pointer into the subject string.
            T is a pointer into the pattern string;
declare NEXT(*) INTEGER;
template 1      STRING,
        2       CURLEN                  INTEGER,
        2       MAXLEN                  INTEGER,
        2       DATA (• MAXLEN)         CHARACTER;
declare M STRING;
declare (S,T) INTEGER;
S := 1;
T := 0;
NEXT(1) := 0;
```

```
while (S < M.CURLEN) do
    begin
            while (T > 0 and M.DATA(S) ≠ M.DATA(T)) do
                T := NEXT(T);
            T := T + 1;
            S := S + 1;
            if (M.DATA(S) = M.DATA(T))
            then NEXT(S) := NEXT(T)
            else NEXT(S) := T
    end;
end COMPUTE _ NEXT;
```

Note that this algorithm requires at most M.CURLEN iterations of the outer *while-do* statement, since S, the variable controlling the outer *while-do* statement, is always incremented by 1. Hence, execution time is proportional to the length of M, the pattern string.

Exercise 3.6. Evaluate NEXT(J) for J from 1 to 5 for the pattern M='ABCAC', and trace through the execution of INDEX and INDEX2 for subject string L='ABCABCA-CAB' and pattern M='ABCAC'. Do the same for the pattern N='ABABC'.

Exercise 3.7. Show that COMPUTE_NEXT gives the correct values for the table NEXT. That is, if N=NEXT(J) and P=J − N+1, then (1) M.DATA(I) = M.DATA (N+I) for each I between 1 and P, and (2) the above equality does not hold for any value of N less than NEXT(J).

Exercise 3.8. There is an even faster string matching algorithm than the one presented in this section, which operates as follows. After the leftmost characters of the subject string and pattern string are aligned, the rightmost characters are compared first. If the comparison is successful, the next characters to the left are compared, and so forth. If comparison fails, the pattern string is advanced to the right as far as possible, using the information gathered during the unsuccessful match. This movement is much like the movement in the previous algorithm. Depending on how far the pattern string is advanced, characters in the subject string may never be compared at all. Thus the algorithm is better than linear. Give an algorithm for this improved string matching procedure.

Exercise 3.9. Suppose that a fixed string (the subject string) is to be searched many times for the presence of various substrings (pattern strings), and further suppose that the substring test will frequently fail. This occurs in text editors while searching for specific words in the current text. (Refer to Project 3.4 at the end of this chapter.) Hashing techniques (see Chapter 5) can be used as a rapid way of determining when the given pattern string is *not* present in the subject string. The *hashed k-signature* of string S is the binary string $b_1 b_2 b_3...b_M$ such that $b_i = 1$ if there is a substring s in string S of length k, such that hash(s)=i, and $b_i = 0$ otherwise. Let P be a pattern string, and let B_P be its hashed k-signature. Then P is a substring of S only if B_P **and** $B_S = B_P$. (Note that this condition may be satisfied even though P is not a substring of S.) Give an algorithm for computing the hashed k-signature of a string. Assuming that m is the length of a computer word, what parameters should influence the choice of k? What parameters should influence the choice of m and k, if m is not restricted to the length of a computer word?

Example. String processing in FORTRAN IV using string identifiers.

This section, which does not present any new concepts, outlines one technique for adding minimal string processing capabilities to FORTRAN IV.

One of the simplest and most uniform methods of implementing variable-length strings is to declare each identifier that is to be a string identifier to be a one-dimensional array having two words more than the maximum size required for containing the characters of the string. The first two words of the string are its *header* and contain its current and maximum length (in characters); the remaining words contain the actual characters of the string. We will call the first two words the CURLEN and MAXLEN fields of the string, respectively. In general, if one word in a computer holds NCHPW characters, then a string identifier that can contain a string of up to M characters would be [(M/NCHPW)] + 2 words long.

Suppose STR1, STR2, STR3, and STR4 are to be string identifiers, and assume that each computer word holds four characters. The strings are to have a maximum length of 10, 20, 20, and 20 characters, respectively. Also assume that STR1 is to have an initial value of 'A TEST' and STR2 is to have an initial value of 'STRING'. The declaration statement in FORTRAN IV for these strings would be:

```
      INTEGER STR1(5) /6,10,'A TE','ST  '/
    *         STR2(7) /7,20,' STR','ING '/
    *         STR3(7) /0,20/
    *         STR4(7) /0,20/
```

The memory representations for these four strings are pictured below, where '?' indicates an unknown character:

STR1	6	10	A T E S T ? ? ? ?
STR2	7	20	S T R I N G ? ? ? ? ? ? ? ? ? ? ? ? ? ?
STR3	0	20	? ? ? ? ? ? ? ? ? ? ? ? ? ? ? ? ? ? ? ?
STR4	0	20	? ? ? ? ? ? ? ? ? ? ? ? ? ? ? ? ? ? ? ?

The string processing operations described earlier are easily implemented in FORTRAN using these data objects. Three primitive subroutines are essential and should be coded as efficiently as possible. This may entail some assembly language coding, or it may involve the use of built in character packing and unpacking operations, depending on the version of FORTRAN and the particular computer. These routines must move and compare characters, independent of the structures being processed. (Note that these routines differ slightly from MOVCH and MOVCHR described earlier.)

> MVCHL(TO,NTO,FROM,NFROM,NUM)
> MVCHL moves exactly NUM characters from the one-dimensional array FROM beginning with character NFROM to the one-dimensional array TO beginning at character NTO. The characters are moved in left-to-right order. There is no check on the validity of the data.
> MVCHR(TO,NTO,FROM,NFROM,NUM)
> Same as MVCHL except that the characters are moved in right-to-left order.
> CMPCH(A1,N1,A2,N2,NUM)
> CMPCH compares the sequence of NUM characters beginning with the N1'st character of the one-dimensional array A1 and the N2'nd character of the one-dimensional array A2. CMPCH returns 0, if all compared characters are identical. Otherwise CMPCH returns the position of the first differing character.

Exercise 3.10. Write the primitives MVCHL, MVCHR, and CMPCH, as appropriate for your computer and FORTRAN compiler.

The following FORTRAN subroutine shows how CONCAT can be implemented using the data structure shown above.

```
      SUBROUTINE CONCAT(A,B,C,OVFLO)
C
C     A BECOMES B || C. THE FLAG OVFLO IS SET IF CHARACTERS
C     ARE LOST DUE TO TRUNCATION.
C
C     A(1)=A.CURLEN=LENA;      A(2)=A.MAXLEN=MAXA;
C     B(1)=B.CURLEN=LENB;      C(1)=C.CURLEN=LENC;
C
      INTEGER A(1), B(1), C(1)
C
C     IN THE DECLARATION STATEMENT FOR THE ARRAYS A, B, AND C,
C     THE SUBSCRIPT 1 IS USED TO INDICATE A ONE-DIMENSIONAL ARRAY.
C     THIS IS EQUIVALENT TO THE '*' USED IN THIS TEXTBOOK. MANY
C     FORTRAN COMPILERS DO NOT ALLOW THIS 'TRICK' AND REQUIRE
C     THE ACTUAL (FIXED) SUBSCRIPTS TO BE USED.
C
      LOGICAL OVFLO
      OVFLO=.FALSE.
      LENA=A(1)
```

```
        LENB=B(1)
        LENC=C(1)
        MAXA=A(2)
        IF(MAXA.LT.LENB+LENC) GO TO 10
C       CASE 1 OF FIGURE 3.2
        A(1) = LENB+LENC
        CALL MVCHR(A(3), LENB+1,C(3), 1, LENC)
        CALL MVCHL(A(3), 1, B(3), 1, LENB)
        RETURN
10      IF (MAXA.GE.LENB) GO TO 20
C       CASE 2 OF FIGURE 3.2
        A (1) = MAXA
        OVFLO = .TRUE.
        CALL MVCHR(A(3), LENB+1, C(3), 1, MAXA-LENB)
        CALL MVCHL(A(3), 1, B(3), 1, LENB)
        RETURN
20      CONTINUE
C       CASE 3 OF FIGURE 3.2
        A(1) = MAXA
        OVFLO = .TRUE.
        CALL MVCHL(A(3), 1, B(3), 1, MAXA)
        RETURN
        END
```

Using the definitions for STR1, STR2, STR3, and STR4 given earlier, a statement of the form:

$$\text{CALL CONCAT(STR3,STR1,STR2,OVFLO)}$$

would cause STR3 to be the string 'A TEST STRING' and to appear this way:

STR3	13	20	A		T	E	S	T			S	T	R	I	N	G	?	?	?	?	?	?	?

Exercise 3.11. Write the procedures INDEX, STRING, COPY, and SUBSTR for this system.

Exercise 3.12. Write a subroutine STINIT(STR, STRVAL, LEN, MAX) (STring INITialization) that initializes the array STR by storing LEN in its current length field, MAX in its maximum length field, and places the first LEN characters of the array STRVAL into STR beginning at character position 1. Using this routine, the statements:

```
        INTEGER STR1(5), STR2(7), STR3(7), STR4(7)
        CALL STINIT(STR1,'A TEST',6,10)
        CALL STINIT(STR2,' STRING',7,20)
        CALL STINIT(STR3,DUMMY,0,20)
        CALL STINIT(STR4,DUMMY,0,20)
```

could be used instead of the data initialization statements shown earlier.

Exercise 3.13. Write an integer function called VERIFY(STR, CHARS) that returns 0 if STR is a string comprised entirely of characters of the string CHARS or returns the index of the first character in STR that is not among the characters of CHARS.

Exercise 3.14. Write a subroutine SUBSP(STR1, STR2, STR3) (SUBstring given SPan characters) that places in STR1 the leftmost substring of string STR2, beginning with a character of the string STR3 and consisting of all adjacent characters comprised entirely of the characters of STR3. (For example, if STR2 = 'A TEST STRING' and STR3 = 'EBSK', then CALL SUBSP(STR1, STR2, STR3) would make STR1 into the string 'ES'.

Exercise 3.15. How would an array ARY have to be dimensioned if it were to be used as an array of 25 strings each having a maximum length of 15 characters? Using the subroutine STINIT described in Exercise 3, give statements that would initialize all 25 strings of ARY to the null string. Give a statement that would make the first string of ARY into the concatenation of the second and third strings of ARY.

3.4.5 Implementing string processing routines using string descriptors

In this section, we will discuss techniques for implementing string operations using dynamic memory allocation without memory reclamation. We will defer until Chapters 6 and 7 detailed discussions of the implementation techniques used by dynamic memory allocation systems that reclaim memory.

There are many circumstances when it is too restrictive to allocate for each string the maximum amount of memory that the string might require. This is true, for example, when a program creates thousands of strings of various lengths most of which are short. One solution is to allocate memory only when a string is created at execution time. When memory is finally used, only the amount of memory that is actually needed for the string is allocated. Systems that dynamically allocate memory at execution time are dynamic memory allocation systems. Dynamic memory allocation systems are of two principle types: those that reclaim memory once the supply is exhausted, and those that do not. Unless memory reclamation is provided, once memory is used up an additional request for memory will cause program termination.

Dynamic memory allocation systems without memory reclamation are ideal for programs that create strings at the beginning of program execution, but once created the strings remain fixed for the duration of the program. Programs that use translation dictionaries are an example, as are programs that create large strings and then use many substrings of the large strings. PASCAL uses dynamic memory allocation without memory reclamation. Dynamic memory allocation systems with memory reclamation are the most powerful and are suited for programs that create and then abandon many strings during execution; parsing systems are an example, as are most natural language question-asnwering systems. SNOBOL4 uses dynamic memory allocation with memory reclamation.

When using dynamic memory allocation, strings are allocated at execution time. Each string is referenced by a string descriptor that points to the structure containing the actual character information. Either the descriptor or the string itself contains the length of the string. A heap of memory called *free space* is initially set aside. A heap is a large block of contiguous memory locations that are allocated dynamically. Memory will be taken from this heap for each string created. A *free space pointer* is maintained by the memory allocation routines. The free space pointer either points to the first available character or to the last used character of free space. When a string is created, the exact amount of memory needed for the string is taken from free space beginning at the first free character. The free space pointer is then incremented by an amount equal to the number of characters (or words) used by the newly created string. Each time a string is created, memory is allocated and the free space pointer incremented. Once the available space is used up, a request for additional memory results in program termination.

The memory representation used for implementing strings in this system is illustrated in Figure 3.3. Each string has a descriptor that has two fields: LENGTH and POINT. The LENGTH field contains the number of characters in the string, and the POINT field contains the subscript in the heap SPACE of the first character of the string. SPACE holds SIZE characters, SPACE(1) thru SPACE(SIZE). Strings are allocated from SPACE sequentially. The pointer FREE holds the subscript of the first unused character in SPACE; hence all characters from SPACE(FREE) to SPACE(SIZE) are available for allocation. The null string is designated by a description with LENGTH field 0.

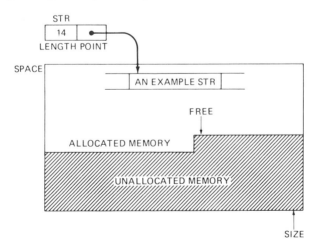

Figure 3.3. The memory representation for a system that allocates strings dynamically. STR designates the string 'AN EXAMPLE STR'.

String definition

The procedure STRING returns a descriptor to a string whose image is contained in the one-dimensional array of characters STRVAL and whose length is LEN.

```
procedure STRING (STRVAL, LEN)
declare STRVAL(*) CHARACTER;
declare LEN INTEGER;
declare (SIZE, FREE) INTEGER global;
declare SPACE(SIZE) CHARACTER global;
template 1      STRINGPTR,
         2    LENGTH    INTEGER,
         2    POINT     INTEGER;
declare STRING STRINGPTR;
if (LEN < 0) then call ABORT ('INVALID LEN ARGUMENT IN STRING') endif;
if (FREE + LEN − 1 > SIZE) then call ABORT ('MEMORY OVERFLOW IN
STRING') endif;
STRING.LENGTH := LEN;
STRING.POINT := FREE;
call MOVCH(SPACE(FREE), STRVAL(1), LEN);
FREE := FREE + LEN;
return;
end STRING;
```

String assignment

There are two ways to perform string assignment: First, a copy of the descriptor to a string can be made; second, the string to be assigned can be copied, and a descriptor to the copy can be made. The procedure COPY for copying a string and returning a descriptor to the copy is given below:

```
procedure COPY(STR);
declare (SIZE,FREE) INTEGER global;
declare SPACE(SIZE) CHARACTER global;
template 1      STRINGPTR,
         2   LENGTH    INTEGER,
         2   POINT     INTEGER;
declare (STR,COPY) STRINGPTR;
if (FREE + STR.LENGTH − 1 > SIZE)
then call ABORT('MEMORY OVERFLOW IN COPY') endif;
COPY.LENGTH := STR.LENGTH;
COPY.POINT := FREE;
call MOVCH(SPACE(FREE), SPACE(STR.POINT), STR.LENGTH);
```

```
FREE := FREE + STR.LENGTH;
return;
end COPY;
```

The statement "B := COPY(A)" would make B into a descriptor to a copy of the string A, whereas the statement "B := A" would make B into a descriptor for the string A. The statement "B := A" could be used instead of "B := COPY(A)," depending on how other string processes are implemented. This issue will be discussed shortly.

Concatenation

CONCAT returns a descriptor to the string A $\|$ B:

```
procedure CONCAT (A, B);
declare (SIZE, FREE) INTEGER global;
declare SPACE(SIZE) CHARACTER global;
template 1      STRINGPTR,
           2      LENGTH      INTEGER,
           2      POINT       INTEGER;
declare (A, B, CONCAT) STRINGPTR;
if (FREE + A.LENGTH + B. LENGTH - 1 > SIZE)
then call ABORT('MEMORY OVERFLOW IN CONCAT') endif;
CONCAT.POINT := FREE;
CONCAT.LENGTH := A.LENGTH + B.LENGTH;
call MOVCH(SPACE(FREE), SPACE(A.POINT), A.LENGTH);
FREE := FREE + A.LENGTH;
call MOVCH(SPACE(FREE), SPACE(B.POINT), B. LENGTH);
FREE := FREE + B.LENGTH;
return;
end CONCAT;
```

Substring

Two different procedures for substring will be presented. The first version, SUBSTR1, copies the substring of string A, beginning at character position START and having length LEN, and returns a descriptor to the newly created substring. The second version, SUBSTR2, simply creates a descriptor to the specified substring of A.

```
procedure SUBSTR1(A, START, LEN);
declare (SIZE, FREE) INTEGER global;
declare SPACE(SIZE) CHARACTER global;
template 1      STRINGPTR,
           2      LENGTH      INTEGER,
           2      POINT       INTEGER;
```

```
declare (A, SUBSTR1) STRINGPTR;
declare (START, LEN) INTEGER;
if (START + LEN − 1 > A.LENGTH or START < 1)
then call ('IMPROPERLY SPECIFIED SUBSTRING IN SUBSTR1') endif;
if (FREE + LEN − 1 > SIZE)
then call ABORT('MEMORY OVERFLOW IN SUBSTR1') endif;
SUBSTR1.LENGTH := LEN;
SUBSTR1.POINT := FREE;
call MOVCH(SPACE(FREE), SPACE(A.POINT + START − 1), LEN);
FREE := FREE + LEN;
return;
end SUBSTR1;
```

The following procedure returns a descriptor to the actual substring of string A, beginning at character position START and having LEN characters. A new string is not created.

```
procedure SUBSTR2(A, START, LEN)
template 1      STRINGPTR,
         2      LENGTH      INTEGER,
         2      POINT       INTEGER;
declare (A, SUBSTR2) STRINGPTR;
declare (START, LEN) INTEGER;
if (START + LEN − 1 > A.LENGTH or START < 1)
then call ABORT('IMPROPERLY SPECIFIED SUBSTRING IN SUBSTR2') endif;
SUBSTR2.LENGTH := LEN;
SUBSTR2.POINT := A.POINT + START − 1;
return;
end SUBSTR2;
```

Two different implementations of string assignment [A := COPY(B) and A := B] and substring [SUBSTR1 and SUBSTR2] were presented. If, once a string is created, the characters of the string are never changed, then either form of assignment and substring would be suitable. The second form of each would be preferred, since it would be faster and require less memory; however, under some circumstances it is advantageous to modify rather than copy existing strings. An example would be a system that frequently modifies strings by changing their characters, one at a time, but infrequently copies an entire string.

The choice of implementation technique depends on the type of processing being done. If a problem requires repeated modifications of the same string, but at no time does it need the previous modification, then an implementation that modifies the existing string would be preferred. If, on the other hand, only a few modifications are going to be made to each string, and if in addition the routines are going to need some or all of the previous versions of the string, then an implementation that creates new strings would be preferred. If the system will make many modifications to strings and will need copies of some, but not all of the versions, then dynamic memory allocation techniques presented in Chapter 6 should be considered.

The procedure MODIFY given below is an implementation of the PL/I pseudo function SUBSTR described earlier (c.f. page 95). MODIFY changes some of the characters in an existing string and hence should not be used in a system that uses the 'A := B' form of assignment. The first parameter A, to MODIFY, is a descriptor for the string to be modified; the second parameter, START, is the character index of the substring to be changed; the third parameter, LEN, is the number of characters to be replaced; and the final parameter, B, is a descriptor for the string containing the replacement characters. If LEN is greater than the length of B, then the specified substring is replaced by B and padded on the right with blanks. If LEN is shorter than the length of B, then only the first LEN characters of B are used. It is an error if START + LEN − 1 > A.LENGTH or START < 1.

```
procedure MODIFY(A, START, LEN, B);
comment The substring of A beginning at position START and having length LENGTH
        is replaced by B, truncated or padded on the right with blanks if necessary;
declare SIZE INTEGER global;
declare SPACE(SIZE) CHARACTER global;
template 1      STRINGPTR,
         2      LENGTH    INTEGER,
         2      POINT     INTEGER;
declare (A,B) STRINGPTR;
declare (START, LEN, I) INTEGER;
if (START + LEN − 1 > A.LENGTH or START < 1)
then call ABORT('IMPROPERLY SPECIFIED SUBSTRING IN MODIFY') endif;
if (LEN ≤ B.LENGTH)
then begin
        call MOVCH(SPACE (A.POINT + START − 1),
                   SPACE(B.POINT), LEN);
        MODIFY := A;
        return
     end endif;
call MOVCH(SPACE (A.POINT + START − 1), SPACE(B.POINT), B.LENGTH):
comment Pad with blanks;
I := A.POINT + B.LENGTH − 1;
while (I < A.POINT + LEN − 1) do
     begin
        SPACE(I) := ' ';
        I := I + 1
     end;
```

MODIFY := A;
return;
end MODIFY;

This procedure can also be written so that it does not modify an existing string: First a copy of the existing string is made; next the specified substring is modified as required; finally a descriptor to the new string is returned.

Exercise 3.16. Write an algorithm for the version of MODIFY described in the above paragraph.
Exercise 3.17. Modify all of the algorithms given in this section so that strings always begin on fullword boundaries. That is, SPACE is declared WORD, and each word can contain some number of characters. (This is beneficial for computers that only have word-oriented instructions, since characters are extracted by shifting and masking operations.)

3.4.6 Implementing strings using linked structures

Historically, string processing systems were first implemented using linked structures; non-linked techniques described in this chapter were developed after the linked techniques. Although under some restricted circumstances linked techniques are faster than non-linked techniques, in general linked techniques are less flexible, slower, use more memory, and are more difficult to program than non-linked systems. In this section, we will present a brief discussion of techniques used for implementing strings using linked systems.

Figure 3.4 shows two different linked memory representations for implementing character strings. The first representation uses fixed-size cells. Each cell has a pointer field that points to the next cell containing characters of the string, and each cell contains from 1 to some maximum number of characters, depending on the size of the cell. An invalid character is used for padding in cells containing fewer than the maximum number of characters, and all routines that process strings of this type must ignore these invalid (or **null**) characters. The second memory representation illustrated in Figure 3.4 uses variable-size blocks instead of cells. In addition to the pointer field, each block has a field that indicates the maximum number of characters that the block can contain. Again, invalid or NULL characters are used for padding.

For each of the illustrated representations, the program identifiers are descriptors that contain pointers to the first block or cell of a string. In addition, a descriptor may contain additional information about the string, such as the address of its last cell or block (e.g. STR9), the number of characters in the string (e.g. STR8), or the number of cells or blocks in the string (not shown). When strings are created, blocks or cells are dynamically allocated using the techniques described in Chapters 6 and 7. Algorithms for string creation are similar to those presented earlier and will not be discussed.

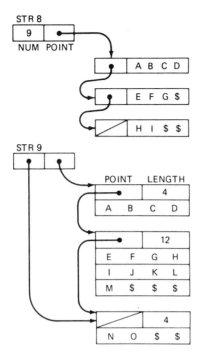

Figure 3.4. Two linked representations of strings. STR9 designates 'ABCDEFGHIJKLMNO'. The symbol '$' is an invalid character (not equivalent to a blank), not treated as part of a string.

Algorithms for string concatenation may be very fast for systems of this type. If a string is referenced by a single program variable, and if the strings to be concatenated are not required after concatenation, then the concatenation operation can be performed simply by changing the link field of the last block of the first string to point to the first block of the second string. For strings of the form of STR8, the descriptor for the concatenated string would have to be changed to indicate the correct number of characters in the string. Also, it would be necessary to trace down the link fields of the blocks of the first string to get the address of its last block so its pointer can be changed. For strings of the form of STR9, concatenation would be faster, since the address of the last block of the first string is contained in its descriptor. However, if both strings to be concatenated are the same string, or if the original strings are needed after concatenation, then copies of the strings would have to be made, and the concatenation operation would be no faster than for the non-linked systems described earlier.

Exercise 3.18. Give algorithms for string concatenation for each of the memory representations defined by Figure 3.4.

Modifications to existing strings can be faster than for non-linked systems provided that each string is referenced by a single program identifier. When that is the case, deleting charcters consists of replacing them by the invalid character, and adding characters is done by linking additional cells or blocks having the desired characters to the string. In the case of deleting characters, if an entire cell or block is filled with the **null** character, then that cell or block can be removed from the string and freed for reallocation.

Exercise 3.19. Give algorithms for the pseudo-function SUBSTR (see page 95) for strings having the representations illustrated in Figure 3.4.

If a string is referenced by more than one program variable, then a copy of the string would have to be made whenever the string is modified. This would be slower than for the corresponding non-linked system.

String searching algorithms are also less efficient since: 1) additional memory references are required for obtaining the characters in each subsequent block or cell in the string; 2) each character must be checked for being a **null** character; and 3) the bookkeeping incurred by the additional checks is costly. (In non-linked systems, simple indexing is used for obtaining subsequent characters.) Memory utility is also less for linked structures, because the link fields (and length fields for blocks) require memory that is not required in non-linked systems.

3.5 SUMMARY

There are two principal techniques used for implementing strings: static allocation techniques, where a block of memory for each string is allocated at compile time and strings are referenced directly by string identifiers, and dynamic allocation techniques, where a block of memory for each string is allocated during program execution and strings are referenced by string descriptors. Static allocation techniques are employed by languages such as PL/I and are more efficient for simple string operations. However, memory for strings must be allocated in advance, which is less efficient on storage and may result in truncation when a string is produced that is larger than the allocated block. Dynamic memory allocation as used by SNOBOL4 is more flexible and does not place restrictions on string length. However, since strings are referenced indirectly, execution may be less efficient, particularly where short strings of a fixed length dominate the computations.

Systems using linked memory representations for strings were also described. However, systems using non-linked memory representations are more flexible, more efficient both for memory usage and time, and in general less complex than systems using linked structures.

Projects

Project 3.1. One representation that can be used for implementing character strings is illustrated below. Each program variable (STR1 and STR2 in the illustration) is a *string index* that holds an integer value used to designate a string. The value of a string index is the subscript in each of two vector arrays POINT and LEN that are used to hold the position of the character string in the array SPACE and its length. The characters of the string are stored in the character array SPACE, which can hold a maximum of SIZE characters. The variable FREE is the subscript of the first unused character in SPACE.

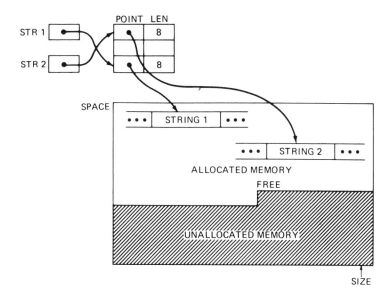

Whenever a string is created, the value of the program variable that will designate the string is set to the subscript in POINT and LEN that will reference the string. Any subscript K can be used, provided that LEN(K) and POINT(K) are both 0. (The arrays LEN and POINT must be initialized to zero.) The statement STR3 := STRING-('TEST',4) would assign to STR3 the index, say K, of the newly created string; LEN(K) would be set to 4; POINT(K) would be set to FREE; SPACE(FREE) thru SPACE(FREE + 3) would be set to 'T', 'E', 'S', and 'T', and FREE would be incremented by 4. However, if FREE + 3 exceeds SIZE, the procedure COLLECT as described below would be called.

During program execution, strings that are no longer used can be 'erased' by a call to the procedure ERASE. The statement ''call ERASE(STR3)'' erases a string by setting its POINT and LENGTH fields to zero and setting the value of the program variable to zero, making it into a null string. The characters of the string are not liberated until the procedure COLLECT is invoked.

The procedure COLLECT liberates memory as follows. It first creates a list of all string indices whose POINT fields are not zero, and then sorts the list according to POINT field values. An efficient sort procedure such as TREESORT3 (pp. 172-177) should be used. Each string is then processed in the order that it appears in the sorted list by shifting its characters left and making them adjacent to the previous string processed in this way. This process is *compaction*. Finally, as a string is shifted, its POINT field is updated to point to its new location in memory.

The procedure COLLECT is invoked whenever one of the following two conditions is sensed: 1) there is insufficient room in SPACE for the characters of the string being created; 2) there are no more free string indices.

Code a complete system of string processing routines using this memory representation. Include at least the following routines:

STRING(CHARS, LEN) — The characters of a new string of length LEN are found in a character array, CHARS, different from SPACE. STRING returns the index of the newly created string.

READS(INPUT) — The characters of a new string are read from input file INPUT. The first character must be a single quote ('). All characters following the single quote are made into a string, until a second single quote is sensed. The character just prior to the second single quote is the last character of the string. The value returned is the index of the new string.

IMAGE(CHARS, STR, LEN, MAX) — STR is the index of a string, and CHARS is a character array different from SPACE whose size is MAX. The characters of STR are copied into the array CHARS. If LENGTH(STR) exceeds MAX, only MAX characters are copied and LEN is set to MAX. If LENGTH(STR) does not exceed MAX, then all characters of STR are copied and LEN is set to LENGTH(STR).

WRITES(STR) — STR is the index of a string. The string is printed in a suitable format.

ERASE(STR) — As described above.

COLLECT — As described above.

LENGTH(STR) — Returns the length of the string.

CONCAT(STR1, STR2) — Returns the index of the string STR1 || STR2.

COPY(STR) — Returns the index of a copy of string STR.

IDENT(STR1, STR2) — A predicate that returns **true** if STR1 and STR2 are identical strings; otherwise IDENT returns **false**.

SUBSTR(STR, INDX, LEN)   Returns the index of a new string whose characters are identical to the substring of STR begin-
ning at character position INDX and having
length LEN. SUBSTR returns 0 if an error
condition is sensed.

INDEX(STR1,STR2)   Returns the index of the leftmost occurrence of
STR1 as a substring of STR2, or 0 if there is no
such substring.

Project 3.1 (alternate). Write the collection of procedures described for Project 3.1. However, instead of having COLLECT create a list of string indices sorted according to POINT field values, make the string descriptors into a doubly linked list by adding a backward and forward link to each descriptor. This descriptor list is kept sorted by POINT field values: ERASE simply removes descriptors from this list; procedures that create strings insert them according to the values in their POINT fields.

Project 3.1 (second alternative). Read Chapter 6. Then write the collection of procedures described for Project 3.1. However, instead of writing ERASE and COLLECT, use garbage collection.

Project 3.2. Develop a collection of procedures for manipulating bibliographic data as follows. Each bibliographic reference will be described on three data cards: a title card, an author card, and a citation card. The data on each card will be in free format. However, if the last non-blank character on a card is a $'+'$, then the following card is a continuation card. Only one continuation card is allowed for any data item. The following actions are to be performed:

1. Create a complete list of references, alphabetized by title. Show the author and citation information.
2. Create a complete alphabetical list of authors, and list all titles by that author.
3. Create a key-work-in-context (KWIC) index listing for each article. A KWIC index shows each word in every title (except as noted below), alphabetized, followed by all article titles containing that word. The procedure should ignore common words such as 'the', 'an', 'is', 'with', and so forth. It should also ignore specific words given as input to the program.

The following data cards illustrate what is required:

PICTURE PROCESSING BY COMPUTER
A. ROSENFELD
NEW YORK: ACADEMIC PRESS, 1969.
GRAPHIC LANGUAGES
F. NAKE, A. ROSENFELD
AMSTERDAM: NORTH-HOLLAND PUBLISHING COMPANY, 1972.

PICTURE LANGUAGE MACHINES
S. KANEFF
NEW YORK: ACADEMIC PRESS, 1970.

The alphabetical list by titles would appear this way:

GRAPHIC LANGUAGES
    F. NAKE, A. ROSENFELD
    AMSTERDAM: NORTH-HOLLAND PUBLISHING COMPANY, 1972.
PICTURE LANGUAGE MACHINES
    S. KANEFF
    NEW YORK: ACADEMIC PRESS, 1970.
PICTURE PROCESSING BY COMPUTER
    A. ROSENFELD
    NEW YORK: ACADEMIC PRESS, 1969.

The author list would appear this way:

KANEFF, S.	PICTURE LANGUAGE MACHINES
NAKE, F.	GRAPHIC LANGUAGES
ROSENFELD, A.	GRAPHIC LANGUAGES
	PICTURE PROCESSING BY COMPUTER

The KWIC index would look like this:

COMPUTER	PICTURE PROCESSING BY COMPUTER
GRAPHIC	GRAPHIC LANGUAGES
LANGUAGE	PICTURE LANGUAGE MACHINES
LANGUAGES	GRAPHIC LANGUAGES
MACHINES	PICTURE LANGUAGE MACHINES
PICTURE	PICTURE LANGUAGE MACHINES
	PICTURE PROCESSING BY COMPUTER

Project 3.3. A *text editor* is an interactive computer program that enables a user to create and manipulate a text file. Some operations that are generally allowed are:

- Retrieve a text file from tape or disk.
- Store a text file on tape or disk.
- Create a new text file.
- Add a new line of text to an already created text file.
- Delete one or more lines of text from an already created text file.
- Move one or more lines from one place to another in an already created text file.
- Modify a line of text in an already created text file.

There are many ways to organize a text file in main memory. One way is to maintain each line of text as a variable length character string, keeping them on a doubly linked list. The first line of text is number 1, the second line of text is number 2, and so forth. Alternatively, the last line of text is number -1, the second line from the end is number -2, and so forth. These numbers are computed implicitly as the text is manipulated. The length of the string appears in the string header, as do forward and backward links to the subsequent and previous lines in the text; this is illustrated below. Three program pointers are maintained: FIRST points to the first line of text, LAST points to the last line of text, and CURRENT points to the current line of text being processed. A single procedure, GETLINE, reads the current line of text that is entered at the terminal. This might be a new line of text to be added, or it may be a control line instructing the text processor what to do next. Control lines are distinguished from lines of text because they start with the special character '@', which is not allowed as the first character of an ordinary line of text.

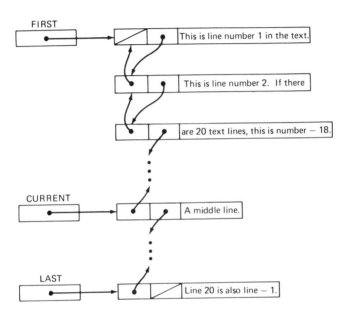

The following control lines are allowed. Lower case letters represent variables that are filled in by the user, and upper case letters stand for themselves.

@CURRENT   Subsequent lines of input that are not command lines are to be inserted following the line pointed at by CURRENT, and CURRENT is to be updated to point to the newly added line. This nullifies the action of the previous @BOTTOM command.

@BOTTOM   Subsequent lines of text that are not command lines are to be added to the bottom of the text. This nullifies the action of the previous @CURRENT command.

@CURRENT; n   Change CURRENT to point to line number n.

@CURRENT; *±n   Increment (decrement) the current line pointer by n lines.

@MOVE; nl   The last line is moved into the text following line number nl.

@MOVE; n1; n2; n3	The lines numbered n2 thru n3 are moved just following line n1. (The value of n1 must not be between n2 and n3.)
@ERASE; n1	Line number n1 is deleted from the text. All lines are subsequently renumbered.
@ERASE; n1; n2	All lines from number n1 thru number n2 are deleted from the text.
@COPY; n1; n2; n3	All lines from number n2 thru number n3 are copied into the text following line number n1. The original lines are not modified.
@n; string1; string2	The leftmost occurrence of string1 in line number n is replaced by string2. No action is taken if string1 is not found.
@n; string1	Line number n is searched for string1. If found, all following characters are deleted from the line.
@LOCATE; n1; n2; s1; s2	The entire text file is searched, beginning from line number n1 and ending with line number n2. If string s1 is found in any of the searched lines, it is replaced by s2 and the remainder of the line searched. (The newly inserted substring s2 is not searched.) All line numbers where changes occur are listed.
@LOCATE; n1; n2; s	All lines from number n1 thru number n2 are searched for string s. Line numbers of all lines containing the string s are listed.
@N	Print the number of lines in the text.
@C	Print the number of the current line of text.
@STORE; filename	Store the current text in the external file named filename.
@GET; filename	Copy the contents of the external file named filename into memory to become the current text file. The previous text file is destroyed.
@DELETE; filename	Delete file filename from the external storage device.
@n	Print line number n.
@PRINT; n1; n2	Print lines numbered n1 thru n2.

You should supply appropriate error and warning messages when the user gives inappropriate or incorrect input. Your memory management procedures should use memory compaction as described in Project 3.1. Note that the commands @STORE, @GET, and @DELETE are really not part of the text editor. You should implement these commands in a reasonable manner for your particular computing system.

Project 3.4. A text formatting routine accepts as input a text file such as described in the previous programming project and prints the file according to several simple rules.
1. Two variables, PAGE_LENGTH and PAGE_WIDTH, specify the number of rows of output per page and the number of characters per line of printed output, not counting the left margin width. The variable LEFT_MARGIN_WIDTH specifies the width, in characters, for the left margin. Finally, HEADING_LENGTH and FOOTING_LENGTH specify how many blank lines are to appear on the top and bottom of each

page of output. These parameters are set by placing the following control lines in the text file:

#PL;number	Sets PAGE _ LENGTH to number.
#PW;number	Sets PAGE _ WIDTH to number.
#LMW;number	Sets LEFT _ MARGIN _ WIDTH to number.
#HL;number	Sets HEADING _ LENGTH to number.
#FL;number	Sets FOOTING _ LENGTH to number.

2. Text is printed either in the formatted or unformatted mode. When #F appears as the only two characters on a line of text, printing of all lines of text until the next #U control line is encountered is in formatted mode. When #U appears as the only two lines of text, printing of all lines of text until the next #F control line is encountered is in unformatted mode. Control lines, lines beginning with the symbol '#' are not printed.

3. When printing in unformatted mode, each line of text is printed exactly as entered, regardless of the PAGE_WIDTH parameter. The LEFT _ MARGIN _ WIDTH parameter is recognized and determines how many leading blanks are to be printed.

4. When printing in the formatted mode, each line must fall within a column of width PAGE _ WIDTH and be preceded by LEFT _ MARGIN _ WIDTH blanks. All lines in a given paragraph are treated as if they were a single line. If a line ends with a hyphen, the hyphen is removed, and the next line is assumed to follow without intervening blanks. Otherwise, a blank character is assumed between lines of text in a paragraph. A paragraph ends when a line consisting entirely of blanks appears, or when either the control line #F or #U appears. When printing a paragraph in formatted mode, the text is broken only at blank characters or at hyphens. The longest initial segment of a paragraph is printed on a line that fits with PAGE_ WIDTH characters. The next initial segment is placed on the next line, and so forth, until the entire paragraph is printed. If a string has no blanks or hyphens and is still too long to fit on a line, the line is broken after PAGE _ WIDTH characters, and the remainder of the paragraph is printed as described herein.

Assume that the text file is represented as a doubly-linked list as described in the previous project, and give all procedures for printing the text file. If you wish, you may add additional formatting procedures, such as tab settings, indentation facilities, headings, footings, footnote facilities, right-justification of text, page numbering facilities, and so forth.

Project 3.5. Write a program that accepts as input a collection of ordered pairs of strings, say (s1, t1), (s2, t2) ,..., (sn, tn). A pair (s,t) is *generated* if it is an input pair, or if there are two generated pairs (s,r) and (r,t). (This definition must be understood recursively.) Your procedure should list all input pairs, all generated pairs, and all pairs (s,t) such that there is no other generated pair (s,t') with t' a substring of t. Indicate for what values of n and for what string lengths your program is computationally feasible. Example:

Input = (A,AA), (AA,A), (AA, BA), (BA, AAB)
Generated = (A, A), (A, BA), (AA, AA), (AA, AAB), (A, AA), (AA, A), (AA,BA), (A, AAB)
Output = (A, A), (AA, A), (BA, AAB)

REFERENCES AND ADDITIONAL READINGS

Books

Griswold, R.E. (1972) *The Macro Implementation of SNOBOL4*. San Francisco: W.H. Freeman and Co.

Griswold, R.E. (1975) *String and List Processing in SNOBOL4: Techniques and Algorithms*. Englewood Cliffs, New Jersey: Prentice-Hall, Inc.

Griswold, R.E., and Griswold, M.T. (1973) *A SNOBOL4 Primer*. Englewood Cliffs, New Jersey: Prentice-Hall, Inc.

Griswold, R.E.; Poage, J.F.; and Polonsky, I.P. (1971) *The SNOBOL4 Programming Language*, Second edition. Englewood Cliffs, New Jersey: Prentice-Hall, Inc.

Maurer, W.D. (1976) *The Programmer's Introduction to SNOBOL*. New York: Elsevier North-Holland, Inc.

Waite, W.M. (1973) *Implementing Software for Non-Numeric Applications*. Englewood Cliffs, New Jersey: Prentice-Hall, Inc.

Articles

Aho, A.V., and Corasick, M.J. Efficient string matching: An aid to bibliographic search. *CACM* Vol. 18, No. 6, June 1975, 333-340.

Baron, R.J., and Critcher, A. STRINGS2: Some FORTRAN-callable string processing routines. Technical Report 75-01, January 1975, Department of Computer Science, The University of Iowa.

Baron, R., and Golini, J. STRINGS: Some FORTRAN callable string processing routines. Technical Report 71-03, September 1970, Department of Computer Science, The University of Iowa.

Berztiss, A.T. A note on storage of strings. *CACM* Vol. 8, No. 8, Aug. 1965, 512-513.

Bowlden, H.J. A list-type storage technique for alphameric information. *CACM* Vol. 6, No. 8, Aug. 1963, 433-434.

Boyer, R.S., and Moore, J.S. A fast string searching algorithm. *CACM* Vol. 20, No. 10, Oct. 1977, 762-772.

Clark, R.K. STRINGS. Argonne National Laboratory Report ANL-76-69, June 1976.

Desantels, E.J., and Smith, D.K. An introduction to the string manipulation language SNOBOL. In Rosen (1967), 419-454.

Farber, D.J.; Griswold, R.E.; and Polonsky, I.P. SNOBOL, a string manipulation language. *JACM* Vol. 11, No. 1, Jan. 1964, 21-30.

Griswold, R.E. Highlights of two implementations of SNOBOL4. Technical Report S4D55, February 1977, Department of Computer Science, The University of Arizona.

Hanson, D.R. A simple technique for representing strings in FORTRAN IV. *CACM* Vol. 17, No. 11, Nov. 1974, 646-647.

Harrison, M.C. Implementation of the substring test by hashing. *CACM* Vol. 14, No. 12, Dec. 1971, 777-779.

Housden, R.J.W. On string concepts and their implementation. *Computer J.* Vol. 18, No. 2, May 1975, 150-156.

Karp, R.M.; Miller, R.E.; and Rosenberg, A.L. Rapid identification of repeated patterns in strings, trees, and arrays. *ACM Symposium on Theory of Computing,* Vol. 4, 1972, 125-136. New York: Association for Computing Machinery.

Knuth, D.E.; Morris, J.H.; and Pratt, V.R. Fast pattern matching in strings. *SIAM Journal on Computing* Vol. 6, No. 2, June 1977, 323-350.

Madnick, S.E. String processing techniques. *CACM* Vol. 10, No. 7, July 1967, 420-424.

Reynolds, R.A. Character string handling in FORTRAN. *Computer J.* Vol. 20, No. 4, Nov. 1977, 325-329.

Yngve, V.H. COMIT. *CACM* Vol. 6, No. 3, March 1963, 83-84.

4
Trees and Graphs

OVERVIEW

In this chapter, we discuss graph structures, beginning with an important class of graph structures called trees. We first examine storage representations and processing algorithms for binary trees and then general trees. We give a variety of examples and algorithms in which trees are used. In the second part of the chapter, we define the general graph structure. We describe matrix and linked implementations for graphs and illustrate the use of these structures in path existence and shortest path algorithms.

4.1 INTRODUCTION

Intuitively, a *graph* is a data structure used to represent relationships among objects. Graphs are used to represent and solve problems in many areas. Some of the application areas of graph processing are artificial intelligence (game trees, problem graphs, semantic networks, robot world models, pictorial relationships), engineering (circuit diagrams, network analysis, force diagrams, flow analyses), physics and chemistry (chemical structures, crystal structures, Feynman diagrams, cloud and bubble chamber track analysis), and computer science (data structures, flowcharts, program schemata, programming language semantics, resource graphs, automata theory, graph theory). Figure 4.1 illustrates pictorially two simple examples of graph structures. The graph of Figure 4.1a represents the adjacency relationship between pairs of regions of a map. The graph (tree) of Figure 4.1b represents a parse, or structural decomposition, of an English sentence. We will begin our discussion of graph structures with the important subset of graphs called *trees*.

4.2 TREES

A tree is a data structure used to represent a hierarchical relationship among items of data. We will give a precise definition of a tree after looking at a few

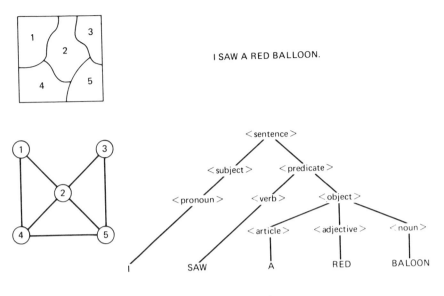

Figure 4.1. Two simple examples of graph structures.
a. A graph representing the adjacency relationships between pairs of regions of a map.
b. A graph (tree) representing a parse of an English sentence.

examples. One simple example of a tree is an outline of a book. The title of the book describes the entire book and is at the top of the hierarchy. The book can be partitioned into chapters which form the second level of the hierarchy. In Figure 4.2, the book BOOK is divided into chapters I, II, III, IV, and V. Each chapter of a book may be subdivided into sections which are one level lower in the hierarchy than the chapters; in Figure 4.2, chapters II, III, IV, and V are divided into two, two, three, and two sections, respectively. Note that section A, chapter II is completely distinct from section A, chapter III; section A, chapter IV; and section A, chapter V. If we follow the hierarchy in Figure 4.2 further, section A, chapter II has three subsections (1, 2, and 3) and subsection 2, section A, chapter II is further divided into parts a and b. Obviously, this process can go on indefinitely depending on the complexity of the book that the outline represents.

A *tree* is a hierarchical structure made up of cells called *nodes*. At the top level (level 0) of the hierarchy is a distinguished node called the *root node*. In Figure 4.2, node BOOK is the root node of the tree. Every node of the tree is the *parent* of zero or more *child* nodes which are connected to the parent. In Figure 4.2, nodes I, II, III, IV, and V are child nodes; they are the *children* of node BOOK. The children of one parent node form an ordered set of nodes called *siblings*, and their position in the hierarchy is one level below the level of their parent (level of

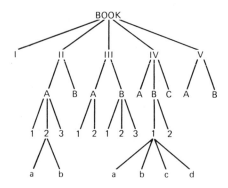

Figure 4.2. A tree representing the outline of a book.

child = level of parent + 1). Thus in Figure 4.2, nodes I, II, III, IV, and V are siblings and are at level 1. A node that has no children is called a *leaf node*; in Figure 4.2, node I is one example of a leaf node. A node that has children is called a *branch node*, and the connection between a branch node and one of its children can be called a *branch* or *link*. In Figure 4.2, node II is a branch node, and the edge connecting node II to node A is a branch or link. Note that there is no sequence of branches that forms a loop in Figure 4.2. This "no loops" property holds for all trees and follows from their hierarchic nature.

Figure 4.3 shows another example of a tree. The nodes of this tree are labeled with arithmetic operators and operands. (We will discuss the semantics of these labels shortly.) The node labeled '+' is the root node of the tree and is at level 0 in the hierarchy. Nodes 'A', '*', and '/' are the children of '+' and are at level 1 in the hierarchy. Nodes '*' and '/' are the siblings of node 'A', nodes 'A' and '/' are the siblings of node '*', and nodes 'A' and '*' are the siblings of node '/'. Node 'A' is the first child of node '+', node '*' is the second child of node '+', and node '/' is the third or last child of node '+'.

Node 'A' is a leaf node and nodes '*' and '/' are both branch nodes, each having two children. The children of '*' and '/' are at level 2 in the hierarchy.

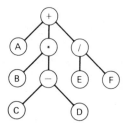

Figure 4.3. A tree representing the arithmetic expression "A+B*(C−D)+ E/F."

Nodes 'B' and '−' are siblings and nodes 'E' and 'F' are siblings. Node '−' is not a sibling of node 'E', since they have different parents. Nodes 'C' and 'D' are the children of node '−' and are at level 3 in the hierarchy.

Notice that if we were to break the connection between any child node and its parent, the child node would be the root of a tree structure. For instance, if we were to remove the connection between '+' and '*' in Figure 4.3, then '*' would be the root of a tree containing nodes 'B', '−', 'C', and 'D'. We call the tree structure whose root is '*' a subtree of the original tree. A *subtree* is a subset of the nodes of a tree that is also a tree structure. All the nodes of a subtree are *descendants* of the root of the subtree, and the root node is the *ancestor* of each node in the subtree. Thus in Figure 4.3, nodes 'C' and 'D' are the descendants of '−'; 'B', '−', 'C', and 'D' are the descendants of '*'; and '+' is the ancestor of every node in the tree.

In Figure 4.3, each node represents an operator or operand of an arithmetic expression. Operand nodes are leaves. The subtrees whose roots are the children of an operator node are the operands of that operator; for example, 'C' and 'D' are the operands of '−'. 'B' and the subexpression represented by the subtree whose root is '−' are the operands of '*'. Thus the tree of Figure 4.3 represents the expression:

$$A + (B * (C - D)) + (E / F).$$

Exercise 4.1. Construct a tree that represents the arithmetic expression "A * B * (E + F) − G / H".

A tree structure that has no nodes is called a *null tree*. Any non-null tree includes a root node and zero or more subtrees, each of which is a tree structure in its own right. This motivates us to formally define a (non-null) tree recursively as an ordered pair (R,S) that satisfies the following:

1. The pair (R, Φ) is a tree consisting of the singleton node R. R is the only node in the tree (R, Φ) and is called the *root node*.

2. If $<T1,...,Tn>$, $n \geq 0$, is an ordered sequence of disjoint trees with root nodes R1,...,Rn and if R is a node that is not in any of the trees T1,...,Tn, then the pair $(R, <T1,...,Tn>)$ is a tree with root node R and *subtrees* T1,...,Tn. The nodes in the tree $(R, <T1,...,Tn>)$ are the nodes of trees T1,...,Tn plus the node R. The node R is the parent of nodes R1,...,Rn. The nodes R1,...,Rn are the *children* of R. The node R1 is the *first* or *leftmost* child, and the node Rn is the *last* or *rightmost* child.

We can also recursively define the level of a node in a tree by:

1. The level of the root node of a tree is 0.

2. The level of any node of a tree that is not the root node is the level of its parent plus 1.

Exercise 4.2. Give recursive definitions for the terms "ancestor" and "descendant".

Trees can be implemented most easily by using a linked structure with pointers forming the connections from a node to its children and sometimes from the children back up to the parent; this structure is illustrated below. This brings up a problem with linked tree representations: If node A has two children and node B has eight children, then node A needs two pointer fields, while node B requires eight pointer fields; thus in the worst case, every node in the tree could have a different structure. There are several solutions to the problem, but for the present we will postpone them and study an important subset of trees where the problem does not exist—binary trees.

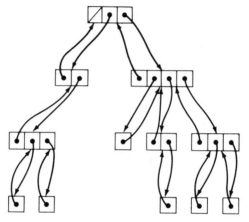

4.2.1 Binary trees

A *binary tree* is a tree in which each node has two subtrees, the *left subtree* and the *right subtree*; either or both of these subtrees may be null. Figure 4.4 shows a

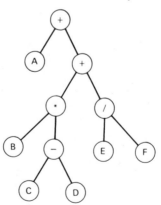

Figure 4.4. A binary tree representing the arithmetic expression "A+B*(C−D)+ E/F."

binary tree which represents the same arithmetic expression as the tree of Figure 4.3.

Figure 4.5 shows a binary tree where some of the nodes have only one child. Note that in a binary tree, we distinguish between the *left child* (root of the left subtree) and the *right child* (root of the right subtree). Thus in Figure 4.5, BILL is the right child of ABE, and the subtree consisting of BILL, BETTY, and DENNIS is the right subtree of ABE. ABE has no left child and therefore no left subtree. PAULA has a left subtree, consisting solely of NANCY, but no right subtree. NANCY is a leaf node and has no subtrees.

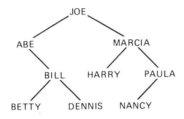

Figure 4.5. A binary tree in which some nodes have a left child but no right child, or a right child but no left child.

Linked representation of binary trees

Since a node in a binary tree can have at most two children, we can represent a node by a cell having two pointer fields and one or more information fields. Figure 4.6 shows a representation for the binary tree of Figure 4.5. Each cell has an INFO field containing a name, an LLINK field pointing to the left subtree, and an RLINK field pointing to the right subtree. Assuming that the INFO field is a fixed size determined by the maximum length character string required, the cells are all the same size.

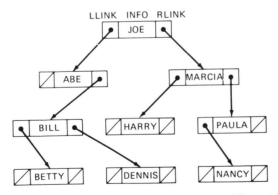

Figure 4.6. A linked representation for the binary tree of Figure 4.5.

Exercise 4.3 Suppose we require forward and backward linkage in a binary tree. Give the format of the cells of such a tree and illustrate your design with the tree of Figure 4.6.

Sequential Representation of Binary Trees

A binary tree can also be implemented sequentially in a block of contiguous memory locations. The nodes are stored as follows: The first memory location contains the root node; the second and third memory locations contain the left and right children of the root node, respectively; the fourth and fifth memory locations contain the left and right children of the left child of the root node. In general, if the root node is stored at address BASE + 1, then the node at address BASE + I has parent node at address BASE + ⌊I/2⌋, left child at address BASE + 2 * I, and right child at address BASE + 2 * I + 1. Figure 4.7 shows the sequential representation for the binary tree of Figure 4.5. Note that unused memory locations in the sequential representation correspond to null pointers in the linked representation.

BASE + 1	JOE
BASE + 2	ABE
BASE + 3	MARCIA
BASE + 4	—
BASE + 5	BILL
BASE + 6	HARRY
BASE + 7	PAULA
BASE + 8	—
BASE + 9	—
BASE + 10	BETTY
BASE + 11	DENNIS
BASE + 12	—
BASE + 13	—
BASE + 14	NANCY
BASE + 15	—

Figure 4.7. A sequential memory representation for the binary tree of Figure 4.5.

The sequential representation is an excellent memory saving representation for the quite rare case of a static binary tree, where every node, except those at the last (bottom) level, has exactly two non-null children and where the entire structure is known prior to its creation. The linked representation becomes more desirable when some child nodes are null, and the tree can dynamically shrink or grow. We will use the more common linked implementation in most of this section, but we will return to the sequential implementation in Section 4.2.3 with a sorting application.

Processing binary trees

It is often necessary to perform some operation on each node of a tree; for example, the tree of Figure 4.4 might be used by an interpreter as an intermediate representation of the original arithmetic expression. In order to evaluate the expression, the interpreter would have to process each node of the tree as follows: If the node represents an identifier, look up the value of the identifier; if the node represents an operator, apply that operator to the value of each subtree of the node. (For example, to process the node $'-'$, subtract the value of D from the value of C.) This brings out an important point: We cannot perform an arithmetic operation on a subtree unless the subtree has already been processed; thus the *order* of processing a tree is important. *Traversing* a tree means processing the nodes of the tree in a systematic order, so that each node is processed exactly once. We will now define three common orders for traversing binary trees.

Preorder traversal

A *preorder traversal* algorithm for binary trees is a traversal algorithm where a node is processed *before* both its children. After the root node is processed, the left subtree is processed and then the right subtree is processed; thus we can define preorder traversal of a binary tree BTREE by the following recursive procedure:

```
procedure PREORDER_TRAVERSAL(BTREE);
if (BTREE = null) then return endif;
ROOT_NODE := root of BTREE;
LEFT_TREE := left subtree of ROOT_NODE;
RIGHT_TREE := right subtree of ROOT_NODE;
call PROCESS(ROOT_NODE);
call PREORDER_TRAVERSAL(LEFT_TREE);
call PREORDER_TRAVERSAL(RIGHT_TREE);
return;
end PREORDER_TRAVERSAL;
```

Suppose we wish to print the operator or variable associated with each node of the tree of Figure 4.4 and that the routine PROCESS(N) prints the data in node N; then traversing the tree in preorder would produce the output:

$$+A +* B - C D / E F$$

which is the *Polish prefix* form of the expression:
$$A + B * (C-D) + E / F$$

Postorder traversal

A *postorder traversal* algorithm for binary trees is a traversal algorithm where a node is processed *after* both its children have been processed, left child first; the procedure for postorder traversal of a binary tree is as follows:

```
procedure POSTORDER _ TRAVERSAL(BTREE);
if (BTREE = null) then return endif;
ROOT _ NODE := root of BTREE;
LEFT _ TREE := left subtree of ROOT _ NODE;
RIGHT _ TREE := right subtree of ROOT _ NODE;
call POSTORDER _ TRAVERSAL(LEFT _ TREE);
call POSTORDER _ TRAVERSAL(RIGHT _ TREE);
call PROCESS(ROOT _ NODE);
return;
end POSTORDER _ TRAVERSAL;
```

If the tree of Figure 4.4 were traversed in postorder, with the PROCESS routine described above, the output would be:

$$A \ B \ C \ D \ - \ * \ E \ F \ / \ + \ +$$

which is the *Polish postfix* form of:

$$A + B * (C-D) + E / F$$

Inorder or symmetric traversal

An *inorder* or *symmetric traversal* algorithm for binary trees is a traversal algorithm where a node is processed *after* its left child and *before* its right child. (The word "inorder" refers to the processing of a node "in between" the processing of its left and right subtrees.)

If the tree of Figure 4.4 were traversed in inorder, with the PROCESS routine again printing the data in each node, the printed output would be:

$$A + B * C - D + E / F$$

which is the original (infix) expression without the parentheses.

Exercise 4.4. Give the procedure for INORDER _ TRAVERSAL.
Exercise 4.5. Show in what order the nodes of Figure 4.5 would be processed in:
a. preorder
b. postorder
c. inorder

Implementing binary tree traversal

The procedures for preorder, postorder, and inorder traversal are recursive procedures and can be easily implemented in languages that support recursion, such as PL/I, SNOBOL, or PASCAL. In order to code these procedures in a language like FORTRAN which does not support recursion, we can use an auxilliary stack. Using the memory representation of Figure 4.6, with BTREE a pointer to the root node of the tree, the following non-recursive algorithm traverses the tree in preorder:

```
procedure PREORDER_TRAVERSAL2(BTREE);
comment Traverse the tree pointed to by BTREE in preorder using the auxilliary stack
        STACK;
template 1    NODE,
              2 INFO   INTEGER,
              2 LLINK  POINTER to NODE,
              2 RLINK  POINTER to NODE;
declare (BTREE, APOINTER) POINTER to NODE;
APOINTER := BTREE;
while (true) do
      if (APOINTER ≠ null)
      then begin
            call PROCESS ([APOINTER].INFO);
            comment Push pointer to right subtree into the stack;
            if ([APOINTER].RLINK ≠ null)
            then call PUSH (STACK, [APOINTER].RLINK) endif;
            comment Move APOINTER to left subtree;
            APOINTER := [APOINTER].LLINK
          end
      else begin
            comment We cannot move left any further;
            comment Pop the stack to traverse the right subtree. If stack is empty, we're
                  done;
            if (EMPTY(STACK)) then return endif;
            APOINTER := POP(STACK)
          end endif;
end PREORDER_TRAVERSAL2;
```

The contents of the stack and output at each iteration of the algorithm on the tree of Figure 4.4 are illustrated below.

In the above procedure, the stack was used to implement backing up. We can get along without a stack by using a more complex data structure to represent the tree. Figure 4.8 shows the tree of Figure 4.5 with two extra fields in each node, the PARENT field and the MARK field. The PARENT field contains a pointer to the parent of the node; the MARK field is a 2-bit field containing the values 0, 1,

ITERATION	STACK	OUTPUT
1		+
2	+⌋	+
3	+⌋	+A
4		+A+
5	/⌋	+A+
6	/⌋	+A+*
7	/̄⌋	+A+*
8	/̄⌋	+A+*B
9	/⌋	+A+*B—
10	D /⌋	+A+*B—
11	D /⌋	+A+*B—C
12	/⌋	+A+*B—CD
13		+A+*B—CD/
14	F⌋	+A+*B—CD/
15	F⌋	+A+*B—CD/E
16		+A+*B—CD/EF

or 2. The value 0 means a node has not yet been processed; the value 1 means the node has been processed and so has its left child; the value 2 means the node and both its children have been processed. With this structure, the following non-recursive procedure implements preorder traversal without a stack:

procedure PREORDER _ TRAVERSAL3(BTREE);
comment Traverse the tree pointed to by BTREE in preorder without using a stack;
declare (APOINTER, BTREE) POINTER **to** NODE;
template 1 NODE,

	2 MARK	2 BITS,
	2 PARENT	POINTER **to** NODE,
	2 INFO	INTEGER,
	2 LLINK	POINTER **to** NODE,
	2 RLINK	POINTER **to** NODE;

comment MARK = 0 for unprocessed node

```
                    1 for processed node and processed left child
                    2 for processed node and processed left and right children;
APOINTER := BTREE;
while (true) do
   begin
      if (APOINTER = null) then return endif;
      case
         ([APOINTER].MARK = 0):
            begin
               comment This node has not been processed yet. Process it and move
                       down left subtree;
               call PROCESS([APOINTER].INFO);
               case
                  ([APOINTER].LLINK ≠ null):
                     begin
                        [APOINTER].MARK := 1;
                        APOINTER := [APOINTER].LLINK
                     end;
                  ([APOINTER].LLINK = null and
                   [APOINTER].RLINK ≠ null):
                     begin
                        [APOINTER].MARK := 2;
                        APOINTER := [APOINTER].RLINK
                     end;
                  ([APOINTER].LLINK = null and
                   [APOINTER].RLINK = null):
                     begin
                        APOINTER := [APOINTER].PARENT
                     end;
               end case
            end;
         ([APOINTER].MARK = 1):
         begin
            comment This node has been processed and its left subtree has been
                    processed. Process right subtree;
            case
               ( [APOINTER].RLINK ≠ null):
                  begin
                     [APOINTER].MARK := 2;
                     APOINTER := [APOINTER].RLINK
                  end;
               ([APOINTER].RLINK = null):
                  begin
                     [APOINTER].MARK := 0;
                     APOINTER := [APOINTER].PARENT
                  end;
```

```
        end case
    end;
( [APOINTER].MARK = 2):
    begin
        comment This node and its left and right subtrees have been processed,
            so just back up;
        [APOINTER].MARK := 0;
        APOINTER := [APOINTER].PARENT
    end;
    end case
end;
end PREORDER _ TRAVERSAL3;
```

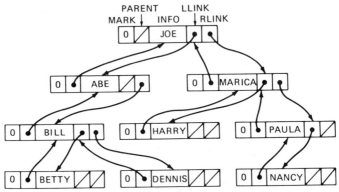

Figure 4.8. A doubly linked memory representation for the binary tree of Figure 4.5.

Exercise 4.6. Trace the three preorder traversal algorithms on the binary tree of Figure 4.5.

Exercise 4.7. Give a non-recursive algorithm that uses a stack for:
  a. POSTORDER _ TRAVERSAL(BTREE)
  b. INORDER _ TRAVERSAL(BTREE)

Exercise 4.8. Give a non-recursive algorithm that doesn't use a stack for:
  a. POSTORDER _ TRAVERSAL(BTREE)
  b. INORDER _ TRAVERSAL(BTREE)

Exercise 4.9. Given two binary trees where each node has fields LLINK, RLINK, and DATA. The variable BT1 points to the first tree, and the variable BT2 points to the second tree. Write a procedure EQTREE(BT1, BT2) which returns **true**, if BT1 and BT2 are identical structures and **false** otherwise.

Threaded binary trees

In the data structure used in the above algorithm, each node of a binary tree has an LLINK field and an RLINK field, even though the node may not have either a left or a right subtree. In Figure 4.6, for example, there are ten fields that contain null LLINK or RLINK fields. If we know the order in which the tree is to be traversed, we can make use of these 'wasted' fields to point to the previous or next node to be processed. The following node structure will be used:

LTAG   LLINK   INFO   RTAG   RLINK

where LTAG and RTAG are two 1-bit fields with the following meaning:

> If LTAG = 0, then LLINK points to the left subtree.
> If LTAG = 1, then LLINK points to the previous node
> (the *predecessor*) in the ordering.
> If RTAG = 0, then RLINK points to the right subtree.
> If RTAG = 1, then RLINK points to the next node
> (*the successor*) in the ordering.

The tree of Figure 4.4 is shown below in the new representation. The dotted lines represent the pointers to predecessor and successor nodes and are called *threads*. The threads are set up to facilitate a preorder traversal of the tree. Note that only node F has a null field, since it has no right subtree and is the last node in preorder. Using this structure, we can rewrite the traversal algorithms to use the threads whenever possible.

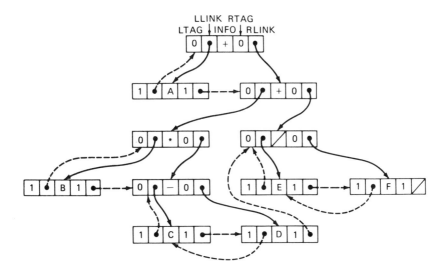

Exercise 4.10. Draw the tree of Figure 4.5 in threaded representation, where the threads are set up to facilitate a postorder traversal of the tree.

Exercise 4.11. Give a data structure for a binary tree threaded to facilitate preorder traversal that includes a header and such that there are *no* null link fields.

Exercise 4.12. Give an algorithm for PREORDER__TRAVERSAL that uses a binary tree threaded to facilitate preorder traversal.

4.2.2 Implementing general trees

The main problem in implementing general trees is that the nodes may have a different number of children and the maximum number of children may be much larger than the minimum or may be unknown prior to generation of the tree. One solution to this problem is to use variable size nodes; Figure 4.9 shows a tree with variable size nodes. The INFO field and SIZE field are present in every node. The INFO field contains an operator or operand, and the SIZE field contains an integer indicating the number of children. The root node has four children, and therefore four pointer fields following the SIZE field. The leaf nodes have no children and therefore have no pointer fields. The nodes must be allocated using dynamic storage allocation techniques such as those described in Chapters 6 and 7.

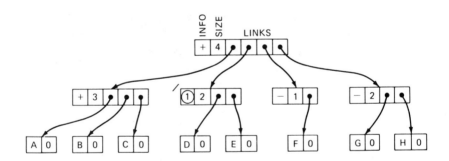

Figure 4.9. A memory representation for a general tree using variable size nodes.

Another method of implementing general trees is known as the *binary tree method*, so called because each node has only two pointer fields. The trick to this method is that a node does not point to all of its children. Each node has two link fields: the FIRST field and the NEXT field. The FIRST field of a node points to its first (leftmost) child. Since the set of children of any one parent is an ordered set, for each child except the last (rightmost) child, there is another child immediately after it in the ordering (directly to its right). The NEXT field of each node points to its next sibling. Thus the NEXT field of each of the children of one parent points to the next child of the same parent, and the NEXT field of the last child is null. Figure 4.10 shows the tree of Figure 4.9 in binary tree representation.

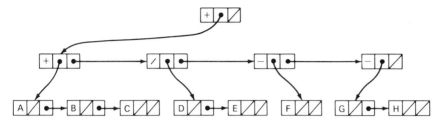

Figure 4.10. The binary tree representation of the general tree of Figure 4.9.

Exercise 4.13. Given the following tree,
a. Show a variable size node representation.
b. Show a binary tree representation.

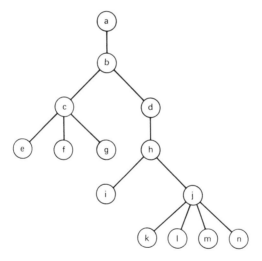

Traversing general trees

A preorder traversal algorithm for general trees is a traversal algorithm where a node is processed before any of its children. A postorder traversal algorithm for general trees is a traversal algorithm where a node is processed after all of its children. Inorder traversal is not well defined for general trees, but we will discuss a subclass of trees called multiway search trees in a later section (c.f. multiway search trees). Preorder traversal of a general tree like the one in Figure 4.9 can be implemented recursively as follows:

```
procedure GENERAL _ PREORDER1(GTREE);
comment Traverse the tree pointed to by GTREE in preorder;
template 1  NODE,
            2 INFO              CHARACTER,
            2 SIZE              INTEGER,
            2 LINKS (• SIZE)    POINTER to NODE;
declare (COUNT, TIMES) INTEGER;
declare (GTREE, ANODE) POINTER to NODE;
call PROCESS([GTREE].INFO);
TIMES := [GTREE].SIZE;
COUNT := 1;
while (COUNT ≤ TIMES) do
    begin
        ANODE := [GTREE].LINKS(COUNT);
        call GENERAL _ PREORDER1(ANODE);
        COUNT := COUNT + 1
    end;
end GENERAL _ PREORDER1;
```

Exercise 4.14. Give a recursive procedure for general postorder traversal of a tree with the data structure of Figure 4.9.

General trees represented in the binary tree representation may be traversed using the algorithms developed for traversal of binary trees. Let us examine the order of such traversals.

Illustrated below are a general tree G and its binary tree representation B. Suppose we traverse the binary tree in preorder. The nodes are processed in the order:

A B F G C H D E I J K

which is exactly the same result as when we traverse the general tree in preorder. If we traverse the binary tree in inorder, the nodes are processed in the order:

F G B H C D I J K E A

which is the same as processing the general tree in postorder. These results turn out to be general. That is, if T is any general tree and B its binary representation, then traversing B in preorder causes the nodes to be processed in the same order as traversing T in preorder. Traversing B in inorder causes the nodes to be processed in the same order as traversing T in postorder.

Thus the procedures for traversing binary trees may be used for traversing general trees in binary tree representation.

general tree G

binary tree B

binary tree B
illustrated to show
binary tree structure

4.2.3 Some applications of trees

Trees are used in most areas of computer science to represent hierarchical structures. We have already seen the use of a binary tree to represent arithmetic expressions in a compiler or interpreter. We will now describe some applications of trees in sorting, searching, game playing, problem solving, and code generation.

Linked treesort

The following procedure reads in a list of numbers and creates a binary tree with one number per node. The numbers are in increasing order when the tree is traversed using inorder traversal, and such a tree is said to be *sorted*. The sorting is achieved as follows: The first number becomes the root node of the tree; each subsequent number is compared with a sequence of nodes, starting with the root node. If the number is less than the value of the node being compared, the next comparison is with the left child of that node; if the number is not less than the value of the node being compared, the next comparison is with the right child of that node. The comparison process goes on until a null pointer is reached. The new number then becomes the left or right child of the leaf node, depending on whether its value is less than or not less than the value in the leaf node. When the tree is traversed in inorder, the numbers are in ascending order.

```
procedure TREESORT(TREE);
comment Read in a sequence of N numbers and add them to the sorted binary tree pointed
        to by the pointer TREE. Then traverse the tree in inorder, printing the number
        at each node. The nodes of the tree have the fields NUMBER, LLINK, and
        RLINK, and the function GETNODE is assumed to return the address of a free
        node;
template 1 NODE,
          2 NUMBER        INTEGER,
          2 LLINK         POINTER to NODE,
          2 RLINK         POINTER to NODE;
declare (TREE, NEWNODE, POINT) POINTER to NODE;
declare FLAG BOOLEAN;
declare (N, ANUM, COUNT) INTEGER;
read N;
if (N ≤ 0) then return endif;
comment Read first number;
read ANUM;
comment Create a first node with ANUM in its number field and null left and right
        children;
comment The routine GETNODE allocates a NODE and returns a pointer to the newly
        allocated NODE;
TREE := GETNODE( );
[TREE].NUMBER := ANUM;
[TREE].LLINK := null;
[TREE].RLINK := null;
COUNT := 1;
while (COUNT < N) do
    begin
    comment Read next number and create node to put it in;
        read ANUM;
        COUNT := COUNT + 1;
        NEWNODE := GETNODE( );
        [NEWNODE].NUMBER := ANUM;
        [NEWNODE].LLINK := null;
        [NEWNODE].RLINK := null;
        comment Find the correct place in tree for NEWNODE;
        POINT := TREE;
        FLAG := true;
        while (FLAG = true) do
            case
            (ANUM < [POINT].NUMBER):
                begin
                    comment If the number is smaller than the one in the current node,
                            move left;
```

```
if ([POINT].LLINK ≠ null)
then POINT := [POINT].LLINK
else
      begin
            comment Insert NEWNODE here;
            [POINT].LLINK := NEWNODE;
            FLAG := false
      end endif
   end;
(ANUM ≥ [POINT].NUMBER):
   begin
      comment If the number is larger than or equal to the number in the
            current node, move right:
      if ([POINT].RLINK ≠ null)
      then POINT := [POINT].RLINK
      else
            begin
                  comment Insert NEWNODE in tree;
                  [POINT].RLINK := NEWNODE;
                  FLAG := false
            end endif;
      end;
   end case
end;
call INORDER_TRAVERSAL(TREE);
end TREESORT;
```

Illustrated below is a sequence of seven numbers to be sorted and the tree at each step of the sort.

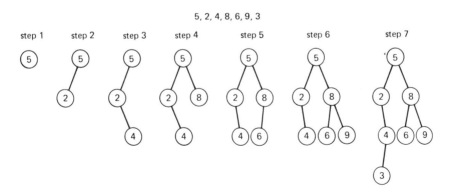

5, 2, 4, 8, 6, 9, 3

step 1   step 2   step 3   step 4   step 5   step 6   step 7

The final tree, processed in inorder, yields the sorted sequence.

2 3 4 5 6 8 9.

Tree-structured tables

One method of implementing a table of attribute-value pairs, where the attributes have a lexicographic ordering is to set up the table as a sorted binary tree with nodes of the form

ATTRIBUTE	VALUE	LLINK	RLINK

This can be achieved by using a minor variation of procedure TREESORT in the previous section. The tree is sorted based on the contents of the ATTRIBUTE fields of the nodes. To find the value associated with a given attribute, the search procedure starts at the top of the tree and compares the contents of the ATTRIBUTE field of the root with the specified attribute. If the root node contains the specified attribute, the contents of the VALUE field is retrieved. If the specified attribute is less than the contents of the ATTRIBUTE field of the root, the procedure goes on to search the left subtree of the root in the same manner. If the specified attribute is greater than the contents of the ATTRIBUTE field of the root, the procedure goes on to search the right subtree of the root. If a null pointer is reached, and the ATTRIBUTE field still does not match the specified attribute, the search fails.

Exercise 4.15. Write the algorithm TREESEARCH(BTREE, ATTR) for the tree search described above. The arguments to TREESEARCH are a pointer BTREE to a binary tree whose nodes have ATTRIBUTE, VALUE, LLINK, and RLINK fields and an attribute ATTR whose value should be returned. Assume the ATTRIBUTE field contains a character string, the VALUE field contains an integer, and the LLINK and RLINK fields contain pointers to other nodes.

Height-balanced trees

The time it takes to search a sorted binary tree depends on the *height* of the tree, the number of nodes on the longest path from the root to a leaf node. (The height of the tree consisting of a single node is 1.) For the sorted binary tree having height 4, shown at the left below, at most four value comparisons must be made to determine whether or not an arbitrary attribute is in the tree. Such a tree is equivalent to a linear list and in general requires time proportional to $\lceil n/2 \rceil$ with a maximum search time n to locate a given attribute. If the tree has 15 nodes, as shown below to the right, the maximum search time is the same as for a linear list having only four elements. For a complete binary tree having n nodes, the search time is proportional to $\lceil \log_2(n) \rceil$, where n is the number of nodes in the tree.

Now consider the process of building a tree-structured table. The procedure TREESORT given earlier is one routine that can be used, but there is no

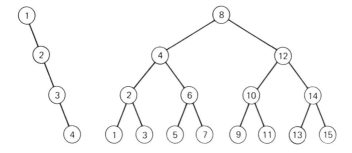

guarantee that the structure of the resulting table will be efficient for searching. For example, if the data is sorted to begin with, the resulting tree will be like the one at the above left: a linear structure that requires search time proportional to the number of elements. To show the variations, the four trees illustrated below result when the TREESORT algorithm is used for the integers 1 thru 10 but presented in different orders.

As a general rule, a tree-structured table will not be completely filled, since there will rarely be exactly $2^n - 1$ table elements, and the tree will usually be unbalanced. The best structure for a partially filled tree is that structure where all levels are filled except the bottom level, which may have some missing leaves.

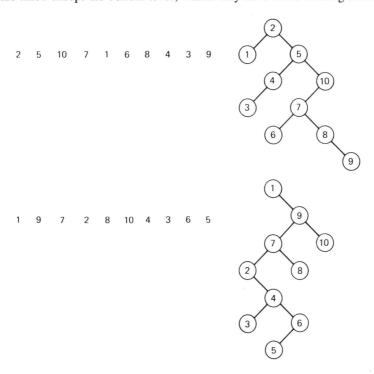

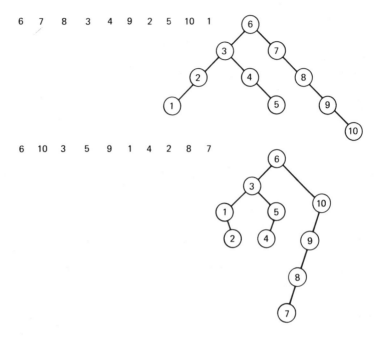

For such a tree, the number of nodes on any path from the root to a leaf is either k or k−1, where k is the height of the tree. When the data to be searched is known in advance, trees of this type are easy to build; however, when the data is known in advance, the hash table techniques presented in Chapter 5 can also be employed and are generally faster.

When the data is not known in advance, such as in many database systems, a data structure should be chosen: 1) so that new elements can be added or old ones deleted efficiently; and 2) for efficiency of search. It is easy to add or delete an element from a linked linear structure, but searching a linked linear structure is inefficient. It is efficient to search a binary tree that is filled except for the lowest level, but there are no known algorithms that enable efficient (execution time proportional to the tree height) additions or deletions. This is an important consideration when the structure may change frequently.

There is, however, a subclass of the binary trees called *height-balanced* or *AVL* trees (named after the researchers who first studied them) for which insertion and deletion operations can be performed in time proportional to the height of the tree and which are reasonably efficient to search. Height-balanced trees are sorted trees that are searched using inorder traversal. In the remainder of this section, we will describe height-balanced trees and present algorithms for insertion and deletion of elements. Intuitively, a height-balanced tree is a tree such that the height of the left and right subtrees at every node differ by at most one. Examples of height-balanced trees appear below.

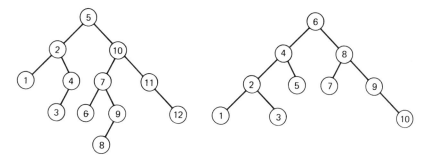

Exercise 4.16. Give a precise recursive definition for tree height, and give a precise recursive definition for height-balanced trees.

The procedure for inserting an attribute-value pair in a height-balanced tree consists of two principle parts. First, the tree is searched for the attribute of the new pair; if the attribute is already present, the value is changed and the tree is otherwise unmodified. However, if the attribute is not already present, the search will terminate either at a leaf node or at a node that has a vacant left or right leaf node position but which is itself not a leaf node. These cases are illustrated below, where A is the value to be added. In each case, memory must be allocated for the new leaf node, and that new node inserted at its proper position.

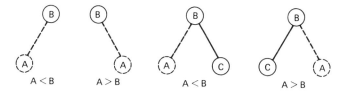

After the new element is added to the tree, the tree must be rebalanced, and rebalancing is the second part of element insertion. If the new element is attached to a node that already has one descendent (the last two cases above), then the tree remains height-balanced, and no further processing is necessary; however, if the new element is added to a leaf node, then rebalancing may be necessary. Rebalancing a tree is done by restructuring the tree at each node that has become unbalanced by the addition of the new node. Since restructuring the tree at a given node will never unbalance the subtrees of that node, the procedure simply moves up the tree toward the root and therefore executes in time proportional to the height of the tree. In fact, we will show that after insertion of a new element, only one node will ever be restructured.

Figure 4.11 shows six restructuring operations R1, L1, R2, L2, R3, and L3, that can be applied to a given node. The important property of each of these

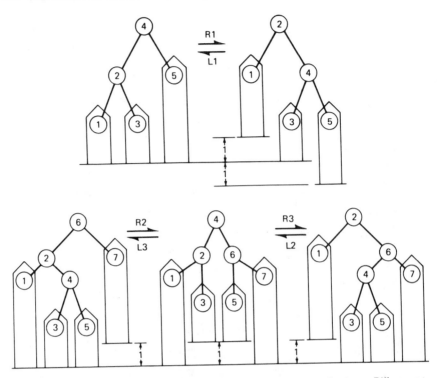

Figure 4.11. Three left and three right rotations are shown for restructuring trees. Differences in the heights of subtrees are noted. Each tree designated by a tree symbol ⌂ is unmodified by the restructuring operations and may be an empty tree. Nodes not within tree symbols must not be null. The rotation R1, for example, consists of making node ② into the root node, with left subtree ① and right subtree having node ④ as its root node. The left and right subtrees of node ④ are ③ and ⑤

restructuring operations is that they do not modify the order in which nodes are processed when using inorder traversal.

Each restructuring procedure takes as its argument a pointer to a node, and it returns a pointer to the root of the restructured tree for which the given node was originally the root. Procedure R1 is given below for trees having nodes with the same structure described in TREESORT; the remaining restructuring operations are left as exercises.

```
procedure R1(TREE);
template    1    NODE,
            2    NUMBER      INTEGER,
            2    LINKL       POINTER to NODE,
            2    LINKR       POINTER to NODE;
```

declare (TREE, R1) POINTER to NODE;
R1 := [TREE].LINKL;
[TREE].LINKL := [R1].LINKR;
[R1].LINKR := TREE;
return;
end R1;

Exercise 4.17. Give algorithms for R2, R3, L1, L2, and L3.

The procedure INSERT is used for inserting a new attribute-value pair in a height-balanced tree-structured table. INSERT first locates the proper place for insertion of the new pair. If the attribute is already in the tree, the new value is inserted and the previous (old) value is returned. Otherwise, a new node is created having the appropriate information and then inserted in the tree; finally the tree is balanced.

In order to balance the tree, it is necessary to know for each node whether or not its two subtrees initially had the same height, and if not, which one was initially higher. However, since the tree was initially balanced, the original heights of the subtrees differed by at most 1. As a result, the balance information requires only two additional bits at each node. The balance information will be held in the field BAL added to each node. The value of the BAL field will be PLUS ('01'B), if the right subtree at that node is higher, EQUAL ('00'B) if both subtrees have the same height, and MINUS ('11'B) if the left subtree is higher. After adding a new node, the balance factor (BAL) of the parent is checked. If the addition of the new node caused the parent to become unbalanced, one of the restructuring procedures is invoked. If not, and the modified subtree became higher, then the balance of the grandparent is checked. This process continues upward in the tree, until the root node is processed or a node is discovered that has become unbalanced. At this point, one of the restructuring procedures must be used. After the proper rebalancing procedure is applied, the height of that restructured subtree is the same as it was before the new node was added, so it is not necessary to further process ancestor nodes. The INSERT procedure simply corrects the balance information in the modified nodes and terminates the procedure.

During the balance procedure, it is necessary to find the parent of each node processed, and it is also necessary to know whether the descent was via the left or right path. One way to keep this information is in a stack or in two independent stacks, as we have chosen to do. The first stack, STACK1, holds a sequence of pointers to the nodes traversed along the descent; the second stack, STACK2, holds the direction of descent (LEFT or RIGHT) at each level. The use of these stacks is easy to understand from the procedure itself.

```
procedure INSERT(TREE, NEWKEY, NEWVALUE);
template     1       NODE,
             2       BAL       2 BITS,
             2       LINKL     POINTER to NODE,
             2       LINKR     POINTER to NODE,
             2       KEY       INTEGER,
             2       VALUE     INTEGER;
declare (NEWNODE, TREE, CURRENTNODE) POINTER to NODE;
declare (GETCELL, LOWERNODE) POINTER to NODE;
declare LEVEL INTEGER;
declare (LINK, LEFT, RIGHT, HIGHER) BOOLEAN;
declare (PLUS, EQUAL, MINUS) 2 BITS;
comment CBAL is the balance factor of CURRENTNODE, the node currently being
          processed.
        LBAL is the balance factor of LOWERNODE, the next lower node on the path
          of descent.
        LINK has value LEFT if LOWERNODE is the LEFT child of CURRENT-
          NODE, and RIGHT if LOWERNODE is the RIGHT child of CURRENT-
          NODE.
        LEVEL is the level of the current node in the tree. The root has level 0, its
          children level 1, and so forth;
PLUS := '01'B;
EQUAL := '00'B;
MINUS := '11'B;
RIGHT := '1'B;
LEFT := '0'B;
LEVEL := 0;
comment Search the tree for a node with KEY equal to NEWKEY;
CURRENTNODE := TREE;
while (CURRENTNODE ≠ null) do
   begin
     call PUSH(STACK1, CURRENTNODE);
     LEVEL := LEVEL + 1;
     case
       (NEWKEY = [CURRENTNODE].KEY):
          begin
            INSERT := [CURRENTNODE].VALUE;
            [CURRENTNODE].VALUE := NEWVALUE;
            return
          end;
       (NEWKEY < [CURRENTNODE].KEY):
          begin
            CURRENTNODE := [CURRENTNODE].LINKL;
            call PUSH(STACK2, LEFT)
          end;
```

```
(NEWKEY > [CURRENTNODE].KEY):
    begin
        CURRENTNODE := [CURRENTNODE].LINKR;
        call PUSH(STACK2, RIGHT)
    end;
  end case
end;
LEVEL := LEVEL - 1;
comment The search is unsuccessful;
comment Create the new node;
NEWNODE := GETCELL( );
[NEWNODE].BAL := EQUAL;
[NEWNODE].LINKL := null;
[NEWNODE].LINKR := null;
[NEWNODE].KEY := NEWKEY;
[NEWNODE].VALUE := NEWVALUE;
INSERT := NEWVALUE;
if (LEVEL = - 1)
then begin
        comment Special case for an initially empty tree;
        TREE := NEWNODE;
        return
    end endif;
comment Insert the new node in the tree;
LINK := POP(STACK2);
LOWERNODE := NEWNODE;
CURRENTNODE := POP (STACK1);
CBAL := [CURRENTNODE].BAL;
LBAL := EQUAL;
comment At this point the situation is like this:
```

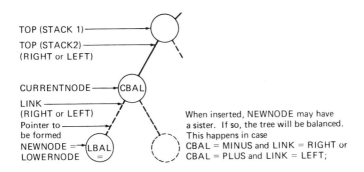

When inserted, NEWNODE may have
a sister. If so, the tree will be balanced.
This happens in case
CBAL = MINUS and LINK = RIGHT or
CBAL = PLUS and LINK = LEFT;

if (LINK = LEFT)
then [CURRENTNODE].LINKL := NEWNODE
else [CURRENTNODE].LINKR := NEWNODE **endif**;
comment Exit if tree does not need rebalancing;
if (LINK = LEFT **and** CBAL = PLUS)
then begin
    [CURRENTNODE].BAL := EQUAL;
    return
    end endif;
if (LINK = RIGHT **and** CBAL := MINUS)
then begin
    [CURRENTNODE].BAL := EQUAL;
    return
    end endif;
comment Addition of NEWNODE caused a change in the height of the subtree, whose
    root is CURRENTNODE;
comment The parent of the new node never needs rebalancing. If it was initially a leaf
    node, set its balance factor and climb one level in the tree;
if (CBAL = EQUAL)
then begin
    if (LINK = RIGHT)
    then begin
        [CURRENTNODE].BAL := PLUS;
        LBAL := PLUS
      end
    else begin
        [CURRENTNODE].BAL := MINUS;
        LBAL := MINUS
      end endif;
    if (LEVEL = 0) **then return endif**;
    LOWERNODE := CURRENTNODE;
    CURRENTNODE := POP(STACK1);
    CBAL := [CURRENTNODE].BAL;
    LINK := POP(STACK2);
    LEVEL := LEVEL − 1
    end endif;
comment Rebalance the tree;
HIGHER := **true**;
comment HIGHER indicates that the subtree whose root is CURRENTNODE has
    increased in height by the addition of the new node;
comment At this point the situation is as shown below. It will be similar each time the
    following **while-do** statement test is performed:
while (LEVEL ⩾ 0 **and** HIGHER = **true**) **do**
    begin
        comment Compare each case with Figure 4.12;

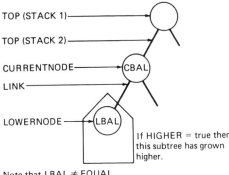

TOP (STACK 1)

TOP (STACK 2)

CURRENTNODE — CBAL

LINK

LOWERNODE — LBAL

If HIGHER = true then
this subtree has grown
higher.

Note that LBAL ≠ EQUAL

case
(LINK = LEFT **and** LBAL = PLUS **and** CBAL = PLUS):
  begin
    comment Figure 4.12, case 1;
    [CURRENTNODE].BAL := EQUAL;
    HIGHER := **false**
  end;
(LINK = LEFT **and** LBAL = PLUS **and** CBAL = EQUAL):
    [CURRENTNODE].BAL := MINUS;
(LINK = LEFT **and** LBAL = PLUS **and** CBAL = MINUS):
  begin
    comment Figure 4.12, case 3;
    CURRENTNODE := R2(CURRENTNODE);
    if ([CURRENTNODE].BAL = MINUS)
    then begin
      comment Subcase 1;
      [[CURRENTNODE].LINKL].BAL := EQUAL;
      [[CURRENTNODE].LINKR].BAL := PLUS
      end endif;
    if ([CURRENTNODE].BAL = EQUAL)
    then begin
      comment Subcase 2;
      [[CURRENTNODE].LINKL].BAL := EQUAL;
      [[CURRENTNODE].LINKR].BAL := EQUAL;
      end endif;
    if ([CURRENTNODE].BAL = PLUS)
    then begin
      comment Subcase 3;
      [[CURRENTNODE].LINKL].BAL := MINUS;
      [[CURRENTNODE].LINKR].BAL := EQUAL;
      end endif;

```
                    CURRENTNODE].BAL := EQUAL;
                    HIGHER := false
                 end
              (LINK = LEFT and LBAL = MINUS and CBAL = PLUS):
                 begin
                    comment Figure 4.12, case 4;
                    [CURRENTNODE.BAL := EQUAL;
                    HIGHER := false
                 end
              (LINK = LEFT and LBAL = MINUS and CBAL = EQUAL):
                 [CURRENTNODE].BAL := MINUS;
              (LINK = LEFT and LBAL = MINUS and CBAL = MINUS):
                 begin
                    CURRENTNODE := R1(CURRENTNODE);
                    comment Figure 4.12, case 6;
                    [CURRENTNODE].BAL := EQUAL;
                    [[CURRENTNODE].LINKR].BAL := EQUAL;
                    HIGHER := false
                 end
              (LINK = RIGHT and LBAL = PLUS and CBAL = PLUS): Exercise 4.18;
              (LINK = RIGHT and LBAL = PLUS and CBAL = EQUAL): Exercise 4.18;
              (LINK = RIGHT and LBAL = PLUS and CBAL = MINUS): Exercise 4.18;
              (LINK = RIGHT and LBAL = MINUS and CBAL = PLUS): Exercise 4.18;
              (LINK = RIGHT and LBAL = MINUS and CBAL = EQUAL): Exercise 4.18;
              (LINK = RIGHT and LBAL = MINUS and CBAL = MINUS): Exercise 4.18;
           end case
           LOWERNODE := CURRENTNODE;
           LBAL := [LOWERNODE].BAL;
           if (LEVEL > 0)
           then begin
                    CURRENTNODE := POP(STACK1);
                    LINK := POP(STACK2);
                    CBAL := [CURRENTNODE].BAL
                 end endif;
           LEVEL := LEVEL - 1;
       end;
comment Change the pointer that points to the restructured subtree;
if (LEVEL = 0)
then TREE := LOWERNODE
else begin
        if (LINK = LEFT)
        then [CURRENTNODE].LINKL := LOWERNODE
        else [CURRENTNODE].LINKR := LOWERNODE endif
     end endif;
return;
end INSERT;
```

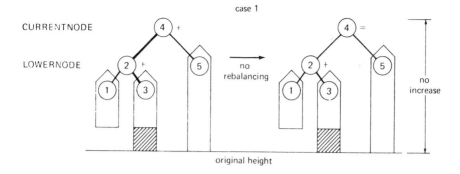

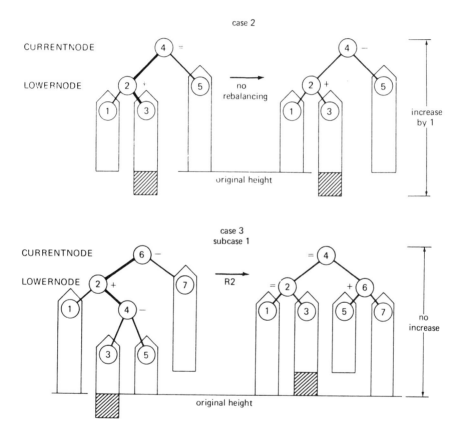

Figure 4.12. When a node is added to a height-balanced tree (indicated by cross hatching), the height of one subtree is increased by one. The six cases that can occur if the node is added to the left subtree of the root node are indicated, and the correct restructuring operation is shown.

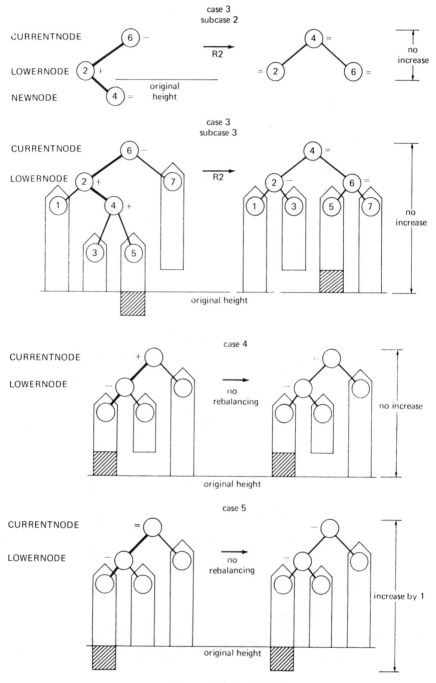

Figure 4.12. (continued)

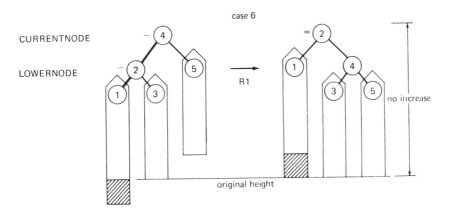

Figure 4.12. (continued)

Exercise 4.18. Fill in the details in the rebalancing phase of the INSERT procedure for the six cases where LINK=RIGHT, and illustrate the cases with a figure similar to Figure 4.12.

Exercise 4.19. Trace through the execution of this procedure for the trees illustrated earlier when given the new value 8.5 to be inserted. Do the same for the value 3.5.

Exercise 4.20. Rewrite the restructuring phase of the INSERT procedure so that the case statement having 12 cases is replaced by a more efficient sequence of branch statements.

Exercise 4.21. Rewrite the procedure INSERT using recursion rather than two stacks.

Removal of a node from the tree can be easily done by noticing that if a given node is to be deleted, then it can be swapped, either with the lowest node in the right subtree reached by following LINKL pointers, or with the lowest node in the left subtree reached by following LINKR pointers, and then the lower node removed. When the lower node is removed, a leaf node may have to be moved upward to take its place. If the balance factor of the node to be removed is PLUS, then the node removed would be in the right subtree, and if the balance factor is MINUS, the node removed would be in the left subtree; otherwise either subtree could be used. Four cases are shown in the illustration below. Once the lower node is deleted from the tree, a rebalancing procedure similar to the one for insertion is followed, rebalancing the tree if necessary for each node along a path to the root node.

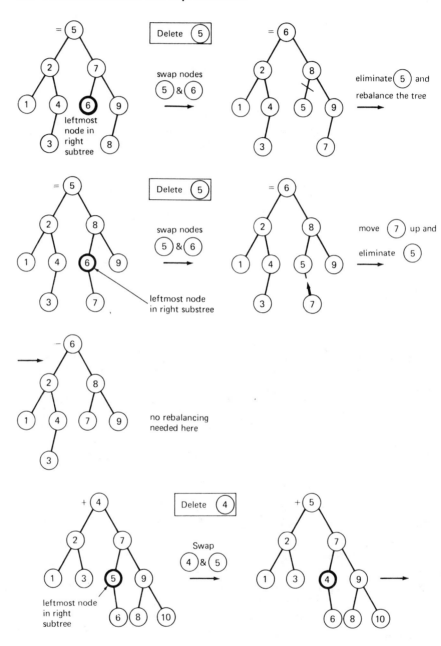

Exercise 4.22. Give the procedure for deletion of an attribute-value pair from a tree-structured table.

Exercise 4.23. A one-sided, height-balanced tree (OSHB tree) is a height-balanced tree such that the right subtree of a given node may have the same height or have height one

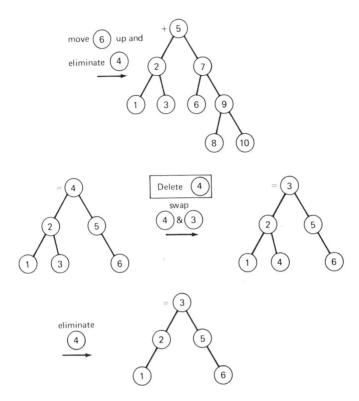

greater than the left subtree of the given node but not vice versa. Write procedures for inserting and deleting elements from OSHB trees. (The best known algorithms at this time require execution time proportional to $(\log_2(n))^2$.)

Exercise 4.24. Fill in the following table:

Structure	Search time	Element insertion	Element deletion
sequential linear linked linear AVL tree OSHB tree			

Multiway search trees

AVL trees are height-balanced binary search trees for which search, insertion, and deletion algorithms have been found that execute in time proportional to $\log_2(N)$, where N is the number of nodes in the tree. AVL trees are useful primarily when they can be maintained in primary memory. When working with large database systems, however, this is often not possible. Instead, the nodes of the tree are maintained on an external storage device, such as a magnetic disk and drum. The items of each node are stored in a contiguous block of words at a particular disk and drum address, and the links between the nodes are disk or drum addresses. When a node is to be processed, all node fields must first be copied into the computer's main memory.

One of the important differences between processing trees that are in main memory and those that are not is the time required to copy the node fields into main memory. In general, a word accessed from main memory has an access time of one microsecond or less, whereas the access time for a random word from disk or drum is on the order of milliseconds. Once a given word is available from disk or drum, however, contiguous words can then be accessed at main memory speeds. The long access time for the first word is due to the time required to position the read head over the desired word and rotate the disk or drum to the proper position.

Because contiguous words can be accessed almost as quickly as a single word, it is beneficial to store as much information as possible in each node. In particular, rather than using a binary tree where each node has one key item and two links, it is beneficial to use a multiway tree. However, multiway trees in general suffer from the same sort of search inefficiencies that binary trees do. In order to overcome these inefficiencies, the notion of a balanced multiway tree is introduced. When a tree becomes unbalanced because of an insertion or deletion operation, it is necessary to rebalance the tree. The issue, of course, is to find insertion and deletion algorithms that have execution time proportional to $\log_2(N)$ while still maintaining an efficient search structure. In the next few paragraphs, we will introduce multiway search trees that have these properties and describe insertion and deletion algorithms that execute quickly. Details of the algorithms will be left as exercises for the reader.

Each node in a multiway search tree contains both pointer data to subtrees of the node and attribute and value data. Since multiway trees are used mainly for database applications, the attributes are called keys, and we will abide by this convention. If a node in a multiway search tree has $N+1$ subtrees, then it also has n keys and n values. Let K_1, K_2, ..., K_N denote the key values, and let L_0, L_1, L_2, ..., L_N denote the addresses of the $N+1$ descendent nodes. Then all keys are ordered so that $K_1 < K_2 ... < K_N$. Furthermore the subtrees are ordered so that all key values in subtree 0 are less than K_1; all key values in subtree i for i less than N fall between the values of key K_i and key K_{i+1}, and all key values in subtree N exceed the value K_N. This ordering property must hold for every node in the tree so the tree can be searched efficiently. Two multiway search trees are shown in the illustration, where the numbers are the keys and the letters are the values.

It should be clear that each different node may have a different number of subtrees, so that each node must contain a value m indicating the number of

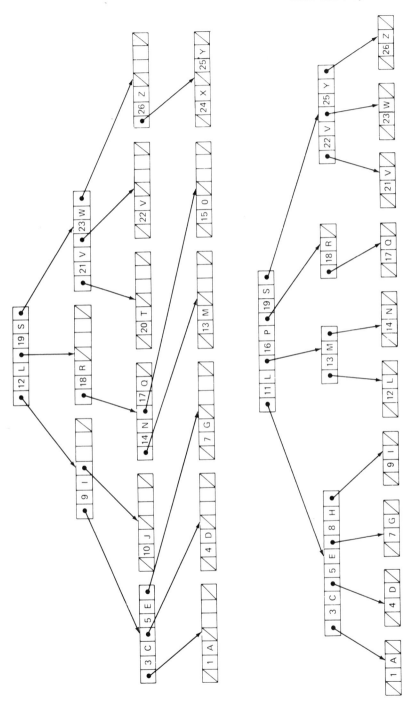

subtrees. If the maximum number of subtrees for a node can vary dynamically, the same techniques that were described in Chapter 3 for variable length strings can also be used here for structuring nodes.

Exercise 4.25. Suppose that a multiway search tree has a node structure defined by the following *template* statement, and also suppose that a buffer NODEBUFFER is declared as in the following *declare* statement.

template	1	NODE,	
	2	MAXLEN	INTEGER,
	2	CURLEN	INTEGER,
	2	KEY(●MAXLEN − 1)	INTEGER,
	2	VALUE(●MAXLEN − 1)	INTEGER,
	2	LINK(●MAXLEN)	INTEGER;
declare	1	NODEBUFFER,	
	2	MAXLEN	INTEGER,
	2	CURLEN	INTEGER,
	2	KEY(99)	INTEGER,
	2	VALUE(99)	INTEGER,
	2	LINK(100)	INTEGER;

Give a search procedure, SEARCH(KEYVAL) that returns the value corresponding to the given key KEYVAL. Assume that if A is declared INTEGER, then the statement:

call DISKREAD(NODEBUFFER,A)

reads all fields of the node whose address is A from external storage into the block called NODEBUFFER declared above. (Note that the largest node on disk must not have more than 100 subtrees.)

Several different multiway search trees for which insertion and deletion times are proportional to $\log_2(N)$ have been studied. AVL trees are one example; a second example are the 2-3 trees proposed by Ullman. For 2-3 trees, every non-leaf node has either two or three children, and all leaf nodes have the same depth. For a 2-3 tree, each node may have one or two key values. An example 2-3 tree is illustrated on page 169.

Exercise 4.26. For a 2-3 tree having height k, what are the maximum and minimum possible number of nodes in the tree? What are the maximum and minimum possible number of key values?

Searching a 2-3 tree is no different than searching a multiway tree. Inserting a new key is done as follows: First the tree is searched for the proper node of insertion; if the key is already present, it will be found, otherwise the search procedure should return the address of a leaf node in which the key should be

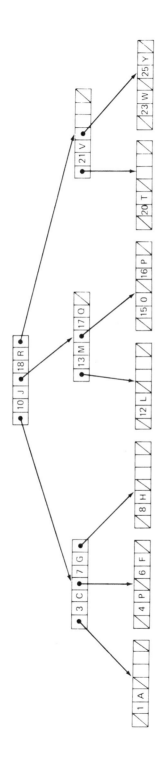

inserted. If the leaf node has one key, the new key is inserted. The new key must be inserted so that the proper key ordering is maintained. If the node already has two keys, however, a new node having three keys is conceptually formed (see illustration), split into two nodes, each having a single key, and the middle valued key made into a new conceptual parent of the two leaves. The conceptual

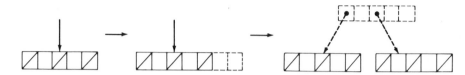

parent is then inserted into the parent of the original leaf node using the same insertion procedure. Three of the five possible cases for inserting the conceptual node in the old parent are illustrated on the following page. This process continues up the tree, until a node is found that does not need to be split, or until the root of the tree is reached. If the root is reached, a new node is allocated, and the conceptual parent is made into a new root for the entire tree.

Exercise 4.27. Show the remaining two cases for inserting a conceptual node into the old parent.

Exercise 4.28. Give an algorithm for node insertion in a 2-3 tree.

Exercise 4.29. Verify that your insertion algorithm from the previous exercise requires time proportional to $\log_2(N)$, where N is the number of nodes in the tree.

Exercise 4.30. Give an algorithm for deleting a key value from a 2-3 tree. Verify that your algorithm requires time proportional to $\log_2(N)$.

The notion of a 2-3 tree generalizes easily to multiway trees, resulting in what are commonly known as B-trees. For a B-tree, the user must supply a branch factor m, indicating the maximum number of branches arising from a given node. An m-way search tree is an *m-way B-tree* in case every non-leaf node in the result has between $\lceil m/2 \rceil$ and m descendents, and all leaf nodes are at the same level. A three-way B-tree is a 2-3 tree. The search algorithms, as well as algorithms for insertion and deletion of keys, are simple extensions of the algorithms for 2-3 trees and are left as exercises.

Exercise 4.31. Give algorithms for insertion and deletion of key values in m-way B-trees. Verify that execution time is proportional to $\log(N)$ in the worst case.

The principle differences between 2-3 trees and m-way B-trees are the number of information fields in each node and the proportionality constants for insertion and deletion operations. The larger the value of m, the larger the constant of proportionality, but the smaller the number of node accesses during search. When the tree will be stored on an external storage device, the user must choose

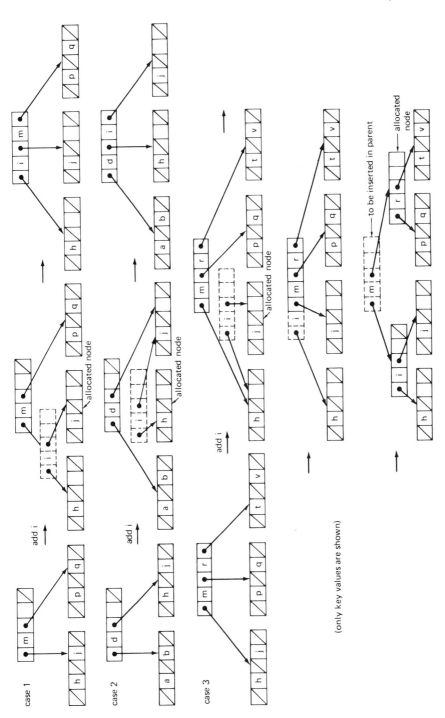

(only key values are shown)

m to optimize the trade-offs between storage utilization and execution time. The reader should consult chapter references for citations to relevant literature on B-tree and related algorithms.

Sequential treesort

The sequential memory representation for binary trees given in Section 4.2.1 leads to a very efficient sorting algorithm which is due to Floyd. The sort, called TREESORT3, also sometimes called a heapsort, takes place in two phases. Prior to the first phase, the N elements to be sorted are placed in an array A. This corresponds to placing them randomly in a binary tree, where all levels, except possibly the lowest one, are full; and the lowest level is full except for the rightmost elements. This is shown in Figure 4.13 for 13 values.

During the first phase of TREESORT3, the tree is partially sorted so that, except for the root node, elements along every path from a leaf to the root are in ascending order. This is done as follows: The nodes are processed moving from right to left and from the next-to-bottom level to the second level, using procedure SIFTUP. The first node processed is the parent of the rightmost node on the bottom level, and the last node processed is the left child of the root. For the tree in Figure 4.13, the nodes are processed in the order specified at the upper-left of the node. The subscripts in A of these nodes are [N/2], [N/2] − 1, [N/2] − 2, ...,2.

A node is processed by SIFTUP as follows: The value of the node is compared with the value of its larger child; if the parent has the larger value, the process

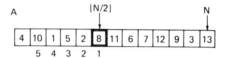

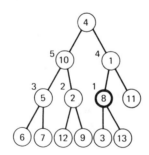

Figure 4-13. Thirteen values have been placed in array A to be sorted. The binary tree represented by this initial configuration is also shown. The order in which nodes are to be processed by SIFTUP is indicated.

terminates. However, if the child has the larger value, the values of the parent and child are swapped, and the new child is processed in the same way. The process terminates either when the parent is larger than its larger child, so that a swap is not performed, or when a leaf node is reached. Figure 4.14 shows the appearance of the tree at each step during phase one of processing. Notice that at the end of phase one of processing, the nodes on all paths from leaf to root, except the root, are in ascending order. When the root node is processed, it will

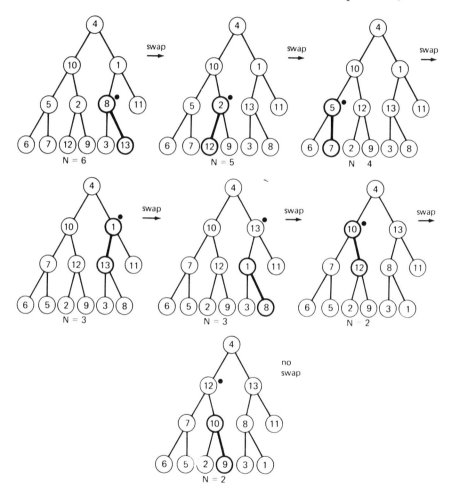

Figure 4.14. The initial, intermediate, and final configurations of the tree shown in Figure 4.15 during phase 1 of TREESORT3. For the final configuration, with the exception of the root, nodes along all paths from leaf to root are in ascending order. The node to which SIFTUP is initially applied is marked by a dot in each illustration. Darkened nodes indicate comparisons.

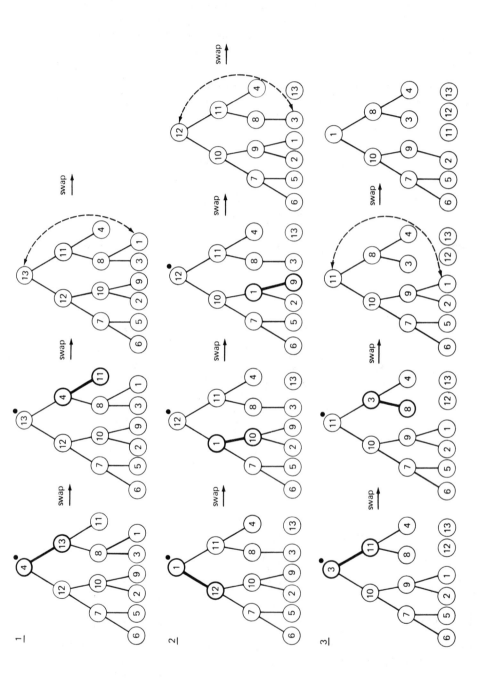

Figure 4.15. The first three applications of SIFTUP to the root node during phase two of TREESORT3 on the tree given in Figure 4.13.

have the highest value, and one of its children will have the second highest value. The second phase of processing consists of applying SIFTUP to the root node to find the largest value in the tree, swapping it with the rightmost leaf node (the last element in the array), and pretending the array has one fewer elements. This process is repeated until the tree has only two nodes. When the larger of them is placed in the second array element, the array A is in sorted order. Figure 4.15 shows each stage during the first three applications of SIFTUP to the root node during phase two. Figure 4.16 shows the appearance of the tree after six applications of SIFTUP to the root node and at the end of TREESORT3.

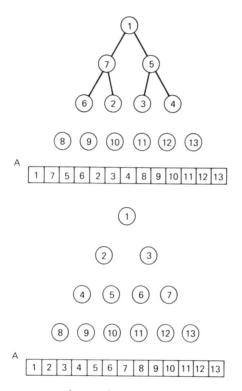

Figure 4.16. The appearance of array A and the binary tree represented by A after 6 applcations of SIFTUP during phase two of TREESORT3 and at the end of TREESORT3.

The algorithm TREESORT3 is shown below.

procedure TREESORT3(A,N);
declare (N,I,A(N)) INTEGER;
comment A is an array having N elements.
   I is the subscript of the element currently being processed;

```
comment Phase 1;
I := ⌊N/2⌋ + 1;
while (I > 2) do
      begin
          I := I - 1;
          call SIFTUP(A,I,N)
      end;
comment Phase 2;
I := N + 1;
while (I > 2) do
      begin
          I := I - 1;
          call SIFTUP(A,1,I);
          call EXCHANGE(A(1),A(I))
      end;
return;
end TREESORT3;

procedure SIFTUP(A,K,N);
declare (I,J,K,N,COPY,A(N)) INTEGER;
comment A(I) is moved upward in the subtree of A(1:N) of which it is the root;
I := K;
COPY := A(I);
J := 2 * I;
while (J ≤ N) do
      begin
         if (J < N)
         then
             begin
                if (A(J + 1) > A(J))
                then J := J + 1 endif
             end endif
         if (A(J) > COPY)
         then begin
                A(I) := A(J);
                I := J;
                J := 2 * I
             end
         else begin
                A(I) := COPY;
                return
             end endif
      end;
A(I) := COPY;
return;
end SIFTUP;
```

```
procedure EXCHANGE(X,Y);
declare (X,Y,T) INTEGER;
T := X;
X := Y;
Y := T;
end EXCHANGE;
```

The number of comparisons and swaps required by this algorithm is proportional to $N*\log_2(N)$, where N is the number of items to be sorted. This can be seen as follows. During phase two, the two children of the root are first compared to find the larger one, and then the root is compared with the larger one. This same process may occur for one descendant of each node moving down the tree, and there are a maximum of $\log_2(N)$ levels. Since this same process (SIFTUP) is repeated N times, the upper bound on comparisons is $2*N*\log_2(N)$. The number is actually smaller, since the tree is reduced by one node after each application of SIFTUP. The same number is an upper bound for phase one, since SIFTUP is applied once to each node except those on the lowest level and the root. Thus the number of comparisons is proportional to $N*\log_2(N)$. The number of swaps is at most half as many, since a swap only occurs between a parent and its larger child.

Game playing

Another use of trees is in game-playing programs. A program that plays a two player board game, such as chess, checkers, or tic-tac-toe will generate a tree consisting of possible moves, down to some maximum depth before it chooses a move. Illustrated on page 178 is a depth-one tree for a tic-tac-toe game with one level-one node expanded to level two. The nodes of level one represent the possible X moves. The nodes of level two represent the possible O moves, if the X is put in the upper left corner of the board.

Figure 4.17 shows a general game tree of depth-four which any game playing program might generate. Board B, the root node, is the current game board, and it is the computer's turn to choose a move. The level-one nodes represent all the possible moves that the computer can make starting at board B. The children of each level-one node B_i represent all the possible moves that the opponent can make if the computer makes move B_i. The children of each level-two node B_{ij} represent all the possible moves that the computer can make at its next turn, if, at the current pair of turns, the computer chooses move B_i, and its opponent chooses move B_{ij}. Finally, the children of each level-three node B_{ijk} represent all the possible moves that the opponent can make at his next turn, if at this pair of turns the computer chooses move B_i and the opponent chooses B_{ij} and at the next

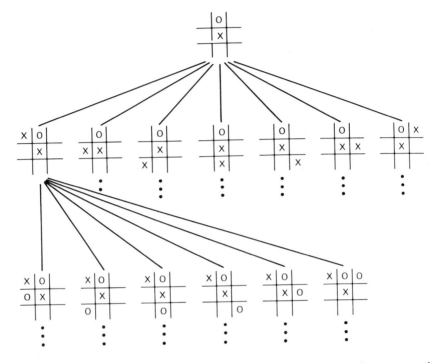

turn the computer chooses B$_{ijk}$. Note that square nodes indicate the computer's turn to move, and round nodes indicate the opponent's turn to move.

Built into the game-playing program is a *static evaluation function* that evaluates a game board and returns a value indicating how good this position is for the computer. For example, in a tic-tac-toe program, one possible evaluation function for a board B is:

$$
F(B) = \begin{cases} +\text{infinity if B is a win for the computer} \\ -\text{infinity if B is a win for the opponent} \\ \text{RCDC} - \text{RCDO, otherwise} \end{cases}
$$

where RCDC is the number of rows, columns, or diagonals still open for the computer, and RCDO is the number of rows, columns, or diagonals still open for the opponent. The program evaluates the leaves of the tree using the static evaluation function. It evaluates the boards at the branch nodes as follows: If a node represents computer's turn to move, the node's *backed up value* is the value of its largest child; the backed up value becomes the value of the node. That is, the computer will always choose the best possible move for itself. If a node represents opponent's turn to move, the node's backed up value is the value of its

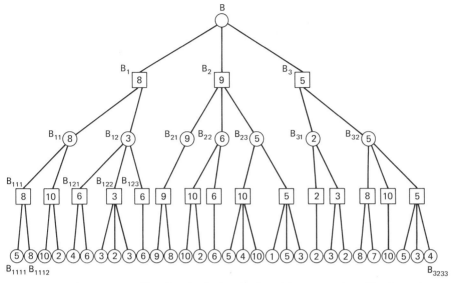

Figure 4.17. A game tree with values backed up by the minimax procedure. Circular nodes indicate human moves, and square nodes indicate computer moves.

smallest child. This means that the computer assumes that its opponent will choose the move that is worst for the computer.

Suppose the numbers in the level-four nodes in Figure 4.17 have been returned by the static evaluation function. The nodes at level three are computer's turn to move, so their values are the maximum values of their children. Thus $B_{111} =$ max $(B_{1111}, B_{1112}) = 8$. The nodes at level two are opponent's turn to move, so their values are the minimum values of their children. Thus $B_{12} = min(B_{121},$ $B_{122}, B_{123}) = 3$. The nodes at level one are again computer's turn to move. Thus B_1 becomes max$(B_{11}, B_{12}) = 8$, B_2 becomes 9, and B_3 becomes 5. Move B_2 is the move the computer finally chooses. The method described here is called the *minimax procedure*. For a more complete description of this procedure and of other procedures which may speed up the search, see Nilsson (1971), Jackson (1974), Slagle (1971), or Winston (1977).

Problem solving

A *state space problem* specifies a set of states $S = \{s_1, s_2, \ldots, s_n\}$, a start state $s \in S$, a goal state $g \in S$, and a set of operators $F = \{f_1, \ldots, f_m\}$ which can be applied to any one state to produce a new state. For example if s_1 is the state "china dish in my hands," and f_3 is the operator "drop what you are holding," then $f_3(s_1)$ is the state "what's left of china dish on floor." The problem is to find a sequence $f_{i1}, \ldots, f_{ik}$ of operators and a corresponding sequence $s_{i0}, \ldots, s_{ik}$ of states, such that:

$s_{i0} = s$, the start state; $s_{ik} = g$, the goal state; and $f_{ij}(s_{i(j-1)}) = s_{ij}$, for j ranging from 1 to k. Less formally, we are to find a sequence of operators that transforms the start state into the goal state. In the above example, if the goal state was "china dish filled with turkey on table in front of guests," then the operator f_3 was not a good choice.

Word puzzles can often be represented as state space problems; for example, in the Tower of Hanoi problem, we are given three pegs 1, 2, and 3 and three discs A, B, and C as shown below. Disc A is smaller than disc B, and disc B is smaller than disc C. A legal move consists of removing the top disc from any peg and putting it on another peg, with the restriction that no disc may rest on top of a smaller disc. The goal is to move all three discs to peg 3.

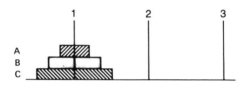

The states in the Tower of Hanoi problem can be represented as triples of the form (PA,PB,PC), where PA, PB, and PC are integers; PA represents the peg that disc A is on, PB the peg that disc B is on, and PC the peg that disc C is on. Thus the initial state is (1,1,1), and the goal state is (3,3,3). The operator O_{ij} represents moving the top disc on peg i to peg j. A sequence of operators that solves the problem is $\{O_{13}, O_{12}, O_{32}, O_{13}, O_{21}, O_{23}, O_{13}\}$.

One method of solving a state space problem is to create a *search tree*. The nodes of a search tree represent states and the branches represent operators. The root is the start state, and the children of each node represent all the states that can be reached from that state by applying one operator. A part of a search tree for the Tower of Hanoi problem is shown below. A search tree can be quite large. If there are m operators and each is applicable to every state, then the first p levels of the tree (not including the root) contain $m + m^2 + m^3 + \ldots + m^p = m(m^p - 1)/(m - 1)$ nodes; thus if there are ten operators, the tree at level 5 contains 111,110 nodes. Instead of creating and storing such a large tree and then searching it, the tree can be searched as it is created. During the search, branches that lead to dead ends (states where no operator is applicable, states where we have already been, or states that just don't seem promising) are discarded. One commonly used search procedure is *depth-first search*. In a depth-first-search, only the first child of each node is created on first encountering that node. If the goal node is reached, the procedure is terminated; if a dead end node is reached, the procedure backs up to the parent of the dead end node and creates the next child of the parent. The following procedure is a depth-first-search that finds the first sequence of operators that transform the start to the goal state:

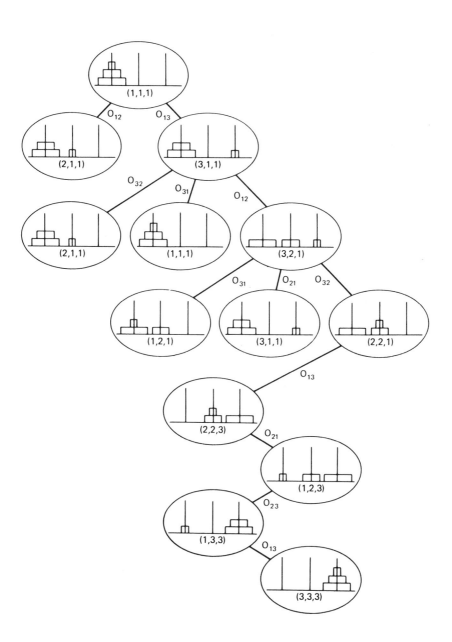

procedure DEPTH_FIRST_SEARCH (START,GOAL,M);
comment Given start state START and goal state GOAL, perform a depth-first-search to find the first sequence of operators that transform START to GOAL. Operators are represented by integers between 1 and M. States are represented by integers;
comment The routine APPLY(N,STATE) applies the N'th operator to STATE and returns the resultant new state;
comment The routine DISPLAY_RESULTS prints the sequence of operators and states;
comment The routine DEAD returns **true**, if its argument is a dead state; otherwise it returns **false**;
declare (ROOT,ANODE) POINTER **to** NODE;
declare (START,GOAL,NEWSTATE,M) INTEGER;
template   1 NODE,
                   2 STATE   INTEGER,
                   2 CHILD   POINTER **to** NODE,
                   2 PARENT   POINTER **to** NODE,
                   2 CURRENT_OP   INTEGER;
comment The routine GETNODE returns a pointer to a cell of type NODE;
if (START = GOAL)
then begin
         call DISPLAY_RESULTS;
         return
     end endif;
ROOT := GETNODE( );
[ROOT].STATE := START;
[ROOT].PARENT := **null**;
[ROOT].CURRENT_OP := 0;
ANODE := ROOT;
while (true) do
   begin
      [ANODE].CURRENT_OP := [ANODE].CURRENT_OP + 1;
      if ([ANODE].CURRENT_OP) > M)
      then begin
             ANODE := [ANODE].PARENT;
             if (ANODE = **null**) **then return endif**
          end
      else begin
             NEWSTATE := APPLY([ANODE].CURRENT_OP,[ANODE].STATE)
             if (NEWSTATE = GOAL)
             then begin
                     call DISPLAY_RESULTS;
                     return
                  end endif;
             if (NEWSTATE ≠ 0 and DEAD (NEWSTATE) ≠ true)
             then begin

```
        NEWCELL := GETNODE();
        [NEWCELL].STATE := NEWSTATE;
        [NEWCELL].PARENT := ANODE;
        [NEWCELL].CURRENT_OP := 0;
        [ANODE].CHILD := NEWCELL;
        ANODE := NEWCELL
      end endif;
    end endif
  end;
end DEPTH_FIRST_SEARCH;
```

Exercise 4.32. Write DISPLAY_RESULTS.

Exercise 4.33 Rewrite DEPTH_FIRST_SEARCH to find all solutions instead of just the first solution.

A second commonly used search procedure is *breadth-first*-search, where searching is done by levels. First the children of the root node are created left to right. If any of these is the goal node, the procedure successfully terminates. If not, each child node that is not a dead end node is expanded further—that is, each of its children is created and checked; thus the tree is created one level at a time. The breadth first search procedure is guaranteed to find a solution if one exists, while the depth-first-search may flounder forever on the wrong path. However, breadth-first-search often uses more storage than depth-first-search and is therefore not as popular. The algorithm for breadth-first-search is left as an exercise.

Exercise 4.34. Write the procedure BREADTH_FIRST_SEARCH(START, GOAL,M).

Code generation

A *one-address machine*, also called an *accumulator machine*, is a computer that has a single register for holding arithmetic results; this register is called an *accumulator*. The machine instructions operate on the value in the accumulator and the value in one storage location in memory, and the result of each operation is placed in the accumulator. Some common assembly language statements for an accumulator machine are given below:

LOAD X   Put the value at location X into the accumulator.

STORE X   Store the contents of the accumulator in location X.

ADD X   Add the contents of location X to the value in the accumulator, and put the result back into the accumulator.

SUB X   Subtract the contents of location X from the value in the accumulator, and put the result back into the accumulator.

MULT X Multiply the contents of the accumulator by the contents of location X, and put the result back into the accumulator.

DIV X   Divide the contents of the accumulator by the contents of location X, and put the results back into the accumulator.

The following is assembly language code for an accumulator machine:

```
LOAD A      *LOAD ACCUMULATOR WITH THE VALUE
            *IN LOCATION A
ADD =5      *ADD 5 TO THE CONTENTS OF THE ACCUMULATOR
MULT C      *MULTIPLY CONTENTS OF ACCUMULATOR BY VALUE
            *IN LOCATION C AND PLACE RESULT IN ACCUMULA-
            *TOR
STORE ANS   *STORE CONTENTS OF ACCUMULATOR IN LOCATION
            *ANS.
```

This code is equivalent to the high-level statement:

$$ANS = (A + 5) * C$$

In the assembly language code, the expression "=5" signifies the constant integer 5, and "A," "C," and "ANS" designate the addresses of three words of memory that will contain the values of the variables A, C, and ANS; the "*" designates the beginning of a comment. Given a binary tree representing an arithmetic expression (see Section 4.2.1), the following algorithm can be used to create the corresponding one-address machine code. The algorithm, CODE(N), generates and returns a string of characters representing assembly language code for the sub-expression represented by the subtree headed by node N:

```
procedure CODE(N);
declare N NODE;
case
        (N is a leaf node representing a variable):
            CODE := the name of the variable;
        (N is a leaf node representing a constant K):
            CODE := '=K';
        (N is a branch node representing an operator OP, NL is the left child of N,and NR
        is the right child of N):
            CODE :=
            CODE(NR)
            'STORE $' || LEVEL(N)
            'LOAD' || CODE(NL)
            OP || '$' || LEVEL(N);
end case;
return;
end CODE;
```

LEVEL(N) is a function that returns the integer level number of node N, and "$\|$" denotes string concatenation. Concatenating the '$' with the integer level number of a node gives a unique variable associated with each level of the tree ($0, $1, $2, ...). The variable whose name is "$ $\|$ LEVEL(N)" provides a storage location where the result of executing the code for the right subtree of N is saved, while the code for the left subtree of N is processed; for example, in the expression '(A+B)/(C+D)', '(A+B)' will be represented by the left subtree of '/', and '(C+D)' will be represented by the right subtree of '/.' The value of the subexpression '(C+D)' is computed and saved in temporary variable $0, then the value of subexpression '(A+B)' is computed and left in the accumulator; finally, the contents of the accumulator is divided by the contents of $0.

The one-address machine code for an entire tree with root node R is given by 'LOAD' $\|$ CODE(R). The code generation for a binary tree representing the expression '(A+1)*(C−D)' is traced below.

tree

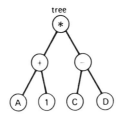

Expression	(A + 1) * (C − D)	
Post order	A1 + CD − *	
code (A)	A	
code (1)	=1	
code (+)	=1	
	STORE	$LEVEL(1)
	LOAD	A
	ADD	$LEVEL(1)
code (C)	C	
code (D)	D	
code (−)	D	
	STORE	$LEVEL(1)
	LOAD	C
	SUB	$LEVEL(1)
code (*)	D	
	STORE	$LEVEL(1)
	LOAD	C
	SUB	$LEVEL(1)
	STORE	$LEVEL(0)
	LOAD	=1
	STORE	$LEVEL(1)
	LOAD	A
	ADD	$LEVEL(1)
	MULT	$LEVEL(0)

The code for the whole tree:

```
LOAD    D
STORE   $LEVEL(1)
LOAD    C
SUB     $LEVEL(1)
STORE   $LEVEL(0)
LOAD    =1
STORE   $LEVEL(1)
LOAD    A
ADD     $LEVEL(1)
MULT    $LEVEL(0)
```

Exercise 4.35. Trace the code generation for the tree shown below.

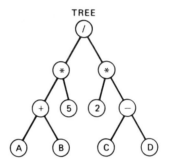

4.3 GRAPHS AND DIGRAPHS

A *graph* G is a set N of objects called *nodes,* together with a set of pairs of nodes called *edges.* If (N1, N2) is one of the pairs, then we say there is an *edge* connecting N1 and N2. Pictorially, a graph is usually represented by drawing a circle for each node and joining two nodes that define an edge by a line segment representing the edge. Figure 4.18 shows a graph where each node represents an English word, and two nodes are joined by an edge, if they have at least one letter in common. The graph of Figure 4.18 is a non-hierarchical graph. A tree is a hierarchical kind of graph.

An *undirected graph* is a graph such that if (N1, N2) is an edge, then (N2, N1) is also an edge. The graph of Figure 4.18 is an undirected graph, since if word W1 has a letter in common with word W2, then W2 has the same letter in common with W1. We will generally refer to undirected graphs simply as graphs.

A *directed graph* or *digraph* is a graph without the above restrictions; thus in a digraph, it is possible for (N1, N2) to be an edge but (N2, N1) not be an edge. In this case, we say there is a *directed edge from* N1 *to* N2. A directed edge is often called an *arc.* If an arc represents the ordered pair (N1, N2), then N1 is called the

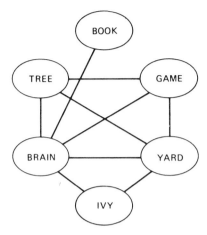

Figure 4.18. A graph whose nodes are words. Two nodes are connected if they have a common letter.

from-node of the arc, and N2 is called the *to-node* of the arc. Pictorially, we draw an arrow on the end of the arc touching the to-node to show the direction of the arc. Figure 4.19 shows a picture of a face and a digraph representation of the picture. The nodes of the digraph represent the picture components CIRCLE, LEFT_EYE, RIGHT_EYE, NOSE, and MOUTH. The arcs represent the spatial relationships between pairs of picture components; for instance, the arc

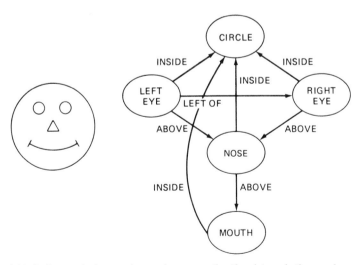

Figure 4.19. A picture of a face and a graph representing the picture. In the graph, each node represents a part of the face, and each arc represents the geometrical relationship between the parts.

from node NOSE to node MOUTH has from-node NOSE and to-node MOUTH and represents the spatial relationship ABOVE. Thus we can determine from the digraph that NOSE is above MOUTH in the picture.

There are several other properties that can be defined for digraphs: The set of all arcs leaving a node is called the *arc-set-out* of the node; the arc-set-out of the node NOSE consists of two arcs representing ABOVE and INSIDE. The set of all arcs entering a node is called the *arc-set-in* of the node; the arc-set-in of the node CIRCLE consists of four arcs, each representing the relation INSIDE. The number of arcs in the arc-set-out of a node is called the *outdegree* of the node, and the number of arcs in the arc-set-in of a node is called the *indegree* of the node. Node CIRCLE has outdegree 0 and indegree 4; node NOSE has outdegree 2 and indegree 2; node LEFT_EYE has outdegree 3 and indegree 0. A node that has outdegree 0 is called a *sink node,* and a node that has indegree 0 is called a *source node;* thus, in Figure 4.19, node CIRCLE is a sink node, and node LEFT_EYE is a source node. In an undirected graph, the number of edges connected to a node is called the *degree* of the node. In Figure 4.18, the degree of node BOOK is 1, and the degree of node BRAIN is 5; thus node BOOK is connected to only one node, while node BRAIN is connected to every other node in the graph.

In working with graphs, we often need to know not only which nodes are directly connected by an edge, but also which nodes are indirectly connected by a sequence of edges. For example, in Figure 4.18, BOOK and GAME are not directly connected, but there is an edge connecting BOOK to BRAIN and an edge connecting BRAIN to GAME; thus BOOK and GAME are indirectly connected. In an undirected graph, we say there is a *path* between nodes A and B, if there is a sequence of nodes $X_0, X_1, X_2, ..., X_n$, such that $A = X_0, B = X_n$, and there is an edge between nodes X_i and $X_{(i+1)}$, for i ranging from 0 to n-1. Since such a path includes n edges, we call it a path of *length n*; in Figure 4.18, there is a path between BOOK and GAME of length 2. Corresponding to this path, $X_0 = $ BOOK, $X_1 = $ BRAIN, and $X_2 = $ GAME. A *loop* is a path from a node to itself where no edge is included more than once. An undirected graph is *connected,* if for every pair of nodes A and B, there is a path between A and B. A *tree* is a connected, undirected graph with no loops.

In a digraph, we say there is a path from node A to node B, if there is a sequence of nodes $X_0, X_1, ..., X_n$, such that $A = X_0, B = X_n$, and there is an arc from X_i to $X_{(i+1)}$ for i ranging from 0 to n $-$ 1. For example, in Figure 4.20, there are two paths of length 2 from node 1 to node 5. A digraph is *strongly connected* if for every pair of nodes A and B, there is a path from A to B; a digraph is *weakly connected* if for every pair of nodes A and B, there is a path from A to B or a path from B to A.

Exercise 4.36. List all the paths of length 6 or less connecting node BOOK and node GAME in Figure 4.18.

A graph can be represented by a complex linked structure or by a simple matrix. A linked structure is used when the graph can grow and shrink dynamically or when the nodes must contain complex information; a matrix is used when the graph has a maximum size and when saving space is important. We will now examine each method in detail.

4.3.1 Matrix representations of graphs

A matrix representation of a graph is a compact representation that shows the structure of the graph but does not contain additional information, such as what a node or arc represents. A graph with N nodes can be represented by an N x N matrix called an *adjacency matrix*. Each element of the matrix has a value of 0 or 1; thus each element requires only one bit of storage. If the element in row I, column J of an adjacency matrix has the value 1, there is an edge between node I and node J; a value of 0 indicates no edge between node I and node J. An undirected graph and its adjacency matrix are shown below. Notice that there is a 1 in row I, column J if and only if there is a 1 in row J, column I. Since an adjacency matrix is symmetric, a triangular matrix can be used to store the adjacency matrix of an (undirected) graph. (See Chapter 5, Section 5.3.)

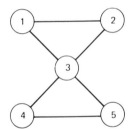

	1	2	3	4	5
1	0	1	1	0	0
2	1	0	1	0	0
3	1	1	0	1	1
4	0	0	1	0	1
5	0	0	1	1	0

A digraph can also be represented by an adjacency matrix; in this case, there may be an arc from node I to node J but no arc from node J to node I. Thus an entire N x N matrix is needed to represent the structure of the graph. Figure 4.20 shows a digraph and its adjacency matrix. The adjacency matrix is the most commonly used matrix representation for graphs.

Example. *Networks*

A *network* is a graph in which there is a value associated with each edge. The nodes in a network often represent positions in time or space, and the arcs represent various constraints, such as processing time or distance. Shown below are three examples of networks. The first example is called a PERT network; the arcs of this network represent the tasks T_1 through T_7 and their completion times. The nodes represent completion states; node S_1 is the initial state in which no tasks have been completed; node S_5 is the final state in which all the tasks have been completed. The tasks represented by arcs leaving a state may be started as soon as all the tasks represented by arcs entering the state have been completed; thus tasks T_3, T_5, and T_6 can be started as soon as task T_2 is completed. The second example is a network of computers. Computer C_i can send information to computer C_j if there is an arc from node C_i to node C_j. In this example, the arcs represent information transmission lines. The third graph represents a network of cities connected by air routes. The arcs represent distances between cities.

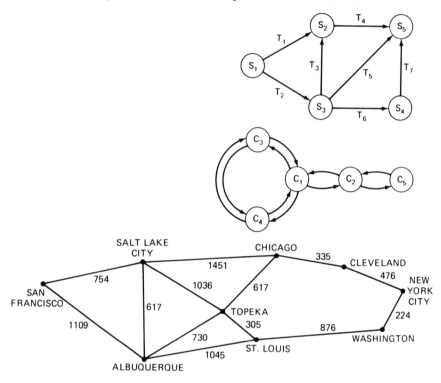

Two questions often asked when working with networks are, for arbitrary nodes A and B:

1. Is there a path from node A to node B?
2. What is the shortest path from node A to node B?

In the case of question 1), we can use the adjacency matrix of the graph to find the answer; for question 2), we need a representation that contains the distance (or time) between each pair of connected nodes. One possible representation is a matrix of numbers. The value 0 denotes no arc between two nodes, and any other

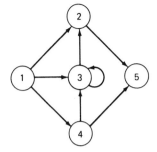

	1	2	3	4	5
1	0	1	1	1	0
2	0	0	0	0	1
3	0	1	1	0	0
4	0	0	1	0	1
5	0	0	0	0	0

Figure 4.20. A digraph and its adjacency matrix. The matrix has a 1 in row i, column j, if and only if there is an arc from node i to node j in the digraph.

number denotes the time or distance between them. A linked structure is another possible representation that we shall describe later. We will first show how to answer question 1), which is the easier of the two questions and can be answered in the context of the simple adjacency matrix. We will describe one method of answering question 2) in the section on linked graph structures.

Determining if there is a path between two nodes of a digraph represented by an adjacency matrix

Let A and B be two N x N matrices; we define the *logical product* A $\wedge$ B of A and B as follows:

$$(A \wedge B)_{IJ} = \overset{N}{\underset{K=1}{V}} A_{IK} \wedge B_{KJ}$$

where $\wedge$ represents the logical AND operator and V the logical OR operator. The *logical sum* A V B of A and B is defined by:

$$(A V B)_{IJ} = A_{IJ} \vee B_{IJ}$$

Suppose G is a directed graph represented by adjacency matrix M. Then $M_{IJ} = 1$ if and only if there is an arc from node I to node J. The logical product matrix M^2 (M x M) is also related to the graph. From the definition of M^2, we can see that $M^2_{IJ} = 1$ if and only if there is at least one node K, such that $M_{IK} = 1$ and $M_{KJ} = 1$. Thus $M^2_{IJ} = 1$ if and only if there is a path of length 2 from node I to node J.

In general, for K = 1 to N, $M^K_{IJ} = 1$ if and only if there is a path of length K from node I to node J. Now regarding the original question, there is a path from node I to node J if and only if there is a path of length N or less from node I to node J. Any longer path would contain loops which, when removed, would leave a path of length N or less. If I $\neq$ J, then there is a path from node I to node J if and only if there is a path of length N $-$ 1 or less. Thus in the general case, there is a path from node I to node J if and only if at least one of M_{IJ}, M_{IJ}^2 ,..., M_{IJ}^N = 1; That is, there is a path from node I to node J if and only if:

$$\underset{K=1}{\overset{N}{V}} \; M_{IJ}^K \; = 1.$$

A graph of 4 nodes, its adjacency matrix A, the product matrices A^2, A^3, A^4, and the logical sum S of the product matrices are shown below. From the matrix S we see that there is a path from every node to every other node with the exception of node 1, which is a source node; there are no paths leading to node 1.

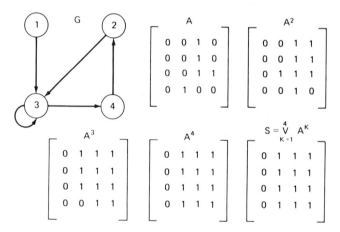

Exercise 4.37. Give an efficient algorithm determining if there is a path between two arbitrary nodes in a network represented by an adjacency matrix.

Exercise 4.38. Suppose a network is very large (1000 or more nodes) but has few arcs. What representation can be used that does not require 1000^2 locations? Using your representation, give an efficient algorithm for determining if there is a path between two arbitrary nodes of a network.

4.3.2. Linked representations of graphs

In this section, we will describe a particular representation for graphs that is based on the GROPE (*Gr*aph *OP*erations *E*xtension to FORTRAN) system. In Chapter 9 we discuss GROPE and its implementation. In this section, we will describe a graph structure that can be used for the problem of finding the shortest path between two nodes. In our structure, a graph is referenced through a *graph header* that has the following format;

NAME	LENGTH	NODESET

The NAME field contains a character string name for the graph; the LENGTH field contains the integer number of nodes in the graph, and the NODESET field contains a pointer to the first node in the graph.

A *node* has the following format:

NAME	MINDIS	PATH	MARK	NEXT_NODE		
LEN_RSETO	FIRST_ARC_OUT		LEN_RSETI	FIRST_ARC_IN		

The NAME field contains the character name of the node. The MINDIS and PATH fields are used in the shortest path algorithm and will be described shortly. The MARK field is a 2-bit field used to describe the status of the node during execution of the shortest path algorithm (or any other algorithm that needs to mark nodes). The NEXT_NODE field contains a pointer to the next node in the graph. All nodes on a graph are linked together using the NEXT_NODE_field. The LEN_RSETO field contains the integer number of nodes in the arc-set-out of the node, and the LEN_RSETI field contains the integer number of nodes in the arc-set-in of the node. The FIRST_ARC_OUT and FIRST_ARC_IN fields contain pointers to the first arcs in the arc-set-out and arc-set-in, respectively.

Finally an arc has the following format:

NAME	DIS	FROMNODE
TONODE	RSETO	RSETI

The NAME field contains the character name of the arc; the DIS field contains an integer representing the distance from the from-node of the arc to the to-node of the arc; the TONODE and FROMNODE fields contain pointers to the to-node and from-node, respectively. The RSETO and RSETI fields of an arc are used to link the arc into the arc-set-out of its from-node and arc-set-in of its to-node.

Figure 4.21 shows a network and its linked representation. G is an identifier (descriptor) that points to the header of the graph. The LENGTH field of the

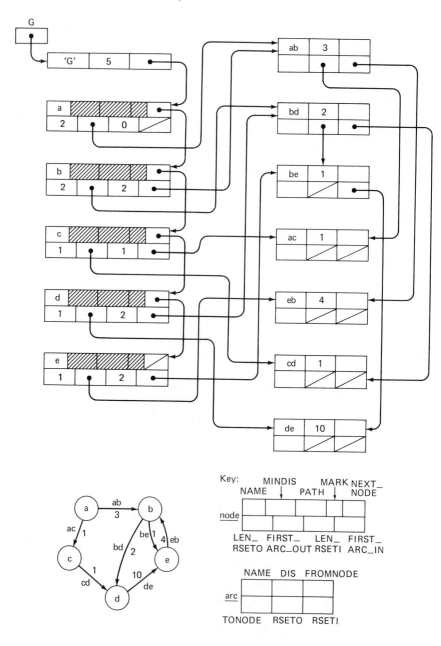

Figure 4.21. A graph and its linked representation.

header contains the value 5, indicating that the graph has five nodes. The NODESET field of the header contains a pointer to the first node of the graph. The MINDIS, PATH, and MARK fields of the node are not yet in use.

We will now use this representation to implement an algorithm for finding the shortest path between two nodes. The algorithm, originally due to Dijkstra (1959) and modified by Johnson (1973), can be summarized as follows: Let V = {V₁, V₂ ,..., Vₙ} be the set of nodes of the graph and let A = {A₁, A₂ ,..., Aₘ} be the set of arcs of the graph; let S∈V be the start node and F∈V be the final node. We wish to find the shortest path from S to F.

Associated with each arc A is a number DIS(A)—the distance from the from-node of A to the to-node of A. Associated with each node V are a number MINDIS(V)—the current shortest distance from S to V, and a path PATH(V)—a character string representing the current shortest path from S to V. The form of PATH(V) is a sequence of node names separated by semicolons. When the algorithm terminates, MINDIS(F) will be the shortest distance from S to F, and PATH(F) will be a character string representing the shortest path from S to F. The set X will be used to hold pointers to all the nodes that still have to be processed. The algorithm can be expressed in a high-level form as follows:

```
MINDIS(S) := 0;
MINDIS(Vi) := + infinity, for Vi ≠ S;
PATH(S) := S;
PATH(Vi) := null, for Vi ≠ S;
X := {S};
while (X is not empty) do
     begin
          Choose node W such that W is in X and MINDIS(W) is smaller than
               MINDIS(U) for all nodes U in X;
          ARCS := arc-set-out of W;
          while (ARCS is not empty) do
               begin
                    Remove one arc R from ARCS;
                    VT := to-node of R;
                    MINDIS(VT) := MIN(MINDIS(VT), MINDIS(W) + DIS(R));
                    if (MINDIS(VT) has changed)
                    then begin
                         X := X U {VT};
                         PATH(VT) := PATH(W) || ';' || VT
                         end
               end;
          X := X - {W}
     end;
```

Given the data structure of Figure 4.21, the following procedure implements the above algorithm. In this procedure, the MINDIS field of each node contains the current minimum distance from the start node N1 to that node. The PATH field contains a character string representing the current shortest path from node N1 to the node. The MARK field is set to $'1'B$, if the node is a member of set X described above and $'0'B$ otherwise.

The algorithm starts by initializing the MINDIS field of each node in the graph to $+$infinity, the PATH field to **null,** and the MARK field to $'0'B$. It then sets the MINDIS field of the start node to 0, its PATH field to its own name, and its MARK field to $'1'B$. Thus the start node is a distance of zero from itself; the path from it to itself consists of its own name; and it is initally the only member of the set X of nodes to be processed. The procedure then enters a loop which does not terminate until no more marked nodes can be found.

In the loop, a marked node with smallest MINDIS field is chosen by examining each node in the node set of G. The chosen marked node is called WNODE. Now for all nodes VNODE that are to-nodes of arcs in the arc-set-out of WNODE, the current MINDIS of VNODE is compared to the sum of the current MINDIS of WNODE and the distance along the arc from WNODE to VNODE. If the sum if smaller, it becomes the new MINDIS of VNODE. In this case, the PATH of VNODE is also changed, and VNODE is marked.

```
procedure SHORTEST_PATH(G, N1, N2);
comment Find the shortest path from node N1 to node N2 in graph G. N1 is a pointer to a
        node, N2 is a pointer to a node, and G is a pointer to the graph header;
declare G POINTER to GRAPH;
declare (N1, N2) POINTER to NODE;
template 1 GRAPH,
            2 NAME              CHARACTER,
            2 LENGTH            INTEGER,
            2 NODESET           POINTER to NODE;
template 1 NODE,
            2 NAME              CHARACTER,
            2 MINDIS            INTEGER,
            2 PATH              CHARACTER,
            2 MARK              1 BIT,
            2 NEXT_NODE         POINTER to NODE,
            2 LEN_RSETO         INTEGER,
            2 FIRST_ARC__OUT    POINTER to ARC,
            2 LEN_RSETI         INTEGER,
            2 FIRST_ARC_IN      POINTER to ARC;
template 1 ARC,
            2 NAME              CHARACTER,
            2 DIS               INTEGER,
            2 TONODE            POINTER to NODE,
```

```
    2 FROMNODE        POINTER to NODE,
    2 RSETO           POINTER to ARC,
    2 RSETI           POINTER to ARC;
declare (COUNT, NUMARCS, MINDIS) INTEGER;
declare (ANODE, WNODE, VNODE) POINTER to NODE;
declare ANARC POINTER to ARC;
comment All nodes in the node set of G that have MARK field = '1'B are in the set X of
        nodes to be processed;
comment For each node in the graph, set its MINDIS field to +infinity, its PATH field to
        null, and its MARK field to '0'B;
COUNT := [G].LENGTH;
if (COUNT = 0) then return endif;
ANODE := [G].NODESET;
while (COUNT > 0) do
    begin
        [ANODE].MINDIS := +infinity;
        [ANODE].PATH := null;
        [ANODE].MARK := '0' B;
        COUNT := COUNT - 1;
        ANODE := [ANODE].NEXT_NODE
    end;
comment Set MINDIS, PATH, and MARK for start node;
[N1].MINDIS := 0;
[N1].PATH := [N1].NAME;
[N1].MARK := '1' B;
while (true) do
    begin
        comment Choose the marked node with smallest MINDIS field from the node set
                of G;
        ANODE := [G].NODESET;
        WNODE := null;
        COUNT := [G].LENGTH;
        while (COUNT > 0) do
            begin
                if ([ANODE].MARK = '1' B)
                then begin
                    if (WNODE = null or [ANODE].MINDIS < [WNODE].MINDIS)
                    then WNODE := ANODE endif
                    end endif;
                ANODE := [ANODE].NEXT_NODE;
                COUNT := COUNT - 1
            end;
        comment If no marked nodes, procedure terminates;
        if (WNODE = null)
            then begin
                SHORTEST_PATH := [N2].PATH;
```

```
                    return
                    end endif;
          comment Now process the arc-set-out of the node WNODE;
          NUMARCS := [WNODE].LEN_RSETO;
          ANARC := [WNODE].FIRST_ARC_OUT;
          while (NUMARCS > 0) do
                begin
                    comment VNODE is a tonode of a node in the arc-set-out of WNODE;
                    VNODE := [ANARC].TONODE;
                    MINDIS := [VNODE].MINDIS;
                    comment Compute the new minimum distance to VNODE;
                    [VNODE].MINDIS := min([VNODE].MINDIS, [WNODE].MINDIS +
                                [ANARC].DIS);
                    comment If the minimum distance to VNODE has changed, then mark it
                                and update its PATH;
                    if ([VNODE].MINDIS ≠ MINDIS)
                    then begin
                                [VNODE].MARK := '1'B;
                                [VNODE].PATH := [WNODE].PATH || ';' || [VNODE].NAME
                                end endif;
                    ANARC := [ANARC].RSETO;
                    NUMARCS := NUMARCS - 1
                    end endif;
                comment Remove WNODE from set X;
                [WNODE].MARK := '0'B
          end;
end SHORTEST_PATH;
```

Shown below is a symbolic representation for the network of Figure 4.21. Each node is partitioned into four parts representing the NAME, PATH, MINDIS, and MARK fields; each arc has a number on it representing its DIS field. The arrow on each arc indicates which nodes are its to-node and from-node. All of these fields have been initialized. The other fields in Figure 4.21 have been left out to simplify the diagram. Figure 4.22 traces the execution of the

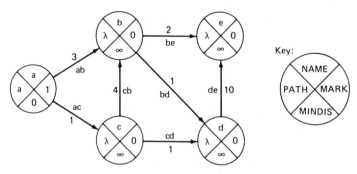

algorithm SHORTEST_PATH(G, a, e) for each iteration of the *while-do* loop. After execution of the algorithm, the PATH field of node e contains 'a;b;e', which is the shortest path from node a to node e.

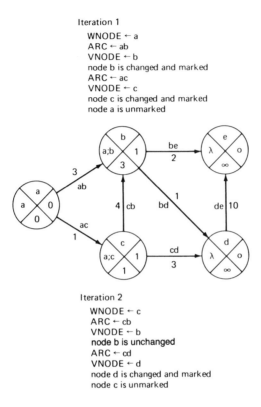

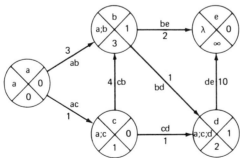

Figure 4.22. A trace of the iterations of the procedure SHORTEST _ PATH (b, a, e). The resultant shortest path is a;b;e.

Iteration 3
   WNODE ← d
   ARC ← de
   VNODE ← e
   node c is changed and marked
   node d is unmarked

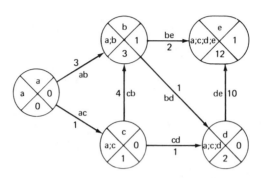

Iteration 4
   WNODE ← b
   ARC ← bd
   VNODE ← d
   node d is not changed
   ARC ← be
   VNODE ← e
   node e is changed and marked
   node b is unmarked

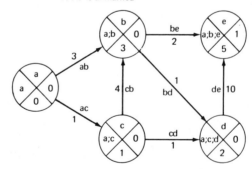

Iteration 5
   WNODE ← e
   there are no arcs in the arc-set-out of e
   node e is unmarked

Iteration 6
   there are no marked nodes; return

Exercise 4.39. Using the representation described above for the airline network illustrated earlier, trace through the execution of the SHORTEST—PATH algorithm to find the shortest path between San Francisco and New York City.

4.4 SUMMARY

Graph structures are used to represent relations among items of data. Trees are graph structures commonly used in compilers, problem solving programs, sorting, searching, and many other applications. Trees may be implemented sequentially or in a linked representation; the sequential implementation requires much less memory, but the linked representation is more flexible and more common. Graphs in general can be represented by matrices or as linked structures. Graphs are commonly used to solve problems in electrical engineering, physics, computer science, geography, and operations research, to name a few applications areas.

Project 4.1. Implement a linked tree sort and search algorithm. The input to the tree sort is a sequence of pairs of attributes and values. The input to the tree search is a sequence of attributes only. Keep all of the nodes in an array that has four columns, one for ATTRIBUTE, one for VALUE, one for LLINK, and one for RLINK. Pointers in the tree structure are the array subscripts of the designated node.

The program should do the following:
1. Create a tree-structured table.
2. Print the table elements in order of attribute, while traversing the tree in inorder.
3. Read in a sequence of attributes and search the table for their values. Print out each attribute, its value or a message indicating that it is not found, and the number of comparisons the search had to make before it found the value or reached the bottom of the tree.

Example:
INPUT1   (8,A)   (2,B)   (5,D)   (1,C)
Resulting tree structure:

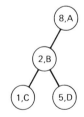

OUTPUT1   (1,C)   (2,B)   (5,D)   (8,A)
INPUT2   2,5
OUTPUT2   2,B   2 COMPARISONS
           5,D   3 COMPARISONS

Project 4.2. The Missionary-Cannibal problem can be stated as follows: There are three missionaries and three cannibals on the left bank of a river; they have one boat capable of holding two people, and they all want to cross over the river to the right bank. The only complication is that if there are ever more cannibals than missionaries on either side of the river, the cannibals will eat the missionaries.

A state in this problem can be represented by a triple (MIS, CAN, BOAT), where MIS is the number of missionaries on the left bank, CAN is the number of cannibals on the left bank, and BOAT is the side of the river that the boat is on (L or R). Thus the initial state is (3, 3, L), and the goal state is (0, 0, R). The operators are the permissible movements of the boat. For example, MCR is the movement of the boat with one missionary and one cannibal from the left bank to the right bank, and CCL is the movement of the boat with two cannibals from the right bank to the left bank.

Write a program that performs depth-first search to find a sequence of operators that transform (3, 3, L) to (0, 0, R). There are four possible answers.

Project 4.3. Suppose you have a digraph representing a PERT network. The nodes of a PERT network represent states of completion, and the arcs represent the time it takes to complete a task. All of the tasks represented by arcs entering a state must be completed before the tasks represented by the arcs leaving the state may be started. There is one node called START which represents the initial state where no tasks have been started, and there is one node called END that represents the completion of the job. A PERT network is loop free; START is the only state with no incoming arcs; and END is the only state with no outgoing arcs. An example is shown below.

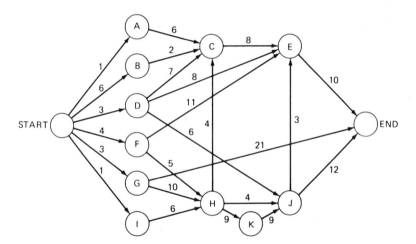

A *critical path* through such a network is a longest time path from START to END. The sum of the times on a critical path is the shortest amount of time required for the completion of all tasks. The algorithm for finding a longest path is similar to the algorithm for finding a shortest path. Write a program that accepts as input a suitable representation of a digraph representing a network, and finds and lists the nodes along the critical path.

Project 4.4. In a previous section (c.f. Code generation), we gave an algorithm (CODE) for producing assembly language code for a one-address machine from a tree representing an arithmetic expression. Section 2.2.3 of Chapter 2 gave an algorithm (CONVERT) which used a stack to convert an expression from infix notation to postfix notation. Design an algorithm POSTFIX_TO_TREE(POSTFIX_EXPRESSION, TREE) that converts a postfix expression into a binary tree representing that expression. (A recursive procedure that scans the postfix expression from right to left is one possibility.) Implement CONVERT, POSTFIX _ TO _ TREE, and CODE to produce a program that takes as input an arbitrary infix expression and produces as output the one-address assembly language code for the expression.

Project 4.5. When working with lists that are searched as often as they are modified by the addition and deletion of elements, neither sequential nor linearly linked memory representations are very efficient. Sequential organizations require execution time proportional to the length of the list for insertions and deletions, while linearly linked representations require search time which is proportional to the length of the list. One suggestion is to maintain the list elements in a height-balanced tree, where the attribute of each node is the element value, and the value of the node is not used.

The difficulty with this suggestion is keeping track of the element number in the list. One way to do this is to add to each node a RANK field whose value is one plus the number of nodes in the left subtree of the node. Using the RANK field, it is easy to determine the order number of an element. Given the order number of an element, it is equally easy to locate the desired element. Furthermore, the time required to search the list as well as add or delete an element is proportional to $n\log_2(n)$, where n is the number of elements in the list.

Design and code a set of procedures for manipulating tree-structured lists. In addition to single element insertions and deletions, discover and code a procedure for list concatenation, inserting all elements of one list, in order, into another list.

Project 4.6. When using minimax evaluation for evaluating a game tree, the value of a maximum node is the largest values of any of its direct descendents, and the value of a minimum node is the smallest. Consider the game tree shown below, and asusme that nodes are generated and evaluated from right to left, using depth-first minimax evaluation. The backed up value of the maximum node M_{31} is 6, as shown. Notice that if one of the backed up values of the second or third maximum nodes, M_{32} or M_{33} exceeds the value 6, then further evaluation of them is not necessary, since the value backed up to the minimum node m_{21} can be no larger than 6. The value 6 is a beta cutoff for nodes M_{32} and M_{33}; a beta cutoff is the largest value that the above minimum node (in this case m_{21}) can be held to.

Referring to the same figure, the backed up value at the root node M1 will be no smaller than 6; hence if the value of one of the minimum nodes m_{22} or m_{23} is less than 6, then the value 6 will be backed up instead. The value 6 in this case is called an alpha cutoff, the smallest value that the above maximum node can be held to. Notice that the alpha and beta values propagate down the tree so that an alpha cutoff of 6 applies to M_{34}. A procedure that uses minimax evaluation is also said to use alpha-beta pruning in case the above concepts are used to restrict the search. In the tree shown above, for example, only seven leaf nodes need to be generated and evaluated to determine its minimax value. This is illustrated below.

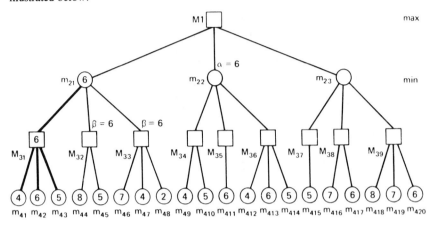

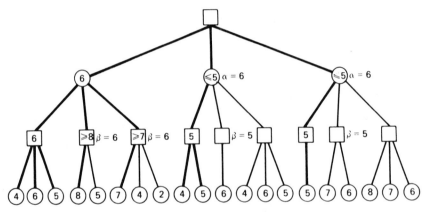

Write a complete procedure MINIMAX(T, M) that has two parameters, a pointer T to a game tree to be evaluated, and an indicator M that specifies whether the root is a maximum node (M = '1') or a minimum node (M = '0'). MINIMAX should return the value of the tree using minimax evaluation and alpha-beta pruning.

REFERENCES AND ADDITIONAL READINGS

Books

Aho, A.V.; Hopcroft, J.E.; and Ullman, J.D. (1976) *The Design and Analysis of Computer Algorithms*. Reading, Massachusetts: Addison-Wesley Publishing Co., Inc.

Aho, A.V., and Ullman, J.D. (1972) *The Theory of Parsing, Translation, and Compiling*. Englewood Cliffs, New Jersey: Prentice-Hall, Inc.

Gries, D. (1971) *Compiler Construction for Digital Computers*. New York: John Wiley & Sons, Inc.

Jackson, P.C., Jr. (1974) *Introduction to Artifical Intelligence*. New York: Petrocelli Books.

Knuth, D.E. (1972) *The Art of Computer Programming, Volume 3/Sorting and Searching*. Reading, Massachusetts: Addison-Wesley Publishing Co., Inc.

Nilsson, N.J. (1971) *Problem Solving Methods in Artificial Intelligence*. New York: McGraw-Hill Book Co., Inc.

Slagle, J.R. (1971) *Artificial Intelligence: The Heuristic Approach*. New York: McGraw-Hill Book Co., Inc.

Tou, J.T. (Ed.) (1974) *Information Systems*, COINS IV. New York: Plenum Press.

Winston, P.H. (1977) *Artifical Intelligence*. Reading, Massachusetts: Addison-Wesley Publishing Co., Inc.

Articles

Adel'son-Vel'skii, G.M., and Landis, E.M. An algorithm for the organization of information. *Soviet Mathematics* Vol. 6, 1963, 1259-1263.

Baecker, H.D. The use of Algol 68 for trees. *Computer J.* Vol. 13, No. 1, Feb. 1970, 25-27.

Baer, J.L., and Schwab, B. A comparison of tree-balancing algorithms. *CACM* Vol. 20, No. 5, May 1977, 322-330.

Baron, R.J.; Friedman, D.P.; Shapiro, L.G.; and Slocum, J. Graph Processing using GROPE/360. Technical Report 73-13, December 1973, Department of Computer Science, The University of Iowa.

Bayer, R. Symmetric binary trees: Data structures and maintenance algorithms. *Acta Informatica* Vol. 1, Fasc. 4, 1972, 290-306.

Bayer, R., and McCreight, E. Organization and maintenance of large unordered indices. *Acta Informatica* Vol. 1, Fasc. 3, 1972, 173-189.

Bentley, J.L. Multidimensional binary search trees used for associative searching. *CACM.* Vol. 18, No. 9, Sept. 1975, 509-517.

Clampett, H.A., Jr. Randomized binary searching with tree structures. *CACM* Vol. 7, No. 3, Mar. 1964, 163-165.

Cohen, D.J., and Gotlieb, C.C. A list structure form of grammars for syntactic analysis. *Computing Surveys* Vol. 2, No. 1, Mar. 1970, 65-82.

Crespi-Reghizzi, S., and Morpurgo, R. A language for treating graphs. *CACM* Vol. 13, No. 5, May 1970, 319-323.

Culik, K., II, and Maurer, H.A. String representations of graphs. *International Journal of Computer Mathematics* Vol. 6, No.4, 1978, 273-301.

Dijkstra, E.W. A note on two problems in connexion with graphs. *Numerische Mathematik* Vol. 1, 1959, 269-272.

Driscol, J.R. A selective traversal algorithm for binary search trees. *CACM* Vol. 21, No. 6, June 1978, 445-447.

Fitzwater, D.R. A storage allocation and reference structure. *CACM* Vol. 7, No. 9, Sept. 1964, 542-545.

Floyd, R.W. Algorithm 245, Treesort 3[M1]. *CACM* Vol. 7, No. 12, Dec. 1964, 70.

Fredkin, E. TRIE Memory. *CACM* Vol. 3, No. 9, Sept. 1960, 490-499.

Friedman, D.P. GROPE: A graph processing language and its formal definition. Technical Report No. 20, August 1973, Department of Computer Science, The University of Texas at Austin.

Garey, M.R. Optimal binary search trees with restricted maximal depth. *SIAM Journal on Computing* Vol. 3, No. 2, June 1974, 101-110.

Ghosh, S.P., and Senko, M.E. File organization: On the selection of random access index points for sequential files. *JACM* Vol. 16, No. 4, Oct. 1969, 569-579.

Hirschberg, D.S. An insertion technique for one-sided height-balanced trees. *CACM* Vol. 19, No. 8, Aug. 1976, 471-473.

Hu, T.C., and Tucker, A.C. Optimal binary search trees. *SIAM Journal of Applied Mathematics* Vol. 2, No. 4, 1971, 514-532.

Hibbard, T. Some combinatorial properties of certain trees with applications to searching and sorting. *JACM* Vol. 9, No. 1, Jan. 1962, 13-28.

Itai, A. Optimal algebraic trees. *SIAM J. Computing* Vol. 5, No. 1, 1976, 9-18.

Johnson, D.B. A note on Dijkstra's shortest path algorithm. *JACM* Vol. 20, No. 3., July 1973, 385-388.

Karlton, P.L.; Fuller, S.H.; Scroggs, R.E.; and Kaehler, E.B. Performance of height-balanced trees. *CACM* Vol. 19, No. 1, Jan. 1976, 23-28.

Knuth, D.E. Optimal binary search trees. *Acta Informatica* Vol. 1, Fasc. 1, 1971, 14-25.

Kosaraju, S.R. Insertions and deletions in one-sided height-balanced trees. *CACM* Vol. 21, No. 3, Mar. 1978, 226-227.

Luccio, F., and Pagli, L. Rebalancing height-balanced trees. *IEEE Trans. on Computers* Vol. C-27, No. 5, May 1978, 386-396.

Martin, W.A., and Ness, D.N. Optimizing binary trees grown with a sorting algorithm. *CACM* Vol. 15, No. 2, Feb. 1972, 88-93.

Maurer, H.A.; Ottmann, Th.; and Six, H.W. Implementing dictionaries using binary trees of very small height. *Info. Proc. Letters* Vol. 5, 1976, 11-14.

Nievergelt, J. Binary search trees and file organization. *Computing Surveys* Vol. 6, No. 3, Sept. 1974, 195-207.

Nievergelt, J., and Reingold, E.M. Binary search trees of bounded balance. *SIAM J. Computing* Vol 2, No. 1, 1973, 33-43.

Nievergelt, J., and Wong, C.K. On binary search trees. *Proc. IFIP Congress 71*. Amsterdam: North-Holland Publishing Company, 1972, 91-98.

Nievergelt, J., and Wong, C.K. Upper bounds for the total path length of binary trees. *JACM* Vol. 20, No. 1, Jan. 1977, 1-6.

Ottmann, Th.; Six, H.W.; and Wood, D. Right brother trees. *CACM* Vol. 21, No. 9, Sept. 1978, 769-776.

Ottmann, Th., and Wood, D. Deletion in one-sided height-balanced trees. *International Journal of Computer Mathematics* Vol. 6, No. 4, 1978, 265-271.

Patt, Y.N. Variable length tree structures having minimum average search time. *CACM* Vol. 12, No. 2, Feb. 1976, 72-76.

Perlis, A.J. and Thornton, C. Symbol manipulation by threaded lists. *CACM* Vol. 3, No. 4, Apr. 1960, 195-204.

Reinboldt, W.C.; Basili, V.R.; and Mesztenyi, C.K. On a programming language for graph algorithms. *BIT* Vol. 12, No. 2, 1972, 220-241.

Rosenberg, A.L. Data encodings and their costs. *Acta Informatica* Vol. 9, Fasc. 3, 1978, 272-292.

Santos, C.S., and Furtado, A.L. G/PL/I—Extending PL/I for graph processing. In Tou (1974), 347-359.

Scidmore, A.K., and Weinberg, B.L. Storage and search properties of a tree-organized memory system. *CACM* Vol.6, No.1, Jan. 1963, 28-31.

Severance, D.G. Identifier search mechanisms: A survey and generalized model. *Computing Surveys* Vol. 6, No. 3, Sept. 1974, 175-194.

Siklóssy, L. Fast read-only algorithms for traversing trees without an auxiliary stack. *Info. Proc. Letters* Vol. 1, No. 4, June 1972, 149-152.

Slocum, J. The graph processing language GROPE. Technical Report NL-22, August 1974, Department of Computer Science, The University of Texas at Austin.

Sussenguth, G.H. Use of tree structures for processing files. *CACM* Vol. 6, No. 5, June 1963, 272-279.

Szwarcfiter, J.L., and Wilson, L.B. Some properties of ternary trees. *Computer*. Vol. 21, No. 1, Feb. 1978, 66-72.

Wood, D. A comparison of two methods of encoding arrays. *BIT* 18, 1978, 219-229.

Yao, A. On random 2, 3, trees, *Acta Informatica* Vol. 9, Fasc. 2, 1978, 159-170.

Zweben, S.H., and McDonald, M.A. An optimal method for deletions in one-sided height-balanced trees. *CACM* Vol. 21, No. 6, June 1978, 441-445.

5
Arrays, Matrices, and Tables

OVERVIEW

In this chapter, we will be concerned with data structures that are generally implemented in single blocks of memory using memory access functions. These structures include arrays, extendible arrays, symmetric and triangular matrices, sparse matrices, and hash tables. We will describe various memory representations, placing particular emphasis on good memory utilization and efficient access procedures.

5.1 INTRODUCTION

Arrays and tables are the most widely used data structures. Arrays are used in nearly all programs, and since arrays are often very large and accesses to array elements very frequent, the memory representations must be conservative and the access functions must be efficient. Although tables are not used as extensively as arrays, the applications for tables are increasing in importance. Because the applications are often in very large systems, such as compilers and database systems that frequently access the tables, it is essential, just as it is for arrays, to use memory representations that are conservative and access functions that are efficient. For some applications, very large arrays are required, but often the arrays have the interesting property that most of the elements are zero. Since it would be particularly wasteful of memory and processing time to reserve memory for each potential array element, special techniques have been developed to minimize the memory requirements yet retain rapid access to the elements. Although the uses of these matrices are rather limited, the techniques have widespread applications and for this reason have been presented in considerable detail.

All high-level programming languages allow the programmer to use variable names to refer to values that are stored in memory, and most high-level languages allow variables to be subscripted. If V is the name of a singly subscripted variable, then V(1), V(2), V(3), and so forth are different variables and therefore refer to different locations in memory. Subscripted variables are called *arrays,* and the number of different subscripts that are required for specifying an element of an array is the *dimension* of the array. One-dimensional arrays are called *vectors;* two-dimensional arrays are often called *matrices.* Very large matrices with the property that most of the elements have the value 0 are *sparse matrices.*

Whenever a variable is to designate an array, a declaration statement is required that specifies the values of the lower and upper bounds of each subscript position. Such a declaration is necessary, first so that space can be allocated for the array and, second so that the addresses of specific elements can be correctly calculated. The following four statements are array declarations in four well known programming languages:

> DECLARE A(10,20);   (PL/I)
> DIMENSION B(10,10,10)   (FORTRAN IV)
> **real array** C(-2:4,1:2,3:5);   (Algol 60)
> D = ARRAY ('0:10')   (SNOBOL4)

These declaration statements specify that: A is a two-dimensional array with subscript bounds 1 to 10 and 1 to 20; B is a three-dimensional array with all subscripts having bounds 1 to 10; C is a three-dimensional array with subscripts having bounds -2 to 4, 1 to 2, and 3 to 5; and D is a one-dimensional array with subscript having bounds from 0 to 10. These structures are shown on p. 210.

Array elements are designated by designational expressions consisting of the array identifier followed by a subscript list; for example, B(1,8,6) is a designational expression designating an element of the FORTRAN array B declared above. When a designational expression for an array element is used in a program statement, the value of each subscript must be within the subscript bounds specified in the declaration statement for that subscript position; otherwise a *subscript error* results. Although some compilers for programming languages generate code to detect subscript errors during program execution, many will not, and it is up to the programmer to insure that this type of error does not occur.

Subscripts used to reference elements of arrays and matrices all have integer values. In contrast, tables are analogous to one-dimensional arrays where the subscripts are not restricted to integer values. When table facilities are provided by the programming language, the table identifier is used in much the same way as an array identifier. In SNOBOL4, for example, the statement T = TABLE ('10') declares T to be a table identifier for a table having (initially) 10 entries. Statements such as A<'CAT'> = 'ANGORA' and A<'DOG'> = 'COLLIE' would place the value 'ANGORA' corresponding to the subscript 'CAT' and the

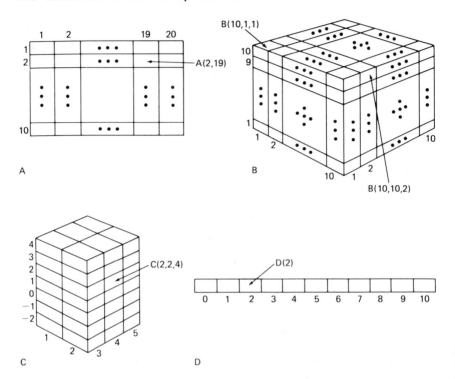

value 'COLLIE' corresponding to the subscript 'DOG' in the table A. However, unlike arrays whose range of subscript values is known in advance, table subscripts are not known in advance and hence must be stored as part of the data in the table. For this reason tables are defined somewhat differently.

A *table* is a collection of *pairs* of *attributes* and *values*. Attributes are also known as *arguments, keys,* or *indicators,* and the values are sometimes called *properties.* Correspondingly, tables are called *attribute-value tables, property lists, association lists, pair lists,* and so forth. Within a table, each attribute-value pair has a distinct attribute, but several pairs may have the same value. Tables need not have numeric attributes and most frequently have string-valued attributes. Symbol tables in assemblers and compilers are examples of tables having string-valued keys. Part of a symbol table is illustrated below.

The subscripts of arrays and matrices and the attributes of tables are used to select specific elements in the array or table and, as a result, are called *element selectors* or *selectors* for short. Given the selector values for an array or table entry, special procedures are used to insert new values in the corresponding array or table or to extract current values from the array or table. An *access function* is a function that maps a selector into a memory address. When inserting a value in a table or array, the access function is used to determine which element is to

NAME	TYPE	LENGTH (WORDS)	ADDRESS
A	2	1	1000
BID	2	50	1001
NUM	1	1	1051
SPEC	2	1	1052
T6	1	1	1053
⋮	⋮	⋮	⋮

receive the new value and where that element is located. When extracting the value of an array or table element, the access function is used to determine the address of the memory location that contains the desired value. Because access functions define a mapping between selector values and memory locations, they define the physical organization of the data within the computer's memory.

5.2 MULTI-DIMENSIONAL ARRAYS

In order to enable access to array elements, a programming language must maintain sufficient information to compute the address of an element when given the subscripts of the element. For programming languages that allocate memory at compile time, each source language statement that designates an array element is compiled into code that evaluates the subscripts and computes the address of the array element. The compiler for the programming language keeps in its symbol table the number of subscripts and the bounds for each subscript, as specified in the array declaration. For programming languages that allow arrays to be specified at execution time, the code for accessing an array element cannot be compiled directly. Rather, the array has a memory representation that contains, in addition to the array elements, the number of subscripts and their bounds. The compiled code must reference the memory representation to retrieve the information needed to calculate the address of an element.

The most frequently used memory representation for a vector array keeps the elements in order in a single block of contiguous memory locations. When represented in this way, the address of the block, which is also the address of the first element of the array (the element having smallest subscript), is the *base address* of the array. If there are NWPE (Number of Words Per Element) words in each array element, and the base address of the array is BASE, then the address of the I'th element is $BASE+(I-1)*NWPE$. This formula is usually computed using the equivalent formula $CONST+I*NWPE$, where CONST is the constant $BASE-NWPE$. CONST is computed only once, so each address computation requires one multiplication and one addition. Since array elements are most frequently one word long, the usual computation requires a single addition. When generating code to access elements of vector arrays, compilers often take advantage of special computer hardware, such as index registers, in order to keep the computation time to an absolute minimum.

For other than one-dimensional arrays, the most common way to represent an array in memory is to keep the elements in a contiguous block of storage in *row major* or *column major* order. Let BASE be the address of the first element of the array. In row major order the element placed at address BASE is the element having the lowest subscripts; the next element is the one whose last subscript is one higher than its lowest value, and so forth, until the last subscript reaches its maximum value. The next element has the last subscript set to its lowest value, and the next-to-last subscript one higher than its previous value. This is shown below for an array declared by the statement:

DECLARE A(0:2, −1:1);   (PL/I)

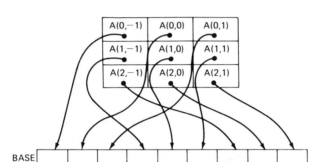

The addresses of the array elements are given below:

@A(0, −1)	is BASE
@A(0,0)	is BASE +1
@A(0,1)	is BASE +2
@A(1, −1)	is BASE +3
@A(1,0)	is BASE +4
@A(1,1)	is BASE +5
@A(2, −1)	is BASE +6
@A(2,0)	is BASE +7
@A(2,1)	is BASE +8

Notice that the array A may be thought of as three separate vector arrays, A(1), A(2), and A(3) stored in sequence, where the elements of A(1) are A(1) (−1), A(1)(0), and A(1)(1); the elements of A(2) are A(2)(−1), A(2)(0), and A(2)(1); and the elements of A(3) are A(3)(−1), A(3)(0), and A(3)(1). Using this memory representation for a two-dimensional array, an assignment statement such as "A(2) := A(1)" can easily be implemented. (In PL/I the equivalent assignment statement, "A(2,*) = A(1,*)," is allowed.)

The access function for a two-dimensional array, when represented in row major order, is as follows. Suppose the array is defined by the following statement:

$$\text{DECLARE } A(L_1:U_1, L_2:U_2);$$

where:

L_1	$=$	the lower bound for the first subscript
L_2	$=$	the lower bound for the second subscript
U_1	$=$	the upper bound for the first subscript
U_2	$=$	the upper bound for the second subscript
NWPE	$=$	the number of words in an array element
BASE	$=$	the base address of the elements of array A

Let D_1 and D_2 be defined as follows:

D_1	$=$	$U_1 - L_1 + 1$	(the number of different first subscripts)
D_2	$=$	$U_2 - L_2 + 1$	(the number of different second subscripts)

Then the address of the element $A(S_1, S_2)$ is given by:

$$\text{BASE} + \text{NWPE} * ((S_1 - L_1) * D_2 + (S_2 - L_2))$$

which can be factored into constant and variable parts so that:

$@A(S_1, S_2)$	$=$	$\text{CONST} + \text{VAR}$

where:

CONST	$=$	$\text{BASE} - \text{NWPE} * (D_2 * L_1 + L_2)$

and:

VAR	$=$	$\text{NWPE} * (D_2 * S_1 + S_2)$

The constant part, CONST, has to be evaluated only once. The variable part requires two multiplications and one addition, so the entire subscript computation requires only two multiplications and two additions; this is better than directly evaluating the original formula, which requires two multiplications and four additions. If, as is most frequently the case, each array element requires only one word of storage, then only one multiplication and two additions are required. For the array given in the example above, it is easy to verify that the access function correctly gives the address of each array element:

$$
\begin{array}{lll}
L_1 & = & 0 \\
L_2 & = & -1 \\
U_1 & = & 2 \\
U_2 & = & 1 \\
D_1 & = & U_1 - L_1 + 1 = 3 \\
D_2 & = & U_2 - L_2 + 1 = 3 \\
\text{NWPE} & = & 1 \\
\text{CONST} & = & \text{BASE} - \text{NWPE} * (D_2 * L_1 + L_2) = (\text{BASE} + 1)
\end{array}
$$

$$
\begin{array}{lll}
@A(I,J) & = & (\text{BASE} + 1) + 1 * (3 * I + J) \\
@A(0,\text{-}1) & = & (\text{BASE} + 1) + 1 * (3 * 0 + (-1)) \\
& = & \text{BASE} \\
@A(0,0) & = & (\text{BASE} + 1) + 1 * (3 * 0 + 0) \\
& = & \text{BASE} + 1 \\
& \bullet & \\
& \bullet & \\
& \bullet & \\
@A(2,1) & = & (\text{BASE} + 1) + 1 * (3 * 2 + 1) \\
& = & \text{BASE} + 8
\end{array}
$$

The same technique can be used for an array having an arbitrary number of subscripts. Assume the array is defined by:

$$\text{DECLARE } A(L_1{:}U_1, L_2{:}U_2, L_3{:}U_3, \ldots, L_K{:}U_K);$$

and:

$$
\begin{array}{lll}
D_1 & = & U_1 - L_1 + 1 \\
D_2 & = & U_2 - L_2 + 1 \\
& \bullet & \\
& \bullet & \\
& \bullet & \\
D_K & = & U_K - L_K + 1
\end{array}
$$

then the address of $A(S_1, S_2, S_3, \ldots, S_K)$ is given by:

$$
\begin{aligned}
@A(S_1, S_2, \ldots, S_K) = \text{BASE} + \text{NWPE} * \\
((S_1 - L_1) * D_K * D_{K-1} * \ldots * D_3 * D_2 \\
+ (S_2 - L_2) * D_K * D_{K-1} * \ldots * D_3 \\
\bullet \ \bullet \ \bullet \\
+ (S_{K-1} - L_{K-1}) * D_K \\
+ (S_K - L_K))
\end{aligned}
$$

When S_K is increased by 1, the address is increased by NWPE; when S_{K-1} is increased by 1, the address is increased by D_K * NWPE; when S_{K-2} is increased by 1, the address is increased by D_K * D_{K-1} * NWPE, and when S_1 is increased by 1 the address is increased by D_K * D_{K-1} *. . . * D_2 * NWPE. This is in agreement with the technique employed by the access function for the two-dimensional array in the example above.

As one can also verify from the formula, a direct computation of the array address requires K differences, K sums, and $1+2+3+ \ldots +(K-1)+1 = 1+((K-1)*K)/2$ products. The same formula can be computed much more efficiently by separating it into variable and constant parts and factoring out the D_i's as follows:

$$@A(S_1,S_2, \ldots ,S_K) = CONST + VAR$$

where:

$$VAR \quad = \quad NWPE * ((\ldots (S_1 * D_2 + S_2) * D_3 + S_3) * D_4 \ldots) * D_K + S_K$$

and:

$$CONST = BASE - NWPE * ((\ldots (L_1 * D_2 + L_2) * D_3 + L_3) * D_4 \ldots) * D_K + L_K$$

The constant part has to be computed only once, so each address computation requires K multiplications and K additions.

An efficient implementation and memory representation for arrays that use this type of access function is described below. The array identifier designates a block of memory that contains the subscript information of the array, also called a *dope vector;* this block is the header of the array. For a K-dimensional array, the header contains $K + 2$ words; the words contain the values $K, D_2, D_3, \ldots, D_K$, NWPE, and CONST. As an example, the representation of the array defined by the declaration statement:

$$DECLARE \ A(0:2, -1:1);$$

is shown in Figure 5.1.

When an element of an array A is to be accessed, the values of the subscripts are placed in a vector S to be passed to the procedure ELEMENT_ADDRESS given below. Procedure ELEMENT_ADDRESS gets as actual parameters the array identifier A and the vector identifier S and evaluates the address of the desired element using the formula given earlier. No checks are made on the validity of the subscripts. Note that the elements of array A are not located at the address of A, since the address of A is the address of the header of the array A.

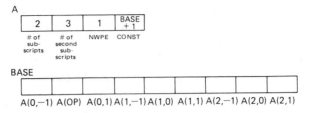

Figure 5.1. The memory representation of array A. The header contains the values of K, D2, NWPE, and CONST. The actual array elements are stored in row order, beginning at address BASE.

The elements are located elsewhere beginning at address BASE, as shown in the illustration. An access procedure for computing the address of an array element is given below.

procedure ELEMENT_ADDRESS(A,S);
declare (I,J,K,A(*),S(*)) INTEGER;
comment A is the header block of the array A.

       S is a block containing the values of the subscripts.
       I is a pointer into S and A:
         S(I) for I≤K is the value of the I'th subscript.
         A(I) for I between 2 and K is UI−LI.
         A(1) is the value of K.
         A(K+1) is the value of NWPE.
         A(K+2) is the value of CONST.
         K is the dimension of the array;
K := A(1);
I := 2;
ELEMENT _ ADDRESS := S(1);
while (I ≤ K) **do**
    begin
        ELEMENT_ADDRESS := A(I) * ELEMENT_ADDRESS + S(I);
        I := I + 1
    end;
comment At this point A(I) is NWPE and A(I + 1) is CONST;
ELEMENT_ADDRESS := A(I) * ELEMENT_ADDRESS + A(I +1)
return;
end ELEMENT_ADDRESS;

We will now trace through the computation of ELEMENT_ADDRESS for the array element A(1,0) for the array illustrated in Figure 5.1. The subscript values 1 and 0 are first placed in vector S so that S(1) = 1 and S(0) = 0 upon entry to ELEMENT_ADDRESS. Just before entering the *while-do* loop the variables K, I, ELEMENT_ADDRESS, S(1) and S(2) have the following values:

K = 2
I = 2
ELEMENT_ADDRESS = 1
S(1) = 1
S(2) = 0

Within the loop the following values change:

ELEMENT_ADDRESS   ← A(2) * ELEMENT_ADDRESS + S(2)
                   = 3 * 1 + 0
                   = 3

I ← 3

Now since I is no longer less than K, the loop is terminated and the final value of ELEMENT_ADDRESS is computed:

ELEMENT_ADDRESS   ← A(3)*ELEMENT_ADDRESS + A(4)
                   = 1 * 3 + BASE + 1
                   = BASE + 4

which is the correct address of the desired element.

Although this representation and access function are efficient, the upper and lower subscript bounds given in the array declaration are not present, and hence it is impossible to check for subscript errors. One way to overcome this difficulty is to store additional subscript information in the array header. The following values are sufficient: $K, L_1, U_1, D_1, L_2, U_2, D_2, . . . , L_K, U_K, D_K$, NWPE, and CONST. When this additional information is available, it is easy to modify ELEMENT_ADDRESS to check for subscript bound errors and invoke an error procedure if necessary.

The array structure used by the SIL implementation of the programming language SNOBOL4 is similar to that described above. The reader is directed to Chapter 6, Section 6.6 for a brief description of the memory representation used.

Exercise 5.1. Modify the procedure ELEMENT_ADDRESS so that it checks subscript bounds, i.e., whether or not the subscripts are within the declared limits. If not, the ELEMENT_ADDRESS procedure should invoke the procedure SUBSCRIPT_ERROR with appropriate diagnostic information. You will have to select a suitable memory representation for your algorithm. Estimate in percent how much longer each subscript computation will take when checking for subscript bounds.

Exercise 5.2. An alternative way of factoring the array access formula is as follows:

$$@A(S_1, S_2, \ldots, S_K) \quad = \quad VAR + CONST$$

where: $\quad VAR \quad = \quad NWPE * (F_1 * S_1 + F_2 * S_2 + \ldots + F_K * S_K)$

$\quad CONST \quad = \quad BASE + NWPE * (F_1 * L_1 + F_2 * L_2 + \ldots + F_K * s_K)$

and: $\quad F_1 \quad = \quad D_K * D_{K-1} * \ldots * D_3 * D_2$

$\quad F_2 \quad = \quad D_K * D_{K-1} \ldots D_3$

$\bullet$

$\bullet$

$\quad F_{K-1} \quad = \quad D_K$

$\quad F_K \quad = \quad 1$

Give a suitable memory representation and access procedure for this formulation. Repeat Exercise 5.1 using this representation, and compare the two representations and access procedures for efficiency.

Although the array representations given above are the most frequently used, it is sometimes convenient to store the elements of each row in a separate block of memory, with row elements stored in ascending order, and to have an independent vector of row pointers to point to these blocks. This storage representation is illustrated below. This representation is particularly useful for large arrays where the elements will be processed in row order and where the entire array will not fit into main memory at one time. This representation is also useful for virtual memory systems where the array elements will not fit in a single page or segment. If the elements are accessed along columns, then a similar representation can be used, only stored by columns rather than by rows. However, if the elements are accessed in random order, then these representations are not particularly beneficial, and one of the representations described earlier should be elected.

declare B(3,5) INTEGER;

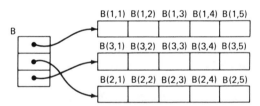

Exercise 5.3. Give suitable *template* and *declare* statements to create an N by M array having the memory representation illustrated above, and give the procedure ELEMENT_ ADDRESS for this representation.

For some applications, such as arrays of characters, where each row is likely to hold a different number of elements, it is convenient to represent the array in one of the two forms shown below. In the first representation, the number of elements of each row is stored along with the row pointer to that row, and, in the second representation, the number of elements of each row is stored as the first element of the block containing the row elements. Arrays of this type are called *ragged arrays*.

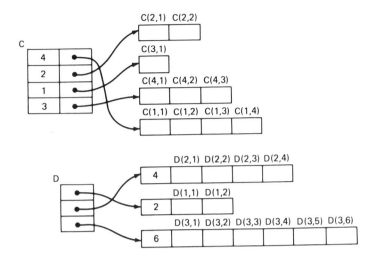

Exercise 5.4. Give suitable *template* and *declare* statements, and define the procedure ELEMENT_ADDRESS for each of the representations in the above illustration. How might ragged arrays be declared in a programming language?

5.3 SYMMETRIC AND TRIANGULAR MATRICES

Symmetric and triangular matrices arise during certain matrix computations and applications and are interesting because, with suitable memory representations and access functions, they require only half as much memory as would be required using conventional two-dimensional array implementations. In this section we describe the memory representations and access functions for these matrices.

A *matrix* is an array having two subscripts. An $N \times N$ *square matrix* is a matrix whose subscripts both vary from 1 to N. A *symmetric matrix* is a square matrix with the property that element (i,j) has the same value as element (j,i). For a symmetric matrix, it is necessary to allocate only $(N + N^2)/2$ memory locations for the array elements instead of N^2. We will assume a memory representation similar to the one described for arrays, where all matrix elements above and including the main diagonal are stored in a contiguous block of memory locations. The following algorithm returns the address of an element of a symmetric matrix A. In this algorithm, block A contains the elements of the matrix and BASE_A is the base address of block A. Only half of the elements of the matrix are stored. The block S is a vector containing the two subscripts that select the element of A.

procedure SYMMETRIC_ADDRESS(BASE_A,N,S);
declare (N,BASE_A,S1,S2,S(2)) INTEGER;
declare A((N + N**2) / 2) INTEGER;
comment BASE_A is the base address of matrix A.
          S is a block containing the values of the subscripts.
          N is the dimension of the matrix;
if (S(2) > S(1))
then begin
          S1 := S(1)−1;
          S2 := S(2)
    end
else begin
          S1 := S(2)−1;
          S2 := S(1)
    end endif;
SYMMETRIC _ ADDRESS := BASE _ A + S2 + N * S1 − (1 + (S1 * (S1 + 1)/2));
return;
end SYMMETRIC_ADDRESS;

Figure 5.2 shows a symmetric matrix M and the computation of the address of M(3,4).

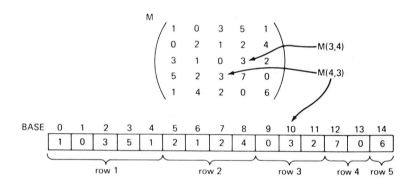

N = 5
S1 = 3−1 = 2
S2 = 4
address = BASE + S2 + N * S1 − (1+(S1*(S1+1)/2))
        = BASE + 4 + 5 * 2 − (1+(2* 3   /2))
        = BASE + 4 + 10 − (1+3)
        = BASE + 10

Figure 5.2. A symmetric matrix M and its memory representation. The computation for the address of M(3,4) is illustrated.

An *upper-triangular matrix* is a square matrix whose elements below the main diagonal all have value 0. Using a memory representation similar to the one described for symmetric matrices, only $(N + N^2)/2 + 1$ memory locations have to be allocated, where $(N + N^2)/2$ memory locations are used for the non-zero element values, and one memory location is used for the constant value 0. The following is an access function for an upper triangular matrix:

```
procedure UP_TRIANGULAR_ADDRESS(BASE_A,N,S)
declare (N,BASE_A,S(2) ) INTEGER;
comment BASE_A is the base address of matrix A.
         S is a block containing the values of the subscripts.
         N is the dimensionality of the matrix;
if (S(2) ≤ S(1) )
then UP_TRIANGULAR_ADDRESS := BASE_A + (N * (N + 1) ) / 2
else  UP_TRIANGULAR_ADDRESS := SYMMETRIC_ADDRESS(BASE_A,N,S)
    endif;
return;
end UP_TRIANGULAR_ADDRESS;
```

An example upper triangular matrix and sample address computation are shown in Figure 5.3.

Exercise 5.5. A *tridiagonal matrix* is a square matrix whose elements are all 0 except along the main diagonal and the diagonals immediately above and below the main diagonal. Evidently, a tridiagonal matrix requires $N + 2 * (N-1) + 1$ memory locations (N elements for the main diagonal; $N-1$ elements for each other diagonal, and one element for the constant value 0.) Find a suitable memory representation and access function for a tridiagonal matrix. An example tridiagonal matrix is shown below.

$$\begin{pmatrix} 7 & 0 & 0 & 0 & 0 & 0 \\ 4 & 7 & 9 & 0 & 0 & 0 \\ 0 & 2 & 4 & 6 & 0 & 0 \\ 0 & 0 & 8 & 8 & 3 & 0 \\ 0 & 0 & 0 & 1 & 2 & 1 \\ 0 & 0 & 0 & 0 & 5 & 7 \end{pmatrix}$$

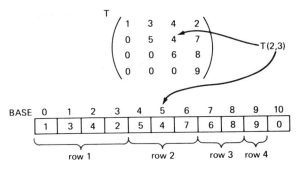

for T(4,2):
  N = 4
  S(1) = 4
  S(2) = 2
address = BASE + N * (N+1)/2
        = BASE + 10

for I(2,3):
  N = 4
  S(1) = 2
  S(2) = 3
address = SYMMETRIC _ ADDRESS (BASE, N, 5)
        = BASE + 5

Figure 5.3 A triangular matrix T and its memory representation. Computations for T(4,2) and T(2,3) are shown.

5.4 EXTENDIBLE ARRAYS

The notion of finding a single access function that can be used for all arrays having a given number of subscripts has been studied by several researchers. When the elements of an array are organized using such an access function, it is not necessary to store subscript information in addition to the number of subscripts, and the array is said to be *extendible*. If an array is implemented as an extendible array, however, enough memory must be allocated to hold all elements that might be accessed, and this generally requires considerably more memory than is actually used. For this reason extendible arrays have limited practical importance. In this section, we will look at several access functions for extendible arrays and discuss the utilization of memory for these implementations.

One-dimensional arrays using the access function described earlier are trivially extendible, since an element's address is given by BASE+NWPE*S, where S is the subscript, and this formula does not depend on the number of elements in the array. Two-dimensional arrays when stored by row are *extendible by row;* that is, additional rows can be added using the same access function. Similarly, two-dimensional arrays when stored by column are *extendible by column*. For an array declared DCL A(1:4, 1:6), the access function for storage by rows is:

$$address1(A(S1,S2)) = (S1 - 1) * 6 + S2$$

assuming that the base address of the array is 1 and each element requires one word of storage. The same access function can be used for any array declared (1:K,1:6), where K is arbitrary. However, $address1(A(1,7))$ is the same as $address1(A(2,1))$; $address1(A(2,7))$ is the same as $address1(A(3,1))$, and so forth. Hence the array is not extendible by columns. By the same argument, an array stored by columns is not extendible by rows.

In order to realize an extendible array in two dimensions, the access function must map all pairs of subscripts in a 1 to 1 fashion into the integers. Two realizations for extendible arrays are described below and illustrated in Figures 5.4 and 5.5; the first is called storage by *diagonal shells,* and the second is called storage by *square shells*. The access functions for diagonal and square shell realizations (in that order) are:

$$address2(A(S1,S2)) = S2 + (S1 + S2 - 1) * (S1 + S2 - 2) / 2$$
$$address3(A(S1,S2)) = (M - 1) * (M - 1) + M + S2 - S1$$
$$where \ M = max(S1, S2)$$

One can easily verify that these two access functions properly map subscript pairs into addresses as shown in Figures 5.4 and 5.5.

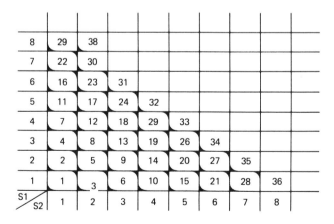

Figure 5.4. The order in memory of the elements of a two-dimensional, extendible array using access formula address2, diagonal shells.

S2 \ S1	1	2	3	4	5	6	7	8	
⋮	⋮	⋮						⋮	⋰
8	50	•••						57	
7	37	•••					43		•••
6	26	27	28	29	30	31			
5	17	18	19	20	21	32			
4	10	11	12	13	22	33			
3	5	6	7	14	23	34			
2	2	3	8	15	24	35			
1	1	4	9	16	25	36	49	64	•••
S1 / S2	1	2	3	4	5	6	7	8	•••

Figure 5.5. The order in memory of the elements of a two-dimensional, extendible array using access formula address3, square shells.

Exercise 5.6. Give the access function for a three-dimensional, extendible array that maps subscripts into addresses as shown below:

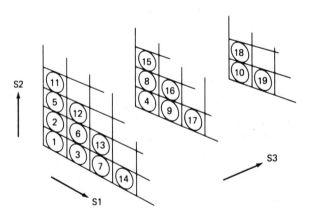

Exercise 5.7. Give the access function for a three-dimensional, extendible array that maps subscripts into addresses as shown below:

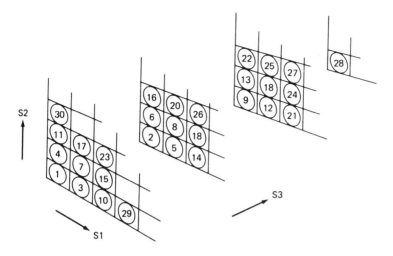

Exercise 5.8. Utilize the formula address3 to define the access function for an extendible, triangular matrix.

For a two-dimensional square array, the access function address3 is optimal in that no memory locations are unassigned by the mapping function; that is, for a N by N array, memory locations 1 thru N**2 are assigned. For the 4-by-6-dimensional array defined by the statement DECLARE A(1:4, 1:6), however, there are 12 unassigned memory locations (17-21, 26-32). For a triangular array, address2 leaves no unassigned memory locations, whereas for the 4 by 6 array, address2 leaves 18 unassigned memory locations (11, 16, 17, 22-24, 28-32, 35-41). In general, for an N by K array, the access function address2 leaves K*(K−N) unassigned memory locations when K⩾N and (N−1)*(N−1−K) when N>K. In contrast, address3 leaves (N−1)*(N−2)/2 + (K)*(K−1)/2 unassigned memory locations when K⩾N or (N)*(N−1)/2 + (K−1)*(K−2)/2 when N>K.

Exercise 5.9. Give an access function that leaves no unassigned memory locations for a two-dimensional array that always has twice as many rows as it does columns.

Exercise 5.10. Verify that the formulas for the number of unassigned memory locations using address2 and address3 given above are correct.

5.5 SPARSE MATRICES

There are several applications areas where it becomes necessary to manipulate matrices of very large order. When there is a high percentage of matrix elements whose value is 0 (or some other constant), the matrix is called a *sparse matrix;* the analysis of large electrical power systems, the analysis of materials for chemical mixtures, and the analysis of large structural systems are three applications areas that use sparse matrices. There are several special storage representations and associated mapping functions for sparse matrices so that it is not necessary to store elements whose value is 0 (or some other constant), and, in this section, we will discuss these implementation techniques.

Our discussion will focus on techniques that store the sparse element values by rows. By reversing the roles of rows and columns in the following algorithms, the same techniques can be employed for storage by columns. For applications that require access to elements in both row and column order, careful consideration should be given to those techniques that enable equally fast access to both row and column elements.

5.5.1 Row and column indexing

One technique for storing the elements of a sparse matrix consists of maintaining a single, one-dimensional array V for the matrix elements that are non-zero, and maintaining two additional one-dimensional arrays IROW and ICOL that give the *row* and *column indices* in ascending order for the elements in V. There is one entry in IROW and one entry in ICOL for each entry in V. The storage

$$M \begin{pmatrix} 0.0 & 0.0 & 0.0 & 0.0 & 4.0 \\ 2.0 & 3.0 & 0.0 & 0.0 & 0.0 \\ 0.0 & 0.0 & 0.0 & 5.0 & 0.0 \\ 7.0 & 0.0 & 0.0 & 0.0 & 8.0 \\ 0.0 & 6.0 & 0.0 & 0.0 & 0.0 \end{pmatrix}$$

	I ROW	I COL	V	
1	1	5	4.0	
2	2	1	2.0	
3	2	2	3.0	
4	3	4	5.0	
5	4	1	7.0	
6	4	5	8.0	
7	5	2	6.0	
8	0	0	0.0	
9	0	0	0.0	unused
⋮	⋮	⋮	⋮	
K	0	0	0.0	

Figure 5.6. A sparse matrix M and its memory representation using column and row indexing.

representation for a 5 by 5 matrix is shown in Figure 5.6. The arrays IROW and ICOL can generally be halfword arrays to conserve memory, in which case each non-zero matrix element requires two words of storage, one for the element value, and one for the column and row indices.

An access function for an element of a sparse matrix stored in this manner is given below.

```
procedure SPARSE_ELEMENT_VALUE(S1,S2,V,IROW,ICOL,K);
declare (I,K,S1,S2,IROW(K),ICOL(K)) INTEGER;
declare (V(K)) REAL;
comment S1 and S2 are the subscripts of the desired element.
        V is the array containing the values of the non-zero elements of the matrix.
        IROW is an array containing the row indices for the elements in V.
        ICOL is an array containing the column indices for the elements in V.
        K is the dimension of V, IROW, and ICOL;
I := 1;
while (I ≤ K and IROW(I) ≠ 0) do
    begin
        case
        (IROW(I) < S1):
            begin
                comment This is not the desired element.
                        Keep looking;
                I := I + 1
            end;
        (IROW(I) > S1):
            begin
                comment The element is not present.
                        Its value must be 0;
                SPARSE_ELEMENT_VALUE := 0;
                return
            end;
        (ICOL(I) < S2):
            begin
                comment IROW(I) must equal S1 but ICOL(I) differs from S2. This is
                        not the desired element;
                I := I + 1
            end;
        (ICOL(I) > S2):
            begin
                comment The element is not present.
                        Its value must be 0;
                SPARSE_ELEMENT_VALUE := 0;
                return
            end;
```

```
        (ICOL(I) = S2):
            begin
               comment IROW := S1 and ICOL := S2.
                        This is the desired element;
               SPARSE_ELEMENT_VALUE := V(I);
               return
            end;
        end case
    end
end SPARSE_ELEMENT_VALUE;
```

Exercise 5.11. Trace the computation performed by SPARSE_ELEMENT_VALUE for the elements (4,5) and (3,3) given in the previous figure.

On the average, an element will be in the middle of the array, so this procedure requires M*N*P/2 passes through the *while-do* loop, where the sparse matrix has dimensions M and N, and P is the percentage of non-zero elements in the matrix. This is somewhat inefficient.

Exercise 5.12. Rewrite the procedure SPARSE_ELEMENT_VALUE using the binary search technique described in Section 2.2.2. Compare the efficiency of your procedure with the one given above.

Exercise 5.13. Write procedures for inserting a new element into a sparse matrix and for removing an element from a sparse matrix. What can you say about the row and column index technique for a system that requires frequent insertions and deletions of matrix elements?

When sparse matrices are used in vector or matrix operations, it is generally not necessary to use an access function to obtain the values of the individual matrix elements. For example, consider the product of a vector with a sparse matrix. Let **C** and **D** be column vectors of length N, and let V be an N by N sparse matrix. The computation:

$$C = V\ D$$

$$\text{defined by} \quad C(I) = \sum_{J=1}^{N} V(I,J) * D(J)$$

can be easily and efficiently carried out by the following algorithm which processes the matrix elements sequentially by rows:

```
procedure VECTOR_PRODUCT(C,V,IROW, ICOL,K,D,N);
declare (I,J,K,L,N,IR,IROW(K), ICOL(K)) INTEGER;
declare (C(N), D(N), C(K), SUM) REAL;
comment C and D are column vectors of dimension N.
        V is a sparse matrix of dimension N by N.
        IROW is a row index array for the values of V.
        ICOL is a column index array for the values of V.
        K is the dimension of V, IROW, and ICOL.
        C(I) = SUMMATION(V(I,J)*D(J));
comment Initialize all elements of the result vector C to 0;
L := 1;
while (L≤K) do
    begin
        C(L) := 0.0;
        L := L + 1
    end;
comment Perform the vector product;
comment SUM contains the accumulated product for each element of C.
        L is the element number in IROW, ICOL, and V.
        IR is the row number of the current row being processed.
        (I,J) are the subscripts of the current matrix element being processed;
SUM := 0.0;
L := 1;
I := IROW(L);
J := ICOL(L);
IR := I;
while (I > 0 and I ≤ K) do
    begin
        comment Continue the computation for all elements in the same row;
        while (I = IR) do
            begin
                comment Memory location V(L) contains the value of V(I,J);
                SUM := SUM + V(L) * D(J);
                L := L + 1;
                I := IROW(L);
                J := ICOL(L)
            end;
        C(IR) := SUM;
        SUM := 0.0;
        IR := I
    end;
end VECTOR_PRODUCT;
```

This algorithm increments K each time through the inner loop and terminates either when the row number is zero or when all matrix elements have been processed. Hence the algorithm requires the same number of iterations as there are non-zero matrix elements and is therefore optimal.

To see how the algorithm works, we will trace through part of the computation of V * **D** for the matrix V shown in Figure 5.6 and the vector **D** := (0.0,1.0,0.0,0.0,2.0). After the procedure is initially entered, the value of vector **C** is initialized to (0.0,0.0,0.0,0.0,0.0). The initial values of the program variables, just before the outer *while-do* loop is entered are given below:

$$L = 1$$
$$I = IROW(L) = 1$$
$$J = ICOL(L) = 5$$
$$IR = I = 1$$
$$SUM = 0.0$$
$$V = 8 \text{ (Assumed since there are seven non-zero matrix entries)}$$

The inner *while-do* loop is entered and the following values are modified:

$$SUM \leftarrow SUM + V(1) * D (5) = 0.0 + 4.0 * 2.0 = 8.0$$
$$L \leftarrow 2$$
$$I \leftarrow IROW(L) = 2$$
$$J \leftarrow ICOL(L) = 1$$

The inner loop test fails, since IR differs from I. The following values are modified within the outer loop:

$$C(IR) \leftarrow C(1) = SUM = 8.0$$
$$SUM \leftarrow 0.0$$
$$IR \leftarrow I = 2$$

Now the inner loop is reentered and the following values modified:

$$SUM \leftarrow SUM + V(2) * D(1) = 0.0 + 2.0 * 0.0 = 0.0$$
$$L \leftarrow 3$$
$$I \leftarrow IROW(3) = 2$$
$$J \leftarrow ICOL(3) = 2$$

at which time the inner loop is again reentered (since IR still equals I). The values are now modified as follows:

$$SUM \leftarrow SUM + V(3) * D(2) = 0.0 + 3.0 * 1.0 = 3.0$$
$$L \leftarrow 4$$
$$I \leftarrow IROW(4) = 3$$
$$J \leftarrow ICOL(4) = 4$$

Now I differs from IR, so the inner loop is exited, and the following values modified in the outer loop:

$$C(IR) \leftarrow C(2) = 3.0$$
$$SUM \leftarrow 0.0$$
$$IR \leftarrow 3$$

The inner loop is once again reentered and the process continues. When the algorithm finally terminates, vector C has value (8.0,3.0,0.0,16.0,6.0), which is the desired result.

Exercise 5.14. Finish tracing through the algorithm.
Exercise 5.15. a) Why was it necessary to initialize the result vector C to 0 at the beginning of the algorithm? b) What restrictions can be placed on the structure so that the test in the outer *while-do* loop can be simplified to (I>0), which is a faster test to perform?
Exercise 5.16. Write a procedure MATRIX_PRODUCT that places the matrix product of V with W in U. Assume U, V, and W are sparse matrices with row and column index arrays IROWU, ICOLU, IROWV, ICOLV, IROWW, and ICOLW. The matrix product of two matrices is defined by:

$$U(I,K) = \sum_{J=1}^{N} V(I,J) * W(J,K).$$

Since V is processed in row order and W is processed in column order, use an efficient sorting algorithm to sort W by column before actually performing the calculations for finding the product. Resort W by rows when finished.

A slight variation in the implementation of a sparse matrix consists of maintaining the same element array and colum index array as before but keeping an indirect row index array instead of the row index array used above. The subscript of an element in the indirect row index array is the same as the row number in the sparse matrix, and the value of the indirect row index is the subscript in the column index array of the first element in that row. A zero value in the indirect row index indicates that the corresponding row has no entries in the sparse matrix. The sparse matrix shown earlier and the corresponding memory representation are shown in Figure 5.7. This technique uses less memory than the previous technique, provided that the sparse matrices have, on the average, more than one element per row. It has furthermore the advantage that rows of the matrix are directly accessible; however, elements can no longer be sorted by columns for efficient column access. This is an important consideration if frequent column operations are required.

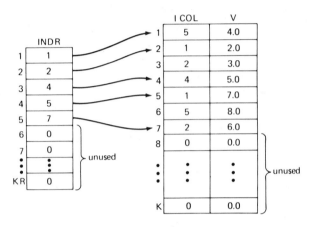

M

$$\begin{pmatrix} 0.0 & 0.0 & 0.0 & 0.0 & 4.0 \\ 2.0 & 3.0 & 0.0 & 0.0 & 0.0 \\ 0.0 & 0.0 & 0.0 & 5.0 & 0.0 \\ 7.0 & 0.0 & 0.0 & 0.0 & 8.0 \\ 0.0 & 6.0 & 0.0 & 0.0 & 0.0 \end{pmatrix}$$

Figure 5.7. A sparse matrix M and its memory representation using indirect row indexing and column indexing.

Exercise 5.17. Write the procedures SPARSE_ELEMENT_VALUE, VECTOR_PRODUCT, and MATRIX_PRODUCT for sparse matrices that use the above memory representation. Compare the efficiency of the MATRIX_PRODUCT procedures for the two implementation techniques discussed so far.

Another variation of the above technique eliminates the row indices entirely and encodes the same information in the column index array. The first column index entry always corresponds to row 1. The magnitude of the column index is the column number of the entry. A magnitude of zero indicates that there are no elements in the row; a negative value indicates that the element is the last element in the current row. The memory representation for the same sparse matrix described earlier is shown in Figure 5.8. Although this representation uses less memory than that of the previous representation, rows are no longer directly accessible.

Exercise 5.18. Repeat exercises 5.13 and 5.17 for the memory representation shown in Figure 5.8.

M

$$\begin{pmatrix} 0.0 & 0.0 & 0.0 & 0.0 & 4.0 \\ 2.0 & 3.0 & 0.0 & 0.0 & 0.0 \\ 0.0 & 0.0 & 0.0 & 5.0 & 0.0 \\ 7.0 & 0.0 & 0.0 & 0.0 & 8.0 \\ 0.0 & 6.0 & 0.0 & 0.0 & 0.0 \end{pmatrix}$$

	I COL	V
1	-5	4.0
2	+1	2.0
3	-2	3.0
4	-4	5.0
5	+1	7.0
6	-5	8.0
7	-2	6.0
8	-0	0.0
	. . .	
K		

Figure 5.8. A sparse matrix M and its memory representation, where row number is encoded in the column index vector.

If we assume halfword row and column indices for the three methods discussed so far and use fullwords for the element values, the number of required memory locations for each technique is given below:

Row index and column index:	$2 * N * M * P$
Indirect row index and column index:	$(3/2) * N * M * P + N/2$
Column index with a sign specifying a new row:	$(3/2) * N * M * P$

In these formulas, N is the number of rows, M is the number of columns, and P is the percent of non-zero entries in the matrix. For a 1000 by 1000 sparse matrix having 5% non-zero elements, the amount of memory required is 100000, 75500, and 75000 words, respectively, for the three techniques.

5.5.2 Bit maps

One technique that may be effective for computers that have efficient bit manipulation hardware consists of maintaining an entire binary matrix or *bit map* that indicates whether or not the corresponding matrix element has value zero or not. The actual matrix values are stored in a second, one-dimensional array, say V, just as they were before. If the matrix is stored by rows, then the first non-zero row element in the bit map corresponds to the first element in V, the second non-zero element in the bit map corresponds to the second element in V, and so forth. Hence the presence or absence of an element is determined by a single bit in the bit map, and the address of a non-zero array element is determined by counting '1' bits in the bit map. Figure 5.9 shows the same array illustrated earlier using this memory representation.

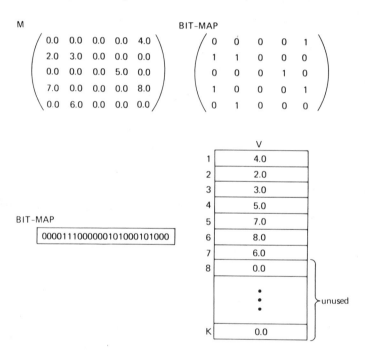

Figure 5.9. A sparse matrix M and its memory representation using a bit map. The bit map is stored in row order.

For an N by M matrix having P percent non-zero elements, N*M*P words are required for the array V, and N*M/NBPW words for the bit map, where NBPW is the number of bits per word. The total is (P+1/NBPW)*N*M words of memory. In case 1/NBPW is greater than P/2 (i.e., P < 2/NBPW) the previous technique requires less memory. For a computer that has 32-bit words, the trade-off comes when P is less than 2/32; that is, when two out of every 32 words are non-zero.

Exercise 5.19. Repeat Exercises 5.13 and 5.17 for this data structure.

Exercise 5.20. Compare the execution speed using this representation with the speeds for the corresponding representations discussed earlier.

The bit map technique has a distinct advantage over the row and column index technique for certain types of row operations. If the elements of two matrices are to be multiplied together, the corresponding bits in the bit maps can be ANDed and the multiplication performed only if the result is '1'B. This is substantially faster than testing row and column index values to determine if both matrices have non-zero elements. On the other hand, the bit map technique has extremely poor access to the column elements of the array and therefore may lead to inefficient execution for certain applications such as matrix product.

5.5.3 Address maps

The address map technique is similar to the bit map technique, except that the address map entries are the addresses of the corresponding elements in V rather than a flag indicating their presence or absence. See Figure 5.10. The address

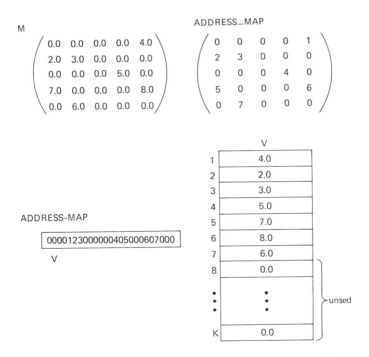

Figure 5.10. A sparse matrix M and its memory representation using an address map. The address map is stored in row order.

map technique requires K times as much memory as the bit map technique, where K is the number of bits required to reference one element of V. For example, for a 1000 by 1000 sparse matrix with 5% non-zero entries, K would have to be 16 (V would require .05*1000*1000=50000 entries). Hence the address map would require 500,000 32-bit words, whereas V would only require 50,000 words! Evidently the address map technique would only be practical for extremely sparse matrices. Although the memory map requires substantially more memory, the access time to find any desired element is now constant. Furthermore, if the entries in the address map are stored by rows, then the addresses of column entries are always a fixed displacement apart, and it is possible to index down columns as fast as indexing down rows. The result is that routines such as MATRIX_PRODUCT can be very efficient.

Exercise 5.21. Write an efficient procedure for performing matrix product using the address map technique.

Exercise 5.22. Repeat Exercise 5.13 for this representation.

5.5.4 Linked memory representation

Figure 5.11 shows a linked memory representation that can be used for sparse matrices. In comparison with other techniques, linked allocation requires considerably more memory and has slower access to random matrix elements. However, linked allocation has the very distinct advantage over other methods of having rapid insertion and deletion of matrix entries. The reader is directed to Knuth (1973) for a more comprehensive discussion of linked allocation techniques for sparse matrices.

Exercise 5.23. Repeat Exercises 5.13 and 5.17 for the linked representation shown in Figure 5.11.

5.5.5 Hash table techniques

A final technique for storing the elements of a sparse matrix is the use of a hash table, where the row and column indices of the non-zero matrix elements are used to form the key into the table. (See the following section for a description of hash tables.) Such a scheme should only be considered when frequent random accesses are made to the individual elements of the matrices. The other techniques discussed are more efficient when matrix rows (or columns) are sequentially processed (as for the majority of matrix applications).

5.6 TABLES

There are several techniques for storing the pairs of a table, including sequential storage, hashed storage, and linked storage, most frequently using tree

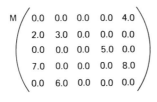

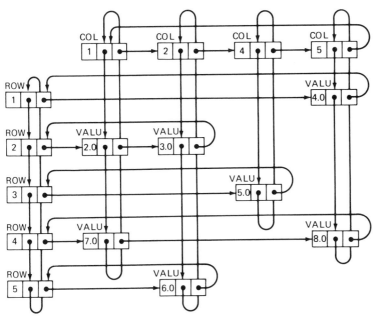

Figure 5.11. A sparse matrix M and its memory representation using a linked structure.

structures. The remainder of this chapter will discuss sequential and hashed storage. Tree-structured tables were discussed in Chapter 4.

5.6.1 Sequential representations

The simplest technique for storing the pairs of a table consists of allocating a single block of memory for the attribute-value pairs (or pointers to the attributes and/or values) and storing the pairs sequentially in the block, first attribute and then value. A symbol table that appears in an assembler is shown below. In the symbol table, the attributes are the mnemonics that the assembler uses for instructions, and the values are the numeric op codes that appear in the assembled instructions. When table entries are stored sequentially, access to the value of a given attribute requires a search for that attribute in the table. When a

T	ATTRIBUTE	VALUE
	A	5A
	AH	4A
	AL	5E
	ALR	1E
	AR	1A
	BAL	45
	BALR	05
	BAS	4D
	BASR	0D
	BC	47
	BCR	07
	BCT	46
	BCTR	06
	BXH	86
	⋮	
	ZAP	F8

stored attribute matches the given attribute, the value is the value associated with the stored attribute. An access function for table values in a sequentially stored table is given below:

```
procedure TABLE_VALUE(ARGUMENT);
declare (K, ATTRIBUTE(K), VALUE(K)) INTEGER global;
declare (I,ARGUMENT) INTEGER;
I := 1;
while (I ≤ K) do
        if (ATTRIBUTE(I) = ARGUMENT)
        then begin
                TABLE_VALUE = VALUE(I);
                return
                end
        else I := I + 1 endif;
TABLE_VALUE := null;
return;
end TABLE_VALUE;
```

Evidently, unless the pairs of a table are stored in the order in which they are most frequently accessed, then access to a table entry will require searching, on the average, half way through the table. For a table having 512 entries that is searched 1000 times, this requires approximately 250000 attribute comparisons!

When the attributes of a table are placed in numeric or alphabetic order as they are in the above illustration, the search time can be substantially reduced by using a binary search rather than a linear search on the table attributes. For a table having K pairs, attribute $\lfloor K/2 \rfloor$ is first compared against the given key. If the table attribute is larger than the given key, attribute $\lfloor K/4 \rfloor$ is next tried; otherwise attribute $\lfloor 3K/4 \rfloor$ is tried. Each comparison divides the remainder of the table in half, so that the entire search requires, in the worst case, $\lceil \log_2(K) \rceil + 1$ comparisons. For a table having 512 entries that is searched 1000 times, approximately 9000 comparisons are made or about $1/18$th the number of a linear search! (See pages 54-55 for the BINARY _ SEARCH algorithm.)

Exercise 5.24. Rewrite procedure TABLE _ VALUE so that it does a binary search on the table attributes.

5.6.2 HASH TABLES

The binary search technique can be used where the elements of a table can be stored sequentially in sorted order. The tree structure techniques described in Chapter 4 are often preferred. The principle alternative to the linear search technique for non-sorted tables is to use an address function that maps the table attributes into 'random' addresses and special techniques to locate the desired pair when given this address. The memory access functions for tables of this type are *hashing functions* or *scatter storage functions* or *randomizing functions* or *key to address transformations,* and the technique in general is called *hashing.*

The idea behind hashing is this: The attribute of a pair to be stored or located is used as a parameter for a hash function which is much like the address computation function used for an array; however, unlike array subscripts, which map directly into sequences of integers, attributes to tables are frequently large and often character strings that do not map into addresses in any methodical way. A hash function takes an attribute as a parameter and, based on the attribute, computes a 'random' number between 0 and $N-1$, where N depends on the size of the particular hash table. This number is not truly random, and, for any given attribute, the number computed by a given hash function is always the same. As an example, suppose the attributes are character strings, and the table can hold 128 pairs. One hash function would be to treat the characters of the string as integers, add them together, and return the low order seven bits of the sum. The resulting value is between 0 and 127, and it certainly appears to be a random value; furthermore, using this hash function, the same value will always be returned for a given string.

It should be noted that a hash function may compute the same value for two different attributes. For example, if the characters are encoded numerically in increasing alphabetical order, then using the above hash function, the hashed values of 'AB' and 'BA' would be the same; this is different from array access functions which compute different values for different sets of subscripts. Special techniques, to be discussed shortly, are used to resolve the conflict that occurs when two attributes hash to the same value.

Once a hash value is computed, it is used in one of several different ways, depending on the organization of the pairs in the hash table. Three different organizations are shown in Figure 5.12. For direct organization, Figure 5.12a, the pairs are all stored in a single block of memory, and the value computed by the hash function is used as the address of a pair in this block. This is the address that the attribute 'hashes to'. If the attribute stored at the hashed address is the same as the given attribute, then the proper pair has been located. If the stored attribute is **null**, then no pair having the given attribute has yet been stored in the table. However, if the stored attribute differs from the given attribute, a *collison* has resulted, and the special techniques to be described must be used to resolve the conflict. In the earlier example, since 'AB' and 'BA' gave the same hashed value, a collision would result in a table using the given hash function. Attributes that hash to the same address are *synonyms* relative to that hash function.

A second technique used to organize the elements of a table is *bucket organization*. See Figure 5.12b. The hash function returns the address of a *hash bucket,* which is a block of attribute-value pairs whose attributes are all synonyms relative to that hash function. After hashing to a bucket, the attributes in the bucket are sequentially searched. Special techniques are used for handling *bucket overflow,* the situation that results when all locations in a bucket are used up.

The third technique to organize the pairs in a table is *list organization.* The hash function returns the address of a linked list (also frequently called a bucket) of attribute-value pairs. (When the lists are sequential, this is equivalent to bucket organization.) In list organization, there are no collisions or overflow, but the elements of the list must be searched by following the list pointers, operations, which are generally fairly slow. (However, see exercise 5.30.)

Two distinctly different problems must be considered: 1) finding good hashing functions that distribute the addresses randomly into the table or set of hash buckets; and 2) detecting and recovering from collisions or bucket overflow. The following sections will deal with these problems independently.

5.6.3 Hashing functions

The following functions have been used as hashing functions for mapping attributes into addresses ranging from 0 to $N-1$:

$$
\begin{aligned}
\text{division:} \quad & h^1(K) = \text{MOD}(K,N); \\
\text{multiplication:} \quad & h^2(K) = \text{EXTRACT}(P,Q,K * L); \\
\text{random:} \quad & h^3(K) = \text{IRAND}(N,K); \\
\text{folding:} \quad & h^4(K) = \text{MOD}(\text{CHARACTER\_SUM}(K), N); \\
& h^5(K) = \text{EXTRACT}(P,Q,\text{CHARACTER\_PROD}(K));
\end{aligned}
$$

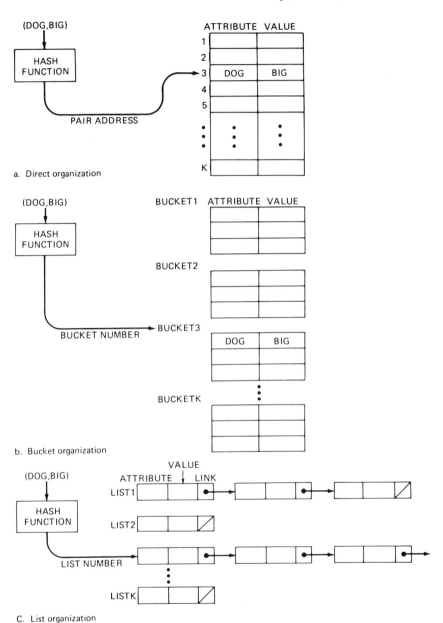

Figure 5.12. Three hash table organizations.

where

MOD(K,N)	is the remainder after dividing K by N.
EXTRACT(P,Q,R)	treats R as a bit string and extracts P bits from R, starting at bit position Q, and pads with leading '0' bits. N, the table size, must be a power of 2, where P=2**N. Q is generally selected so that the middle P bits are extracted from R.
IRAND(N, K)	returns a pseudo random number on the interval from 0 to N−1.
CHARACTER_SUM(K)	K refers to a character string. The words of string K are treated as integers and summed. The sum is returned.
CHARACTER_PROD(K)	K refers to a character string. The words of the string are treated as integers and multiplied together. The product is returned.

The choice of a hashing function should be influenced by: the speed of execution; any knowledge of the distribution of attributes in the table; the hardware on which the function is to be executed; the lengths of the keys; and the length of the table. For example, when a hash table used as a directory into a large data base file is consulted (relatively) infrequently, a different hash function is likely to be selected than when a hash table is used as a symbol table in an assembler: The symbol table is consulted very frequently, the keys are all short, and their distribution is known in advance. If N is a power of two, then the division algorithm can easily be implemented by a shifting operation, which can be very fast; however, division is often used after one of the other hashing procedures. For example, if the keys are strings and the division algorithm is used directly, then all strings having the same leading characters will hash to the same address. The folding function is most suitable for long keys, whereas a random number function is better suited for keys of uniform length. The division function performs relatively well under many conditions and is therefore frequently used.

5.6.4 Hash table organizations

Direct organization

When hashing directly to the address of a pair, collisions are detected by comparing the given attribute against the attribute at the computed address. Initially all table attributes are set to *null,* a special symbol that differs from all valid attributes. When inserting an attribute-value pair in a table, if the given attribute hashes to an address that contains the *null* attribute, the attribute and value are stored at that address in the table. If the computed address contains the given attribute, either an error condition results or the new value replaces the previous value in the table, depending on the way the table is to be used. When retrieving a value from a table, if the given attribute hashes to an address that has the same attribute, the value of the attribute is returned; if the attribute hashes to a location containing the *null* attribute, *null* is returned. If during either storage or retrieval the attribute at the hashed address differs from the given attribute, the result is a collision.

There are several techniques for obtaining an alternative address when a collison results, including:

1. using a procedure that returns the address of the first free location following the one hashed to, wrapping around to the beginning of the table if necessary;
2. using a procedure that searches the table in a non-sequential order and returns the address of the first free location;
3. rehashing—using alternate hash functions to compute alternate addresses until no collision results;
4. placing all pairs that collide into a single, overflow area.

If the size of the table is large in comparison with the number of table entries, then few collisions will result, and any of the above techniques could be used. The fourth technique would be the slowest in recovering from collision, since all pairs stored as the result of a collision would be searched sequentially. As the table becomes fuller, the number of collisions increases. When using technique 1, pairs that collide are placed in adjacent memory locations, and the ultimate result is the formation of clusters where collisions result even for attribues that are not synonyms; this causes additional sequential searching and a resulting inefficiency. Techniques 2 and 3 overcome this difficulty. Rehashing reduces clustering at the expense of additional execution time for computing alternate addresses. A combination of these techniques seems to be a good compromise.

As a specific example, we will implement a hash table that is divided into two parts, a primary area and an overflow area. The attributes and values are character strings having variable length as described in Chapter 3. The primary table area holds 512 pairs of pointers to strings, and the overflow area holds 20 pairs of pointers. See Figure 5.13. The hash algorithm for the primary table area uses folding, where the characters of the string (each character is an 8-bit quantity) are treated as integers and added. If a collision results, then the attribute is placed in an overflow area which is linearly organized. The hash function for entering values in the table is given below.

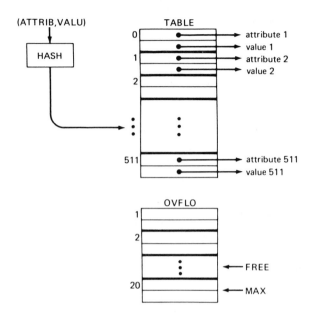

Figure 5.13. The memory representation of the table used by HASHIN.

procedure HASHIN(ATTRIB, VALU);
template   1 STRING,
                  2 MAXLEN   INTEGER,
                  2 CURLEN   INTEGER,
                  2 DATA(● MAXLEN)   CHARACTER;
template   1 PAIR,
                  2 ATTRIBUTE   POINTER to STRING,
                  2 VALUE   POINTER to STRING;
declare (HASHIN,ATTRIB,VALU) POINTER to STRING;
declare TABLE (512)   PAIR   **global**;
declare OVFLO (20)   PAIR   **global**;
declare (HASH,ADDRESS)   8 BIT INTEGER;
declare (MAX, FREE)   INTEGER **global**;
comment MAX is set to 20, the size of the overflow area OVFLO.
          FREE is the number of the next pair in OVFLO to be used.
          FREE is initially set to 1.
          EQUAL is a predicate for testing string equality.
          See Chapter 3;
ADDRESS := HASH(ATTRIB);
if (EQUAL(TABLE(ADDRESS).ATTRIBUTE,ATTRIB) **or** TABLE(ADDRESS).AT-
    TRIBUTE = **null**)
then begin

```
        comment No collision. Insert pair in table;
        HASHIN := TABLE(ADDRESS).VALUE;
        TABLE(ADDRESS).ATTRIBUTE := ATTRIB;
        TABLE(ADDRESS).VALUE := VALU;
        return
    end
else begin
        comment Collision in primary area. Search for attribute in overflow area;
        ADDR := 1;
        while (ADDR < FREE) do
            if (OVFLO(ADDR).ATRRIBUTE = ATTRIB)
            then begin
                    comment The pair is located. Return old value and insert new value;
                    HASHIN := OVFLO(ADDR).VALUE;
                    OVFLO(ADDR).VALUE := VALU;
                    return
                end
            else ADDR := ADDR + 1 endif;
        if (ADDR > MAX)
        then begin
                comment The overflow area is full. Abort;
                call ABORT ('TABLE OVERFLOW IN HASHIN')
            end
        else begin
                comment Insert the new pair in the table;
                HASHIN := OVFLO(ADDR).VALUE;
                OVFLO(ADDR).VALUE := VALU;
                OVFLO(ADDR).ATTRIBUTE := ATTRIB;
                FREE := FREE + 1
                return
            end endif
    end endif;
end HASHIN;

procedure HASH(STR);
template    1 STRING,
                2 MAXLEN                 INTEGER,
                2 CURLEN                 INTEGER,
                2 DATA (• MAXLEN)        8 BIT INTEGER;
declare STR POINTER to STRING;
declare HASH 8 BIT INTEGER;
declare I             INTEGER;
I := 1
HASH := 0;
while (I ≤ [STR].CURLEN) do
        begin
```

HASH := HASH + [STR].DATA(I);
I := I + 1
end;
return;
end HASH;

Exercise 5.25. Write a function GETVAL that returns the value of an attribute for the table described above. If the attribute is not in the table, 0 should be returned.

Bucket organization

When hash tables are organized into buckets of synonyms, the process of storing or retrieving the value of an attribute consists of hashing to a bucket and sequentially searching thru all pairs in the bucket. During storage, if an identical attribute is found in the bucket, the value is stored in the value field of that attribute. If *null* is found, the attribute and value are both stored in that pair. However, if none of the attributes in the bucket is *null* or is equal to the given attribute, then overflow has resulted. The usual way to recover from overflow is to provide a single, overflow area where all pairs are stored that caused overflow. Since a good hash function will distribute all attributes uniformly into all buckets, overflow is an unusual condition, and the number of pairs in the overflow area should be small. The technique for handling the overflow area was described in the previous example.

Exercise 5.26. Give an implementation of a hash table that has 256 hash buckets with 8 pairs in each bucket. The hash function should use multiplication, extracting the middle 8 bits of the product and padding on the right with 3 '0' bits.

Exercise 5.27. Using hashing techniques, implement a 1000 by 1000 sparse matrix that has 1% non-zero elements. Compare the access time for your algorithm with the SPARSE _ ELEMENT _ VALUE algorithm given on page 227.

List organization

The third technique for organizing the pairs in a table consists in placing all synonyms on a linked list. The hash function is used to obtain the address of the appropriate list, and the list is searched sequentially for the appropriate pair. When inserting an element in the table, memory for the pair is obtained from available storage (see Chapters 6 and 7), and the new pair is linked into the appropriate list (see Chapter 4). The new pair can be inserted at the beginning, end, or in the middle of the list, depending on the desired organization. For example, each pair might contain an indication of the number of accesses made to that pair by the system, and the list can be ordered according to frequency of accesses. This would reduce the access time of the most frequently accessed pairs, while increasing the time for the infrequently accessed pairs. In contrast, the list might be kept in alphabetic or numeric order of the attributes. In this case, on the average, only half of the list would have to be searched for each access. An interesting modification of this technique is used by the SNOBOL4 programming language as described below. A further modification is suggested in Exercise 5.29.

All strings in SNOBOL4 (called natural variables) are kept in a single table. This includes program identifiers, statement labels, and strings created by the program during execution. As a result, the sizes of the strings vary greatly and special techniques are required. A linked organization is used, where the links pass through the string headers. See Figure 5.14. The table uses a hash function that selects for each string one of 256 lists (i.e., buckets). A second hash function is used to obtain an order number for each string. The strings on each list are sorted according to their order number. When searching for an entry in the table,

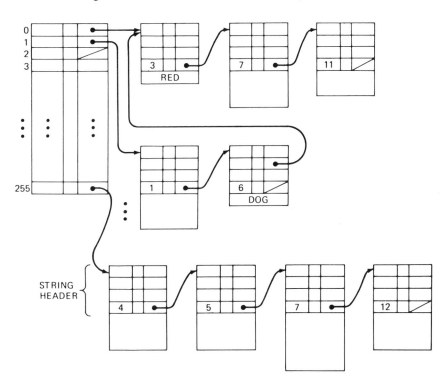

h_1 ('DOG') = 1 h_1 ('RED') = 0
h_2 ('DOG') = 6 h_2 ('RED') = 3

Figure 5.14. The table of natural variables in SNOBOL4. The value of a natural variable is referenced indirectly through the string header of the natural variable. In the above figure, the value of DOG is 'RED' (i.e., DOG = 'RED').

it is only necessary to compare order numbers until entries are found that share the same order number. Only at that time must the entire attribute strings be compared. The result is that string comparisons are kept to a minimum. If the hash function that computes order numbers returns (random) numbers on the range 0 to 256, then up to 256 x 256 different bucket number-order number pairs are possible. When there are 4K different strings in the hash table, two hash numbers and, on the average, eight order number comparisons will be needed to locate the desired string. This follows since there will be, on the average, 16 strings on each chain, and the desired string will be, on the average, in the middle of the chain. It would be unlikely that two strings share the same order number when there are only 4K strings in the table. The specific hash functions used for two different computers are described in Griswold (1972).

Exercise 5.28. Suppose that a fixed string (the subject string) is to be searched many times for the presence of various substrings (pattern strings), and further suppose that the substring test will frequently fail. This occurs in text editors while searching for specific words in the current text. Hashing techniques can be used as a rapid way of determining when the given pattern string is *not* present in the subject string. The *hashed k-signature* of string S is the binary string b_1, b_2, b_3...b_m, such that $b_i = 1$ if there is a substring s in string S of length k such that hash(s)=i, and $b_i = 0$ otherwise. Let P be a pattern string, and let B_P be its hashed k-signature. Then P is a substring of S only if B_P **and** $B_S = B_P$. (Note that this condition may be satisfied even though P is not a substring of S.) Give an algorithm for computing the hashed-k signature of a string. Assuming that m is the length of a computer word, what parameters should influence the choice of k? What parameters should influence the choice of m and k if m is not restricted to the length of a computer word? (This is the same as Exercise 3.9.)

Exercise 5.29. Substantial improvement in search time can be realized if instead of using a simple linked list for the attribute value pairs, height-balanced trees are used. Give a suitable memory representation for a hash table of this variety, and give the procedures for entering pairs in the table and looking up the value of an attribute.

5.6.5 External tables

In this section, we give a very brief introduction to the special problems that arise when tables are kept on external storage devices such as disk packs or drums.

Indexed sequential access files

In previous sections, we discussed implementation techniques for tables that reside in main memory. Tables that reside in external storage devices may use modified or completely different methods of organization. As a specific example, we will briefly describe the indexed sequential access method available on the IBM series 360 and 370 computers. This method in particular shows how file organization is influenced by the nature of the hardware device on which the data are kept.

A *file* is a collection of related data items called records that are treated as a unit. *Records* are contiguous chunks of external storage containing several (and often many) fields of information. In an *indexed sequential file*, each record has a special field called a *key*, and the records are arranged in sequence according to the values of their keys. A set of indices is maintained by the system as described below, which gives the location (disk address) of certain principal records in the file. An *index* is simply a table whose attributes are key values and whose values are addresses. The addresses are the disk addresses of other indices or data areas. Since these indices reside on the disks, they are *external tables*. Indices simply permit a quasi-direct access to each record in the file.

An indexed sequential file is stored on a *direct access* storage device, such as a disk pack. A disk pack is a storage device which can access a record directly when given the disk address of the record. A disk pack contains several platters called *disks* which are arranged on a single spindle. See Figure 5.15. The top and bottom surface of each disk is covered with a magnetic material on which information can be stored. A read/write head for each surface is attached to a fixed arm, and the heads for each surface are arranged in a vertical stack. The arm can be positioned at one of a fixed number of horizontal positions, frequently 100 or more, by the hardware. For a given horizontal position, the recording surface on each disk is called a *track*, and the set of tracks at a given horizontal position is called a *cylinder*. Each track may (logically) contain a number of records, say N, so that each cylinder can contain N * K records, where K is the number of surfaces on the given disk pack.

For a given disk storage device, the time it takes to move the heads from one cylinder to another and to rotate the disks to a desired position is substantial, on the order of milliseconds, whereas the time it takes to read contiguous words on a given cylinder is comparable to main memory access speeds, on the order of microseconds. For this reason, the tracks on a cylinder can be thought of as contiguous data areas, whereas the data on different cylinders are not contiguous. When a file is stored on a disk pack, it is generally partitioned into cylinders; cylinders are further partitioned into tracks; and finally tracks are partitioned into records. The records are the logical entities that contain useful information in the file.

An indexed sequential file residing on a disk pack can occupy up to three different (logical) areas: a prime area; an overflow area; and an index area. The *prime area* always exists and contains *track indices* that describe the data records on the tracks and the corresponding data records. An *overflow area* is optional

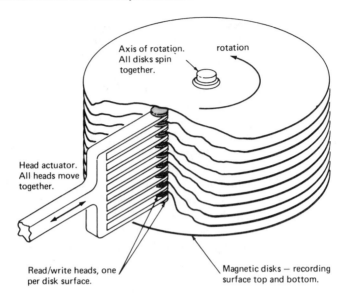

Figure 5.15. The essential components of a disk storage device. All read/write heads move together and stop at one of a fixed number of positions, typically around 100. The information from all tracks of one such position form a cylinder. If each track holds same number of records, say K, then each cylinder holds K*N records, where N is the number of disk surfaces on the device.

and if present contains records that overflow the prime area when new data records are added to the file. The *index area* contains indices associated with the file.

The indices of an indexed sequential data set are analagous to the card catalog of a library: If you know the name of a book, you can look up its shelf code in the card catalog. Once the shelf code (library address) of a book is known, the book can be located by finding the correct room in the library, finding the first shelf marked with the proper call letters (generally alphabetical), and sequentially searching for the book with the proper shelf code.

The indexed sequential access method can use three indices: a master index; cylinder indices; and track indices. The master index is optional and describes locations in the cylinder index where the search for a record should begin. This is analagous to a map of the library which indicates what room in the library contains a given range of shelf codes. If more than one cylinder is used for the file, a cylinder index is used. Each entry in the cylinder index identifies the key of the last entry in a cylinder and the address of the track index for that cylinder. This makes it possible to restrict a search to a given cylinder and is analagous to the shelf code labels appearing on the ends of each row of book cases in a library.

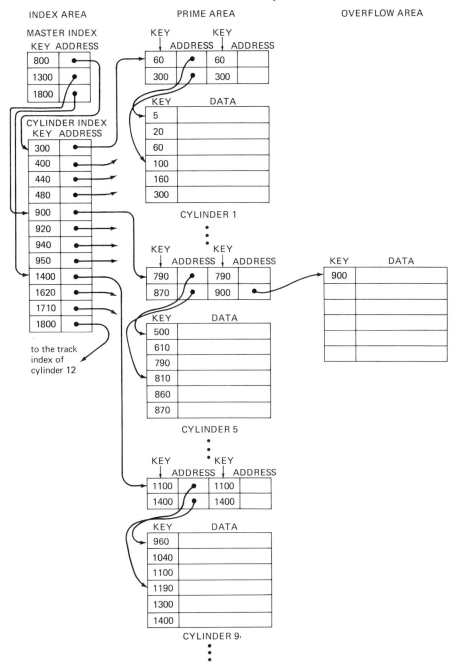

Figure 5.16. The structure of an indexed sequential file. The record with KEY = 900 is the only overflow record in the file.

Finally, each cylinder has a track index. Each entry in the track index identifies the key of the last record on a particular track; this would be analagous to placing the shelf code of the last book on a shelf at the end of the shelf. See Figure 5.16 for an illustration of an indexed sequential file.

With these three levels of indices, the search process for a record starts with the master index. A sequential search of the relatively small ordered master index locates the address of a starting point to search the cylinder index; a second search of part of the ordered cylinder index produces the address of the track index of the appropriate cylinder. The track index consists of pairs of entries: a normal entry and an overflow entry. The normal entry contains the key of the highest record on a track and the address of the last record on the track. If the record being sought is not in an overflow area, the track on which to start searching sequentially is obtained from the track index. The overflow entry contains the key of the highest overflow record and the address of the lowest overflow record on the track. Initially, the overflow entry is the same as the track index entry. If a record being sought has a key higher than the key of the highest (normal) record on the track, then the record is in an overflow area. It can be found by starting at the address of the lowest overflow record on the track and searching the ordered linked list of overflow records.

When an indexed sequential file is first set up, there is no overflow area, and the records pointed to by each track index are contiguous and ordered by key. When a record is added, it is inserted in the proper place, and the other records moved down. When there is no longer enough room for the last records on the track, they are placed in the overflow area. Initially, looking up a record is very fast. As more records are put in the overflow area, look-up becomes slower. This can be helped some by specifying separate overflow areas for each cylinder, but eventually a complete reorganization of the file is necessary. The same thing happens in a library when book shelves become filled: Ultimately, books are moved from shelf to shelf, and, when a room becomes filled, the entire collection is reorganized.

We must point out that the indexed sequential access method is designed for use by files which are ordered according to a single key. When more than one key is present, and the file is to be searched based on the values of different keys, the indexed sequential access method is no longer useful. The reader should consult a textbook on data base systems for a discussion of the special problems associated with multi-key files.

External hash tables

In previous sections on hash tables, it was implicitly assumed that the hash tables resided in main memory so that accesses to table entries are fast. When using a hash table as an index into a large data base, however, it is often not possible to store the entire table in primary memory. Instead, the table entries, whether they be attribute-value pairs in a direct or list organization or buckets in a bucket organization, reside on a rotating storage device, such as disk or drum. Because of the long access time of a disk or drum relative to main memory, the choices of a table organization plays a crucial role in the efficiency of the table.

As we described earlier, when accessing words from a drum or disk, the access time for a random word is slow, but the access times for subsequent, contiguous words are fast. It is therefore beneficial to choose a table organization which can take advantage of this fact, such as a bucket-organized hash table, where each bucket has several attribute-value pairs, or a linked table, where each list element contains several pairs.

If the number of pairs in a bucket or list element is chosen too large, then the time required to copy the contents of the bucket or list element into main memory plus the time required to search through them for the desired attribute will exceed, on the average, the time required to access and search several buckets or elements having fewer attribute-value pairs. The following factors should be taken into consideration when selecting a specific table organization and bucket or element size:

- access time for a single random word from external storage;
- access time for subsequent words from contiguous words of external storage;
- time required to search for the desired attribute in a bucket or list element;
- the effectiveness of the hashing function;
- the table loading factor (percentage of words in use).

Each of these parameters depends on particular hardware characteristics, as well as on the distribution of table attributes, so that the optimum choice will differ for different applications.

The techniques for handling overflow must likewise be chosen carefully. If rehashing is used, each subsequent access will be in a random disk location, and maximum access time will be required; this is clearly a poor choice. If a single overflow area is used, then sequential accesses within that area will require minimum access time; however, a sequential search through a large overflow area is very costly. When using a table with direct organization, a good compromise is to have several overflow areas, each one for a different collection of buckets. The address of the overflow area for each bucket can be contained within the bucket, and the overflow area can be located on the disk so that if the desired pair is not in the bucket, the time required to position the heads at the overflow area will be minimum; if additional overflow areas are required, they can be chained together in the same way.

5.7 SUMMARY

Arrays and matrices are used so extensively that both efficient access procedures and efficient memory representations are necessary. In this chapter, we described how these structures are effectively implemented. Although sparse matrices are examples of two-dimensional arrays, the standard implementation techniques result in extremely poor memory utilization and are therefore not practical, especially for large matrices. Special techniques for implementing sparse matrices were described which, although slower for accessing elements, utilize memory much more efficiently. When array elements are accessed by rows or columns, these techniques are almost as efficient as the standard techniques used for ordinary arrays. By extending the concept of an address computation function to a hashing function, we have shown how to efficiently implement tables. Hash tables are particularly useful when the attributes are not required in any particular order and when frequent insertions and deletions are not necessary. When stored externally, however, particular care should be taken in the choice of an efficient table organization suited for the external storage device.

Projects

Project 5.1. In typical block structured languages (e.g. ALGOL, PL/I), blocks determine the scope of identifiers. Identifiers declared within nested blocks are local to (defined only within) the nested block, and if such an identifier were also declared in an outer block, the identifiers designate different variables. As an example, in the following program skeleton, I designates one variable at statements 1 and 4 and a different variable at statements 2 and 3. Similarly, J designates one variable at statements 1, 2 and 4 and another variable at statement 3.

```
begin
DECLARE (I,J) INTEGER;
        •
        •
<statement 1>
        •
        •
    begin
        DECLARE I INTEGER;
            •
            •
        <statement 2>
            •
            •
    begin
        DECLARE J INTEGER;
            •
```

```
                •
        <statement 3>
                •
                •
        end;
                •
                •
        end;
                •
                •
<statement 4>;
        •
        •
end
```

A symbol table used by a compiler when translating a block structured language must be able to distinguish between different variables having the same name. One way to do this is to use a *block structured table*. Each defined block is given a number as soon as it is encountered. Each block is also given a nesting level, which is the nesting level of the immediately surrounding block plus 1. Whenever a new block is encountered, any identifiers declared within that block are inserted in the table, together with information used by the compiler. When table lookup of the information for an identifier is requested, the lookup procedure must return the information associated with the correct variable. The lookup procedure is given the block number of the requested identifier, and if the identifier were declared within that block, the requested information is returned. Otherwise, the lookup procedure must look for the declared variable in the surrounding block, and so forth, until the declaration is found. If no declaration is found for the identifier, an error condition results.

The illustration below shows the skeleton of a complicated block and the corresponding block structured table. The block number and nesting level is given for each block. The block structured table consists of a *block list* and *symbol table*. The block list gives the surrounding block number for each block, the number of symbols defined within that block, and a pointer to the first symbol table entry for those symbols. The symbol table itself is linearly organized.

```
begin
    declare (I,J,K) INTEGER;
    declare (X,Y) REAL;
        •
        •
        •
    begin
        declare (I,M) INTEGER;
        declare Z     REAL;
            •
            •
            •
        begin
```

```
            declare (X, Z) REAL;
            declare (I,J) INTEGER;
                    •
                    •
                    •
      end
        •
        •
        •
      begin
            declare (I,K) INTEGER;
            declare Y REAL;
                    •
                    •
                    •
      end
        •
        •
        •
  end
    •
    •
    •
end
```

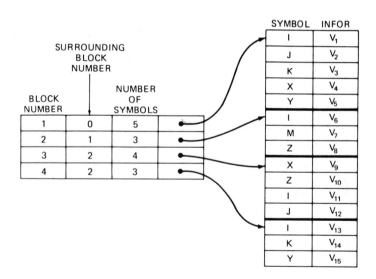

Assume that all entries for a given block are made before the next block is encountered. (Declarations must appear at the beginning of each block.) Give procedures as described below for manipulating the symbol table:

NEW _ BLOCK( ) A parameterless procedure that is invoked when a new block is encountered. This procedure makes initial entries in the block list and returns the block number of the new block.

ENTER(ID,INFO) A procedure that enters the symbol ID in the symbol table and assigns the value INFO to that symbol. The block list is also updated.

CLOSE( ) A parameterless procedure that is invoked when the end of a block is encountered. This procedure makes the final entries in the block list.

GET(ID,BLKNO) A procedure that returns the value of the symbol ID corresponding to block number BLKNO. An error condition results if there is no symbol ID defined for (not necessarily within) BLKNO.

The symbol table shown in the previous illustration would be formed by the following sequence of statements:

```
call  NEW _ BLOCK( );
call  ENTER('I',V1);
call  ENTER('J',V2);
call  ENTER('K',V3);
call  ENTER('X',V4);
call  ENTER('Y',V5);
call  NEW _ BLOCK ( );
call  ENTER('I',V6);
call  ENTER('M',V7);
call  ENTER('Z',V8);
call  NEW _ BLOCK ( );
call  ENTER('X',V9);
call  ENTER('Z',V10);
call  ENTER('I',V11);
call  ENTER('J',V12);
call  CLOSE( );
call  NEW _ BLOCK;( )
call  ENTER('I',V13);
call  ENTER('K',V14);
call  ENTER('Y',V15);
call  CLOSE( );
call  CLOSE( );
call  CLOSE( );
```

After the table is created, the statements:

$$Z := GET('I',4);$$
$$Z := GET('J',2);$$
$$Z := GET('Z',4);$$
$$Z := GET('I',1);$$
$$Z := GET('K',3);$$

would assign to Z the values: V13, V2, V8, V1, and V3.

Project 5.2. Digitized pictures are generally represented in memory as two-dimensional arrays of integers whose values range from 0 to 7, 0 to 15, 0 to 31, and so forth. The individual picture elements are called *pixels*. One operation that is frequently performed on pictures is to take their spatial gradient. Let P (I,J) be the I-J'th pixel of a picture (row I, column J), and let G designate its gradient. The values of G(I,J) are given by:

$$G(I,J) = P(I,J) - .25 * P(I - 1,J)$$
$$- .25 * P(I + 1,J)$$
$$- .25 * P(I \quad ,J - 1)$$
$$- .25 * P(I \quad ,J + 1)$$

which can easily be implemented as follows:
```
I := 2;
J := 2;
while (I < NUMROWS) do
     begin
          while (J < NUMCOLUMNS) do
               begin
                    G(I,J) := P(I,J) - .25 * ( P(I - 1,J) + P(I + 1,J)+
                                                P(I,J - 1 ) + P(I,J + 1));
                    I := I + 1
               end;
               J := J + 1
     end;
```

where NUMROWS and NUMCOLUMNS are the number of rows and columns in the picture. (Notice that the gradient has two fewer rows and columns than the initial picture.)

A large percentage of the computation time is involved with the two-dimensional subscript computations. Assume that the picture is stored by rows. The same result can be obtained much more efficiently by using one-dimensional subscripts for determining the addresses of the array elements. Design and code such a procedure. The following support routines should also be coded:

INPUT(P,I,J)   A procedure that reads an I by J picture into the array P. Assume that the values of the pixels are between 0 and 15.

OUTPUT(P,I,J)   A procedure that prints picture P on a line printer. The print characters should be determined by the pixel value as follows:

Pixel value

	0	1	2	3	4	5	6	7	8	9	10	11	12	13	14	15
character	ƀ	-	.	/	C	O	Q	U	U	D	O	O	O	O	O	O
overprint 1	ƀ	ƀ	ƀ	ƀ	ƀ	ƀ	ƀ	C	G	B	.	/	0	0	0	0
overprint 2	ƀ	ƀ	ƀ	ƀ	ƀ	ƀ	ƀ	ƀ	ƀ	ƀ	ƀ	ƀ	ƀ	-	=	#

Project 5.3. A *triple* is a data structure of the form (attribute, object, value), where the relation "attribute *of* object = value" is said to hold. For example, if (color, ball, red) is a triple, then the relation "color *of* ball = red" is said to hold. The following operations are to be performed on triples and sets of triples:

ADD(S,T)   The triple T is to be added to the set of triples S. The set S is returned.

DELETE(S,T)   The triple T is to be removed from the set of triples S. The set S is to be returned.

VALUE(A,O,S)   The value of attribute A of object O is to be returned, where S is the set of triples containing a triple of the form (A,O,V).

FINDA(S,A)   A set of triples is returned. The set is comprised of all triples of set S having attribute A. The set S is not modified.

FINDO(S,O)   A set of triples is returned. The set is comprised of all triples of set S having object O. The set S is not modified.

FINDV(S,V)   A set of triples is returned. The set is comprised of all triples of set S having value V. The set S is not modified.

FINDAO(S,A,O)   A set of triples is returned. The set is comprised of all triples of set S having attribute A and object O.

FINDAV(S,A,V)   A set of triples is returned. The set is comprised of all triples of set S having attribute A and value V. The set S is not modified.

FINDOV(S,O,V)   A set of triples is returned. The set is comprised of all triples of set S having object O and value V. The set S is not modified.

CHANGEV(S,A,O,V)   The value of the triple of set S having attribute A and object O is changed to V. The old value is returned.

INPUTS( )   A set of triples is input in suitable format.

OUTPUTS(S)   The triples of set S are listed in suitable format.

INPUTT( )   A single triple is input in suitable format.

OUTPUTT (T)   A single triple is printed in suitable format.

Select a suitable memory representation for triples and sets of triples whose attributes, objects and values are strings, and implement the above operations.

REFERENCES AND ADDITIONAL READINGS

Books

Bunch, J.R., and Rose, D.J. (Eds.) (1976) *Sparse Matrix Computations*. New York: Academic Press, Inc.

Gries, D. (1971) *Compiler Construction for Digital Computers*. New York: John Wiley & Sons, Inc.

Griswold, R.E. (1972) *The Macro Implementation of SNOBOL4*. San Francisco: W.H. Freeman and Co.

IBM (1973) *OS Data Management Service Guide*, File No. S360/370-30, Order No. GC 26-3746-2, International Business Machines.

Rose, D.J., and Willoughby, R.A. (1972) *Sparse Matrices and Applications*. New York: Plenum Press.

Articles and Technical Reports

Amble, O. and Knuth, D.E. Ordered hash tables. *Computer J*. Vol. 17, No. 2, May 1974, 143-147.

Atkinson, L.V. Hashing matrix subscripts. *BIT* Vol. 15, No. 3, 1975, 328-330.

Baecker, H.D. Mapped list structures. *CACM* Vol. 6, No. 8 Aug. 1963, 435-438.

Batagelj, V. The quadratic hash method when the table size is not a prime number. *CACM* Vol. 18, No. 4, Apr. 1975, 216-217.

Bays, C. A note on when to chain overflow items within a direct-access table. *CACM* Vol. 16, No. 1, Jan. 1973, 46-47.

Bays, C. The reallocation of hash-coded tables. *CACM* Vol. 16, No. 1, Jan. 1973, 11-14.

Bays, C. Some techniques for structuring chained hash tables. *Computer J*. Vol. 16, No. 2, May 1973, 126-131.

Bell, J.R., and Kaman, C.H. The linear quotient hash code. *CACM* Vol. 13, No. 11, Nov. 1970, 675-677.

Bobrow, D.G. A note on hash linking. *CACM* Vol. 18, No. 7, July 1975, 413-415.

Brent, R.P. Reducing the retrieval time of scatter storage techniques. *CACM* Vol. 16, No. 2, Feb. 1973, 105-109.

Chung-Phillips, A., and Rosen, R.W. A note on dynamic data storage in FORTRAN IV. *Computer J*. Vol. 18, No. 4, Nov. 1975, 342-343.

Harrison, M.C. Implementation of the substring test by hashing. *CACM* Vol. 14, No. 12, Dec. 1971, 777-779.

Hoffman, S.A. Data structures that generalize rectangular arrays. AFIPS Conference Proceedings 1962 Joint Computer Conference, 325-333.

Hopgood, F.R.A., and Davenport, J. The quadratic hash method where the table size is a power of 2. *Computer J*. Vol. 15, No. 4, Nov. 1972, 314-315.

Jennings, A. A compact storage scheme for the solution of symmetric linear simultaneous equations. *Computer J*. Vol. 9, No. 3, 1966, 281-285.

Larson, Per-Ake. Dynamic hashing. *BIT* 18, Nr. 2, 1978, 184-201.

Lawrence, E.E. Remarks on Algorithm 408 [F4]. A Sparse Matrix Package. *CACM* Vol. 16, No. 9, Sept. 1973, 578.

Mallach, E.G. Scatter storage techniques: A unifying viewpoint and a method for reducing retrieval times. *Computer J*. Vol. 20, No. 2, May 1977, 137-140.

Maurer, W.D., and Lewis, T.G. Hash table methods. *Computing Surveys* Vol. 7, No. 1, Mar. 1975, 5-19.

McNamee, J.M. Algorithm 408. A sparse matrix package. (Part I) [F4]. *CACM* Vol. 14, No. 4, Apr. 1971, 265-273.

Morris, R. Scatter storage techniques. *CACM* Vol. 11, No. 1, Jan. 1968, 38-44.

Pooch, V.W., and Nieder, A. A survey of indexing techniques for sparse matrices. *Computing Surveys* Vol. 5, No. 2, June 1973, 109-133.

Price, C.E. Table lookup techniques. *Computing Surveys* Vol. 3, No. 2, June 1971, 49-66.

Rosenberg, A.L. Preserving proximity in arrays. *SIAM J. Computing* Vol. 4, No. 4, Dec. 1975, 443-460.

Severance, D.G. Identifier search mechanisms: A survey and generalized model. *Computing Surveys* Vol. 6, No. 3, Sept. 1974, 175-194.

Tewarson, R.P. Computations with sparse matrices. *SIAM Review* Vol. 12, No. 4, Oct. 1970, 527-543.

Tewarson, R.P. Row column permutations of sparse matrices. *Computer J.* Vol. 10, No. 4, 1968, 300-305.

deVilliers, E.v.d.S., and Wilson, L.B. Hashing the subscripts of a sparse matrix. *BIT* Vol. 14, No. 3, 1974, 347-358.

Wood, D. A comparison of two methods of encoding arrays. *BIT* 18, 1978, 219-229.

6
Dynamic memory management using sequential allocation and compaction

OVERVIEW

In this chapter, we discuss two dynamic memory management systems that sequentially allocate blocks of variable size from a pool of contiguous memory locations called a heap and compact memory during memory regeneration. The first system can easily be coded in almost any programming language and is ideally suited for simple string processing operations where the allocated blocks do not contain pointers to other allocated blocks. The second system is more general and is based on the memory management system used by SNOBOL4 (Griswold, 1972).

6.1 INTRODUCTION

Since the late fifties, a great deal of effort has gone into the development of high-level programming systems and languages, and two fundamentally different philosophies have emerged. For the algorithmic languages, such as FORTRAN, BASIC, PL/I, ALGOL, and PASCAL, memory allocation is, for the most part, related to the static structure of the program. In FORTRAN and BASIC, memory for variables is allocated at compile time, although there are some implementations of FORTRAN that allocate memory upon FUNCTION or SUBROUTINE entry. In PL/I, ALGOL, and PASCAL, programs are block-structured, and memory for variables is allocated at block entry and liberated at block exit. The exceptions are CONTROLLED and BASED variables of PL/I and dynamic variables of PASCAL.

In contrast, the symbolic processing languages, notably LISP and SNOBOL, were designed so that variables are not declared, and memory for all program variables is allocated and liberated dynamically. In LISP, for example, the fundamental data structures are atoms (integers, real numbers, and fixed-length strings called symbolic atoms) and binary structures formed by using arbitrarily many binary cells. Lists are a special case of these structures, and lists are the most frequently used structure in LISP. For these languages, memory for structures is allocated as required, and no explicit procedures are available to notify the memory management routines that a structure is being abandoned. For languages of this type, it is absolutely essential to have efficient procedures for allocating memory and reclaiming memory that has been abandoned during program execution.

Numerous other systems use dynamic memory management: discrete simulation languages, such as GPSS and GASP IV; artificial intelligence languages, including numerous dialects of LISP; graphics languages; operating systems; disk management routines; and virtual memory computer systems. The importance of the various dynamic memory allocation techniques cannot be over emphasized.

There are several different techniques that are used for dynamic memory management. This chapter will be concerned with systems that sequentially allocate variable sized blocks of memory from a block of available memory called a *heap* or *free space*. Once free space is used up, the system regenerates memory by *compaction,* moving all blocks that are in current use to contiguous low addresses. This frees all high address memory locations for reallocation. Systems in which all references to blocks are made indirectly can use this technique. Programming languages like SNOBOL4 are also able to use this technique, since the memory management routines have a complete list of addresses of all identifiers that point to allocated blocks of memory. When the locations of all block pointers are known, they can be updated during memory regeneration. There are some dynamic memory allocation environments where it is impossible, impractical, or unnecessary to move blocks once they are allocated. A comprehensive discussion of memory management techniques for those systems is given in Chapter 7.

6.2 MEMORY REGENERATION

In a dynamic memory allocation environment, a block is *active* in case a) it is referenced directly by a program variable, or b) it is referenced by an active block. This definition must be understood recursively. It follows that if a given block is active, there is a chain of pointers that originates at a program variable and continues through a sequence of active blocks until it reaches the given block.

During memory regneration, the first problem is to determine which blocks are active and which are not. This is done by a *marking procedure* that follows chains of pointers beginning at program variables and marks all blocks that it encounters. A single bit called a 'mark bit' is kept in the header of each block. The mark bits are set to '0' when the blocks are allocated, otherwise, the first time memory is to be regenerated, all blocks would be found marked, no memory would be liberated, and the program would be terminated. Said another way, all blocks are assumed to be inactive unless discovered to be active by the marking procedure. Each block that is found to be active by the marking procedure is *marked:* Its mark bit is set to '1'.

Marking is the first phase of memory regeneration. After marking is completed, the second phase, *compaction* (also called *compression),* is initiated. Memory compaction consists of moving all marked blocks into one contiguous region in the low-address portion of memory and adjusting all block pointers accordingly. At the same time, the mark bits are set to '0' in anticipation of subsequent marking. As a result, after memory compaction, free space occupies a single region at the high-address end of memory, and all blocks are unmarked. Memory from this region can be allocated quickly and easily using a sequential allocation algorithm. Memory compaction can be used by systems that use variable-sized blocks, as well as by those that use fixed-sized blocks (cells), although the examples presented in this chapter all use variable-sized blocks.

Marking is done in all dynamic memory allocation systems that do not provide explicit procedures for freeing blocks that are no longer wanted (e.g. FREE in PL/I), and it is even used by some systems that do. Historically, LISP was the first system to use dynamic memory management using a marking algorithm. Several marking procedures are discussed in Section 6.5.

Each system that uses a marking procedure must maintain an *initial address list,* a list of addresses of memory locations that contain pointers to active blocks. In programming languages like SNOBOL, the initial address list includes all program variables, but it also includes system variables, as well. Marking procedures always begin by marking blocks that are directly accessible from the initial address list. Blocks that are not accessible by following a chain from the initial address list are not marked and are therefore eliminated during memory regeneration.

Memory compaction, the second phase of memory regeneration, is an important technique for several reasons. It eliminates *fragmentation,* the situation where there are numerous small blocks of unused memory, separated by the active blocks. Although the total amount of unused memory may be large when fragmentation occurs, there is often no single block of adequate size to meet an allocation request. The result is premature program termination. Memory compaction reorganizes the active blocks in memory so that all available space is in a single contiguous block; memory compaction also tends to localize memory references, which can be particularly beneficial if the program is to be run on a computer that uses virtual memory. Locality of references reduces page thrashing, a common problem for list processing systems that do not use memory compaction. Finally, memory compaction enables sequential memory allocation, a considerable saving of time over systems that maintain lists of available space from which blocks or cells are allocated. (C.f. Chapter 7.)

6.3 DYNAMIC MEMORY MANAGEMENT USING INDIRECT ADDRESSING

In this section, we present a very simple, dynamic memory management system that can easily be coded in languages like FORTRAN that do not otherwise provide dynamic memory management. This system is ideally suited for simple string processing operations, as described in Chapter 3, but has other applications as well.

In this system, program variables reference allocated blocks indirectly. Each program variable that is used to reference a block points to an *indirect block pointer,* a pointer maintained by the memory management procedures. Indirect block pointers point directly to the allocated blocks. By using indirect block pointers, the memory management routines do not need to have access to the program variables.

The following assumptions are made for this system:

1. Each block has one and only one indirect block pointer.
2. All references to a block are made through its indirect block pointer.
3. There is at least one reference on the initial address list to every active block.

The first assumption is necessary because only one indirect block pointer for each block gets changed to point to the block's new position during memory regeneration. If a block had two indirect block pointers, then, after memory compaction, one of them would be incorrect. The second assumption is made, since the system only updates indirect block pointers. If a reference were made directly to a block by a program variable, then after memory regeneration that reference would be incorrect. (The memory management routines do not have access to the program variables.) The third assumption is necessary to insure that every active block is marked.

The memory representation is illustrated in Figures 6.1 and 6.2. Three blocks of memory called SPACE, PTABLE, and IALIST are used; SPACE is the heap from which BLOCKs are allocated, PTABLE *(P*ointer *TABLE)* is used for indirect block pointers, and IALIST *(I*nitial *A*ddress *LIST)* is used for the initial address list. The pointer FREE points to the first character in SPACE that is available for allocation; all memory locations between SPACE (FREE) and SPACE (SIZE) are available for allocation. The pointer PUSED, in contrast to

FREE, points to the last allocated indirect block pointer in PTABLE. Initially, FREE is set to the address of the first word of SPACE; SIZE is the number of words in SPACE; and PUSED is set to 0. The variable NLIST indicates how many words are on the initial address list and is initially set to 0.

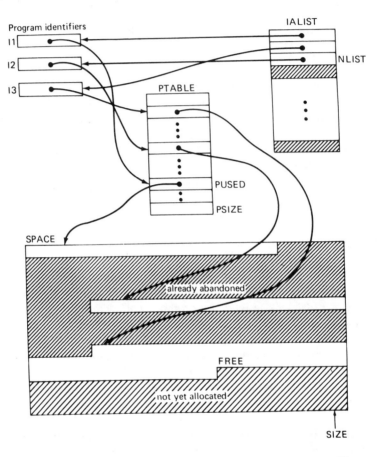

Figure 6.1. The storage representation when three blocks are in current use. The program variable I3 designates the last block that was allocated.

Allocation of blocks of memory is done by the procedure GETBLK1 to be given shortly. The procedure GETBLK1 has one parameter, the number of words required in the allocated block. We assume that addresses are word addresses, and we use the data type WORD to denote one word of memory. GETBLK1 allocates the required block of memory from SPACE; allocates an indirect block pointer from PTABLE; places the address of the allocated block in

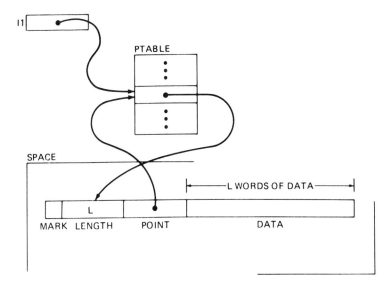

Figure 6.2. The memory representation of an allocated block.

the indirect block pointer; and sets up a block header in the first two words of the block. The block header contains three fields: MARK, LENGTH and POINT; the LENGTH field contains the length of the block (not including its header), and the POINT field contains the address (subscript in PTABLE) of the block's indirect block pointer; the MARK bit is used by the memory regeneration routines and is initally set to '0'. We assume that the LENGTH field plus mark bit together require one word of storage. The subscript in PTABLE of the indirect block pointer is the value returned by GETBLK1. Each allocated block has one and only one indirect block pointer. Figure 6.3 shows part of the structure that results if the last allocated block: has three data words; starts at SPACE(372); has its indirect block pointer at PTABLE(22); and is referenced by the program variable I1.

One key point to note about this memory representation is that it is possible to sequentially process the blocks in the order in which they were allocated (and hence appear in SPACE). This is true first because they are allocated contiguously in SPACE and second because the LENGTH field is the first field of each block. Hence the location of a subsequent block can be calculated from the location of the current block by adding the current block's total length to its address. (The first block always begins at SPACE(1).) The ability to process allocated blocks sequentially is essential for the memory regeneration routines.

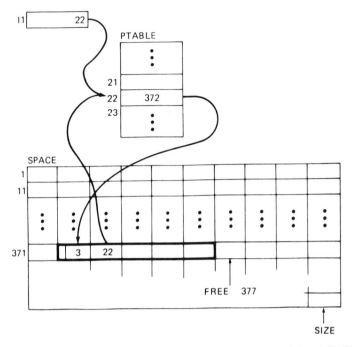

Figure 6.3. Part of the structure that results if: the last allocated block has 3 DATA words, begins at SPACE(372), and is designated by I1.

6.3.1 Memory allocation

Allocation of a block of memory from SPACE consists of incrementing the pointer FREE by an amount given by the sum of the number of words in the block plus 2 (the number of words in the block header). If there is not enough room in SPACE to allocate the requested block, the memory regeneration routine REGEN1 is invoked. If there is still insufficient space after memory regeneration, ABORT is invoked which prints an error message and aborts the program; see GETBLK1 below. The procedure for allocating an indirect block pointer is somewhat different. All words in PTABLE beginning at subscript PUSED+1 are sequentially checked for value zero. If a word is found that has value zero, that word is allocated as the indirect block pointer; if there are no free block pointers, then memory regeneration is initiated; if the memory regeneration routines do not free an indirect block pointer, ABORT is invoked. The procedure GETBLK1 for allocating a block from storage is given below.

procedure GETBLK1(NWORDS);
comment Pointers are word addresses. If P is a pointer, then P+1 is the address of the
           following word;
comment The header (MARK-LENGTH-POINT fields) is two words long;
template   1 BLOCK,
        2 MARK   BIT,
        2 LENGTH   INTEGER,
        2 POINT   POINTER,
        2 DATA ($\bullet$ LENGTH)   WORD;
declare SPACE (SIZE)   WORD **global**;
declare (PTABLE(PSIZE),FREE)   POINTER to BLOCK **global**;
declare (SIZE,PSIZE)   INTEGER **global**;
declare (I,NWORDS,GETBLK1)   INTEGER;
comment Set I to the subscript of the first unused, indirect block pointer;
I := PUSED + 1;
while (PTABLE(I) $\neq$ 0 and I$\leqslant$PSIZE) **do**
      I := I + 1;
if (I = PSIZE + 1)
then begin
       comment All indirect block pointers are in use. Regenerate memory;
       call REGEN1;
       I := 1;
       comment Search for a free indirect block pointer;
       while (PTABLE(I) $\neq$ 0 and I$\leqslant$PSIZE) **do**
             I := I + 1;
       if (I = PSIZE + 1)
       then begin
             comment No indirect block pointers were made free;
             call ABORT('NO INDIRECT BLOCK POINTERS IN
             GETBLK1')
          end endif
    end endif;
PUSED := I;
comment Allocate the block from SPACE;
if (FREE + 1 + NWORDS > @SPACE(SIZE))
then begin
       comment SPACE is used up. Regenerate memory;
       call REGEN1;
       if (FREE + 1 + NWORDS > @SPACE(SIZE))
       then begin
             comment Even after memory regeneration there is not enough
                  memory to satisfy the request;
             call ABORT('MEMORY OVERFLOW IN GETBLK1')
          end endif
    end endif;

comment Create the header and indirect block pointer;
[FREE].MARK := '0';
[FREE].LENGTH := NWORDS;
[FREE].POINT := I;
PTABLE(I) := FREE;
FREE := FREE + 2 + NWORDS;
GETBLK1 := I;
return;
end GETBLK1;

The routine GETBLK1 creates the block header and indirect block pointer but does not place any values in the data portion of the block; routines that invoke GETBLK1 are left with that responsibility.

Exercise 6.1. A routine similar to GETBLK1 could be used for memory allocation in a string processing system. In such a system, the formal parameter would be the number of required characters rather than words. How would you modify GETBLK1 for such a system?

The single requirement imposed by this system on the user is that an initial address list be maintained. All blocks not referenced by variables whose addresses are on the initial address list will be eliminated during memory regeneration. Generally, program variables determine which blocks are active. The procedures SAVE and FREE (left as exercises for the reader) place on and remove from the initial address list the addresses of program variables that contain pointers (subscripts) to indirect block pointers. It is up to the user of the routines to notify the system about which program variables contain such pointers. This is done by invoking the functions SAVE and FREE as follows: The statement "**call** SAVE(X)" places on the initial address list the address of identifier X, and the statement "**call** FREE(X)" removes the last occurrence of the address of X from the initial address list. In programming languages that do not have statements for obtaining the addresses of program variables, assembly language routines must be written for that purpose. An alternative is to require that all program variables pointing to indirect block pointers be kept in a single region of memory, such as a COMMON block in FORTRAN. The memory management procedure uses the variables in the specified region as the list of available space.

Exercise 6.2. Give algorithms for the procedures SAVE and FREE for this system.

6.3.2 Memory regeneration

After sufficiently many blocks of memory have been allocated, either all available indirect block pointers in PTABLE will be in use, or all of SPACE will have been allocated. When either of these situations arise, the routine REGEN1 is invoked. The procedure REGEN1 must do four things: 1) determine, using the initial address list, which blocks are active and *mark* them; 2) determine where active blocks will be placed during memory compaction and *adjust all indirect block pointers* to point to the new block locations (after compaction); 3) if a block is not marked, *set the value of its indirect block pointer to 0* in order to free it for re-use; and 4) *compact memory* by shifting all marked blocks to their new locations at the low subscript end of SPACE.

Marking consists of setting a *mark bit* or *flag* in the header of each block pointed to by elements on the initial address list. Blocks of storage that are not marked during the marking phase of memory regeneration are *garbage* and will

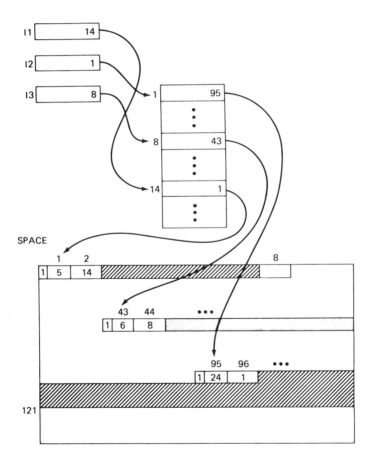

Figure 6.4. The memory representation if I1, I2, and I3 after marking but before compaction. The initial address list is not shown.

be lost during compaction. After compaction, the pointer FREE is adjusted to point to the first free word of SPACE. Memory compaction is illustrated in Figures 6.4 and 6.5. The marking procedure is given below:

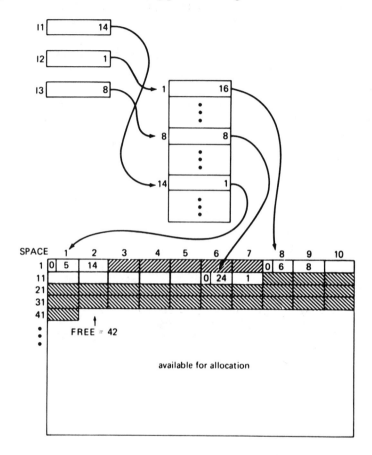

Figure 6.5. The memory representation of I1, I2, and I3 just after memory regeneration.

```
procedure MARK1;
comment Let IALIST be the initial address list, and let NLIST be its length;
template   1 BLOCK,
                2 MARK                BIT,
                2 LENGTH              INTEGER,
                2 POINT               INTEGER,
                2 DATA(• LENGTH)      WORD;
```

```
declare PTABLE (PSIZE)          POINTER to BLOCK global;
declare IALIST (NLIST)          POINTER global;
declare PSIZE                   INTEGER global;
declare (IBP,I)                 INTEGER;
declare ADDR                    POINTER to INTEGER;
I := 1;
while (I ≤ NLIST) do
        begin
                    comment ADDR is the address of a program variable;
                    ADDR: = IALIST(I);
                    comment IBP is the value of the identifier at address ADDR;
                    IBP := [ADDR];
                    comment mark the current block;
                    [PTABLE(IBP) ].MARK := '1';
                    I := I + 1
        end;
return;
end MARK1;
```

Memory regeneration consists of marking each block that is active, changing all current indirect block pointers to point to the new (future) locations of their blocks, setting to 0 all indirect block pointers for unmarked blocks, and then physically moving and unmarking the blocks. The complete procedure REGEN1 is given below.

```
procedure REGEN1;
comment Pointers are word addresses. If P is a pointer, then P+1 is the address of the
            following word;
comment The header (MARK-LENGTH-POINT fields) is two words long;
comment I is a pointer to the current block being processed.
            FREE is a pointer to the first free word of SPACE before and after memory
            regeneration.
            FREE1 is a pointer to the first free word of SPACE at the current time during
            memory regeneration.
            LEN is the length ([I].LENGTH) of the block which starts at address I. The
            length of a block does not include the length of its header.
            [I].POINT is the subscript in PTABLE of the block's indirect block pointer
            (IBP).
            Note that I=PTABLE([I].POINT);
template   1 BLOCK,
              2 MARK              BIT,
              2 LENGTH            INTEGER,
              2 POINT             INTEGER,
              2 DATA(● LENGTH)    WORD;
declare SPACE(SIZE)              WORD global;
```

```
declare (FREE1,I)              POINTER to BLOCK;
declare (PTABLE (PSIZE),FREE)  POINTER to BLOCK global;
declare IBP                    POINTER to BLOCK;
call MARK1;
I := @SPACE;
FREE1 := @SPACE;
while (I < FREE) do
        begin
            LEN := [I].LENGTH;
            IBP := [I].POINT;
            if ( [I].MARK = '1')
            then begin
                    comment Block I is marked. Change its indirect pointer to
                        point to its new location;
                    PTABLE(IBP) := FREE1;
                    FREE1 := FREE1 + LEN + 2
                end
            else begin
                    comment Block I is not marked. Set its indirect pointer to
                        0;
                    PTABLE(IBP) := 0
                end endif;
            comment Process the next block;
            I := I + LEN + 2
        end;
comment Now move the blocks to their new location;
I := @SPACE;
FREE1 := @SPACE;
while (I<FREE) do
        begin
            LEN := [I].LENGTH;
            if ( [I].MARK = '1')
            then begin
                    comment The block is marked. Move it to its new
                        location;
                    J := 0;
                    while (J < LEN + 2) do
                            begin
                                [FREE1 + J] := [I + J];
                                J := J + 1
                            end;
                    comment Unmark the block;
                    [FREE1].MARK := '0';
                    FREE1 := FREE1 + LEN + 2
                end endif;
```

            comment Process the next block;
            I := I + LEN + 2
    end;
comment Now update FREE;
FREE := FREE1;
return;
end REGEN1;

Exercise 6.3. Trace the execution of REGEN1, beginning just following the statement **call** MARK1, for the structure given in Figure 6.4. Assume I1 has address 176, I2 has address 422, and I3 has address 217.

Exercise 6.4. The procedure REGEN1 can be speeded up by combining the process of computing new addresses with the process of physically moving the blocks to their new locations. Give this improved algorithm.

Exercise 6.5. An alternative implementation of this system is to have the list of available space consist of pointers that point directly to the indirect block pointers of the active blocks rather than to the program variables. Modify the procedures MARK1 and REGEN1 for this alternative system. What are some of the advantages and disadvantages of this alternative system?

6.4 DYNAMIC MEMORY MANAGEMENT USING DIRECT ADDRESSING

The previous system is ideally suited for string processing operations. A reference to every block appears on the initial address list, and blocks are referenced through only the indirect block pointers. In this way, many program variables can designate the same block, and the memory regeneration routines do not have to know which program variable refers to which block.

In programming languages such as SNOBOL4 that use dynamic memory allocation, it is not practical to keep a reference to every active block on the initial address list. One major reason is that structures are created that consist of blocks pointing to other blocks in a complicated and unpredictable way. If a program variable is a pointer to one block of a structure, then all blocks of the structure are active; if a structure is large, it would be unreasonable to have a pointer to each active block of the structure. A second and perhaps more important reason is that it is extremely difficult to discover (in general) whether or not a block is made available when a data structure is modified. As a result, it would be impractical to maintain an initial address list having pointers to every active block.

Having ruled out the practicality of maintaining a complete list of active blocks, the central problem for memory reclamation consists of discovering which blocks are active and which are not. This can be done by employing a marking procedure that starts at each element on the initial address list and marks every block that can be reached by following a chain of pointers. In order to do this, the marking procedure must know which fields within any block point to other blocks and which fields contain non-pointer data. The only additional requirement, which turns out to be useful for memory compaction, as well, is to have sufficient workspace in each block to store the field number of the last field containing a pointer that was followed. The workspace will be used during compaction to keep track of the future address of the block.

In the system presented here, references to blocks by program variables are direct, and the initial address list consists of the addresses of all *external block pointers,* pointers that are not in the DATA fields of the allocated blocks. Program variables are examples of external block pointers. Variable sized blocks are used, and memory compaction is part of memory regeneration. In summary, the following assumptions are made:

1. Each block header indicates which DATA words in the block are pointers to other blocks.
2. The addresses of all external pointers to blocks are on the initial address list.
3. Each block header contains a field that can hold the future address of the block after compaction.

The memory representation used by this system is illustrated in Figures 6.6 and 6.7. Each block has a header that has a LENGTH field, a POINT field, a MARK bit, a field of USE bits, and a DATA field. As illustrated in Figure 6.6, references to blocks are direct, and all pointers to blocks not within the data fields of the blocks themselves have their addresses on the initial address list. The LENGTH field contains the length of the block in words, not including the length of its header. The POINT field is used by the memory regeneration routines and during memory compaction will either contain a word number (during marking) or a pointer to the block's new (future) position. The MARK bit of a block is set by the marking routine to indicate that the block is active. There is one USE bit for each DATA word in a block. The USE bits specify which DATA words of the block are used as pointers to other blocks. USE bits are set by routines that place data in the blocks. Finally, the DATA field of the block is aligned on a word boundary and is used to contain either pointers to other blocks or non-pointer data. Each DATA word that is used as a pointer must have its corresponding USE bit set, and each DATA word whose USE bit is set must be either a pointer to a block or have value 0 (indicating a null pointer). When a block is allocated, its LENGTH field is set, and its MARK bit and USE bits are initialized to '0'.

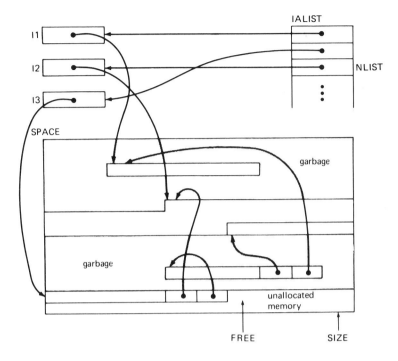

Figure 6.6. The memory representation when five block are active. The program variables, I1, I2, and I3 designate three blocks. The block is designated by I3 references another block, which in turn references a third block not directly referenced by program variables.

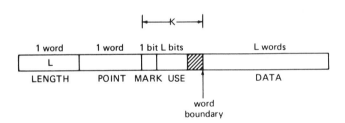

$$K = \lceil L+1)/\text{NBPW} \rceil \text{ words}$$
$$\text{NBPW} = \text{number of bits per word}$$

Figure 6.7. The memory representation of a block.

A structure having two program identifiers and four allocated blocks is shown in Figure 6.8. Notice that for this system, the size of a block header is not fixed. In particular, if there are K DATA words in the block and NBPW (Number of Bits Per Word) bits in a word, then the MARK and USE bit fields together are

[(K+1)/NBPW] words long. Hence, if I is the address of a block having K words, the address of the J'th data word is given by I+2+[(K+1)/NBPW]+J−1. Notice also that because the LENGTH field is the first field of each block, blocks can be processed sequentially in the order in which they appear in memory. Just as in the previous system, this capability is essential for memory compaction and is used as well by several marking algorithms (to be described).

Block allocation for this system is done by GETBLK2 in much the same way that GETBLK1 allocated blocks in the previous system. There are four differences: 1) the indirect block pointers are no longer used; 2) the value returned by GETBLK2 is the address of the block; 3) the length of a block header is influenced by the number of DATA words in the block; and 4) the USE bits are initially set to '0' when the block is allocated. The block allocation procedure is given below:

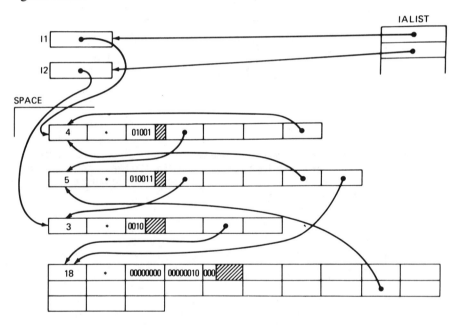

Figure 6.8. The storage representation of two program variables I1 and I2. Eight bits per word are assumed, and the first bit of the third word of each block is the mark bit.

procedure GETBLK2(NWORDS);
comment Pointers are word addresses. If P is a pointer, then P+1 is the address of the following word;
comment NBPW is the number of bits in one word.
NWDSTOT is the total number of words in the requested block.

SPACE is the heap of memory being allocated.
FREE is a pointer to the first available word in SPACE at the current time;

```
template  1 BLOCK,
             2 LENGTH              INTEGER,
             2 POINT               POINTER to BLOCK,
             2 MARK                BIT,
             2 USE(● LENGTH)       BIT,
             2 filler              WORD,
             2 DATA (● LENGTH)     POINTER to BLOCK;
declare FREE                       POINTER to BLOCK global;
declare SPACE(SIZE)                WORD global;
declare SIZE                       INTEGER global;
declare (NWDSTOT,NWORDS,COUNT)     INTEGER;
NWDSTOT := NWORDS + 2 + [(1 + NWORDS) / NBPW];
if (NWDSTOT + FREE − 1 > @SPACE(SIZE)
then begin
    call REGEN2;
    if (NWDSTOT + FREE − 1 > @SPACE(SIZE)
    then call ABORT ('MEMORY OVERFLOW IN GETBLK2') endif
    end endif;
comment Allocate the block and initialize its header;
GETBLK2 := FREE;
[FREE].LENGTH := NWORDS;
[FREE].MARK := '0';
COUNT := 1;
comment Set USE bits to '0';
while (COUNT ≤ NWORDS) do
    begin
        [FREE].USE(COUNT) := '0';
        COUNT := COUNT + 1
    end;
FREE := FREE + NWDSTOT;
return;
end GETBLK2;
```

Implementation note

The algorithm GETBLK2 presented above directly modifies the LENGTH, MARK, and USE bits of the allocated structure. An alternative approach is to declare a static block within procedure GETBLK2 that is as large as the header of any block that will be allocated. (If this is not practical, then GETBLK2 as described above should be used.) When a block is allocated, GETBLK2 first modifies the fields in the local static block. After the header is created, GETBLK2 then copies the header into the dynamic region where the block is allocated. In that way, only the final copy procedure would be directly accessing dynamic memory. This would be advantageous in a virtual memory environment. (We assume that the copy procedure would copy the header information in the most efficient way possible.)

6.5. MARKING ALGORITHMS

A marking algorithm must mark all blocks referenced either directly or indirectly by words whose addresses are on the initial address list. There are many different algorithms that can be used; we will present four: MARK2, MARK3, MARK4, and MARK5. MARK2 is a recursive algorithm that is presented for pedagogical reasons; although short, MARK2 requires memory for the recursion stack which may not be available. MARK3 is an iterative algorithm that assumes that the blocks can be processed sequentially. MARK4 is a stack algorithm that uses a breadth-first marking strategy. (Refer to Chapter 4 for a discussion of breadth-first search.) Although memory is not available for a large stack, the technique can be used with a limited sized stack to speed up the other marking algorithms. MARK5 is also a stack algorithm; however, MARK5 uses a 'depth-first' strategy and keeps the stack within the pointer fields of the structure being marked. A combination of the techniques of MARK5 and MARK4 is faster than either algorithm and is left as an exercise for the reader.

For the following discussion, we assume that an initial address list has been established containing the addresses of all external references to blocks that are active. It is further assumed that if I is a block address and [I].USE(J) is '1', then [I].DATA(J) is a pointer to another block. (For a system that uses cells rather than blocks, the USE bit information is generally implicit in the structure. See Chapter 7.) An example block is shown below:

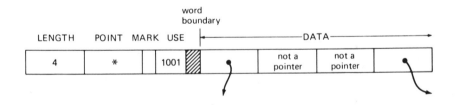

The following algorithm is recursive and marks all blocks that are referenced by pointer A. This procedure must be invoked for each block referenced by the initial address list.

procedure MARK2(BLK);
comment Pointers are word addresses. If P is a pointer, then P+1 is the address of the following word;

```
template  1 BLOCK,
          2 LENGTH          INTEGER,
          2 POINT           INTEGER,
          2 MARK            BIT,
          2 USE(• LENGTH)   BIT,
          2 filler          WORD,
          2 DATA (•LENGTH)  POINTER to BLOCK;
declare BLK POINTER to BLOCK;
declare J INTEGER;
if ( [BLK].MARK = '1') then return;
[BLK].MARK := '1';
J := 1;
while (J ≤ [BLK].LENGTH) do
        begin
            if ( [BLK].USE(J) = '1' and [BLK].DATA(J) ≠ null)
            then call MARK2([BLK].DATA(J))endif
        end;
end MARK2;
```

Although simple, the procedure defeats the purpose for which it was written! When memory is exhausted, the problem is to recover those blocks of memory that are not in use. The algorithm correctly marks the active blocks, but it does so at the cost of maintaining all linkage necessary for recursion. Since memory is already exhausted, there is no memory left for maintaining the recursive linkage; the problem, therefore, is to discover an algorithm that does not require memory in excess of what is already in use.

The following procedure satisfies the memory requirement and can be used in any environment in which the blocks can be processed sequentially, in the order in which they appear in memory. This is true not only for the system being described, but also for systems that use fixed size cells with a uniform internal structure. The procedure first marks all blocks referenced directly by the initial address list. Next, starting with the first block in memory, the algorithm sequentially processes each block as follows: If a block is marked, then the procedure marks all unmarked blocks that are directly referenced by that block. After all blocks in memory are processed, the process is repeated until no more blocks are marked during an entire scan of memory. The process then terminates. The algorithm is as follows:

```
procedure MARK3;
comment  Pointers are word addresses. If P is a pointer, then P+1 is the address of the
         following word;
comment  Let IALIST be the initial address list, and let NLIST be its length.
         DONE is a flag that is set when a block is marked during the current pass of
         memory;
```

```
template  1 BLOCK,
          2 LENGTH              INTEGER,
          2 POINT               INTEGER,
          2 MARK                BIT,
          2 USE(• LENGTH)       BIT,
          2 filler              WORD,
          2 DATA(• LENGTH)      POINTER to BLOCK;
declare       FREE                  POINTER to BLOCK global;
declare       BLK                   POINTER to BLOCK;
declare       IALIST (NLIST)        POINTER to POINTER global;
declare       SPACE(SIZE)           WORD global;
comment Mark all directly referenced blocks;
I := 1;
while (I ≤ NLIST) do
        begin
                BLK := [IALIST(I) ];
                [BLK].MARK := '1';
                I := I + 1
        end;
comment Mark all indirectly referenced blocks;
DONE := false;
while (DONE = false) do
  begin
     BLK := @SPACE;
     DONE := true;
     while (BLK < FREE) do
        begin
           if ( [BLK].MARK = '1')
           then begin
                   J := 1;
                   while (J ≤ [BLK].LENGTH) do
                      begin
                         if ( [BLK].USE(J) = '1' and
                            [BLK].DATA(J) ≠ 0 and
                            [ [BLK].DATA(J) ].MARK≠ '1')
                         then begin
                                 [[BLK].DATA(J)].MARK := '1';
                                 DONE := false
                              end endif;
                         J := J + 1
                      end
                end endif;
           comment Process the next block;
           BLK := BLK + [BLK].LENGTH + 2
                      + [(1 + [BLK].LENGTH)/NBPW]
```

```
      end
    end;
return;
end MARK3;
```

Exercise 6.6. Algorithm MARK3 is slow and requires repeated passes of memory in order to mark all active blocks. In the worst case, an entire pass of memory will be required for marking each block. Prove that this algorithm, therefore, requires execution time proportional to $N**2$, where N is the number of blocks which are finally marked.

Exercise 6.7. Some efficiency can be gained by recording the low and high addresses of blocks marked during any pass of memory and, on the next pass, limiting processing to blocks whose addresses fall within the recorded range. Give an algorithm for this improved marking procedure.

Exercise 6.8. Modify MARK3 so that it is correct for the system described in Chapter 7, page 310. (MARK3 will replace the call to MARK6.)

We will now give an algorithm that, although fast, suffers from the same difficulty that the recursive marking algorithm described above did: namely, it requires memory (a stack) for its implementation, and memory is not available. If, however, the entire marking procedure can be executed using a stack of limited size, then this algorithm marks all active blocks in time proportional to the number of blocks that are marked; hence it is an ideal algorithm as far as execution speed. (Refer to Chapter 2 for the details of the PUSH and POP procedures.) The basic procedure is as follows. Push the address of each block directly referenced by the initial address list on a stack, and mark it. Repeat until the stack is empty: pop the stack and place on the stack the address of each unmarked block that is referenced. Mark it as it is pushed in the stack. The algorithm for this procedure follows.

```
procedure MARK4;
comment  Let BSTACK be a stack on which addresses can be placed and retrieved by the
         routines PUSH and POP.
         Let IALIST be the initial address list, and let NLIST be its length;
template  1 BLOCK,
             2 LENGTH            INTEGER,
             2 POINT             INTEGER,
             2 MARK              BIT,
             2 USE(● LENGTH)     BIT,
             2 filler            WORD,
             2 DATA(● LENGTH)    POINTER to BLOCK;
declare BLK                      POINTER to BLOCK;
declare IALIST(NLIST)            POINTER to POINTER global;
declare (NLIST,I,K)              INTEGER;
comment Mark all directly referenced blocks;
I := 1;
```

```
while (I ≤ NLIST) do
        begin
                    BLK := [IALIST(I)];
                    [BLK].MARK := '1';
                    call PUSH(BSTACK,BLK);
                    I := I + 1
        end;
comment Mark all indirectly referenced blocks;
while ([EMPTY(BSTACK) ) do
        begin
                    BLK := POP(BSTACK);
                    LEN := [BLK].LENGTH;
                    K := 1;
                    while (K ≤ LEN) do
                            begin
                              if ([BLK].USE(K) = '1' and
                                  [BLK].DATA(K) ≠ null
                                  and [[BLK].DATA(K)].MARK ≠ '1')
                              then begin
                                    [ [BLK].DATA(K) ].MARK := '1';
                                    call PUSH(BSTACK,[BLK].DATA(K) )
                                  end endif;
                              K := K +1
                            end
        end;
return;
end MARK4;
```

Exercise 6.9. Some efficiency can be gained by combining the techniques of MARK3 and MARK4, but using a fixed size stack. If the stack overflows, then the elements at the bottom of the stack are lost, and after the stack is emptied, another pass of memory is required. If, however, a complete pass of memory is made without stack overflow, the procedure terminates. Give an algorithm for this improved marking procedure.

As mentioned earlier, the difficulty with MARK4 is that there may not be memory for the maintenance of the stack BSTACK. The following algorithm is a stack algorithm but does not require an independent stack! The 'stack' is maintained by changing the direction of each pointer as the routine descends into the structure. Changing the directions of the pointers enables MARK5 to ascend from the structure. When ascending, MARK5 again reverses the directions of the pointers, thereby restoring the original structure. In contrast to MARK4 which marks blocks in a breadth-first fashion, MARK5 employs a depth-first marking strategy. (See Chapter 4). In order to do this, however, it is necessary to keep track of which DATA word the routine is currently processing. This is done by storing the word number in the POINT field of the block header while descending. The value that is left in the POINT field after the routine finishes is irrelevant for other parts of memory regeneration. Figures 6.9 to 6.15 show how the structure of Figure 6.8 would look during various stages of processing of the routine MARK5.

```
procedure MARK5(A);
comment A is a pointer to the current block being processed.
        B and C are temporary pointers that point to the previous two blocks in the
        structure during the ascending and descending steps.
        ASCEND is a flag that is set to false when returning to the top cell of the
        structure during ascent;
template  1 BLOCK,
          2 LENGTH              INTEGER,
          2 POINT               INTEGER,
          2 MARK                BIT,
          2 USE(• LENGTH)       BIT,
          2 filler              WORD,
          2 DATA(• LENGTH)      POINTER to BLOCK;
declare (A,B,C)                 POINTER to BLOCK;
declare ASCEND                  BOOLEAN;
if ( [A].MARK ≠ '1')
then begin
        ASCEND := true;
        [A].POINT := 1;
        [A].MARK := '1';
        B := null;
        C := null;
        while (ASCEND = true) do
          begin
            comment Descend as far as possible;
            while ( [A].POINT ≤ [A].LENGTH) do
              begin
                if ( [A].USE( [A].POINT) = '1'
                and [A].DATA( [A].POINT) ≠ null
                and [ [A].DATA( [A].POINT) ].
                  MARK = '0')
                then begin
                        comment Descend one level;
                        B := A;
                        A := [A].DATA( [A].POINT);
                        [B].DATA( [B].POINT) := C;
                        C := B;
                        [A].MARK := '1';
                        [A].POINT := 1;
                    end
                else [A].POINT := [A].POINT + 1 endif
              end;
```

comment Now ascend one level if possible;
if (B ≠ **null**)
then begin

    comment Ascend one level;
    C := [B].DATA([B].POINT);
    [B].DATA([B].POINT) := A;
    A := B;
    B := C;
    [A].POINT := [A].POINT + 1

end
else begin

    comment The entire structure is now marked;
    ASCEND := **false**

    end endif

  end
  end endif;
return;
end MARK5;

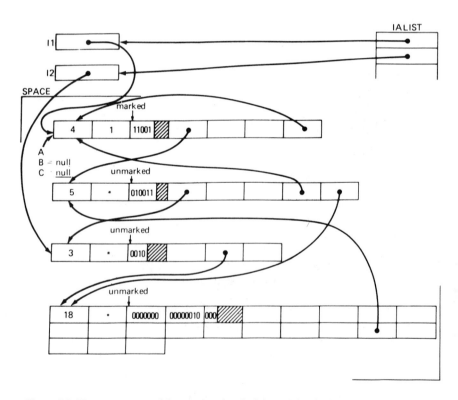

Figure 6.9. The appearance of the structure just before entering the inner **while-do** statement.

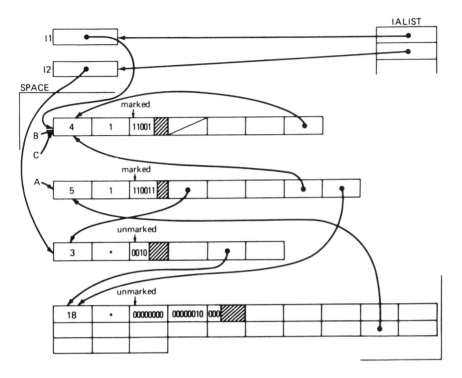

Figure 6.10. The appearance of the structure just before reentering the inner **while-do** statement. The pointers A, B, and C are maintaining the linkage information for the removed link, and the null pointer [B].DATA(1) indicates the 'top' of the structure.

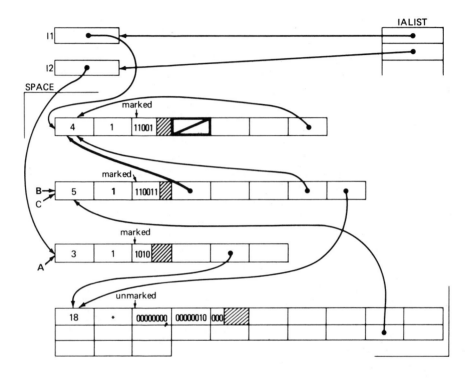

Figure 6.11. The appearance of the structure just before reentering the inner **while-do** statement. The darkened area represents stack information.

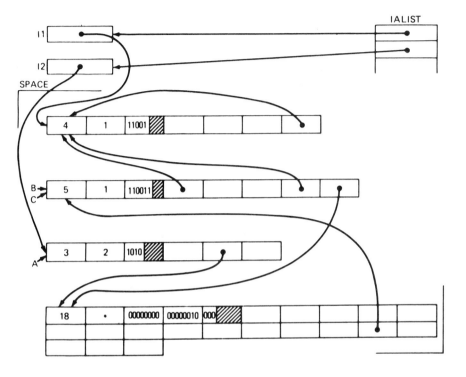

Figure 6.12. The appearance of the structure after entering the inner **while-do** statement once, but not the second time, at the current level.

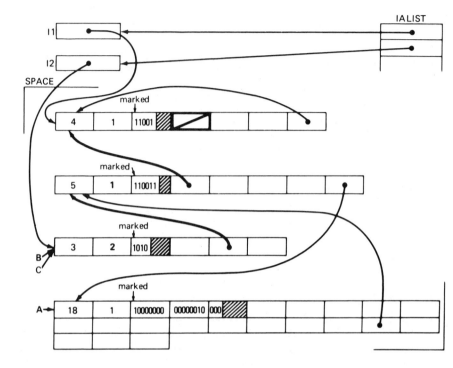

Figure 6.13. The appearance of the structure just before entering the inner **while-do** statement at the current level of descent. Note that all blocks have now been marked; hence the ascent will begin. The darkened area again represents stack information.

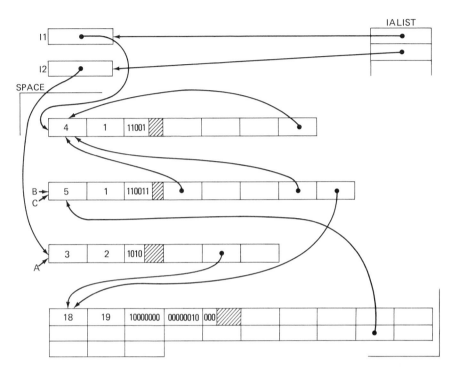

Figure 6.14. The appearance of the structure after ascending one level. Note that one link has already been reset.

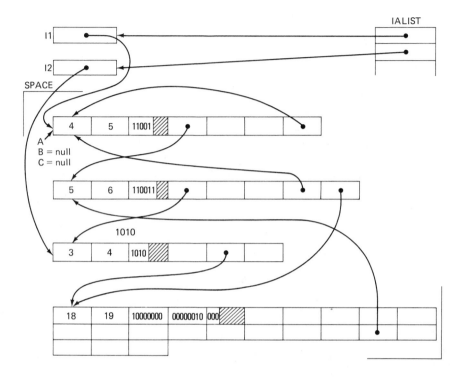

Figure 6.15. The appearance of the structure when marking is complete.

Exercise 6.10. Indicate the order in which MARK4 and MARK5 would mark the blocks in the structures shown below:

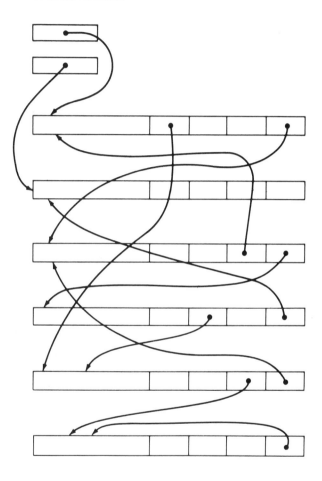

Exercise 6.11. As written, MARK5 must be invoked for each block that is referenced by the initial address list. Modify MARK5 to process all blocks on the initial address list.

Exercise 6.12. Modify MARK5 so that: 1) it does not require the POINT field but uses instead a single bit, B; and 2) the blocks are all uniform-size cells having the following structure:

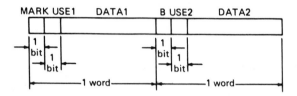

If USE1=$'1'$, then DATA1 is a pointer; otherwise DATA1 is not a pointer. Similarly, if USE2=$'1'$, then DATA2 is a pointer; otherwise DATA2 is not a pointer.

Exercise 6.13. Some execution time can be saved by providing the marking routine MARK5 with a limited size stack and combining the techniques of MARK4 and MARK5. If it turns out that all of the data structures can be marked using the limited stack and following the technique of MARK4, then the ideal situation would result. However, if it turns out that the stack overflows, then the technique of algorithm MARK5 can be employed. Give a marking procedure, MARK6, which combines a limited size stack with the technique of algorithm MARK5.

6.6 MEMORY COMPACTION

Memory compaction for this system is somewhat more complicated than for the first system described in this chapter. The difficulty is not in relocating the blocks that were marked; in fact, that is done just as before. The difficulty is in updating all the block pointers. For this system, memory compaction is done in several stages. First, all blocks are sequentially processed to determine where they will be located after compaction. During this process, the new address of each block is placed in the POINT field of its header. (Recall that the POINT field was used as a temporary memory location by the marking routine MARK5, but the information left by MARK5 is no longer needed.) Next, the initial address list is used once more, this time for updating the external block references. In particular, each pointer referenced by the initial address list is given the value in the POINT field of the block to which it refers (the location that the block will have after compaction). Next, the blocks are processed sequentially. This time, each DATA word whose corresponding USE bit is set is changed to the value of the POINT field of the block that it points to; this updates all the pointers contained within the blocks themselves. Finally, the blocks are moved to the position indicated by their POINT fields. The pointer FREE is updated just before exiting the procedure. An algorithm for memory compaction is given below:

```
procedure COMPACT2;
comment Pointers are word addresses. If P is a pointer, then P+1 is the address of the
        following word;
template  1 BLOCK,
            2 LENGTH            INTEGER,
            2 POINT             POINTER to BLOCK,
            2 MARK              BIT,
            2 USE(• LENGTH)     BIT,
            2 filler            WORD,
            2 DATA(• LENGTH)    POINTER to BLOCK;
declare (FREE1,BLK)         POINTER to BLOCK;
declare (SIZE,N,LIST)       INTEGER global;
declare FREE                POINTER to BLOCK global;
declare (LEN,J)             INTEGER;
declare SPACE(SIZE)         WORD global;
declare IALIST(NLIST)       POINTER global;
comment Compute new block addresses and place in POINT field;
FREE1 := @SPACE;
BLK := @SPACE;
while (BLK < FREE) do
        begin
                LEN := [BLK].LENGTH +2 +[( [BLK].
                LENGTH + 1) / NBPW];
                if ( [BLK].MARK = '1')
                then begin
                        [BLK].POINT := FREE1;
                        FREE1 := FREE1 + LEN
                     end endif;
                BLK := BLK + LEN
        end;
comment Update block pointers referenced by the initial address list;
J := 1;
while (J ≤ NLIST) do
        begin
                BLK := [IALIST(J) ];
                IALIST(J) := [BLK].POINT;
                J := J + 1
        end;
comment Update the block pointers that are within the DATA fields of the blocks;
BLK := @SPACE;
while (BLK < FREE) do
        begin
                if ( [BLK].MARK = '1')
                then begin
                        J := 1;
                        while (J ≤ [BLK].LENGTH) do
```

```
                              begin
                                if ( [BLK].USE(J) = '1' and [BLK].DATA
                                (J) ≠ null)
                                then [BLK].DATA(J) :=
                                     [[BLK].DATA(J)].POINT endif;
                                J := J + 1
                              end
                  end
                  BLK := BLK + [BLK].LENGTH + 2 +[( [BLK].
                  LENGTH + 1) / NBPW]
         end;
comment Relocate the blocks;
BLK := @SPACE;
FREE1 := @SPACE;
while (BLK < FREE) do
         begin
                  LEN := [BLK].LENGTH + 2 +[( [BLK].
                  LENGTH + 1) / NBPW];
                  if ( [BLK].MARK = '1'
                  then begin
                       [BLK].MARK := '0';
                       J := 0;
                       while (J < LEN) do
                       begin
                          comment Blocks are moved 1 word at a time;
                          [FREE1 + J] := [BLK + J];
                          J := J + 1
                       end;
                       FREE1 := FREE1 + LEN
                       end endif;
                  BLK := BLK + LEN
         end;
comment Update FREE;
FREE := FREE1;
return;
end COMPACT2;
```

The complete memory regeneration routine can now be easily written using MARK5 and COMPACT2 as follows:

```
procedure      REGEN2;
declare        IALIST(NLIST)              POINTER global;
declare        NLIST                      INTEGER global;
declare        BLK                        POINTER;
comment Mark all blocks referenced by the initial address list;
```

```
I := 1;
while (I ≤ NLIST) do
      begin
            BLK := [IALIST(I) ];
            call MARK5(BLK);
            I := I + 1
      end;
call COMPACT2;
end REGEN2;
```

Exercise 6.14. Suppose that the blocks in the first system presented in this chapter are allowed to contain pointers to other blocks. That is, assume that the header contains MARK and USE bits that are used as described for the above system. However, assume that pointers in the DATA words point to secondary block pointers rather than directly to blocks. Modify the routine MARK1 so that it properly marks all blocks that are active. What changes, if any, would have to be made to REGEN1 for such a system to work?

Example. SNOBOL4 arrays.

The memory management techniques employed by the macro implementation of SNOBOL4 are similar to those described above. The primary difference is that there are no USE bit fields in the block headers. Instead, each block has a header (called its 'title') that has a type field. The type field specifies how the data is organized in the block and hence is used to determine which fields may contain pointers to other blocks. The marking and compaction routines inspect the type field of each block as it is processed and then determine if further processing of the block's data elements is necessary.

As a specific example, the illustration below shows the basic structure of an array in SNOBOL4. Arrays are created by source statements of the form A = ARRAY('<dimensions>','<initial value>'). The first parameter to the ARRAY function is called the array *prototype* and is stored in memory (in an

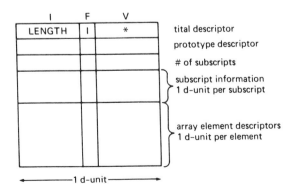

allocated block) as a string. In the illustration, a string is indicated by a pointer to the characters of the string enclosed in brackets ({ and }). The second parameter is used to set the initial values of the array elements and will not be of concern here. The first parameter is a string composed of subscript bounds separated by commas. Each subscript bound is of one of two forms: a simple, positive integer or a pair of integers separated by a colon with the restriction that the first is smaller than the second. For example, A = ARRAY('3,4,5') allocates an array having three subscripts whose bounds are 1 to 3, 1 to 4, and 1 to 5, respectively; thus the array has a total of 60 elements. If a subscript bound is a pair of integers separated by a colon, then the range of subscripts is from the first to the second. Thus, B = ARRAY('−3:5') allocates an array having one subscript and a total of nine elements.

Instead of using words as the basic data units, SNOBOL4 uses descriptor units, or d-units, which, depending on the computer to be used, may be a single word, several words, or some other machine unit. Each d-unit is divided into three fields, T, F, and V. The array itself requires one d-unit for each array element; an additional d-unit for each subscript; one d-unit to point to the array prototype; and one d-unit for the block title. The memory representation of the array created by the statement ARRAY('2,3:5,11:13') is shown below. The array has 23 d-units plus a title. The title of the array has the value 23d in its T field, which specifies the total length of the allocated block (not including its title). The F field of the title is a flag that indicates that the following 23 d-units

23d	I	*
S	A	• → {2, 3:5, 11:13}
0	0	3
3	0	11
3	0	3
2	0	1
⋮	⋮	⋮

18 descriptors, one for each array element

may be pointers, and the V field is used by the memory regeneration routines just as the POINT field is in the last system described in this chapter. In general, if a d-unit contains a pointer to a block in allocated memory, then its F field contains the flag 'A' (for allocated). If the d-unit contains immediate data, then the F field contains the flag '0'. The T field of a descriptor is a datatype flag that contains a code for the type of item referenced by the descriptor (S for string, I for integer, R for real, and so on). Hence the memory regeneration routines can process the 23 d-units following the title and determine whether or not they point to other blocks which are to be further processed.

Other data structures in SNOBOL4 are similar in that the title is always the first d-unit of an allocated block, and, by inspecting the title, the memory regeneration procedures can immediately determine 1) how long the block is; and 2) how the d-units of the block should be processed; Hence memory regeneration can take place in a manner almost identical to that described in this chapter.

Exercise 6.15. Give suitable **template** and **declare** statements for the SNOBOL4 array representation, and give efficient procedures for storing and retrieving element values. In particular, ENTVAL(A,S,V) stores the descriptor V in the element of array A whose subscripts are given in S, and GETVAL(A,S) returns the descriptor that is stored in the same array element. In case of a subscript error, ENTVAL and GETVAL should return the special value *failure*.

6.7 SUMMARY

Dynamic memory management using sequential memory allocation and compaction is a useful technique provided that: 1) all external references are known; 2) all internal references can be determined; 3) there is sufficient memory available to maintain a block header in each block; and 4) compaction does not occur so frequently that execution time is prohibitive. When using memory regeneration with compaction, the time required is proportional to the amount of memory in use when regeneration begins. Memory compaction eliminates fragmentation and tends to localize memory references, two important considerations for many practical systems. String processing systems and programming languages, such as SNOBOL4, effectively utilize these techniques, but their usefulness extends to a much wider range of applications.

Projects

Project 6.1. One feature common to many string processing systems is that strings which are created early during program execution are either liberated early, or they remain fixed during the entire program execution; constant string definitions and strings used as labels during output are two examples. The memory management routines can be speeded up if that part of memory which remains essentially constant during one memory regeneration is not modified during subsequent memory regenerations. Design a memory management system, and give a complete set of memory management algorithms that incorporates this idea.

Project 6.2. Design and code a collection of procedures for performing arbitrary precision arithmetic. The following discussion indicates the nature of the procedures and suitable encodings for arithmetic data.

An integer can be represented by a string of numerals. For instance '123' represents the integer 123, and '335647298800' represents the integer 335647298800, which is too big to be processed directly by most computers. Such a string is an *integer string*. Let A designate some integer string, and let v(A) be the integer value of the designated string. The following routines should be coded:

PLUS(A,B) Returns a pointer to an integer string designating the value v(A) + v(B).

TIMES(A,B) Returns a pointer to an integer string designating the value v(A) * v(B).

MINUS(A,B) Returns a pointer to an integer string designating the value v(A) − v(B).

POWER(A,I) Returns a pointer to an integer string designating the value v(A)**I.

CVITS(I) (*ConVert Integer To String*) Returns a pointer to an integer string designating the value of the integer I.

CVSTI(A) (*ConVert String To Integer*) Returns the integer v(A). If v(A) cannot be represented in a single computer word, then CVSTI invokes an error procedure OVFLO that prints an appropriate error message before returning control to CVSTI. CVSTI then returns the value 0.

ENCODE(I,J) I is an array of characters that is not a part of the memory management routines being written. I must contain a sequence of J characters consisting entirely of the digits, possibly preceded by the character '-'. ENCODE returns a pointer to an integer string that designates the integer whose character representation is in the array I.

READI(Q) Q is a file number for input. READI reads a character string as input data and creates an integer string whose value is the integer in the input stream. (The input must be a valid integer.)

PRINTI(A,Q) The character representation of the integer v(A) is printed in the output file Q.

As an example, consider the code given below:

$$A = ENCODE('123456',6)$$
$$B = ENCODE('765432',6)$$
$$C = PLUS(A,B)$$
$$D = TIMES(C,A)$$
$$CALL\ PRINTI(A,6)$$
$$CALL\ PRINTI(B,6)$$
$$CALL\ PRINTI(C,6)$$
$$CALL\ PRINTI(D,6)$$

The output corresponding to these statements would appear in output file number 6 as follows:

123456
765432
888888
109738556921

Base your procedures on a dynamic memory allocation system. You may either use garbage collection and compaction or include procedures for explicitly liberating unwanted strings; however, you must compact memory.

Project 6.3. When working with a cell-oriented system that uses one size of cell, the following memory compaction procedure, which relocates some but not all of the cells that are active during memory regeneration, may be used. First, a standard marking procedure is invoked. After marking, imagine that memory is divided into two blocks, as illustrated below, where the number of inactive cells in the left (low-address) block equals the number of active cells in the right block. Beginning at the leftmost active cell in the right block, copy its contents into the first available, inactive cell in the left block. Replace the contents of the active cell by the address of the formerly inactive cell. Repeat this process until all active cells have been copied from the right block into the left block and all old cells in the right block have been replaced by the addresses of their copies. See the second illustration below. Now process all cells in the left block sequentially as follows. If one of the fields of a cell contains a pointer to a cell in the right block, replace that pointer with the pointer in the cell pointed to; this updated address is now the correct address for the referenced cell's new location. Give a complete set of algorithms for this memory regeneration technique. How does this algorithm compare for speed and memory usage with the compaction algorithm?

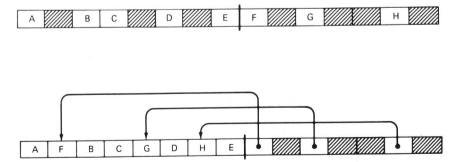

REFERENCES AND ADDITIONAL READINGS

Books

Griswold, R.E. (1972) *The Macro Implementation of SNOBOL4*. San Francisco: W.H. Freeman and Co.

Knuth, D.E. (1973) *The Art of Computer Programming, Volume 1/Fundamental Algorithms*, Second Edition. Reading, Massachusetts: Addison-Wesley Publishing Co., Inc.

Peck, J.E.L. (Ed.) (1971) *ALGOL 68 Implementations*. Amsterdam: North-Holland Publishing Co.

Pratt, T.W. (1975) *Programming Languages: Design and Implementation*. Englewood Cliffs, New Jersey: Prentice-Hall, Inc.

Articles and Technical Reports

Balkovich, E.; Chiu, W.; Presser, L.; and Wood, R. Dynamic memory repacking. *CACM* Vol. 17, No. 3, Mar. 1974, 133-138.

Bailey, M.J.; Barnett, M.P.; and Burleson, P.B. Symbol manipulation in FORTRAN—SASP I. *CACM* Vol. 17, No. 3, June 1964, 339-346.

Berztiss, A.T. A note on storage of strings. *CACM* Vol. 8, No. 8, Aug. 1965, 512-513.

Branquart, P., and Leur, J. A scheme of storage allocation and garbage collection for ALGOL 68. In Peck (1971), 199-238.

Britton, D.C. Heap storage management for the programming language Pascal. Master's Thesis, 1975, Department of Computer Science, The University of Arizona.

Cheney, C.J. A nonrecursive list compacting algorithm. *CACM* Vol. 13, No. 11, Nov. 1970, 677-678.

Fenichel, R.R. List tracing in systems allowing multiple cell-types. *CACM* Vol. 14, No. 8, Aug. 1971, 522-526.

Griswold, R.E. Highlights of two implementations of SNOBOL4. Technical report S4D55, February 1977, Department of Computer Science, The University of Arizona.

Griswold, R.E. SNOBOL4 internal structures, a source book for the macro implementation. Technical Report S4D46, December 1974, Department of Computer Science, The University of Arizona.

Hanson, D.R. Dynamic allocation and reclamation of variable-size storage elements in SITBOL. Technical Report S4D52a, July 1975, Department of Computer Science, The University of Arizona.

Hirschberg, D.S. A class of dynamic memory allocation algorithms. *CACM* Vol. 16, No. 10, Oct. 1973, 615-618.

Kain, R.Y. Block structures, indirect addressing, and garbage collection. *CACM* Vol. 12, No. 7, July 1969, 395-398.

Marshall, S. An ALGOL 68 garbage collector. In Peck (1971), 239-244.

Morris, F.L. A time- and space-efficient garbage compaction algorithm. *CACM* Vol. 21, No. 8, Aug. 1978, 662-665.

Nielsen, N.R. Dynamic memory allocation in computer simulation. *CACM* Vol. 20, No. 11, Nov. 1977, 864-873.

Steele, G.L., Jr. Multiprocessing compactifying garbage collection. *CACM* Vol. 18, No. 9, Sept. 1975, 495-508.

Thorelli, L-E. A fast compactifying garbage collector. *BIT* Vol. 16, No. 4, 1976, 426-441.

Wegbreit, B. A generalized compactifying garbage collector. *Computer J.* Vol. 15, No. 3, Aug. 1972, 204-208.

Weinstock, C.B. Dynamic storage allocation techniques. Technical Report, April 1976, Department of Computer Science, Carnegie-Mellon University.

Wodon, P.L. Methods of garbage collection for ALGOL 68. In Peck (1971), 245-262.

7
Dynamic memory management using lists of available space

OVERVIEW

In this chapter, we discuss dynamic memory management systems that maintain linked lists of available space, out of which cells or blocks are allocated and into which cells or blocks are placed when liberated. The first part of the chapter deals with cell-oriented memory management techniques used by list processing systems and discusses how to maintain lists of available space, using either garbage collection or reference counts. The second part of the chapter discusses two different block-oriented memory management techniques used by operating systems: buddy systems and systems that maintain blocks with boundary tags.

7.1 INTRODUCTION

There are several different techniques for dynamic memory management. In the previous chapter, we discussed systems that allocate memory sequentially and, during memory regeneration, compact all active blocks so that available space is in one contiguous area of memory. Memory compaction, however, requires substantial execution time and one full field per block for the future address of the block; furthermore, because it is necessary to adjust essentially all block pointers during memory compaction, the memory management procedures must know which fields contain pointers to other blocks and which do not.

There are several different classes of systems where it is either impractical or impossible to use sequential memory management techniques: cell-oriented systems where the cells are small and therefore the cost in memory of maintaining the future address pointers is prohibitive; cell-oriented systems that allocate and liberate memory so frequently that the time required for memory compaction is prohibitive; and block-oriented systems where it is not known which fields contain pointers to other blocks, and therefore memory cannot be compacted at all. These systems have in common the fact that available space is not a heap at all but is organized into lists from which blocks are allocated and into which blocks are placed when liberated.

The first part of this chapter discusses memory management for cell-oriented systems. List processing systems, such as LISP, are cell-oriented systems that use available space lists. LISP programs require many thousands of cells, and the memory requirements often prohibit the cells from having the extra, future pointer field. Finally, since all cells are the same size, fragmentation does not occur and therefore memory compaction is not necessary.

The second part of this chapter describes dynamic memory management for operating systems. Operating systems that dynamically allocate memory generally use lists of available space. Operating systems are block-oriented systems, the blocks being allocated for programs, when requested by programs, for input-output buffers, and so on. In this case, memory compaction is usually not feasible because of the large amount of time that would be required. In fact, in some cases memory compaction is impossible (often depending on the particular hardware), because the operating system does not know which words in the allocated blocks are pointers and which are not; hence sequential memory management techniques cannot be used. In these cases, linked lists of available space are generally employed.

A *list of available space* or *free list* is a linked structure that contains all blocks or cells that are available for allocation. For systems that use cells, the list of available space consists of linked cells. For systems that allocate cells having a few different sizes, independent lists of available space are frequently maintained for each different cell size. For systems that allocate blocks of arbitrary size, a single list of available space is maintained, where each block on the list is the largest, contiguous collection of memory locations between two adjacent blocks that are in use. Figures 7.1 to 7.3 illustrate the lists of available space for these three types of system.

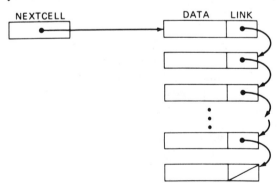

Figure 7.1. A list of available space for a system that uses cells of one size.

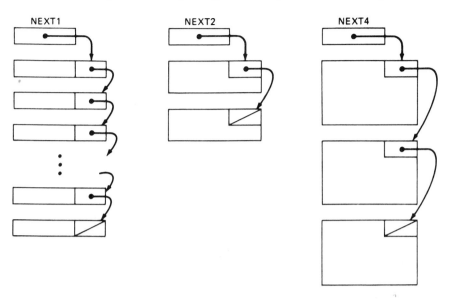

Figure 7.2. Lists of available space for a system that uses three sizes of cells.

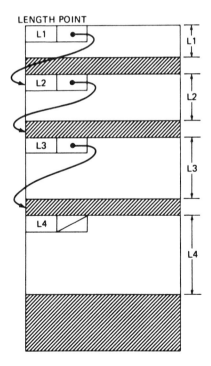

Figure 7.3. A list of available space for a system that allocates blocks of arbitrary size. The shaded areas are blocks that are currently active.

7.2 MEMORY MANAGEMENT TECHNIQUES USED BY LIST PROCESSING SYSTEMS

7.2.1 Allocating cells

The simplest, dynamic memory management systems are those that allocate and liberate cells of a single size. In general, at the beginning of program execution a single block of memory is set aside. The block is divided into cells of the desired size, which are then linked together to form the initial list of available space. Figure 7.1 shows the structure of a cell and the structure of the list of available space. NEXTCELL is a pointer to the top of the list of available space, and the LINK field of the last element of the list of available space is **null**. The procedure FORMLAVS (*FORM* *L*ist of *AV*ailable *S*pace) that initially creates the list of available space is given below:

```
procedure FORMLAVS(SPACE,SIZE,CELLSIZE);
comment SPACE is the block out of which CELLS are to be allocated.
        SIZE is the size of SPACE in words.
        CELLSIZE is the number of words in a cell;
template    1 CELL,
            2 LINK      POINTER to CELL,
            2 DATA      WORD;
declare (NEXTCELL,I)    POINTER to CELL;
declare SPACE(SIZE)     WORD;
declare (SIZE,CELLSIZE) INTEGER;
NEXTCELL := @SPACE;
I := @SPACE;
while (I + CELLSIZE − 1 ≤ @SPACE(SIZE)) do
    begin
        [I].LINK := I + CELLSIZE;
        I := I + CELLSIZE
    end;
I := I − CELLSIZE;
[I].LINK := null;
return;
end FORMLAVS;
```

Once the list of available space is created, it is a simple matter to allocate cells and place liberated cells back on the list. To allocate a cell, the value of NEXTCELL is returned, and NEXTCELL is changed to [NEXTCELL].LINK. To liberate a cell pointed to by A, [A].LINK is set to NEXTCELL, and then NEXTCELL is set to A. Since cells are placed on the top of the list of available space and removed from its top, in this system the list of available space is a stack. ABORT is invoked in case a request is made for a cell when the list of available space is empty. Procedure GETCELL1 for allocating cells and procedure FREECELL1 for liberating cells are given below:

```
procedure GETCELL1;
comment GETCELL1 returns a pointer to the allocated cell;
template    1 CELL,
            2 LINK      POINTER to CELL,
            2 DATA      WORD;
declare (NEXTCELL,GETCELL1)   POINTER to CELL;
if (NEXTCELL = null)
then call ABORT('MEMORY OVERFLOW IN GETCELL1') endif;
GETCELL1 := NEXTCELL;
NEXTCELL := [NEXTCELL].LINK;
return;
end GETCELL1;
procedure FREECELL1(A);
comment A is a pointer to the cell being liberated;
template    1 CELL,
            2 LINK      POINTER to CELL1,
            2 DATA      WORD;
declare (A, NEXTCELL)   POINTER to CELL;
[A].LINK := NEXTCELL;
NEXTCELL := A;
return;
end FREECELL1;
```

The procedures for allocating and liberating cells in this system are short and fast. However, in list processing systems, it is often not practical to liberate cells one at a time. Although the cell is the basic memory unit that is allocated, cells are linked together to form lists, and lists point to other lists to form list structures. Once formed, list elements (cells) are occasionally liberated, but lists and list structures are often liberated as well.

Exercise 7.1. Suppose that a system creates circular lists of the form shown below. Write a procedure, FREELIST, that liberates all cells of a given list. For example, the statement **call** FREELIST(A) would liberate all cells of the illustrated list and set the value of A to **null**.

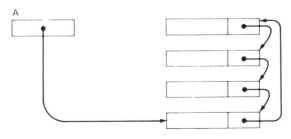

7.2.2 Dangling references

Figure 7.4 below shows a list structure having several lists and sublists. If a program constructs such a structure and then wishes to liberate list L2, for example, one major difficulty becomes evident: should the cells of the indirectly referenced lists, in this case lists L3 and L4, also be liberated? As the figure shows, the fourth cell of list L2 points to list L3, which is not otherwise referenced; however, the fifth cell points to list L4 which is referenced by another structure, list L1. How is the procedure that liberates list L2 to know which case pertains to each sublist?

A cell, list, or list structure is *active* if it is referenced directly by one or more

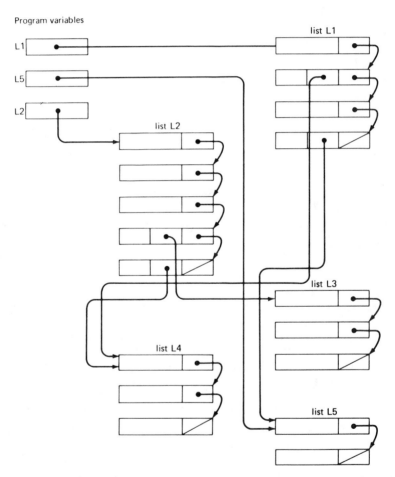

Figure 7.4. The memory representation of three program variables, L1, L2, and L5, and five lists. List L3 is a sublist of list L2; list L4 is a sublist of lists L1 and L2; and list L5 is a sublist of list L1.

program variables; a cell, list, or list structure is also active if it is referenced by one or more active cells. If a cell is active, there is a chain of pointers that begins at a directly referenced cell and ends (or passes through) the active cell; otherwise it is *isolated* or *free*. Using these definitions, it should be clear that when a given cell or list is freed, cells of all other structures that become isolated should also be liberated.

Now suppose that a program variable is a pointer to a list or list structure; an example is L5 which points to list L5 in Figure 7.4. Further suppose that at some point during program execution the program variable L5 is assigned a new value. Should list L5 be liberated? Again, the answer is 'yes', if that program variable was the only reference to the list, and 'no', if the list remains active by virtue of some other reference. If a list or structure is liberated which was not isolated, then all outstanding references to the structure will point to cells which are either no longer being used (i.e., they are part of the list of available space) or which are being used for different purposes (i.e., they have been reallocated). Those references became *dangling references* when the structure was liberated. In contrast, if a structure that becomes isolated is not liberated, for example list L3 if list L2 is liberated, then the cells become wasted, as they are no longer available for reallocation. This may cause early program termination because memory becomes used up prematurely, but the problem is not so severe as creating a dangling reference.

Two different techniques have been employed for liberating cells in memory management systems: *garbage collection* and *reference counts;* each of these techniques will be discussed independently below.

7.2.3 Garbage collection

Garbage collection is the process of locating all cells that were isolated during program execution and adding them to the list of available space. Systems that use garbage collection do not generally use procedures that liberate cells, lists, or structures, so the user is relieved of that responsibility. The user program simply abandons old cells, lists, or structures as program variables change value. When the list of available space becomes exhausted, the garbage collection procedures are invoked.

Each system that uses garbage collection must maintain an *initial address list,* a list of addresses of program identifiers that point to structures comprised of allocated cells. It is frequently the user's responsibility to place the addresses of program identifiers on the initial address list by invoking an appropriate routine with each program variable as an actual parameter. A second requirement is that each cell must have a single, reserved bit called a *mark bit* that is used exclusively by the garbage collection routines. The mark bits are initially set to '0' when cells are allocated.

Garbage collection consists of two parts. First, all cells of each structure referenced directly or indirectly by a program variable are *marked*. Marking is done by setting the mark bits of all active cells to '1'. Isolated cells are not marked, so their mark bits remain at '0'. See Chapter 6 for a complete discussion of marking. After all active cells are marked, all cells in memory are processed sequentially. Cells that are not marked are linked together to form a new list of available space, and, at the same time, cells that are marked are unmarked. Thus immediately after garbage collection, all isolated cells are on the list of available space and all cells, both active and inactive, are unmarked.

In order for the marking procedure to be able to mark all active cells, it is necessary to determine which cells point to other structures and which cells contain non-pointer data. In cell-oriented systems, cells are generally of a limited number of types, and a few bits in each cell are used to specify the type of cell. All cells of the same type have pointer data in the same fields. The illustration below shows how the cells of a list processor may appear:

```
TYPE 0
     TYPE  MARK      DATA        LINKU    LINKD
      ┌──┬───┬──────────────┬─────────┬────────┐
      │ 0│   │              │         │        │
      └──┴───┴──────────────┴─────────┴────────┘

TYPE 1
     TYPE  MARK  POINT1   POINT2    LINKU    LINKD
      ┌──┬───┬───────┬────────┬─────────┬────────┐
      │ 1│   │       │        │         │        │
      └──┴───┴───────┴────────┴─────────┴────────┘

TYPE 2
     TYPE  MARK      LENGTH       LINKU    LINKD
      ┌──┬───┬──────────────┬─────────┬────────┐
      │ 2│   │              │         │        │
      └──┴───┴──────────────┴─────────┴────────┘
```

TYPE 0   cells contain non-pointer data.
TYPE 1   cells contain pointers to other lists in the POINT1 and POINT2 fields.
TYPE 2   cells are list headers. LENGTH is the number of cells in the list.

Exercise 7.2. Modify the procedure MARK5 given on page 285 to properly mark all structures referenced by a pointer at address A, where the cells of the structures are of the three types illustrated above. Call this new procedure MARK6.

Once the cells of a structure have been marked, it is not difficult to form a new list of available space. The procedure GARCOL1 given below invokes the marking procedure, MARK6, and then forms a new list of available space:

procedure GARCOL1;
comment SPACE is the heap of memory being processed.
          SIZE is the size of memory, in words.
          NEXTCELL is a pointer to the first available cell.
          CELLSIZE is the size of a cell, in words;

```
template    1 CELL,
            2 TYPE      2 BITS,
            2 MARK      BIT,
            2 DATA      WORD,
            2 LINKU     POINTER to CELL,
            2 LINKD     POINTER to CELL;
declare (I,NUCELL)      POINTER to CELL;
declare SPACE(SIZE)     WORD global;
declare (SIZE,CELLSIZE) INTEGER global;
declare FIRST           BOOLEAN;
call MARK6;
comment See Exercise 7.2 for MARK6;
FIRST := true;
NEXTCELL := null;
I := @SPACE;
while (I + CELLSIZE ≤ @SPACE(SIZE) + 1) do
    begin
        case
        ([I].MARK = '1'):
            begin
                comment The cell is active. Unmark it;
                [I].MARK := '0'
            end;
        ([I].MARK = '0'):
            begin
                comment The cell is not active. Add it to the list of available space;
                [I].LINKD := NEXTCELL;
                NEXTCELL := I
            end;
        end case;
        I := I + CELLSIZE
    end;
return;
end GARCOL1;
```

The garbage collection process is illustrated in Figures 7.5 to 7.8.

Exercise 7.3. Procedure GARCOL1 could abort the program, if no cells are placed on the list of available space. Modify procedure GARCOL1 to do this. Can you think of any reasons why this would be advantageous? Disadvantageous?

7.2.4 Reference counts

In this section we discuss the use of reference counts for memory management. As a specific example, we will discuss memory management in SLIP, a FORTRAN based list processing system that uses reference counts. Later, we

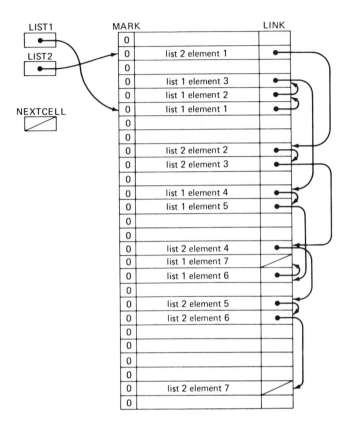

Figure 7.5. The appearance of memory before the garbage collector has been invoked.

will discuss how to implement an efficient reference count system that also employs garbage collection.

For some cell-oriented systems, reference counts are used to determine when a cell is no longer active. A *reference count* for a cell is an integer that indicates how many times that cell is currently referenced by other cells or external pointers. (In some systems such as SLIP (to be described), lists rather than individual cells have reference counts.) Whenever a reference to a cell is created, the reference count for the cell is incremented by 1. When a reference to a cell is eliminated, the reference count for the cell is decremented by 1; a cell is freed when its reference count becomes 0.

There are both advantages and disadvantages in using reference counts as opposed to employing a garbage collector. The principle advantage is that

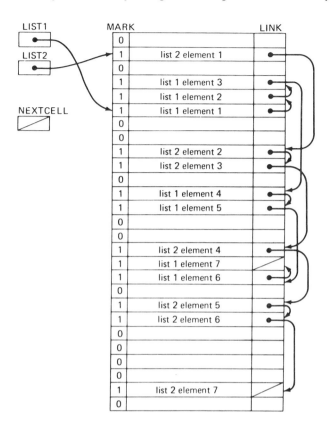

Figure 7.6. The appearance of memory after marking but before formation of the new list of available space.

liberation of free cells is incremental. There is never the single large interval of time devoted to garbage collection, and hence the system is better suited for interactive applications. There are four major disadvantages in using reference counts: 1) Reference counts require more memory than mark bits; 2) whenever cells are added to or deleted from a structure, the reference counts must be changed; this requires execution time not required by a system that uses garbage collection; 3) if a recursive list structure is created, the cells of that structure may never get reclaimed, even though the structure is not active. See page 322. (A structure is *recursive* if it points to itself either directly or indirectly through a chain of pointers through other structures); 4) the programmer must explicitly 'free' structures that are no longer referenced; otherwise the system would not know when to decrease the reference counts of the cells referenced by external pointers.

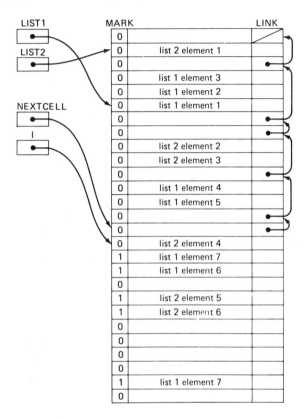

Figure 7.7. The appearance of memory during the formation of the new list of available space. List linkage is not shown.

7.2.5 Memory management in SLIP

We will now describe in detail how memory is managed in SLIP (*Symmetric LIst Processor*). In SLIP, a program identifier that points to a list is called a *name*. A name is a variable whose LNKL (*LiNK Left*) and LNKR (*LiNK Right*) fields both contain a pointer to the same list; see below. Names of lists are sometimes stored

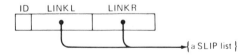

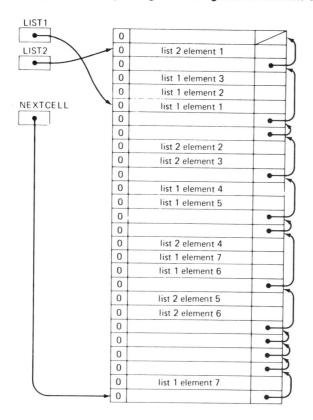

Figure 7.8. The appearance of memory after garbage collection terminates. Only the linkage for the list of available space is shown.

in cells of other lists. A list pointed to by another list in this way is a *sublist* of the first list. See Weizenbaum (1963) for a detailed presentation of SLIP.

SLIP uses cells of three different types as shown on the following page. The first cell of every list is a type 2 cell and is the header of the list. The elements of a list are cells of type 0 or 1. Cells of type 1 contain names in their NAME field; cells of type 0 contain non-pointer data in their DATA field.

Lists in SLIP are doubly linked circular structures (c.f. Chapter 2, Section 2.3.3). List headers are part of the structure so that if the LNKL and LNKR fields of a header both point to the header itself, the list is empty. In addition, SLIP lists may point to special lists called *descriptor lists* (also known as *property sets, attribute-value pair lists,* or *tables).* Descriptor lists are linearly organized tables. If a list does not have an associated descriptor list, the DLIST fields of a header both point to the header itself, the list is empty. In addition, the descriptor list. Descriptor lists have a header plus an even number of data cells. The DATA field of each odd numbered cell contains an *attribute,* and the

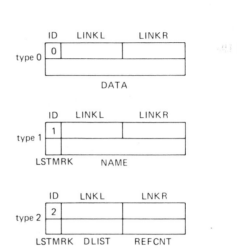

DATA field of the following cell contains the *value* of that attribute. SLIP provides special functions (not discussed here) for working with attribute-value pairs on descriptor lists. Figure 7.9 shows the memory representation of a SLIP list having five elements and an associated descriptor list. The list also has a sublist consisting of three elements.

SLIP is a list-oriented system; lists, not cells, have associated reference counts. In the header of each SLIP list is a REFCNT (*REF*erence *C*ou*NT*) field that indicates the number of times the list occurs as a sublist of another list. When a list is initially created, its REFCNT field is initialized to 0. This indicates that the list is referenced by a program variable but not by any other lists. When a list cell of type 1 is created, the REFCNT field of the list to which the type 1 cell points is incremented by 1. This indicates that the list is referenced by another list. Just before a program identifier that contains a list name is assigned a new value, it is the responsibility of the user program to invoke the procedure ERALST (*ERA*se *L*i*ST*) with that program identifier as an argument. (ERALST was called IRALST in the original implementation of SLIP.) ERALST does one of two things: If the reference count of the list is not zero, the reference count is simply decremented by 1; if the reference count of the list is 0, then this call to ERALST eliminates the last outstanding reference to the list, and the cells of the list may be liberated. The cells of the list, not including the list header, are placed

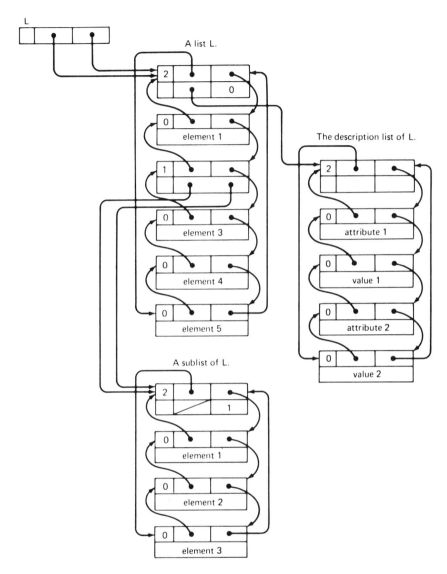

Figure 7.9. The storage representation of a SLIP list L, its descriptor list, and a sublist. Note that the descriptor list and the sublist are lists also.

on the bottom of the list of available space. This is done when ERALST calls the routine MTLIST (eMpTy the *LIST*). Since cells are always removed from the top of the list of available space and placed on the bottom, the list of available space in SLIP is a queue. Next, if the list does not have a descriptor list, the header cell is placed on the bottom of the list of available space. However, if the list does have a descriptor list, the header cell is made into a type 1 cell that points to the descriptor list, and the type 1 cell is placed on the bottom of the list of available space. The associated descriptor list may be liberated when the former header cell is later allocated by NUCELL. Figure 7.10 shows the appearance of memory before and after execution of the statement "**call** ERALST(LIST)."

The only cells that are placed on the bottom of the list of available space are those cells of lists whose reference count is 0. As a result, only cells that have no outstanding references are liberated, and no dangling references are created. When a type 1 cell is placed on the list of available space, the cells of the list to which it points may be liberated by NUCELL, as described below. This is true both for descriptor lists and for sublists of lists that are liberated.

Exercise 7.4. Figure 7.10 shows the memory representation of list LIST just before and just after execution of the statement **call** ERALST(LIST). Trace through the execution of ERALST and the procedures it invokes, and show every change that occurs between the 'before' and 'after' figures. Do the same for the structure illustrated in Figure 7.9 if the statement "**call** ERALST(L)" is executed.

There are five SLIP routines that are responsible for managing memory. The first is INITAS (*INIT*ialize *A*vailable *S*pace list); INITAS sets up the list of available space and also creates pointers to its top and bottom cells. Cells are always removed from the top and placed on the bottom of the list of available space. The routine ERALST is responsible for returning the cells of an entire list to the list of available space. Since SLIP lists use the LNKR fields of cells in the same way that the list of available space does and because SLIP lists are circular, the address of the last cell of the list is immediately known. All cells of a list can therefore be liberated at once in an amount of time independent of the length of the list. See Exercise 7.1. The routine RCELL (Return *CELL*) returns a single cell to the bottom of the list of available space; RCELL does not check on the type of the cell. Finally, NUCELL allocates cells from the list of available space. NUCELL first checks the type of cell. If it is type 0 or 2, then NUCELL allocates that cell and advances the top cell pointer to the next cell on the list of available space; however, if the cell is type 1, then NUCELL invokes ERALST with the NAME field of that cell as its actual parameter. NUCELL is therefore responsible for liberating sublists of previously liberated lists. After NUCELL invokes ERALST, the cell is allocated, and the top cell pointer is advanced to the next cell on the list of available space. By giving NUCELL the responsibility for placing sublists and descriptor lists on the list of available space, the process of freeing sublists is deferred until the last possible minute, at which time they are most likely to be free. On the negative side, keeping lists around for the longest possible time tends to prevent memory references from becoming localized and

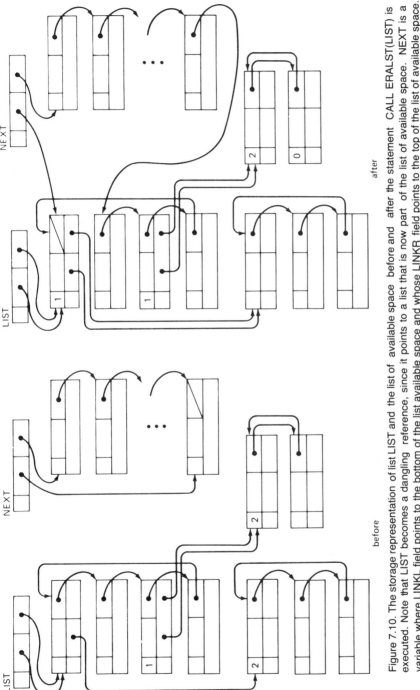

Figure 7.10. The storage representation of list LIST and the list of available space before and after the statement CALL ERALST(LIST) is executed. Note that LIST becomes a dangling reference, since it points to a list that is now part of the list of available space. NEXT is a variable where LINKL field points to the bottom of the list available space and whose LINKR field points to the top of the list of available space.

may be disadvantageous if SLIP is run on a computer that uses virtual memory. Algorithms for INITAS, ERALST, MTLIST, RCELL, and NUCELL are given below. The template statements are given once to conserve space.

comment The following declarations are global to the procedures INITAS, ERALST, MTLIST, RCELL, and NUCELL.

SPACE is the heap of memory out of which cells are to be allocated.

SIZE is the size of SPACE in words.

CELLSIZE is the size of a cell in words and depends on the computer being used.

NEXT is a word whose LNKL field points to the last cell on the list of available space and whose LNKR field points to the first word on the list of available space;

```
template      1  CELL,
              2  ID          2 BITS,
              2  LNKL        POINTER to CELL,
              2  LNKR        POINTER to CELL,
              2  filler      WORD,
              2  DATA,
                 3  LSTMRK   2 BITS,
                 3  DLIST    POINTER to CELL,
                 3  REFCNT   POINTER to CELL,
                 3  filler   WORD;
template      1  DESCRIPTOR,
              2  ID          2 BITS,
              2  LNKL        POINTER to CELL,
              2  LNKR        POINTER to CELL;
declare SPACE (SIZE)        WORD global;
declare NEXT                DESCRIPTOR global;
declare (SIZE, CELLSIZE)    INTEGER global;

procedure INITAS;
declare I                   POINTER to CELL;
declare (SIZE, CELLSIZE) INTEGER global;
declare SPACE (SIZE)        WORD global;
declare NEXT                DESCRIPTOR global;
CELLSIZE := the number of words in a CELL;
NEXT.LNKR := @SPACE;
I := @SPACE;
while (I + CELLSIZE − 1 ≤ @SPACE (SIZE) ) do
      begin
           [I].LNKR := I + CELLSIZE;
           [I].ID := 0;
           I := I + CELLSIZE
      end;
```

```
I := I - CELLSIZE;
[I].LNKR := 0;
NEXT.LNKL := I;
return;
end INITAS;


procedure ERALST(L);
comment L is a list name;
declare L DESCRIPTOR;
comment LST contains a pointer to the list referenced by L;
declare LST POINTER to CELL;
LST := L.LNKR;
if ([LST].REFCNT > 0)
then [LST].REFCNT := [LST].REFCNT - 1
else begin
        comment Place all list elements on the list of available space;
        call MTLIST(L);
        if ([LST].DLIST = null)
        then begin
                call RCELL(L);
                return
                end
        else begin
                [LST].ID := 1;
                [LST].REFCNT := [LST].DLIST;
                call RCELL(L)
                end endif
    end endif;
return;
end ERALST;


procedure MTLIST(L);
comment L is the name of a list being emptied.
        LIST is a pointer to the list being emptied;
declare (L,TOP,BOT)     DESCRIPTOR;
declare LIST            POINTER to CELL1;
declare NEXT            DESCRIPTOR global;
LIST := L.LNKR;
if ([LIST].LNKR = LIST and [LIST].LNKL = LIST)
then begin
        comment The list is already empty. Return;
        return
        end endif;
comment The list is not empty. Empty it;
TOP := [LIST].LNKR;
BOT := [LIST].LNKL;
```

```
[LIST].LNKR := LIST;
[LIST].LNKL := LIST;
[BOT].LNKR := null;
[NEXT.LNKL].LNKR := TOP;
NEXT.LNKL := BOT;
return;
end MTLIST;


procedure RCELL(C);
comment C.LNKR is a pointer to a cell being liberated;
declare  C          DESCRIPTOR;
declare  NEXT       DESCRIPTOR global;
[NEXT.LNKL].LNKR := C.LNKR;
[C.LNKR].LNKR := null;
NEXT.LNKL := C.LNKR;
return;
end;


procedure NUCELL;
comment NUCELL returns a pointer to the allocated cell;
declare  NUCELL DESCRIPTOR;
declare  NEXT DESCRIPTOR global;
if (NEXT.LNKR=null)
then call ABORT ('MEMORY OVERFLOW IN NUCELL') endif;
NUCELL := NEXT.LNKR;
if ([NUCELL].ID = 1) then call ERALST([NUCELL].DATA) endif;
[NUCELL].ID := 0;
NEXT.LNKR := [NUCELL].LNKR;
return;
end NUCELL;
```

The reference count technique described here may lead to the situation where an isolated list is never liberated. Consider the case where a list is created having name L, and further suppose that during program execution the list is made to reference a second list which references a third list which finally references the initial list; that is, a circular structure is created. When L was initially created, its reference count was set to 0, and when it was made a sublist of itself, its reference count was incremented to 1. Now suppose that L is liberated by the statement **call** ERALST(L) and that the identifier L is assigned a new value. The reference count of L is reduced by 1, and since the reference count was initially positive, no cells are placed on the list of available space. Since the identifier L no longer points to the list, there are no program variables that refer to the list. Thus the cells of the list are lost forever; they are never liberated.

The inability of the reference count technique to properly handle recursive structures is common to all reference count systems. Although there are techniques that can be used to liberate memory when recursive structures are created, those techniques are either very restricted or similar to garbage collection procedures. Hence, standard garbage collection procedures might just as well be used.

Exercise 7.5. Explain why the following technique is not a solution to the problems introduced when recursive list structures are created: Whenever a list is made a sublist of itself, the reference count of the list is not incremented.

7.2.6 Maintaining lists of available space in real time

There are several modifications to the reference count and garbage collection techniques that have been proposed for maintaining lists of available space for interactive systems. One proposal combines the techniques of maintaining reference counts with the techniques of garbage collection. That will be the topic of this section.

One of the principal advantages of using reference counts for memory management is that cells are liberated throughout list processing. There is no large interval of time during which garbage collection occurs. Whenever a cell is liberated, it is immediately made available for reuse. The principal disadvantage is that if a recursive structure is created, cells can become permanently 'lost'. A second disadvantage stems from the fact that the program must explicitly 'free' structures that are abandoned by program variables. Both of these disadvantages can be overcome if the memory management routines use both reference counts and garbage collection. Reference counts are used until all of memory is used up; garbage collection is then used to liberate structures that were abandoned by the program or that were lost because recursive structures were created.

We will now describe a specific proposal for an efficient implementation of the reference count technique. We leave the details of the proposed system as an exercise for the reader. We first assume that list structures will be singly linked. When this is the case, the vast majority of cells will contain a single pointer which points to the successor cell in the structure. (If a system uses double linkage, then the vast majority of cells would contain two pointers rather than one, and the techniques presented here would have to be modified accordingly.) Since the vast majority of cells have reference count 1, it is practical to keep in a hash table the addresses of all cells whose reference count differs from 1 and to keep the actual reference count as the associated value of the cell address in the hash table. In order to save time, two different tables will be maintained: a *zero count table* (ZCT) and a *multiple reference table* (MRT). The ZCT contains the address of each cell whose reference count is 0; there is no value associated with this address. The MRT contains the address and reference count of each cell whose reference count exceeds 1. Cells whose reference count is exactly 1 do not appear in either table. Finally, an initial address list is maintained for each external reference; however, external references do not influence the reference counts of the cells.

The execution of the system is based on the fact that only a limited number of operations cause the reference counts to change; these are: 1) cell allocation, 2) creating a pointer to a cell, and 3) destroying a pointer to a cell. Whenever a cell is allocated, an entry for the cell is made in the ZCT. However, this entry need not be made if the operation that causes the cell to be allocated also places a pointer to the cell in another cell. This happens frequently in list processing systems, for example, when a cell is appended to a list. Whenever a pointer to a cell is created (either in a cell or in the initial address list), the reference count of the cell is incremented by 1. This is done as follows: First, the ZCT is checked to see if the address of the cell is present; if it is, the entry is deleted; if there is no entry in the ZCT, the MRT is checked. If an entry is present, the associated value is incremented; finally, if an entry is not present in the MRT, an entry is made in the MRT with initial value 2. (Since the address of the cell did not appear either on the ZCT or the MRT, the reference count of the cell was initially 1 and must be incremented to 2.)

When a pointer to a cell is deleted, the MRT is first checked. If an entry is present, its associated value is decremented; if the decremented value is 1, then the entire entry is deleted; if, however, there is no entry on the MRT for the cell, then an entry is made for the cell in the ZCT. A cell that is referenced by the ZCT but not by the initial address list is isolated. Isolated cells are reclaimed by appending them to the list of available space. When a cell is appended to the list of available space, its entry is eliminated from the ZCT.

The entire system works as follows: As list processing procedes, references to free cells are placed on the ZCT; occasionally the memory management routines are invoked. This could be done, for example, when an interactive terminal is idle, or it may be done when the ZCT becomes full. When called, the memory management routines append all liberated cells on the bottom of the list of available space and remove those entries from the ZCT. If a cell is ever requested and the list of available space is empty, the garbage collector is invoked; if no cells are liberated by the garbage collector, then program execution is terminated and an appropriate error message given.

Exercise 7.6. Give algorithms for the memory management system described above. Assume that the structure of a cell is as illustrated below, and make all the necessary assumptions regarding the structure of the ZCT, the MRT, the initial address list, and the garbage collection routines. Finally, assume that the ZCT can contain up to 100 entries. When the ZCT is full, all liberated cells are placed on the list of available space.

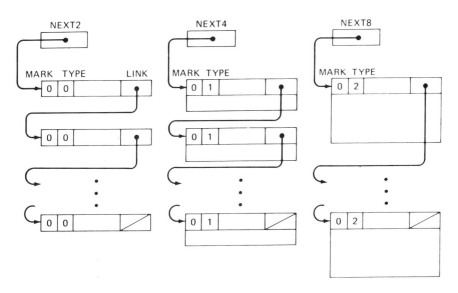

7.2.7 Systems that use cells of several sizes

Some systems use cells of several sizes rather than cells of one size. These systems generally maintain independent lists of available space, one for each cell size. In order to be specific, we will present memory management algorithms for a system that uses cells having two, four, and eight words. The memory representation used by the system is shown below. As illustrated, there are three pointers, NEXT2, NEXT4, and NEXT8: one to the top of each list of available space. Each cell has two reserved fields: a 1-bit MARK field that is used by the garbage collection routines, and a 2-bit TYPE field that indicates how long the cell is. If TYPE=0, the cell is two words long; if TYPE=1, the cell is four words long; and if TYPE=2, the cell is eight words long.

Requests for cells are handled in much the same way that they are for systems that have a single list of available space. One procedure, GETCELL2, will be used for allocating cells. The actual parameter to GETCELL2 will be the size of the desired cell; GETCELL2 returns a pointer to the allocated cell. When a request for a small cell is made, and the list of available space for that size cell is empty, a cell is removed from one of the lists having larger cells. The larger cell is split into smaller cells, and one of the smaller cells is allocated as requested. The remaining smaller cells are attached to the lists of available space for the appropriate smaller sized cells. See Figure 7.11. If all lists of available space for the requested size cell and larger cells are exhausted, then the garbage collection routines are invoked.

One garbage collection routine, GARCOL2, first calls MARK (not given) to mark the cells, and then it creates new lists of available space; marking is done as

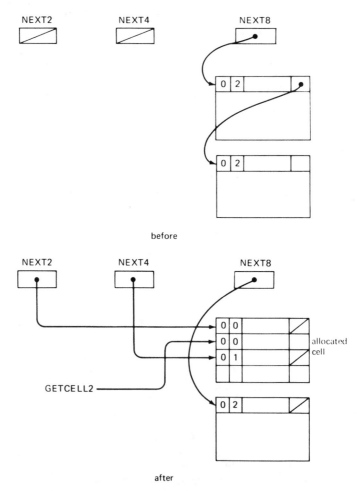

Figure 7.11. The changes that occur when GETCELL2 is invoked with argument 2 if the lists of available space for cells of types 0 and 1 are initially empty.

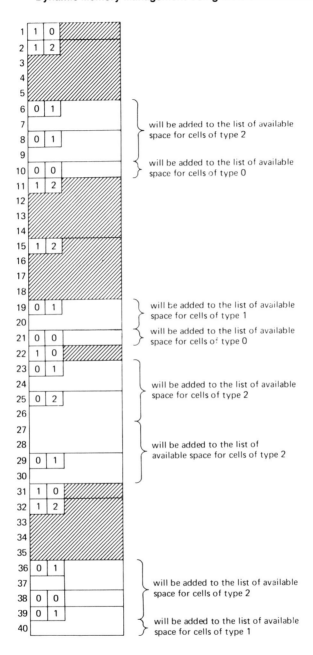

Figure 7.12. The appearance of memory after marking but before forming the new lists of available space. Shaded areas are cells that are currently active.

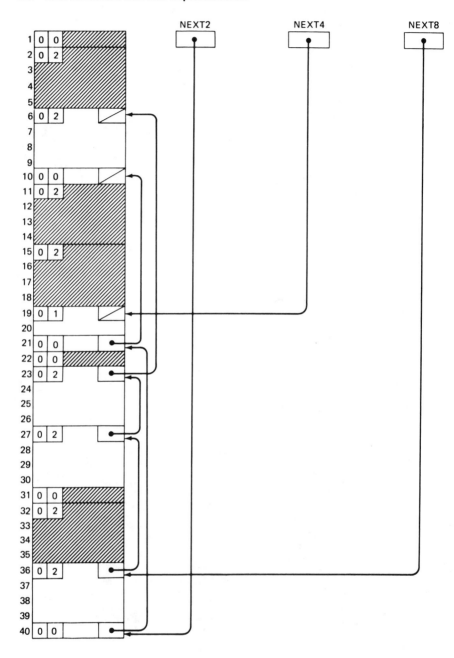

Figure 7.13. The appearance of memory after garbage collection.

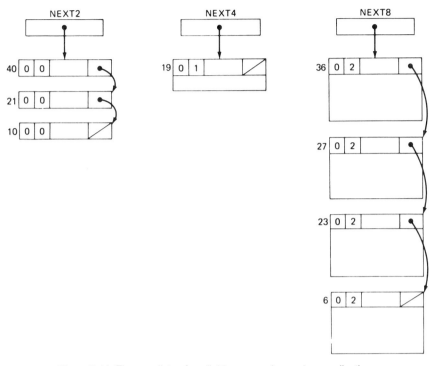

Figure 7.14. The new lists of available space after garbage collection.

described elsewhere (c.f. Chapter 6). Creating the new lists of available space is done by processing unmarked cells sequentially until either enough adjacent cells are found to form a single cell of the largest size, in which case it is added to the list of available space for that size cell, or a marked cell is detected, in which case the cells up to that point are added to lists of available space for smaller size cells. The procedures GETCELL2 and GARCOL2 are given below. The routine MARK is left as an exercise for the reader. Figures 7.12 to 7.14 show how the lists of available space are created by GARCOL2.

```
procedure GETCELL2(SIZE);
template 1 CELL,
          2 MARK                BIT,
          2 TYPE                2 BITS,
          2 LINK                POINTER,
          2 DATA(*)             WORD;
declare (NEXT2,NEXT4,NEXT8)     POINTER to CELL;
declare SIZE                    INTEGER;
declare (ADDR,GETCELL2)         POINTER to CELL;
```

```
case
    (SIZE = 2):
        begin
            if (NEXT2 = null and NEXT4 = null and NEXT8 = null)
            then call GARCOL2 endif;
            case
                (NEXT2 ≠ null):
                    begin
                        GETCELL2 := NEXT2;
                        NEXT2 := [NEXT2].LINK
                    end;
                (NEXT4 ≠ null):
                    begin
                        GETCELL2 := NEXT4 + 2;
                        [GETCELL2].MARK := '0';
                        [GETCELL2].TYPE := 0;
                        NEXT2 := NEXT4;
                        [NEXT2].TYPE := 0;
                        [NEXT2].LINK := null
                        NEXT4 := [NEXT4].LINK;
                    end;
                (NEXT8 ≠ null):
                    begin
                        GETCELL2 := NEXT8 + 2;
                        [GETCELL2].MARK := '0';
                        [GETCELL2].TYPE := 0;
                        NEXT4 := NEXT8 + 4;
                        [NEXT4].TYPE := 1;
                        [NEXT4].MARK := '0';
                        [NEXT4].LINK := null;
                        NEXT2 := NEXT8;
                        [NEXT2].TYPE := 0;
                        [NEXT2].LINK := null
                        NEXT8 := [NEXT8].LINK;
                    end;
                (true): call ABORT('MEMORY OVERFLOW IN GETCELL2');
            end case;
        end;
    (SIZE = 4):
        begin
            if (SIZE4 = null and SIZE8 = null) call GARCOL2 endif;
            case
                (NEXT4 ≠ null):
                    begin
                        GETCELL := NEXT4;
                        NEXT4 := [NEXT4].LINK
                    end;
```

```
    (NEXT8 ≠ null):
      begin
        GETCELL2 := NEXT8 + 4;
        [GETCELL2].MARK := '0';
        [GETCELL2].TYPE := 1;
        NEXT4 := NEXT8;
        [NEXT4].TYPE := 1;
        [NEXT4].LINK := null
        NEXT8 := [NEXT8].LINK;
      end;
      (true): call ABORT('MEMORY OVERFLOW IN GETCELL2');
    end case;

  end;
  (SIZE = 8):
    begin
      if (NEXT8 = null) then call GARCOL2 endif;
      if (NEXT8 = null)
      then call ABORT('MEMORY OVERFLOW IN GETCELL2') endif;
      GETCELL2 := NEXT8;
      NEXT8 := [NEXT8].LINK
    end;
end case;
return;
end GETCELL2;


procedure GARCOL2;
comment BLOCK is the heap out of which CELLS are allocated.
        SIZE is the size of memory.
        COUNT is the current number of adjacent free, two-word units found so far.
        I is the address of the first of the COUNT two-word units;
template 1   CELL,
             2  MARK              BIT,
             2  TYPE              2 BITS,
             2  LINK              POINTER,
             2  DATA(*)           WORD;
declare SIZE                      INTERGER global;
declare BLOCK(SIZE)               WORD global;
declare (NEXT2,NEXT4,NEXT8)       POINTER to CELL global;
declare (I,ADDR)                  POINTER to CELL;
declare (COUNT)                   INTEGER;
declare MARKED                    BOOLEAN;
I := @BLOCK;
call MARK;
NEXT2 := null;
NEXT4 := null;
NEXT8 := null;
```

```
COUNT := 0;
while (I ≤ @BLOCK(SIZE)) do
    begin
        if (COUNT = 0) then MARKED := false endif;
        while (MARKED = false and I + 1 + COUNT ≤ @ BLOCK(SIZE)) do
        begin
            ADDR := I + COUNT;
            if ([ADDR].MARK = '0')
            then begin
                    case
                        ([ADDR].TYPE = 0):
                            COUNT := COUNT + 2;
                        ([ADDR].TYPE = 1):
                            COUNT := COUNT + 4;
                        ([ADDR].TYPE = 2):
                            COUNT := COUNT + 8;
                    end case
                end
            else begin
                    comment The cell is marked;
                    [ADDR].MARK := '0';
                    if (COUNT > 0)
                    then MARKED := true
                    else begin
                            case
                                ([ADDR].TYPE = 0):
                                    I := I + 2;
                                ([ADDR].TYPE = 1):
                                    I := I + 4;
                                ([ADDR].TYPE = 2):
                                    I := I + 8;
                            end case
                        end endif
                end endif
        end;
        case
            (COUNT ≥ 8):
                begin
                    [I].LINK := NEXT8;
                    [I].TYPE := 2;
                    [I].MARK := '0';
                    NEXT8 := I;
                    I := I + 8;
                    COUNT := COUNT - 8
                end;
            (COUNT = 6):
```

```
           begin
               [I].LINK := NEXT4;
               [I].TYPE := 1;
               [I].MARK := '0';
               NEXT4 := I;
               I := I + 4;
               [I].LINK := NEXT2;
               [I].TYPE := 0;
               [I].MARK := '0';
               NEXT2 := I;
               I := I + 2;
               COUNT := 0
           end;
         (COUNT = 4):
           begin
               [I].LINK := NEXT4;
               [I].TYPE := 1 ;
               [I].MARK := '0';
               NEXT4 := I;
               I := I + 4;
               COUNT := 0
           end;
         (COUNT = 2):
           begin
               [I].LINK := NEXT2;
               [I].TYPE := 0;
               [I].MARK := '0';
               NEXT2 := I;
               I := I + 2;
               COUNT := 0
           end;
         end case
       end;
return;
end GARCOL2;
```

Exercise 7.7. Modify the above algorithms so that they work for a system that uses cells of sizes 1, 2, 4, 8, ... 2^K for some fixed K. You may assume that the TYPE field of a cell is K- bits long.

7.3 MEMORY MANAGEMENT TECHNIQUES USED BY OPERATING SYSTEMS

One of the major responsibilities of an operating system is the allocation and deallocation of memory. Depending on the complexity of the operating system, memory management algorithms can range from very simple algorithms, as in the case of a batch operating system with no multiprogramming, to very sophisticated strategies, such as those used in demand paging systems. As a particular example we will investigate the memory management algorithms used by multiprogramming systems using partitioned memory allocation. Paging and segmentation algorithms will not be discussed here because of their reliance on particular hardware. The interested reader should consult a standard textbook on operating systems, such as Madnick & Donovan (1974).

In a single-processor multiprogramming system, several processes reside in memory at once, but only one process can execute at a time. While one process is executing, the other processes are performing I/O operations or awaiting resources. In a *partitioned allocation system*, memory is divided into a number of contiguous blocks. In a *fixed partition* scheme, the sizes and locations of the blocks never change. Figure 7.15 shows a fixed partition scheme with four blocks. One block is 32K words long and will be used for small jobs, such as student programs; two of the blocks are 64K words long and will be used for average size jobs; the fourth block is 128K words long and will be used for very large jobs.

Memory management for a fixed partition scheme is simple. The most common method is to keep a table containing one entry for each block. Each entry contains the size and location of the block, plus a use bit indicating if the block is currently available or not. Shown below is a table for the partition of Figure 7.15. In this table, blocks 1, 2, and 4 are in use and block 3 is available. Jobs waiting to enter the system are grouped according to the maximum amount of memory that they will need. Within these groups, they can be ordered according to some priority scheme; for instance, jobs with small execution time estimates may have high priority. Whenever a block is freed, the job scheduler chooses a new job that will fit in the block and allocates the block to the job. This

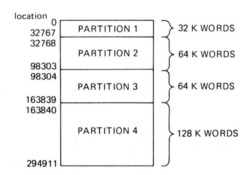

Figure 7.15. A fixed partition memory management scheme with four blocks.

involves setting the use bit to 1 and setting a pointer associated with the job to the entry in the block table.

	LOC	SIZE	USE
1	0	32 K	1
2	32768	64 K	1
3	98304	64 K	0
4	163840	128 K	1

One question that should be asked at this point is how do we decide which block to run a job in? Clearly a 128K job can only run in the 128K block, but a 30K job could run in any of the blocks. If we let the 30K jobs run in the 128K block, the 128K jobs may have to wait a long time, because they will probably have a lower priority. On the other hand, if very few 128K jobs are run, the 128K block is essentially wasted. Another problem with the fixed partition scheme is

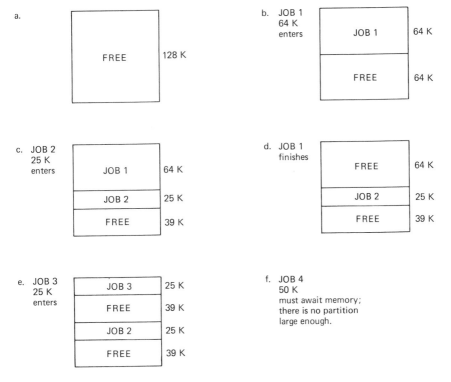

Figure 7.16 A sequence of jobs entering and leaving a system with dynamic partitions. The situation in f is called fragmentation—there is enough total memory for JOB4, but memory is fragmented and a contiguous 50K block does not exist.

that most jobs will not correspond closely to any block size. A job of length 65K words must run in the 128K block with 63K words of storage wasted while it is running!

In a *dynamic partition* scheme, the sizes and locations of the blocks vary dynamically as jobs of different sizes are run. In such a scheme, one large job could use all of memory, or a lot of small jobs could be core-resident at one time. Figure 7.16 shows a sequence of jobs entering and leaving a system and one way that memory might be allocated to accommodate them. Figure 7.16e shows how memory appears when JOB4 tries to enter the system. It cannot be accommodated, even though 78K words of memory are free, since there is no single block big enough to hold a 50K job; this situation is called *fragmentation*. Avoidance of fragmentation is an important factor in the success of a memory management algorithm.

We can represent the state of a dynamic partition with a table like that used in a fixed partition. A problem with this representation is that the size of the table will vary as the number of jobs in the system varies. One solution to this problem is to fix the maximum table size. This is a reasonable solution, since there will probably be a maximum number of jobs which can run concurrently without system performance being downgraded.

A more general solution is to keep a linked list of the free blocks; such a list is similar to the lists of available space described earlier in this chapter. In operating systems, the list of available space is usually called a *free list*. When a block is allocated to a program, it is removed from the free list. When the program terminates, the block is added to the free list again. Since blocks may be inserted or removed from the middle of the list, it is convenient to use a doubly linked, circular list; a doubly linked, circular free list is shown below. There is a header at the beginning of each block of memory for system use. The TAG field of the header is a 1- bit field that specifies whether the block is in use (TAG=$'1'$) or free (TAG=$'0'$). The SIZE field contains the size of the block, *not* including the header. The FLINK and BLINK fields are used only in free blocks and contain pointers to the next block and previous block on the free list, respectively. The pointer FREE contains the address of the first block on the free list.

In the remainder of this section, we will describe allocation and deallocation strategies using free lists. We will begin with the easiest algorithms—first-fit and best-fit allocation. We will then describe a deallocation scheme that uses an ordered free list. Finally, we will discuss two techniques—the boundary tag method and the buddy system—and discuss their advantages and disadvantages.

7.3.1 First-fit allocation

In a *first-fit* algorithm, the first block on the free list that can accommodate an incoming job is allocated for that job. If the block used is larger than the size

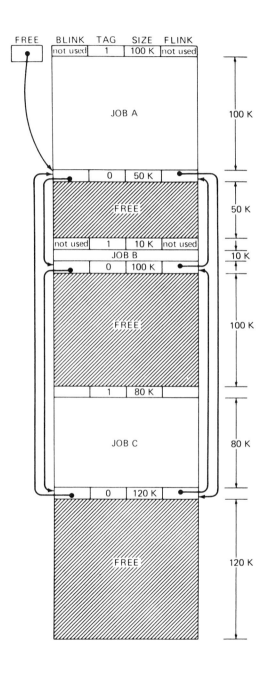

required and is big enough so that removing a piece of the required size leaves a useable size block, then only the bottom portion is allocated, and the unused top portion of the block remains on the free list. The free list does not have to be kept in any particular order. The following first-fit algorithm tries to allocate a block of size N from the free list.

procedure FIRSTFIT(N);
comment This procedure searches for a free block of size N. If it finds such a block, it returns a pointer to the header. Otherwise it returns **null**;
template 1 BLOCK,
        2 HEADER,
           3 SIZE   INTEGER,
           3 TAG   BIT,
           3 FLINK   POINTER to BLOCK,
           3 BLINK   POINTER to BLOCK,
        2 SPACE(●SIZE)   WORD;
declare (BLOCKPTR,FIRSTFIT) POINTER to BLOCK;
declare (LEFTOVER,N) INTEGER;
declare FREE POINTER to BLOCK **global**;
declare (HEADERSIZE,SMALLESTSIZE) INTEGER **global**;
comment HEADERSIZE is the size of a block header.
        SMALLESTSIZE is the smallest size block that is still useable.
        LEFTOVER will be the size of the unused top portion of a block from which some space is allocated.
        The routine DELETE(PTR,FREE) deletes the block pointed to by PTR from the doubly linked circular list pointed to by FREE;
FIRSTFIT := **null**;
if (FREE = **null**) **then return endif**;
BLOCKPTR := FREE;
while (true) do
    begin
        case
           ([BLOCKPTR].SIZE < N):
             begin
                comment Move on to next block;
                BLOCKPTR := [BLOCKPTR].FLINK;
                if (BLOCKPTR=FREE) **then return endif**
             end;
           ([BLOCKPTR].SIZE ⩾ N **and** [BLOCKPTR].SIZE < N
              + HEADERSIZE + SMALLESTSIZE):
             begin
                comment A block has been found that is either the exact size required or a little bigger, but not big enough to leave the remainder on the free list;
                [BLOCKPTR].TAG := '1';
                FIRSTFIT := BLOCKPTR;

```
            call DELETE(BLOCKPTR,FREE);
            return
        end;
        ([BLOCKPTR].SIZE ≥ N + HEADERSIZE + SMALLESTSIZE):
        begin
            comment A block of more than enough space has been found;
            LEFTOVER := [BLOCKPTR].SIZE - (HEADERSIZE + N);
            FIRSTFIT := BLOCKPTR + HEADERSIZE + LEFTOVER;
            [FIRSTFIT].TAG := '1';
            [FIRSTFIT].SIZE := N;
            [BLOCKPTR].SIZE := LEFTOVER;
            return
        end;
    end case
  end
end FIRSTFIT;
```

7.3.2 Best-fit allocation

In a best-fit algorithm, the block that can accommodate the request and is nearest in size to the requested size is used. If the free list is unordered, the entire list must be searched, since the best-fitting block may be anywhere on the list. For this reason, a system using a best-fit algorithm will generally keep the free list in descending order according to size of block. When the free list is in descending order, the search starts with the largest block on the list and continues until a block B, which is smaller than the requested block, is encountered. The block on the free list just prior to B is used (if one exists), and any leftover memory is inserted into the free list in the proper place according to its size.

Exercise 7.8. Illustrate an ordered, free list with blocks of sizes 10, 20, 30, 50, 80. Show where the search starts and ends for a block of size 25.

Exercise 7.9. Give an algorithm called BESTFIT which, given a request for a block of size N, returns a portion of the best-fitting block on the (ordered) free list and moves the remainder of the block to the proper place in the free list according to its size or fails if no such block exists.

7.3.3 Deallocation

Deallocation of storage presents a problem not encountered in allocation. The blocks on the free list should be the largest possible contiguous blocks. Thus when a block is to be returned to the free list, the deallocation algorithm must determine whether the blocks directly preceding it and directly following it in storage are also free; if so, they must be merged with the newly freed block to form a larger free block. This situation is illustrated below.

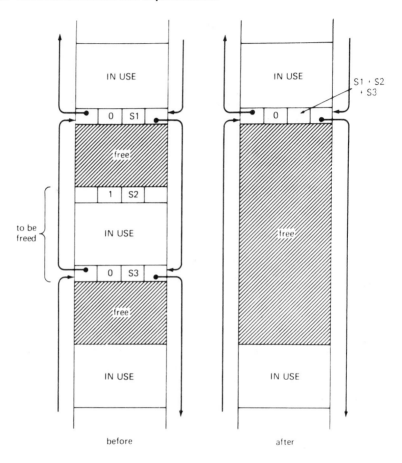

before   after

Suppose the free list is unordered, or ordered by size of block as in the last section; then it may be necessary to search the entire free list for the adjacent free blocks, since they could be anywhere on the list. If best-fit allocation is not being used, the free list should be ordered by the address of the first storage location of each block. Then it is only necessary to search half the free list, on the average, and if both the preceding and following blocks are free, they will be next to each other on the free list. The following algorithm returns a block of memory to the free list, which is ordered according to address in memory.

procedure RETURNBLOCK(ADDRESS);
comment Return the block pointed to by ADDRESS to the free list which is ordered by address of block. Merge the block with the block preceding it and the block following it in storage if they are free;

```
template 1 BLOCK,
         2 HEADER,
           3 SIZE        INTEGER,
           3 TAG         BIT,
           3 FLINK       POINTER to BLOCK,
           3 BLINK       POINTER to BLOCK,
         2 SPACE(•SIZE)  WORD;
declare (ADDRESS,BLOCKPTR) POINTER to BLOCK;
declare FREE POINTER to BLOCK global;
declare (SIZE,FULLSIZE,HEADERSIZE) INTEGER;
declare END BOOLEAN;
comment END will be set to true if the entire free list has been searched and the block
        must be inserted at the end of the list;
if (FREE = null)
then begin
        FREE := ADDRESS;
        [ADDRESS].FLINK := ADDRESS;
        [ADDRESS].BLINK := ADDRESS;
        [ADDRESS].TAG := '0';
        return
     end endif;
SIZE := [ADDRESS].SIZE;
FULLSIZE := SIZE + HEADERSIZE;
BLOCKPTR := FREE;
END := false;
while (true) do
   case
     (BLOCKPTR < ADDRESS and END = false):
        begin
          comment Keep searching;
          BLOCKPTR := [BLOCKPTR].FLINK;
          if (BLOCKPTR = FREE) then END := true endif
        end;
     (BLOCKPTR > ADDRESS and END = false or
      BLOCKPTR < ADDRESS and END = true):
        begin
          comment If BLOCKPTR > ADDRESS and END = false, then the block
                  must be inserted just prior to [BLOCKPTR].
                  If BLOCKPTR < ADDRESS and END = true, then the block
                  must be inserted at the end of the list—again just prior to
                  [BLOCKPTR] since [BLOCKPTR] is the first element of the list
                  and the list is circular;
          PREVPTR := [BLOCKPTR].BLINK;
          NEXTPTR := [BLOCKPTR].FLINK;
          case
            (PREVPTR + HEADERSIZE + [PREVPTR].SIZE = ADDRESS and
```

```
ADDRESS + FULLSIZE = BLOCKPTR):
    begin
        comment Merge all three blocks;
        [PREVPTR].SIZE := [PREVPTR].SIZE + SIZE +
            [BLOCKPTR].SIZE + 2 * HEADERSIZE;
        [PREVPTR].FLINK := NEXTPTR;
        [NEXTPTR].BLINK := PREVPTR
    end;
    (ADDRESS + FULLSIZE = BLOCKPTR):
    begin
        comment Merge current block with next;
        [ADDRESS].SIZE := SIZE + HEADERSIZE +
            [BLOCKPTR].SIZE;
        [ADDRESS].TAG := 0;
        [ADDRESS].FLINK := NEXTPTR;
        [ADDRESS].BLINK := PREVPTR;
        [NEXTPTR].BLINK := ADDRESS;
        [PREVPTR].FLINK := ADDRESS
    end;
    (PREVPTR + [PREVPTR].SIZE + HEADERSIZE = ADDRESS):
    begin
        comment Merge current block with previous block;
        [PREVPTR].SIZE := [PREVPTR].SIZE + FULLSIZE
    end;
    (true):
    begin
        comment The block is not merged;
        [ADDRESS].TAG := '0';
        [ADDRESS].FLINK := BLOCKPTR;
        [ADDRESS].BLINK := PREVPTR;
        [BLOCKPTR].BLINK := ADDRESS;
        [PREVPTR].FLINK := ADDRESS
    end;
    end case;
    if (ADDRESS < FREE) then FREE := ADDRESS;
    return
    end;
    end case
end RETURNBLOCK;
```

The above algorithm is an improvement over searching the whole list, but is not ideal. Searching even half the list is too time consuming in a busy system, but even if search time is unimportant, the method of ordering the free list by address makes best-fit allocation unfeasible. The free list was ordered so that the blocks adjacent to a block being returned could be found more easily if they were also free. In the current data structure, given a block at address B, it is possible to locate the next contiguous block in memory with a simple calculation; it is located at address B+[B].SIZE+HEADERSIZE. There is no similar way to locate the beginning of the previous contiguous block in memory, since we have no way of knowing how far above the current block to look.

7.3.4 The boundary tag method

It is possible to change the data structure slightly so that the block above a given block can be located just as easily as the one below. This is done by adding a *footer* containing two fields of information to the *bottom* of each block. The new block structure is shown below. Now the address of the block above the block whose address is B is B−([B−FOOTERSIZE].SIZE+HEADERSIZE+FOOT-ERSIZE) and that block is free if [B−FOOTERSIZE].TAG is zero. The address of the block below the block at address B is B+[B].SIZE+HEADERSIZE+FOOTERSIZE. This representation is called the *boundary tag representation*.

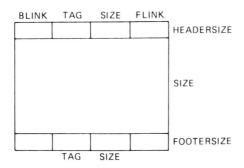

The boundary tag representation does not require an ordered free list and the free list is not searched at all when returning a block. Given the block structure above, the following algorithm returns a block at location ADDRESS, merging it with adjacent blocks if they are free. The details of merging, deleting, and inserting in this algorithm are left as an exercise.

procedure RETURNBLOCK2(ADDRESS);
template 1 BLOCK,
        2 HEADER,
           3 SIZE   INTEGER,
           3 TAG   BIT,
           3 FLINK   POINTER to BLOCK,
           3 BLINK   POINTER to BLOCK,
        2 SPACE(•SIZE)   WORD,
        2 FOOTER,

```
                3 SIZE                        INTEGER,
                3 TAG                         BOOLEAN;
declare ADDRESS POINTER to BLOCK;
declare FREE POINTER to BLOCK global;
declare (HEADERSIZE,FOOTERSIZE) INTEGER global;
comment The free list is not ordered;
case
        ([ADDRESS − FOOTERSIZE].TAG = '0' and
        [ADDRESS + [ADDRESS].SIZE + HEADERSIZE + FOOTERSIZE].TAG =
        '0)':
            begin
                comment Remove the block above and the block below from the free list,
                        merge them with the current block and add the result to the end of
                        the free list;
                    •
                    •
                    •
            end;
        ([ADDRESS − FOOTERSIZE].TAG = '0'):
            begin
                comment Merge the current block with the block above it which is already
                        on the free list. In this case the merging can be easily done
                        without removing anything from the free list;
                    •
                    •
                    •
            end;
        ([ADDRESS + [ADDRESS].SIZE + HEADER SIZE + FOOTERSIZE].TAG =
        '0')
            begin
                comment Remove the block below from the free list, merge it with the
                        current block, and add the result to the end of the list:
                    •
                    •
                    •
            end;
        (true):
            begin
                comment No merging. Add the block to the end of the free list;
                    •
                    •
                    •
            end;
end case;
end RETURNBLOCK2;
```

Exercise 7.10. Complete the details in procedure RETURNBLOCK2.

7.3.5 The buddy system

Another interesting method for splitting and merging blocks is the *buddy system*. In this scheme, all blocks are required to have length 2**K for some non-negative integer K. The storage pool is of length 2**M for some M, and addresses range from 0 to 2**M − 1. Instead of one, there are M+1 free lists, one for each possible block size. Figure 7.17 shows the memory representation for this system.

When a block of size 2**K is requested, free list K is the first to be checked. If free list K is not empty, the first block on it is returned; if free list K is empty, free list K+1 is checked next. Eventually, either a free block is found on some free list J, J≥K or failure is reported. When a block of size J>K is found, it is split into two equal parts called *buddies*. Each buddy is of size 2**(J−1). One buddy is placed on free list J−1 for future use. If J−1=K, the other buddy is

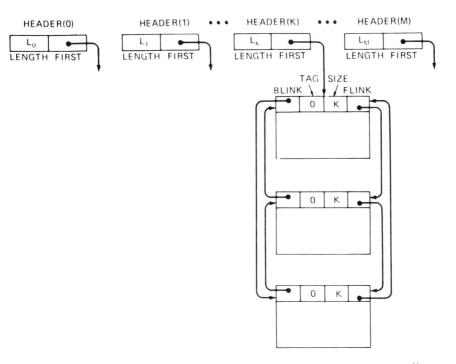

Figure 7.17. A memory representation for the buddy system. For a memory of size 2^M-1, there are M headers pointing to the M free lists. The K'th free list contains all the blocks of size 2^K.

returned; if not, it is split into two more buddies. This process continues until a block of size 2**K is produced. When a block of size 2**K is liberated, it is merged with its buddy if the buddy is available. This is where the scheme is most interesting: it is not necessary to search any of the free lists to find the buddy; instead, the address of the buddy can be calculated directly.

If B is the address of a block of size 2**K, then the address of its buddy can be calculated from the formula:

$$\text{buddy(B,K)} = \begin{cases} B + 2**K \text{ if remainder}(B/2**(K+1)) = 0 \\ B - 2**K \text{ if remainder}(B/2**(K+1)) = 2**K \end{cases}$$

In the first case, B is the address of the top block of the two buddies, and, in the second case, it is the address of the bottom block. For example, suppose M = 10. Then initially, there is a block of size $2^{10} = 1024$, and the addresses range from 0 to $2^{10} - 1$ or 1023. This big block can be divided into two buddies of size $2^9 = 512$ each. The first buddy starts at address 0. Since remainder(0/1024) is 0, we have buddy(0,9) = 0 + 2^9 = 512; thus the second buddy's address is 512. Working backwards, since remainder(512/1024) is 512, we have buddy(512,9) = 512 - 2^9 = 0.

In implementing the buddy system, we note that:

$$\text{buddy(B,K)} = 2**K \; xor \; B$$

where *xor* is the exclusive-or operation on two binary numbers. Thus the computation can generally be carried out with a single machine instruction and hence is very fast.

Once the header of the buddy is located, its TAG field is examined. If TAG=$'1'$, the buddy is in use; in this case the block being returned is just added to free list K. If TAG=$'0'$, and the SIZE field of the header is the same as the SIZE field of the block being returned, the buddy is free, and the two buddies are merged. The previously free buddy must, of course, be removed from the free list where it previously resided. Now the search continues for the buddy of this new larger block. Eventually after all merging is completed, a block is added to free list J for some J⩾K.

Exercise 7.11. Give the algorithm for allocating a block of size 2**K, given the memory representation of Figure 7.17 and the buddy system.
Exercise 7.12. Give the algorithm for returning a block of size 2**K, given the memory representation of Figure 7.17 and the buddy system.
Exercise 7.13. Give an example of fragmentation caused by the failure of the buddy system to merge two contiguous blocks that are not buddies.

7.3.6 Comparison of methods

We have described several different techniques that can be used with dynamic allocation in operating systems. Free lists may be ordered by address of block, by size of block, or unordered; the ordering policy depends on the allocation and deallocation algorithms chosen. The first-fit and best-fit allocation algorithms are simple and easy to implement. First-fit requires no ordering of the free list and is generally a little faster and simpler than best-fit, but it may break up large blocks that are needed later and that the best-fit algorithm would not choose. The best-fit algorithm with a free list ordered by size of block searches half the free list (on the average) before choosing a block. It will often choose a better fitting block than the first fit algorithm, but it may create *splinters* (very small blocks) in the process.

The boundary-tag representation can use either a first-fit or best-fit allocation algorithm and has these advantages: 1) the free list need not be ordered by address of block; and 2) the deallocation procedure does not have to search the free list. The main disadvantage is the extra storage used by the footer. The buddy system requires the blocks to be grouped by size and provides a fast allocation algorithm; however, the fit may not be very good, and a block may be split several times during allocation. Deallocation requires no searching but may require several merge operations. The chief disadvantages are the restriction of the block sizes to powers of two and the fragmentation that can occur, because only buddies can be merged; generalizations to the buddy system have been explored by Peterson and Norman (1977). In the final analysis, the best way to determine which scheme is best for a particular computer system and application is by simulation, a topic beyond the scope of this text.

Exercise 7.14. One way to keep track of allocated memory, as an alternative to maintaining a free list, is to maintain a bit string having the same length as there are words in memory. Bit I in the bit string is set to '1' in case the I'th word is allocated; it is set to '0' otherwise. If a block of memory consisting of K words is to be allocated, a search is made of the bit string for a substring of length K having all '0' bits. Allocation consists of setting the bits of the allocated words to '1' and returning the address of the first word. Deallocation consists simply of resetting the bits of the words being liberated to '0'.
   a. Give a first-fit allocation algorithm for the bit string management technique.
   b. Discuss the merits and demerits of this technique in comparison with the buddy system and the boundary tag technique.

7.4 SUMMARY

Dynamic memory management systems use linked lists of available space when sequential allocation with compaction is not practical either for space or for time reasons. Cell-oriented systems are one example: compaction is not necessary since fragmentation does not occur, and the memory overhead of the future address pointers is prohibitive. Cell-oriented systems use either garbage collection or reference counts to liberate memory. The memory management routines employed by operating systems also use linked lists of available space and frequently utilize either the buddy system or boundary tags to aid in memory liberation. The free lists are generally doubly linked to enable rapid insertion of liberated blocks, and, when best-fit allocation is used, the free list is generally ordered by block size. Best-fit allocation and liberation require, on the average, searching through half the free list. When first-fit allocation is used and the free list is ordered by memory address, allocation is simpler and often faster than best-fit; however, memory fragmentation is much more likely to result. When boundary tags are used, liberation requires a constant amount of time.

The choice of a memory management discipline depends on these factors but can also be aided by a simulation when the statistics of the job stream are known.

Projects

Project 7.1. A disk is an external storage device in which memory locations are linearly ordered from some low address, generally 0, to some high address $N-1$ for a disk with a capacity of N words. The first block of words on a disk is used to contain a *disk directory* that indicates the name of each data set on the disk, its low and high addresses, and other information, such as: data set format; when the data set was last accessed; the user's data set project number, and so forth. A *disk management procedure* is a procedure that allocates memory for new data sets and places the appropriate information in the disk directory. In addition, the disk management procedure deletes unwanted data sets or moves data sets from one location to another and updates the disk directory accordingly. The disk management procedure maintains a list of available space on the disk for this purpose.

There are several memory management techniques that are used by disk management procedures:

1. Best fit: The new data set is placed on disk in that slot whose size is closest to the size of the data set. (A slot is a block of available space between two data sets.)
2. First fit: The new data set is placed in the first slot in which it will fit.
3. Sequential allocation with compaction.

Describe efficient memory management algorithms for each of these disciplines. Indicate for each discipline when it would be substantially better than the other two. Discover what disk management discipline your computing system uses, and try to discover why that policy was elected over other policies.

Project 7.2. A *polynomial* is an expression consisting of a sum of *terms*, each term being a product of *constants* (real numbers or integers) and *variables* (unknowns) raised to positive integer powers. Examples of polynomials are given below:

$$6X^2 + 5X + 17$$
$$19X^2Y + 11XY^3 + 22X - 11Y$$
$$12.3XYZ - 14.2XZ - 16.0Z^2$$

Polynomials can be added, subtracted, multiplied, and evaluated. When adding or subtracting polynomials, the constants of terms having identical variables to the same powers are added or subtracted, while other terms are left unchanged; for example, $(X^3 + 2X + 6) + (X^2 + 6X - 5)$ yields $X^3 + X^2 + 8X + 1$. When multiplying polynomials, all terms are multiplied together, and the resulting polynomial is reduced by adding or subtracting the coefficients of terms having identical variables raised to identical powers; for example, $(6X + Y)*(X + 3Y)$ yields $6X^2 + 18XY + XY + 3Y^2$ which reduces to $6X^2 + 19XY + 3Y^2$. Polynomial evaluation consists of replacing all occurrences of a given variable by the value of that variable. For example, if the polynomial $X^2Y + 3XY + 2Y + 7Y^2 + 6$ is evaluated for X having value 1, the result is $Y + 3Y + 2Y + 7Y^2 + 6$, which reduces to $7Y^2 + 6Y + 6$.

A polynomial can be represented as a doubly linked linear list of cells, where each cell contains either a coefficient of a term or a variable name and its exponent. A polynomial is in *normal form,* if within each term variables appear in alphabetical order and, within the polynomial, terms appear in lexicographic order; this is illustrated below:

$$1.0X^2 + 3.1XY + 6.1Y^2$$
$$4.0A^3B + 2.1A^2B^2C + 3.1A^2CD + 2.7AC + 7.2B + 9.4C^3$$

Note that $XX > XY > YY$ so that $X^2 > XY > Y^2$, and similarly, $AAAB > AABBC > AACD > AC > B > CCC$ so that $A^3B > A^2B^2C > A^2CD > AC > B > C^3$.

Two types of cells are used:

template 1 COEFFICIENT _ CELL,
          2 COEFFICIENT   REAL,
          2 BLINK   POINTER,
          2 FLINK   POINTER;
template 1 TERM _ CELL,
          2 TERM _ NAME   CHARACTER,
          2 TERM _ EXPONENT   INTEGER,
          2 BLINK   POINTER,
          2 FLINK   POINTER;

Design and code a collection of procedures for polynomial manipulation. Choose an encoding so that the length of a COEFFICIENT _ CELL is the same as the length of a TERM _ CELL. Using this structure, the polynomial $X^2 + 3.1XY + 6.2Y^2$ would appear this way:

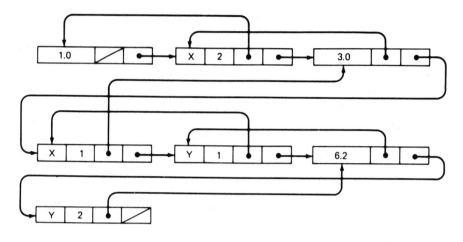

You are to provide all memory management routines necessary for the allocation and liberation of cells. In addition, you should provide the following routines:

INPUT( )	A procedure that reads one or more data cards and creates the polynomial described on the cards. The procedure returns a pointer to the newly created normal form polynomial.
OUTPUT(P)	A procedure having one argument P, a pointer to a polynomial. The indicated polynomial is printed in the output stream.
EQUAL(P, Q)	A predicate that returns **true,** if polynomial P is equal to polynomial Q; otherwise, EQUAL returns **false.**
PLUS(P, Q)	A procedure that creates a polynomial which is the sum of the two polynomials designated by P and Q. PLUS returns a pointer to the new polynomial.
MINUS(P, Q)	A procedure that creates a polynomial which is the difference of the polynomials designated by P and Q. MINUS returns a pointer to the new polynomial.
TIMES(P, Q)	A procedure that creates a polynomial which is the product of the polynomials designated by P and Q. TIMES returns a pointer to the new polynomial.
REDUCE(P, V, X)	A procedure that evaluates the polynomial designed by P and returns a pointer to the reduced polynomial. The argument V is a variable name, and the argument X is a real number which is the value assigned to V.

Additional procedures should be written as necessary, including memory management routines, routines for putting a polynomial in normal form, and so forth.

REFERENCES AND ADDITIONAL READINGS

Books

Findler, N.V.; Pfaltz, J.L.; and Bernstein, H.J. (1972) *Four High-Level Extensions of FORTRAN IV: SLIP, AMPPL-II, TREETRAN, SYMBOLANG*. New York: Spartan Books.

Knuth, D.E. (1973) *The Art of Computer Programming, Volume 1/Fundamental Algorithms*, Second Edition. Reading, Massachusetts: Addison-Wesley Publishing Co., Inc.

Madnick, S.E., and Donovan, S.J. (1974) *Operating Systems*. New York: McGraw-Hill Book Co., Inc.

Newell, A.; Tonge, F.M.; Feigenbaum, E.A.; Green, B.F. Jr.; and Mealy, G.H. (1964) *Information Processing Language-V Manual*, Second Edition. Englewood Cliffs, New Jersey: Prentice-Hall, Inc.

Rosen, S. (1967) *Programming Systems and Languages*. New York: McGraw-Hill Book Co., Inc.

Articles

Baecker, H.D. Garbage collection for virtual memory computer systems. *CACM* Vol. 15, No. 11, Nov. 1972, 981-986.

Barth, J.M. Shifting garbage collection overhead to compile time. *CACM* Vol. 20, No. 7, June 1977, 513-518.

Bobrow, D.G., and Murphy, D.L. A note on the efficiency of a LISP computation in a paged machine. *CACM* Vol. 11, No. 8, Aug. 1968, 558.

Bowlden, H.J. A list-type storage technique for alphameric information. *CACM* Vol. 6, No. 8, Aug. 1963, 433-434.

Clark, D.W. Copying list structures without auxiliary storage. Technical Report, October 1975, Department of Computer Science, Carnegie-Mellon University.

Clark, D.W. An efficient list-moving algorithm using constant workspace. *CACM* Vol. 19, No. 6, June 1976, 352-354.

Cohen, J., and Trilling, I. Remarks on "garbage collection" using a two-level storage. *BIT* Vol. 7, No. 1, 1967, 22-30.

Collins, G.E. A method for overlapping and erasure of lists. *CACM* Vol. 3, No. 11, Nov. 1960, 655-657.

Comfort, W.T. Multiword list items. *CACM* Vol. 7, No. 6, June 1964, 357-362.

Cranston, B., and Thomas, R. A simplified recombination scheme for the Fibonacci buddy system. *CACM* Vol. 18, No. 6, June 1975, 331-332.

Deutsch, L.P., and Bobrow, D.G. An efficient, incremental, automatic garbage collector. *CACM* Vol. 19, No. 9, Sept. 1976, 522-526.

Feiler, P.H. Evaluation of the bit string algorithm. Technical Report CMU-CS-78-111, Department of Computer Science, Carnegie-Mellon University, April 1978.

Fenichel, R.R. List tracing in systems allowing multiple cell-types. *CACM* Vol. 14, No. 8, Aug. 1971, 522-526.

Fenichel, R.R., and Yochelson, J.C. A LISP garbage-collector for a virtual memory computer. *CACM* Vol. 12, No. 11, Nov. 1969, 611-612.

Hansen, W.J. Compact list representations: definitions, garbage collection, and system implementation. *CACM* Vol. 12, No. 9, Sept. 1969, 499-507.

Hinds, J.A. An algorithm for locating adjacent storage blocks in the buddy system. *CACM* Vol. 18, No. 4, Apr. 1975, 221-222.

Hinds, J.A. A design for the buddy system with arbitrary sequences of block sizes. Technical Report 74, March 1974, Department of Computer Sciences, SUNY Buffalo.

Hirschberg, D.S. A class of dynamic memory allocation algorithms. *CACM* Vol. 16, No. 10, Oct. 1973, 615-618.

Hsu, H.T. A note on weighted buddy systems for dynamic storage allocation. *BIT* Vol. 16, No. 4, 1976, 378-382.

Iliffe, J.K., and Jodeit, J.G. A dynamic storage allocation scheme. *Computer J.* Vol. 5, No. 3, Oct. 1962, 200-209.

McCarthy, J. Recursive functions of symbolic expressions and their computation by machine. *CACM* Vol. 3, No. 4, Apr. 1960, 184-195.

Knowlton, K.C. A fast storage allocator. *CACM* Vol. 8, No. 10, Oct. 1965, 623-625.

Knowlton, K.C. A programmer's description of L⁶. *CACM* Vol. 9, No. 8, Aug. 1966, 616-625.

Nair, R.K. Dynamic storage allocation—Simulation techniques and efficient algorithms. Technical Report UIUCDCS-R-76-785, February 1976, Department of Comptuer Science, University of Illinois, Urbana.

Newell, A., and Tonge, F.M. An introduction to Information Processing Language V. *CACM* Vol. 3, No. 4, Apr. 1960, 205-211.

Nielsen, N.R. Dynamic memory allocation in computer simulation. *CACM* Vol. 20, No. 11, Nov. 1977, 864-873.

Peterson, J.L., and Norman, T.A. Buddy systems. *CACM* Vol. 20, No. 6, June 1977, 421-431.

Randell, B., and Kuehner, C.J. Dynamic storage allocation systems. *CACM* Vol. 11, No. 5, May 1968, 297-306.

Rochfeld A. New LISP techniques for a paging environment. *CACM* Vol. 14, No. 12, Dec. 1971, 791-795.

Ross, D.J. The AED free storage package. *CACM* Vol. 10, No. 8, Aug. 1967, 481-492.

Scattley, K. Allocation of storage for arrays in ALGOL 60. *CACM* Vol. 4, No. 1, Jan. 1961, 60-65.

Schorr, H., and Waite, W.M. An efficient machine-independent procedure for garbage collection in various list structures. *CACM* Vol. 10, No. 8, Aug. 1967, 501-506.

Shore, J.E. On the external storage fragmentation produced by first-fit and best-fit allocation strategies. *CACM* Vol. 18, No. 8, Aug. 1975, 433-440.

Smith, D.K. An introduction to the list processing language SLIP. In Rosen (1967), 393-418.

Tou, J.T., and Wegner, P. (Eds.) Proceedings of a symposium on data structures in programming languages. *SIGPLAN Notices* Vol. 6, No. 2, Feb. 1971.

Wadler, P.L. Analysis of an algorithm for real time garbage collection. *CACM* Vol. 19, No. 9, Sept. 1976, 491-500.

Waite, W.M., and Schorr, H. A note on the formation of free list. *CACM* Vol. 7, No. 8, Aug. 1964, 478.

Weinstock, C.B. Dynamic storage allocation techniques. Technical Report, April 1976, Department of Computer Science, Carnegie-Mellon University.

Weizenbaum, J. More on the reference counter method of erasing lists. *CACM* Vol. 7, No. 1, Jan. 1964, 38.

Weizenbaum, J. Recovery of reentrant list structures in SLIP. *CACM* Vol. 12, No. 7, July 1969, 370-372.

Weizenbaum, J. Symmetric list processor. *CACM* Vol. 6, No. 9, Sept. 1963, 524-544.

Wise, D.S., and Friedman, D.P. The one bit reference count. *BIT* 17. No. 3, 1977, 351-359.

Woodward, P.M., and Jenkins, D.P. Atoms and lists. *Computer J.* Vol. 4, No. 1, Apr. 1961, 47-53.

8
Recursion

OVERVIEW

In this chapter, we discuss recursion both as a tool for the definition and evaluation of recursively defined arithmetic expressions and as a tool for working with data structures. We will introduce the LISP programming language, describe how data structures are manipulated using recursive procedures, and illustrate recursive procedures with numerous LISP examples.

8.1 INTRODUCTION

Recursion is the general process of defining mathematical objects, such as functions, procedures, trees, graphs, geometric patterns, and languages by enumerating one or more specific cases and building other cases in terms of one or more of the previous cases. As an example, a *recursive procedure* is a procedure that invokes itself either directly or indirectly through a sequence of procedure calls. It is, in essence, defined in terms of itself.

Recursion is the most powerful data structure facility provided by many programming languages. The appearance of recursion as a tool in programming can be traced to McCarthy's (1960) seminal paper "Recursive functions of symbolic expressions and their computation by machine." Recursion was first introduced in the LISP programming language (McCarthy et. al., 1962) and about the same time in ALGOL 60 (Naur et. al., 1963). Recursion is a powerful tool for working with data structures, as many of the algorithms in this text have proven. It is for this reason that we devote an entire chapter to recursion and programming in LISP.

8.2 RECURSIVE DEFINITIONS AND RECURSIVE PROCEDURES

Recursive definitions are frequent in mathematical and formal systems. In this section, we will look at how several arithmetic expressions are defined recursively and the definitions translated into code. We will present iterative procedures for some recursive functions and show why iterative procedures are often preferred to recursive procedures.

Recursive definitions consist of three clauses: a *basis clause* that enumerates one or more values of the function being defined; an *inductive clause* that specifies how additional values can be obtained in terms of previously found values; and an *extremal clause* that limits functional values to those derived from the basis and inductive clauses. The extremal clause is generally understood and hence omitted from the definition.

Example 8.1. *Factorial*

> *basis clause:*   factorial(0)=1;
> *inductive clause*   factorial(N) = N*factorial(N−1), N⩾1;

The factorial function, with which you are probably familiar, occurs frequently in probability and statistics. From its definition, one can directly evaluate factorial(N); for any positive integer N; some values are calculated below:

> factorial(0)=1
> factorial(1)=1*factorial(0)=1
> factorial(2)=2*factorial(1)=2*1=2
> factorial(3)=3*factorial(2)=3*2=6
> factorial(4)=4*factorial(3)=4*6=24
>
> •
> •
>
> factorial(15)=15*factorial(14)=1307674368000
>
> •
> •

The following recursive procedure also defines the factorial function:

```
procedure FACTORIAL(N);
declare (N,FACTORIAL) INTEGER;
if (N = 0)
then FACTORIAL := 1
else FACTORIAL := N * FACTORIAL(N − 1) endif;
return;
end FACTORIAL;
```

The recursive procedure call occurs when the *else* clause of the *if* statement is evaluated. In that clause, the procedure *calls itself recursively.*

It is not difficult to show that factorial(N) can easily be written iteratively using the formula factorial(N)=1*2*3...*(N−1)*N. A corresponding iterative procedure can be coded as follows:

```
procedure FACTORIAL(N);
declare (I,N, FACTORIAL) INTEGER;
FACTORIAL := 1;
I := 1;
while (I ≤ N) do
    begin
        FACTORIAL := FACTORIAL * I;
        I := I + 1
    end;
return;
end FACTORIAL;
```

This procedure is somewhat more efficient than the previous procedure, in that it avoids maintaining the linkage necessary for recursive procedure calls (discussed later in this chapter). However, we showed earlier that factorial(15) evaluates to 1307674368000, a number that requires a word size of at least 41 bits, which is larger than the word size for most computers. Hence writing the procedure to do table lookup would be faster yet. Such a procedure coded in FORTRAN appears below:

```
INTEGER FUNCTION FACTL(I)
INTEGER J(15)/1,2,6,24,120,720,5040,40320,362880,3628800,
              39916800,479001600,6227020800,87178291200,
              1307674368000/
FACTL=1
IF (I.LT.0) CALL ARGERR(I)
IF (I.LE.1) RETURN
IF (I.GT.15) CALL TOOBIG(I)
FACTL=J(I)
RETURN
END
```

Here, TOOBIG and ARGERR are error functions that print an appropriate error message and abort the program.

Example 8.2 *Ackermann's function*
  basis clause: $acker(0,N)=N+1$;
  induction clause: $acker(M,0)=acker(M-1,1)$;
                       $acker(M,N)=acker(M-1,acker(M,N-1)),M\geqslant 1, N\geqslant 1$;

Ackermann's function is probably not among the functions with which you are familiar and was initially introduced primarily for its theoretical significance. (See Rogers, 1967.) Ackermann's function grows extremely rapidly as a function of its arguments and much much more rapidly than polynomials, exponentials, factorials, and other familiar functions. Some values of Ackermann's function are evaluated below:

$$acker(0,0)=1$$
$$acker(0,1)=2$$
$$acker(0,2)=3$$
   •
   •
$$acker(1,0)=acker(0,1)$$
$$=2$$
$$acker(2,0)=acker(1,1)$$
$$=acker(0, acker(1,0))$$
$$=acker(0,2) \text{ [an above result]}$$
$$=3$$
$$acker(3,0)=acker(2,1)$$
$$=acker(1,acker(2,0))$$
$$=acker(1,3) \text{ [an above result]}$$
$$=acker(0,acker(1,2))$$
$$=acker(0,acker(0,acker (1,1)))$$
$$=acker(0,acker(0,acker (0,acker (1,0))))$$
$$=acker(0,acker(0,acker(0,2))) \text{ [an above result]}$$
$$=acker(0,acker(0,3))$$
$$=acker(0,4)$$
$$=5$$
   •
   •

The reader who is not already familiar with Ackermann's function might try to evaluate acker(2,2) and then acker(3,3). The following table gives the values of Ackermann's function for selected, small arguments:

	N=0	N=1	N=2	N=3	N=4
M=0	1	2	3	4	5
M=1	2	3	4	5	6
M=2	3	5	7	9	11
M=3	5	13	29	61	125
M=4	13	65533	$2^{65533}-3$	*	*
M=5	65533	*	*	*	*
M=6	*	*	*	*	*

where '*' indicates that the value of the function is too large to be represented in binary on *any* current computer.

Ackermann's function can be easily written recursively; one recursive encoding of Ackermann's function is as follows:

```
procedure ACKER(M,N);
declare (M,N,ACKER) INTEGER;
case
    (M = 0): ACKER := N + 1;
    (N = 0): ACKER := ACKER(M - 1,1);
    (true): ACKER := ACKER(M - 1,ACKER(M,N - 1));
end case;
return;
end ACKER;
```

Before discussing techniques for implementing recursive procedures in general, we would like to point out that recursive definitions, although easy to program, are generally not as efficient as non-recursive implementations. It is not easy to write a non-recursive procedure for Ackermann's function. However, an algebraic analysis of the recursive definition does give a closed form for some values of M and N as follows:

$$ACKER(0,M)=M+1$$
$$ACKER(1,M)=M+2$$
$$ACKER(2,M)=2*M+3$$
$$ACKER(3,M)=(2**(M+3))-3$$

$$ACKER(4,M)= \left. 2^{2^{2^{\cdot^{\cdot^{\cdot^{2}}}}}} \right\} M+3 \text{ 2's} - 3$$

Using these formulas we can easily compute the entries in the previous table. Those entries designated by '*' are so large that they are not computable in any practical sense. For example, ACKER(4,2) (which is given in the table) would require a 65536 bit field, and ACKER(4,3) would require approximately 2**ACKER(4,2) bits!! A partial function can be written for Ackermann's function as follows:

```
procedure ACKER(M,N);
declare (I,M,N,ACKER) INTEGER;
case
    (M = 0): ACKER := N + 1;
    (M = 1): ACKER := N + 2;
    (M = 2): ACKER := 2 * N + 3;
    (M = 3):
        begin
            ACKER := 8;
```

```
            I := 1;
            while (I ≤ N) do
               begin
                  ACKER := ACKER * 2;
                  I := I + 1
               end;
            ACKER := ACKER - 3;
         end;
      (M = 4):
         case
            (N = 0): ACKER := 13;
            (N = 1): ACKER := 65533;
            (true): call TOOBIG;
         end case;
      (M = 5 and N = 0): ACKER := 65533;
      (true): call TOOBIG;
   end case;
   return;
end ACKER;
```

If we assume that the computer detects integer overflow, then the above procedure quickly gives the correct value of Ackermann's function whenever the value does not cause integer overflow, and the computer either raises an integer overflow interrupt or the procedure TOOBIG is invoked when overflow would result. Not only was an algebraic analysis of the function useful in deriving this procedure, but calculating the first few values of the function by hand shows the practical limit of computability of the function and hence enables an efficient implementation.

Exercise 8.1. Write recursive code for Ackermann's function in PL/I, Algol, or some other language that allows recursion. How many function calls are required for computing ACKER(3,6)? Estimate how many function calls are necessary to compute ACKER (M,N).

Exercise 8.2. Consider the following recursively defined function:

$$\textit{basis clause:} \quad f(0,N)=0;$$
$$\textit{inductive clause:} \quad f(M,N)=f(M-1,N) + N,$$
$$M>0, N \geq 0;$$

Give a non-recursive implementation of the same function. How much more efficient is your non-recursive implementation than the recursive implementation?

Not all recursively defined functions should or even can be written iteratively rather than recursively. Consider the function that computes the greatest common divisor between two integers:

basis clause: gcd(M,0)=M;
inductive clause: gcd(M,N)=gcd(N,M), N>M;
                     gcd(M,N)=gcd(N,mod(M,N)),
                     N≤M;
                     where mod(M,N) is the remainder
                     after dividing M by N.

This procedure, like factorial, executes nearly as fast when written recursively as when written iteratively. Furthermore, this function cannot be written using table lookup, since it is defined and computable for all pairs of positive integers.

Exercise 8.3. Calculate gcd(21,27) by hand.
Exercise 8.4. Give a non-recursive procedure for gcd.

8.3 IMPLEMENTING NON-RECURSIVE PROCEDURES

A procedure that invokes itself either directly or indirectly through a sequence of procedure calls is a *recursive procedure*. Some programming languages, such as FORTRAN, do not allow recursive procedure calls. This restriction is due primarily to the fact that FORTRAN uses static memory allocation. Other programming languages, such as PL/I, ALGOL, PASCAL, and SNOBOL4, support recursive procedure calls. When a recursive procedure is first invoked, its *depth of recursion* is 1, and the procedure executes at *level* 1. If the depth of recursion of a procedure is N and the procedure calls itself, it *descends* one level of recursion to level N+1. When the procedure executes a *return* statement, it *ascends* one level of recursion. Any attempt to return from level 0 is a program error.

When a procedure is converted into machine language instructions by a compiler, it is roughly correct to say that each statement in the procedure is expanded into several machine language instructions. When a procedure is invoked, one of the machine language instructions is a branch (or branch and link) to the machine codes for the called procedure. In general, the machine language instruction immediately following the branch is the instruction to which control is returned when the called procedure finishes executing, and the address of that instruction is the *return address* for the procedure call. It is the responsibility of the calling procedure to make the return address known to the called procedure. (This is done by code generated by the compiler and is generally invisible to the programmer.)

Parameter passage between calling and called procedures is the combined responsibility of both procedures. We will restrict our attention in the following discussion to parameter passage by reference (c.f. Chapter 1, Section 1.3.6). (For a more detailed treatment of parameter passage, and a discussion of alternative parameter passage techniques, the reader is directed to any standard text on programming languages or compiler theory such as Gries [1971] or Pratt [1975].)

In general, different computer systems use different techniques for passing information between called and calling procedures. The details of program linkage are generally determined by the systems programmers for the particular system, and the conventions used are *linkage conventions*. It is sometimes possible for one programming language to invoke procedures written in another programming language, and the ideal situation would be if procedures coded in any given language could invoke procedures coded in any other language; unfortunately this is not the case. However, for any given programming language, it is usually possible to invoke procedures written in the machine's assembler language, and, by writing assembler language primitive routines, it is frequently possible to write and invoke procedures written in several different programming languages. In general, linkage conventions specify how the computer's registers are to be used during procedure calls and returns, how the actual parameters are passed to the called procedure, and how the called procedure returns values to the calling procedure. We will discuss some typical linkage conventions in the following paragraphs.

One responsibility of the calling procedure is creating a structure, defined by the linkage conventions, that contains all information necessary to describe the actual parameters passed to the called procedure. One way in which this is done is to create a sequential list of addresses of the actual parameters, in the order in which they appear in the calling statement, and to pass the address of this list to the called procedure; this is a *parameter address list*. In case an actual parameter is an expression, however, the calling procedure must evaluate that expression, place the value in a temporary memory location, and place the address of that temporary memory location in the parameter address list. As an example, a compiler would generate a parameter address list for the statement "Z:=ACK-ER(I,5+K)". The parameter address list would have two entries: the address of identifier I and the address of a temporary memory location containing the value of the expression "5+K".

The address of the parameter address list is passed to the called procedure in the way specified by the linkage conventions; some commonly used techniques are:

1. It is placed in a specified register.
2. It is placed in a designed memory location.
3. It is placed in an execution stack.
4. It is stored at a specified offset from the entry point of the called procedure, that is, it is stored at a specified place within the called procedure.

5. It is stored in a designated place within the calling procedure. The called procedure can use the return address to find the address of the parameter address list.

It is not a good programming practice for one procedure to directly modify or place values within a second procedure. Furthermore, in some programming systems, the called procedure is not loaded into the computer's main memory until the procedure is actually invoked. For these reasons, we will not consider 4) above to be a viable alternative to 1)-3) above. Similarly, technique 5) above is not always suitable, since the calling procedure may be removed from main memory after the called procedure is invoked.

Regardless of the chosen technique, the called procedure must be able to determine the address of each actual parameter whenever a reference is made to a formal parameter within the body of the called procedure; this is called *address resolution*. Consider the non-recursive procedure FACTORIAL given earlier and shown below:

```
procedure FACTORIAL(N);
declare (I,N,FACTORIAL) INTEGER;
FACTORIAL := 1;
I := 1;
while (I≤N) do
      begin
          FACTORIAL := FACTORIAL * I;
          I := I+1
      end
return;
end FACTORIAL;
```

The clause "**while** $(I \leq N)$ **do**" requires that the value of I be compared against the value of the actual parameter N, and hence the address of the actual parameter must be resolved. Once the linkage conventions are established, the code for resolving the address of an actual parameter is straightforward. The called procedure uses the parameter address which is found in the parameter address list. Linkage conventions also specify how the return address will be passed to the called procedure and how the result will be passed back to the calling procedure. The techniques are similar to those used for parameter passage and will not be further elaborated.

We shall now select a particular set of linkage conventions and show how a simple procedure such as FACTORIAL would be converted into machine language instructions. Let us assume that there are four registers, say R1, R2, R3, and R4, available for use. The calling procedure will create a parameter address list for each statement that invokes a procedure, and the address of the

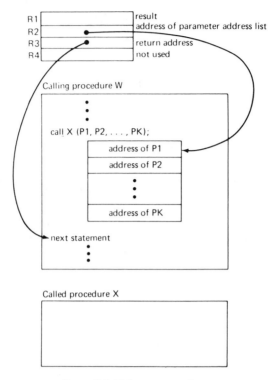

Figure 8.1. Linkage conventions.

parameter address list will be placed in register R2 before the calling procedure branches to the called procedure. The return address will be placed in register R3, and the called procedure must place its result in register R1 before returning control to the calling procedure; register R4 is not used in this example. In addition, the called procedure must save all the registers from the calling procedure in an internal save area immediately after being called and restore those registers just prior to returning. These conventions are illustrated in Figure 8.1.

Once again consider the procedure FACTORIAL, and suppose that FACTORIAL is invoked by the statement "X := FACTORIAL(3)." When the statement "X := FACTORIAL(3)" is converted into machine language instructions, the following approximate sequence of statements result in the calling procedure:

M1. Place the constant 3 in a temporary memory location, say T. (We assume that when a constant appears as an actual parameter, it is treated like a simple expression. T is a temporary memory location that holds the value of the expression, in this case 3.)

M2. Place the address of T in location S. (S is the parameter address list.)

M3. Place the address of S in register R2. (R2 contains the address of the parameter address list.)

M4. Place the address of the next instruction in register R3, and branch to procedure FACTORIAL. (R3 contains the return address.)

M5. After the return from FACTORIAL, store the contents of register R1 in memory location X. (This statement executes immediately after FACTORIAL returns control. The value returned by FACTORIAL is found in register R1.)

Let R designate the value in register R, [[R]] designate the value in the memory location whose address is contained in the memory location pointed to by register R (see illustration below), and c(I) designate the value in memory location I. (Note that [[R2]] designates the value of the first and in this case only actual parameter.) The procedure FACTORIAL roughly translates to machine instructions as follows:

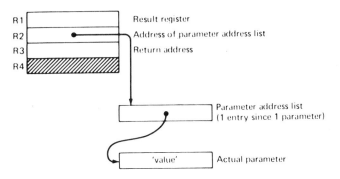

R2	designates the contents of register 2.
[R2]	designates the address of the first actual parameter.
[[R2]]	designates the value of the first actual parameter

F0. Save the contents of all the registers except R1 in internal save area SA. (R1 will return the result.)

F1. Place the constant 1 in register R1.

F2. Place the constant 1 in memory location I.

F3. If c(I)>[[R2]], then branch to statement F7.

F4. Place in register R1 the product of R1 and c(I).

F5. Increment the contents of memory location I by 1.

F6. Branch to statement F3.

F7. Restore the contents of all the registers except R1 from SA.

F8. Branch to the statement whose address is in register R3. (This is often called a *return jump*.)

Figure 8.2a shows the situation just before FACTORIAL executes F1, and Figure 8.2b shows the situation just after FACTORIAL terminates execution. Although the exact sequence of machine language instructions will differ from computer to computer, the above sequence illustrates typical code for linking one procedure to another when the procedures do not call themselves recursively.

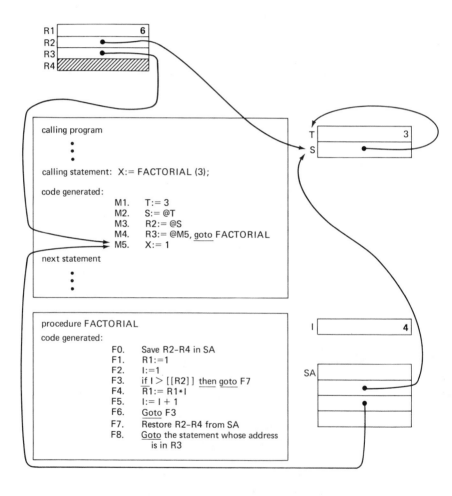

Figure 8.2a. The appearance of memory just before FACTORIAL(3) begins execution.

There are several reasons why procedures, when implemented as described above, cannot be used recursively. In order to see why this is the case, consider the sequence of machine instructions that would result if the recursive version of FACTORIAL were being considered. The procedure is as follows:

procedure FACTORIAL(N);
declare (N,FACTORIAL) INTEGER;
if (N = 0)
then FACTORIAL := 1
else FACTORIAL := N * FACTORIAL(N − 1) **endif**;
return;
end FACTORIAL;

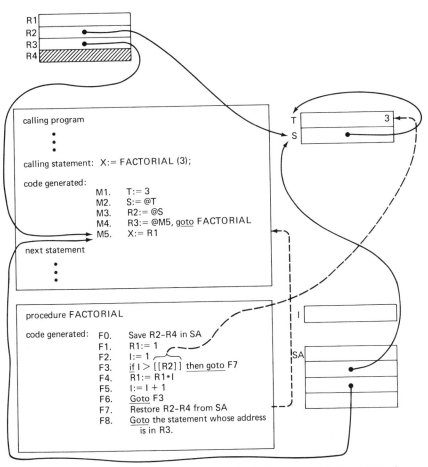

Figure 8.2b. The appearance of memory just after FACTORIAL(3) finishes execution.

Let TEMP1 be the address of a temporary memory location. TEMP1 will hold the value of the expression "N−1". Let TEMP2 be the address of a second temporary memory location. TEMP2 is the parameter address list. The factorial procedure expands into machine language statements roughly as follows:

F0. Save the contents of all registers except R1 in internal save area SA.

F1. If [[R2]]≠0, then branch to statement F4.

F2. Place the constant 1 in register R1.

F3. Branch to statement F9.

F4. Place in TEMP1 the value [[R2]]. Decrement the contents of TEMP1 by 1.

F5. Place in TEMP2 the address of TEMP1.

F6. Place the address of TEMP2 in register R2.

F7. Place in register R3 the address of the next instruction, and branch to procedure FACTORIAL.

F8. Multiply [[R2]] by R1, and place the result in register R1. (This is the value returned by the procedure.)

F9. Restore the contents of all registers except R1 from SA.

F10. Branch to the statement whose address is in register R3.

Now consider what happens if the statement "X := FACTORIAL(3)" is invoked. First, the value 3 is placed in the temporary memory location T. Next, the address of T is placed in the parameter address list S [statement M2 in the calling procedure]; the address of S is placed in R2; the address of statement M4 is placed in register R3; and a branch is made to procedure FACTORIAL. Procedure FACTORIAL immediately saves the calling procedure's registers (statement F0).

Statement F1 in FACTORIAL is executed, and since [[R2]] does not equal 0, the branch is taken to statement F4. Next, the value of [[R2]], namely 3, is placed in TEMP1. This is the value of the actual parameter. The value in TEMP1 is decremented by 1 (to a new value of 2), which becomes the new, actual parameter for the recursive call. The address of TEMP1 is placed in TEMP2. This is the parameter address list. The address of TEMP2 is placed in register R2. At statement F7, the address of statement F8 is placed in register R3. Procedure FACTORIAL is now entered once again recursively, and saves all the registers in SA. Registers R2 and R3 have been changed from the values that the calling procedure put in them, and those values are now destroyed in SA as well. Thus the value 3 and the return address of the calling procedure are lost permanently. This situation is shown in Figure 8.3.

At statement F1, a comparison is made between the constant 0 and [[R2]] (which now refers to location TEMP1 in procedure FACTORIAL). The value in TEMP1 is 2, so the test fails, and the branch is taken to statement F4. At this

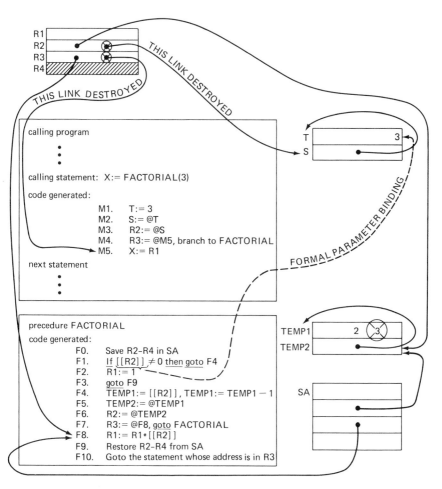

Figure 8.3. The destroyed contents of registers R2 and R3 are shown. The location TEMP1 originally received a 3 from [[R2]] which was then decremented to 2.

point, the value in TEMP1 is placed once again in memory location TEMP1, which is subsequently decremented to 1. The address of TEMP1 is again placed in TEMP2, and the address of TEMP2 is (again) placed in register R2. The address of statement F8 is placed in register R3, and the branch is again taken to FACTORIAL. This situation is shown in Figure 8.4. The same sequence of statements is repeated two more times, and FACTORIAL is invoked first with actual parameter having value 1 and finally with actual parameter having value 0. During the final entry to FACTORIAL, when statement F1 is executed, [[R2]] equals 0, so the branch to statement F4 is not taken; instead, the value 1 is placed in register R1, and the branch is taken to statement F9. At statement F9, registers

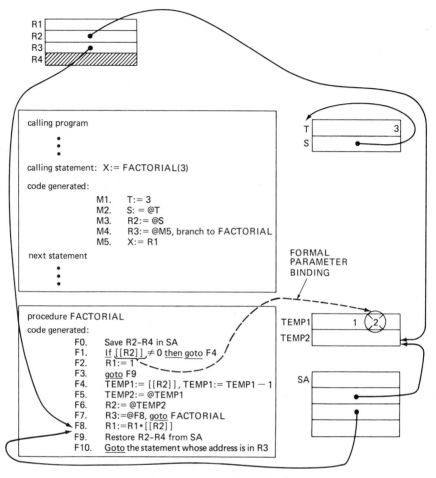

Figure 8.4. The old value in [[R2]] was destroyed when TEMP1 was decremented at F4.

R2 and R3 are restored from SA. R2 still contains the address of TEMP2 which contains the address of TEMP1 which contains 0. R3 still contains the return address in FACTORIAL of statement F8. At statement F10, the return branch is taken which passes control to statement F8. Now [[R2]] is multiplied by R1 and the result (in this case 0) placed in register R1. Notice that memory location [[R2]] had value 1 when the procedure originally invoked FACTORIAL recursively, but upon return it has the new (incorrect) value 0; hence the result at this level of recursion is incorrect. Continuing, registers R2 and R3 are restored from SA again and the branch to statement F8 (currently in register R3) is taken. Again the multiplication is performed, the result, again 0, is placed in register

R1, and the branch is taken to statement F8. The procedure is now in an infinite loop, and the process continues forever. The return linkage was destroyed when the procedure first invoked itself recursively so it can never return to the calling procedure.

What went wrong? Several things. First when the procedure called itself recursively, the return address for the previous call was lost. Second, the value of the temporary expression (N − 1, held in TEMP1) for a given level of recursion was lost as the function descended to the next deeper level of recursion. Third, the values of the actual parameters were lost as the function descended recursively. As a result, when the function ascended one level of recursion, the incorrect actual parameter was used. All of these things occurred because only a single save area (SA) was used to save the return address, and several save areas were needed, one for each call to the procedure.

8.4 IMPLEMENTING RECURSIVE PROCEDURES

In this section, we will discuss one method of implementing recursive procedures so that these difficulties do not arise. We will initially restrict our attention to actual parameters that are simple program identifiers (not arrays, structures, field references, etc.) and defer until the following section a more general discussion of parameter passage.

When implementing recursive procedures, it is necessary to preserve for each level of recursion the addresses of all actual parameters, the values of all local variables, all return addresses, and the values of all temporary expressions. When the procedure returns from one level of recursion to the next higher level of recursion, all information preserved for that level of recursion must be restored. This suggests the use of a stack for preserving the required information, and the use of such a *recursion stack* is our next topic of discussion.

When a procedure is to be called recursively, it is necessary for the compiler to generate appropriate machine instructions to preserve all information as described above; that information is the *current environment* of the procedure. One way this can be done is as follows: First, all memory locations used for local variables, temporary expression values, and parameter address lists are allocated dynamically upon entry to a procedure; the block of memory containing them is the *activation record* for the current procedure invocation. Dynamic memory allocation techniques that can be used are discussed in Chapter 7. If a procedure is invoked ten times without returning to the calling procedure, then ten independent activation records would be allocated. During execution, a procedure uses a single memory location or register to point to the current activation record; this is the *current environment pointer*. The value of the current environment pointer is determined when the current activation record is allocated. All statements within the procedure always refer to memory locations within the current activation record by referring to addresses relative to the current environment pointer. All references to actual parameters, local variables, etc. are made to the appropriate field in the current activation record. Just before the procedure calls another procedure (or itself), the address of the parameter address list, return address for the current procedure invocation, and the current environment pointer are pushed into a recursion stack. The new return address and the address of the current parameter address list are passed to the procedure just as they were in the nonrecursive implementation. Upon return from a called procedure, however, additional code is required to restore the address of the parameter address list, the return address, and the current environment pointer after obtaining their values from the recursion stack. An illustration of this situation is given in Figure 8.5, where register R4 holds the current environment pointer.

In order to see how this technique works, we will once again consider the procedure FACTORIAL. Now, however, the machine language instructions for FACTORIAL are slightly different as described below:

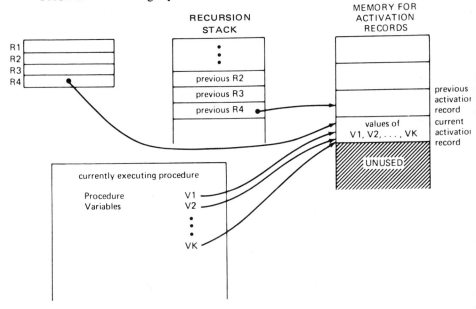

Figure 8.5. Register R4 points to the current environment; the recursion stack holds pointers to the environments of calling procedures.

procedure FACTORIAL(N);
declare (N,FACTORIAL) INTEGER;

if (N = 0)
then FACTORIAL := 1
else FACTORIAL := N * FACTORIAL(N − 1) **endif**;
return;
end FACTORIAL;

This procedure expands into machine language statements roughly as follows, where statements FA thru FC are those statements which have been added to the previous version of the same procedure:

FA.   Allocate 2 words of memory for the current activation record. This includes memory for the expression N−1 (TEMP1) and the newly allocated parameter address list (TEMP2). Place the address of the activation record in register R4.

F1.   If [[R2]]≠0, then branch to statement F4.

F2.   Place the constant 1 in register R1.

F3.   Branch to statement F9.

F4.   Place in TEMP1 the value [[R2]]. Decrement the contents of TEMP1 by 1.

F5.   Place in TEMP2 the address of TEMP1.

FB.   Push the contents of registers R2, R3, and R4 in the recursion stack.

F6.   Place the address of TEMP2 in register R2.

F7.   Place in register R3 the address of the next instruction (the return address) and branch to procedure FACTORIAL.

FC.   Restore registers R4, R3, and R2 from the recursion stack, and pop the stack.

F8.   Multiply [[R2]] by R1, and place the result in register R1. (This is the value returned by the procedure.)

F9.   Branch to the address in register R3.

The machine language statements corresponding to the statement X := FACTORIAL(3) also differ from those presented before. The revised statements follow:

M1.   Place the constant 3 in a temporary memory location, say T.

M2.   Place the address of T in location S.

MB.   Push the contents of registers R2, R3, and R4 in the recursion stack.

M3.   Place the address of S in register R2.

M4.   Place the address of the next instruction in register R3 (the return address) and branch to procedure FACTORIAL.

MC.   After the return from FACTORIAL, restore the contents of registers R4, R3, and R2 from the recursion stack, and pop the stack.

M5.   Store the contents of R1 in memory location X.

Consider once again what happens if the statement "X := FACTORIAL(3)" is invoked. Just as before, the value 3 is placed in memory location T, and the address of memory location T is placed in the parameter address list S. Now, unlike before, the contents of registers R2, R3, and R4 are pushed in the recursion stack to preserve their values while FACTORIAL executes. The address of S, the parameter address list, is placed in register R2, the return address, now the address of statement MC, is placed in register R3, and the branch is taken to procedure FACTORIAL. This is shown in Figure 8.6.

Upon entry to procedure FACTORIAL (statement FA), a block of memory for the current environment is allocated, and its address is placed in register R4, the current environment pointer. At statement F1, a comparison is made between [[R2]], the actual parameter (value 3), and the constant 0. The test fails, so the branch to statement F4 is taken. Statements F4 and F5 evaluate N − 1 and leave the value in TEMP1 of the current environment. The value of TEMP1 is 2; this is the actual parameter for the recursive call. The address of the temporary is placed in TEMP2, which is the new parameter address list. This situation is shown in Figure 8.7. At statement FB, the address of the old parameter address list (register R2), the old return address (register R3), and the current environment pointer (register R4) are pushed in the recursion stack. This preserves them until the called procedure returns control. At statement F6, the address of the new parameter address list is placed in R2, and, at statement F7, the return address is placed in register R3, and the branch is taken to procedure FACTORIAL. This situation is shown in Figure 8.8.

The above sequence of events is repeated two more times until FACTORIAL is entered with actual parameter 0. Figure 8.9 shows this situation. Now, however, after the current activation record is allocated, the test at statement F1 fails. Hence statements F2, F3, and then F9 are executed. Statement F2 determines the value of the function [FACTORIAL(0) = 1] and places that value in register R1, and statement F3 is a branch to statement F9, which is a return branch from the procedure. The return address is the address of statement FC, so the branch is taken to statement FC. At statement FC, the registers R4, R3, and R2 are restored; these are the parameter address list address, the return address, and the current environment pointers, respectively. Hence all references within the procedure are to the correct environment for the current level of recursion, and the return address is also correct for the current level of recursion. This is shown in Figure 8.10.

At statement F8, the value in register R1 (value 1) is multiplied by [[R2]] (TEMP1) and the product placed in register R1. This is the value of FACTORIAL(1) to be returned to the next higher level of recursion. This process continues until, as shown in Figure 8.11, the return is made to the first (original) function call. The final value 6 is computed, and the final return from the function is properly made to the calling procedure.

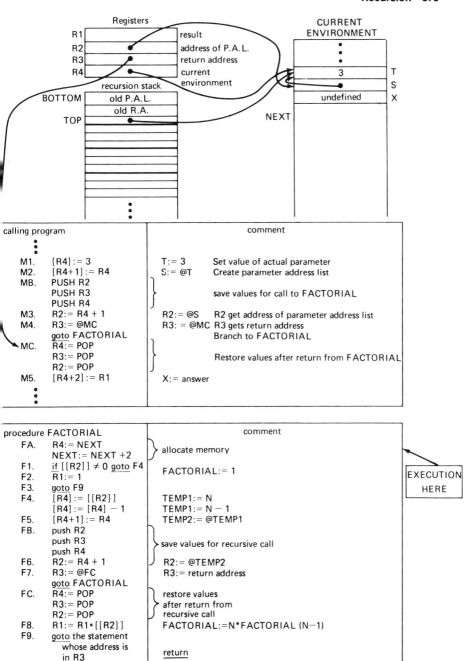

Figure 8.6. The appearance of the linkage registers, recursion stack, and current environment just after entering FACTORIAL.

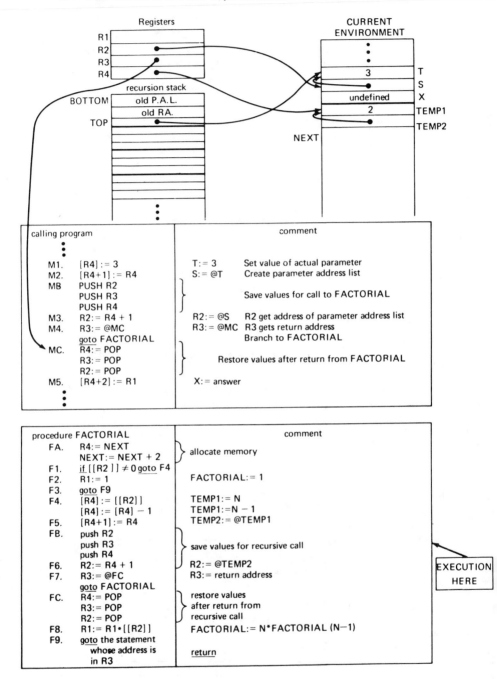

Figure 8.7. The appearance of the linkage registers, recursion stack, and current environment just prior to calling FACTORIAL recursively for the first time.

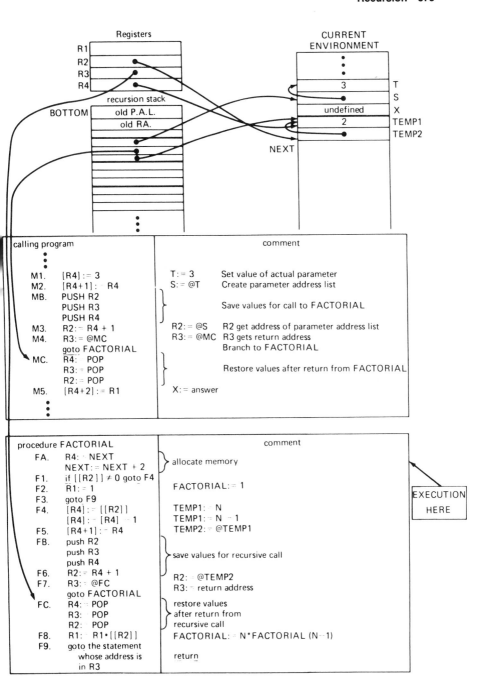

Figure 8.8. The appearance of the linkage registers, recursion stack, and current environment just after entering FACTORIAL recursively for the first time.

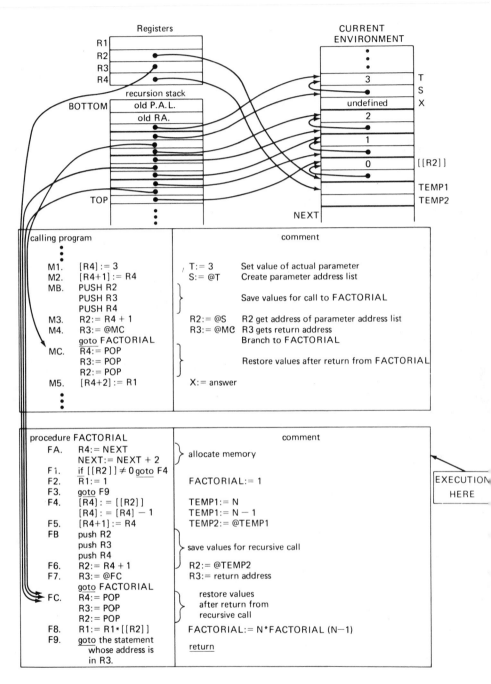

Figure 8.9. The appearance of the linkage registers, recursion stack, and current environment just after entering FACTORIAL recursively for the third time.

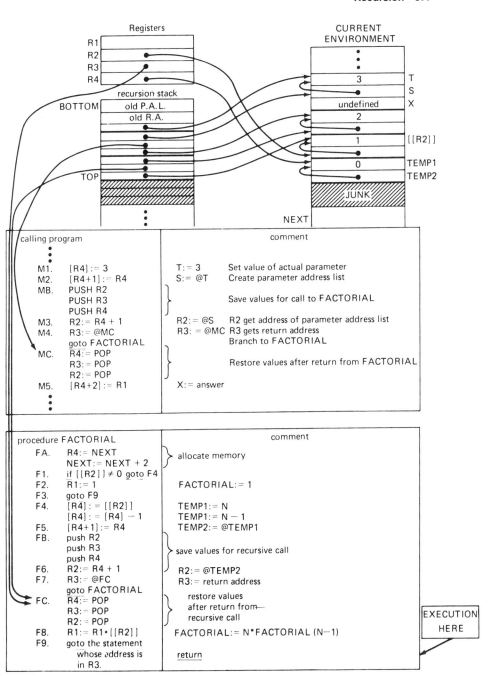

Figure 8.10. The appearance of the linkage registers, recursion stack, and current environment just before returning from FACTORIAL for the fourth time.

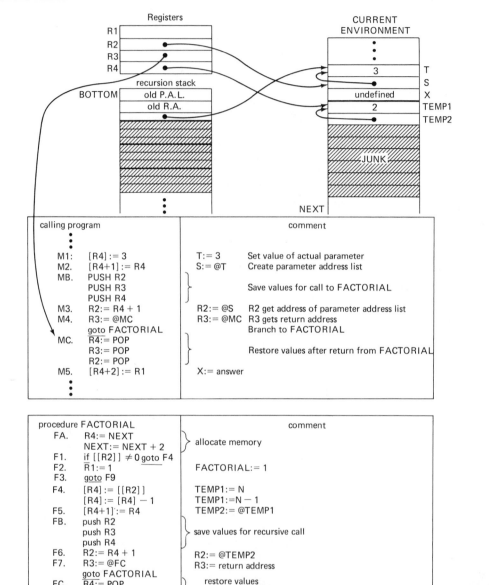

Figure 8.11. The appearance of the linkage registers, recursion stack, and current environment just prior to returning to the calling procedure.

Exercise 8.5. How should FACTORIAL be modified so that it liberates (frees) the memory that it allocated during its execution? Will this deallocation procedure work in general? Why?

Exercise 8.6. Consider the procedure gcd given earlier. In the style used above for procedure FACTORIAL, indicate roughly what the machine language statements would look like. Illustrate in a figure, and identify all local variables, temporaries, and parameter address lists.

8.5 DATA STRUCTURES AS ACTUAL PROCEDURE PARAMETERS

When an actual parameter in a procedure call is an array identifier, field referencing operation, descriptor for a structure, or other non-simple variable identifier, the problems associated with parameter passage are somewhat more complex than in the simple case described in the previous section. As an example, consider a procedure call with an array identifier as an actual parameter. Any reference to a formal parameter within the called procedure is understood to be a reference to some element in the array within the calling procedure. This is illustrated below:

procedure MAIN;
declare A(100) INTEGER;
    •
    •
Z := F(A);
    •
    •
end MAIN;
procedure F(B);
declare B(100) INTEGER;
    •
    •
B(20) := 2;
    •
    •
end F;

The procedure called MAIN declares A to be an array having 100 elements. The array identifier A is passed as the first actual parameter to the procedure F. The formal parameter in procedure F is also declared to be an array having 100 elements. Since it is a formal parameter, memory is not allocated for an array. Instead, code is generated for resolving the references to elements in the structure. In the above example, the formal parameter B is declared to be an array. Hence the reference B(20) in procedure F refers to element A(20) of the array A in the calling procedure.

Procedure F must assume that the actual parameter is the address of an array that has 100 elements; otherwise the reference within the called procedure might be incorrect. (This could be checked dynamically, of course, but we consider only the simplest case here.) As an example of an incorrect reference, suppose that the statement "Z := F(A(90))" were to appear in procedure MAIN. The actual parameter A(90) could be treated in one of two ways depending on the semantics of the particular programming language. It could be treated as an expression, and hence the value of A(90) would be copied into a temporary memory location whose address would be passed to the called procedure. In this case, the reference within the called procedure F would be incorrect, because F would get the address of a temporary memory location and not an array. The second alternative is that the actual parameter A(90) could be treated as the address of a field to be passed to the procedure F. In this case the reference B(20) in procedure F would be incorrect, since B(20) would refer to the element A(109) which does not exist, (B(1) refers to A(90), B(2) refers to A(91) etc.) and an incorrect reference would also result.

In order to be consistent with most programming languages that pass parameters by reference, including the algorithmic language used in this text, let us assume that simple, subscripted variables and field references cause the address of the designated field to be passed to the called procedure; that is, statements like F(A.E(10)) and G(A.B) would result in the *address* of the designated field being passed to the called procedures. As a general rule, programming languages should check for agreement between the data type of an actual parameter and the declared type of the corresponding formal parameter; when they don't, it is the responsibility of the programmer to insure that there is type agreement. As a simple example showing such agreement, consider the procedures shown below:

```
procedure MAIN;
declare 1   A,
            2      B(10)      INTEGER,
            2      C(10)      INTEGER;
Z := G(A.C);
    •
    •
end MAIN;
procedure G(A1);
declare A1(10) INTEGER;
    •
    •
A1(3) := 7;
    •
    •
return;
end G;
```

The MAIN procedure declares A to be a structure. The actual parameter A.C in the procedure call statement is compiled into code so that the address of the designated field is passed to procedure G. In the above example, the address of the ten-word array A.C is passed to procedure G. Procedure G assumes that it receives the address of a ten-word structure, which it does. Hence the reference A1(3) in procedure G is a reference to A.C(3) in the MAIN procedure.

8.6 RECURSIVE PROCEDURES FOR MANIPULATING DATA STRUCTURES

One of the primary reasons for using recursive procedures when working with data structures is to take advantage of the recursive stack mechanism used in the recursive procedure calls. We will illustrate the use of recursion for manipulating data structures in the framework of the LISP programming language, our choice for several reasons: LISP was one of the first languages to introduce recursion; LISP was the first language to allow convenient manipulation of structures recursively; LISP provides a convenient and concise notation for manipulating structures; LISP is actively used today and is an important language in programming language theory and artificial intelligence; and LISP is based on sound mathematical principles. Before describing LISP, however, we will present a tree searching algorithm that uses a data structure which is similar to the data structure used by the LISP language. In this example, unlike in LISP, the programmer directly manipulates pointers and datatype flags.

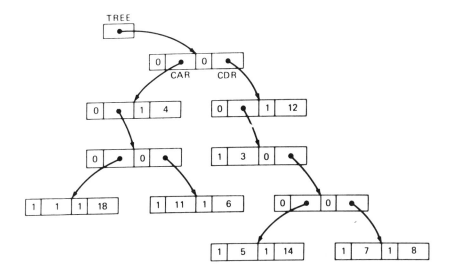

The tree structure illustrated below shows the form of the structure we wish to search. Each cell in the structure has two similar fields called the CAR and the CDR of the cell. (The names CAR and CDR are borrowed from LISP. They originally stood for "contents of the address register" and "contents of the decrement register," which are 15-bit fields of the accumulator register on the IBM 7090 computer. These terms have stuck and are still in common use today.) Each cell corresponds to one node of a tree and is defined by the following structure declaration:

template 1	CELL1,	
2	TYPECAR	BOOLEAN,
2	CAR	CELLPOINTER,
2	TYPECDR	BOOLEAN,
2	CDR	CELLPOINTER;
template 1	CELL2,	
2	TYPECAR	BOOLEAN,
2	CARI	15 BIT INTEGER,
2	TYPECDR	BOOLEAN,
2	CDRI	15 BIT INTEGER;
template	CELLPOINTER	15 BIT POINTER **to** (CELL1,CELL2);

This structure is similar to the cell structures used in many LISP implementations and has the essential features of the LISP cell structure. For a CELL structure, if the TYPECAR (TYPECDR) field has value $'0'$, then the CAR (CDR) field is a pointer to a CELL. If the TYPECAR (TYPECDR) field has value $'1'$, then the CARI (CDRI) field contains a 15-bit integer. (In LISP, the data field of a cell does not in general contain the actual data, depending of course on the specific implementation, but rather a pointer to a cell; Furthermore, several data types are allowed and the type fields are therefore several bits long. A mark bit for garbage collection is also included.)

Let us suppose that an arbitrary tree structure of the type illustrated earlier has been constructed. Our goal will be to write a procedure to search the entire tree structure for a cell whose CAR or CDR field contains the integer N and return a pointer to that cell. We will write a procedure that has two formal parameters, a 16-bit pointer to a cell, and the 15-bit value being sought. The procedure for searching the tree is given below:

```
procedure SEARCH(FIELD,VALUE);
```

template 1	CELL1,	
2	TYPECAR	BOOLEAN,
2	CAR	CELLPOINTER,
2	TYPECDR	BOOLEAN,
2	CDR	CELLPOINTER;

```
template 1     CELL2,
         2     TYPECAR      BOOLEAN,
         2     CARI         15 BIT INTEGER,
         2     TYPECDR      BOOLEAN,
         2     CDRI         15 BIT INTEGER;
template   CELLPOINTER    15 BIT POINTER to (CELL1, CELL2);
declare    FIELD      CELLPOINTER;
declare    VALUE      15 BITS;
comment This case statement searches the CAR half of the structure pointed to by
        FIELD;
case
    ([FIELD].TYPECAR = '1'):
        begin
            comment FIELD points to a cell whose CAR field contains data. Test that
                    data;
            if ([FIELD].CARI = VALUE)
            then begin
                comment The test succeeds. Return FIELD;
                TEMP := FIELD
                end
            else begin
                comment The test fails. Continue the search;
                TEMP := null
                end
            end;
    ([FIELD].TYPECAR = '0'):
        begin
            comment FIELD points to a cell whose CAR field points to a structure.
                    SEARCH the structure;
                    TEMP := SEARCH([FIELD].CAR,VALUE)
            end;
end case;
comment This case statement searches the CDR half of the structure pointed to by
        FIELD;
case
    (TEMP ≠ null):
        begin
            comment The CAR search succeeded. Return the value found;
            SEARCH := TEMP
            end;
    ([FIELD].TYPECDR = '1'):
        begin
            comment The VALUE was not found in the CAR half of the structure and
                    FIELD points to a cell whose CDR field contains data. Test that
                    data;
            if ([FIELD].CDRI = VALUE)
```

```
            then begin
                 comment The search succeeds. Return FIELD;
                 SEARCH := FIELD
            end
        else begin
                 comment The search fails. Return null;
                 SEARCH := null
            end
    end
    ([FIELD].TYPECDR = '0'):
        begin
            comment The VALUE was not found in the CAR half of the structure and
                    FIELD points to a cell whose CDR field points to a structure.
                    SEARCH that structure and return the result of that search;
            SEARCH := SEARCH ([FIELD].CRD,VALUE)
        end
end case;
return;
end SEARCH;
```

Initially the procedure is entered with a pointer to a tree as the first actual parameter. If the CAR field of the cell pointed to by FIELD contains an integer, then the value of that integer is compared for equality with the desired value. If the comparison succeeds, then the value of TEMP is set to FIELD which is a pointer to the desired cell; if the comparison fails, however, then TEMP is set to null. Next suppose that FIELD points to a cell whose CAR field is a pointer. Then SEARCH is called recursively to search that part of the structure, and the value returned is assigned to TEMP. The first entry in the second *case* statement

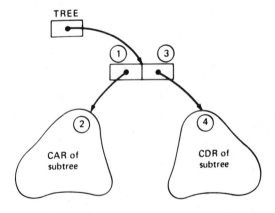

Figure 8.12. The order of searching elements in the structure.

tests whether or not the search of the CAR half of the structure succeeded. If the search succeeded, then the value found is returned; otherwise the CDR half of the referenced structure is searched in exactly the same way that the CAR half was searched. See Figure 8.12.

The problem of searching the entire tree is reduced to searching the left part of the tree and then searching the right part of the tree. However, the right part of the tree is only searched if the desired data item is not located in the left part of the tree. Since the left and right parts of the tree are themselves trees, recursive application of the procedure is possible. The procedure ultimately terminates since, after each recursive call, there are fewer nodes to be searched, and no node is ever searched more than one time.

Exercise 8.7. Trace the procedure calls that would result if SEARCH were invoked with a pointer to the tree illustrated earlier as the first actual parameter and the value 14 as the second actual parameter. Perform a similar trace if the value 15 is the second actual parameter.

Exercise 8.8. Now suppose that a tree is modified so that it is no longer a tree but has the structure shown below. Show that the procedure gets into an 'infinite recursion' loop. How can infinite recursion be avoided?

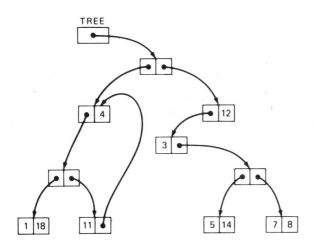

8.7 RECURSIVE DEFINITIONS AND LISP

The LISP (*LIS*t *P*rocessor) programming language, although developed in the late fifties, is still a very important programming language used in artificial intelligence research. In this section, we will indicate very briefly some of the important features of the LISP language, and we will present enough information about LISP to illustrate how recursive definitions are used for manipulating data structures. It is not our goal to give the reader a writing knowledge of LISP. For that, the interested reader should consult one of the standard textbooks or manuals cited at the end of this chapter.

In LISP, all structures are manipulated by the LISP system rather than by the programmer. It is true for most LISP implementations that program variables, values returned by procedures, actual parameters to procedures, and so forth, are descriptors to the actual data items. These descriptors either point to LISP *cells*, or they point to *atomic data items*. The type field of a descriptor is set by the LISP system according to the type of the object referenced by that descriptor. LISP atomic data items, or *atoms* for short, are either atomic symbols, fixed point numbers (integers), floating point numbers (reals), or the Boolean values T (**true**) or NIL (**false**). (The value NIL is also used as the null pointer and designates the empty list.) Atomic symbols are strings of numerals and capital letters and are from 1 to 30 characters long, beginning with a letter.

LISP cells are similar to the cells described in the previous section; they contain two major fields, a CAR field and a CDR field. The principle data structure used by the LISP programmer is the *list*. A list consists of any number of LISP cells linearly linked together by their CDR fields. The CDR field of the last cell of a list must contain a NIL pointer. Several LISP lists are illustrated below:

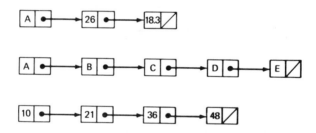

LISP structures are illustrated by showing the cells as rectangles divided into two parts, the CAR on the left and the CDR on the right. When one of the fields contains a null pointer (NIL), a slash is shown in that field; when one of the fields contains a descriptor to an atomic data item, the *value* of that data item is shown in the field of the cell. Thus the first list shown above consists of three elements, the symbolic atom 'A', the integer 26, and the floating point number 18.3.

Symbolically, LISP lists are described in *list notation* by placing the element values within parentheses that are separated by blanks. Using list notation, the lists illustrated above would be denoted:

(A 26 18.3)
(A B C D E)
(10 21 36 48)

The elements of a list may themselves be lists, and each list element is called a sublist of the list. This is illustrated below:

(A (B C) D)

((A B) (C D))

((A((B((C D) E)) F)) G)

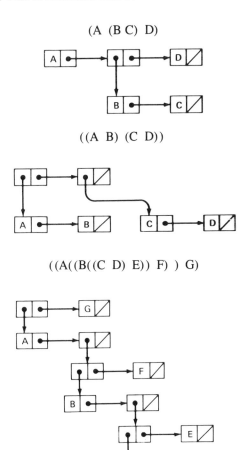

Exercise 8.9. For each of the lists described below in list notation, show the resulting cell structure:
  a. ((A) (B) (C))
  b. (A (B (C)))
  c. (((A) B) C)

For each of the following structures, give the corresponding list notation.

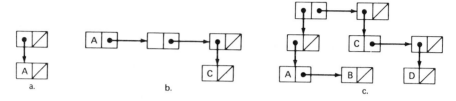

a.   b.   c.

Some LISP structures are not lists. For example, the single-cell structure is not

A | B

a list, because the CDR field of the last cell (the only cell) does not contain the NIL pointer. This structure is a *dotted pair*, which is the most general form of LISP cell. Lists are made of dotted pairs whose CDR fields all contain pointers. Any structure that contains a dotted pair like the one above cannot be represented in list notation; in fact, such a structure is a binary tree. In order to have a notation that is completely general, the concept of *dot notation* was introduced. The structure illustrated above is denoted "(A.B)" ('A dot B'). Every list structure can be described using dot notation. To illustrate this principle, each list described earlier is designated below in dot notation:

(A.(26.(18.3.NIL))) = (A 26 18.3)
(A.(B.(C.(D.(E.NIL))))) = (A B C D E)
(10.(21.(36.(48.NIL)))) = (10 26 36 48)
(NIL.NIL) = NIL
(A.((B.(C.NIL)).(D.NIL))) = (A (B C) D)
((A.(B.NIL)).((C. (D.NIL)).NIL)) = ((A B) (C D))
((A.(((B.(((C.(D.NIL)).(E.NIL)).NIL)).(F.NIL)).NIL)).(G.NIL))
    = ((A ((B ((C D) E)) F)) G)

Exercise 8.10. For each structure designated below in dot notation, show the LISP cell structure:
a. (A.(B.(C.NIL)))
b. (A.((B.((C.NIL).NIL)).NIL))
c. (((A.NIL).(B.NIL)).(C.NIL))

Give the dot notation that designates each of the following structures.

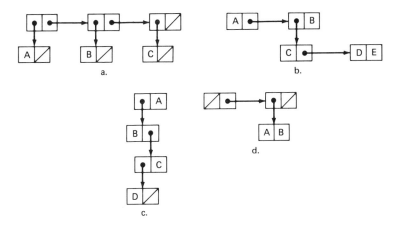

Structures are usually designated in list notation unless they contain dotted pairs, in which case a mixture of list and dot notations is used. For example, the list of dotted pairs shown below would be designated as ((A.B) (C.D) (E.F)).

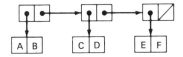

Lists of dotted pairs are sometimes used, and we will illustrate their use later.

As a programming language, LISP is unique: There are no declarations, few control structures, and syntactically, all LISP constructs are written as lists. To begin with, LISP function calls appear as lists, where the first element of the list is the function name, and the remaining elements of the list are the actual parameters to the function. For example, (PLUS 10 11) designates the function PLUS with actual parameters 10 and 11. The value returned by this expression is the integer value 21. The statement (TIMES (PLUS 1 3) 7) returns the value 28, which is the value of (PLUS 1 3) times 7, or 4 times 7. All arithmetic and logical values are specified in the above way, and, in fact, there are no arithmetic or boolean operators like those provided in most programming languages. The following table describes some simple LISP functions to operate on numeric values:

LISP expression	semantics
(PLUS x1 x2 x3 . . . xn)	x1+x2+x3+. . . +xn
(ADD1 x)	x+1
(DIFFERENCE x1 x2)	x1−x2
(SUB1 x)	x−1
(MAX x1 x2 x3 . . . xn)	maximum of x1, x2, . . . xn
(MIN x1 x2 x3 . . . xn)	minimum of x1, x2, . . . xn
(TIMES x1 x2 x3 . . . xn)	x1*x2*x3. . .*xn
(QUOTIENT x1 x2)	x1/x2
(REMAINDER x1 x2)	mod(x1,x2) if x1 and x2 are integers; else the residue after dividing x1 by x2.
(LESSP x1 x2)	T if x1<x2; NIL if x1 ≥ x2
(GREATERP x1 x2)	T if x1>x2; NIL if x1 ≤ x2
(ZEROP x1)	T if x1 = 0;NIL if x1 ≠ 0
(EQUAL x1 x2)	T if x1 = x2; NIL otherwise

In the above expressions, the value of the result is assumed to be floating point, unless all arguments are integer, in which case the result is integer.

Unless the evaluation of an identifier or list is explicitly inhibited by the function QUOTE (see below), all identifiers and lists are evaluated. Lists are evaluated by treating the first element of the list as the name of a function and treating the remaining elements as actual parameters for the function. The actual parameters are first evaluated and their values passed to the procedure.

The special function QUOTE must be used when an actual parameter is not to be evaluated. For example, the statement (F (A B C)) invokes the function F with one actual parameter, the *value* of the list (A B C). In contrast, the statement (F (QUOTE (A B C))) invokes the function F with one actual parameter, the list (A B C). Similarly, (G A) invokes the function G with one actual parameter, the value of the identifier A, whereas (G (QUOTE A)) invokes the function G with the atom A as the actual parameter.

There are six primitive functions in LISP that are central to all list processing operations; they are: CONS, CAR, CDR, EQ, ATOM, and NULL. Each of these functions is described below:

(CONS x y) CONS allocates and returns a new LISP cell and places a descriptor to the value of x in its CAR field and a descriptor to the value of y in its CDR field. The actual parameters to CONS can be atoms or cells.

(CAR x) The actual parameter x is evaluated. If x evaluates to a dotted pair, the value in the CAR field of that dotted pair is returned. If x evaluates to an atom then (CAR x) is undefined.

(CDR x)   The actual parameter x is evaluated. If x evaluates to a dotted pair, the value in the CDR field of that dotted pair is returned. If x evaluates to an atom, then (CDR x) is undefined.

(EQ x y)   EQ is a predicate that returns T (**true**) only if x and y evaluate to identical non-numeric atoms; otherwise EQ returns NIL (**false**).

(ATOM x)   ATOM is a predicate that returns T, if x evaluates to an atom and NIL if x evaluates to a dotted pair.

(NULL x)   NULL is a predicate that returns T, if and only if x evaluates to NIL. (Note that the empty list evaluates to NIL.)

Thus, for example,

(CONS (QUOTE A) (QUOTE B))	yields (A.B)
(CONS (QUOTE A) NIL)	yields (A)
(CONS (QUOTE (A)) (QUOTE (B))	yields ((A).B)
(CONS (QUOTE A) (QUOTE (B)))	yields (A B)
(CAR (QUOTE (A.B)))	yields A
(CONS (CAR (QUOTE (A.B))) (QUOTE C))	yields (A.C)
(CAR ( ))	yields NIL
(CAR (QUOTE A))	yields *undefined*
(CDR ( ))	yields NIL
(CDR (QUOTE (A B C)))	yields (B C)
(CDR (QUOTE A))	yields *undefined*
(ATOM (QUOTE A))	yields T
(ATOM (QUOTE (A)))	yields NIL
(ATOM (CAR (QUOTE (A.B))))	yields T
(EQ (QUOTE A) (QUOTE A))	yields T
(EQ (QUOTE A) (QUOTE B))	yields NIL
(EQ (QUOTE (A)) (QUOTE (A)))	yields NIL
(EQ (QUOTE A) (CAR (QUOTE (A.B))))	yields T
(NULL (QUOTE A))	yields NIL
(NULL (QUOTE ( )))	yields T
(NULL ( ))	yields T

LISP provides one conditional statement called COND. The function COND (*COND*itional) has an arbitrary number of lists as its actual parameters, but these lists must be of a special form: Each of the lists must have two elements, a predicate (a function that evaluates to T or NIL), and an arbitrary expression. A call to COND has the form:

$$(COND\ (p1\ e1)\ (p2\ e2)\ .\ .\ .\ (pn\ en)\ )$$

which is often written this way:

$$\begin{aligned}
&\text{(COND} \\
&\quad \text{(p1 e1)} \\
&\quad \text{(p2 e2)} \\
&\qquad \bullet \\
&\qquad \bullet \\
&\qquad \bullet \\
&\quad \text{(pn en))}
\end{aligned}$$

Each pi is a predicate and each ei is an expression. The value of the above COND statement is the value of e1, if p1 evaluates to T; otherwise, the value of e2, if p2 evaluates to T, and so forth. If none of the pi evaluate to T, then the value of the entire expression is undefined. The COND function can be defined in algorithmic notation as follows:

```
procedure COND(p1,e1,p2,e2,. . .pn,en);
        case
            (p1)    :  COND := e1;
            (p2)    :  COND := e2;
            (p3)    :  COND := e3;
                •
                •
                •
            (pn)    :  COND := en;
            (true)  :  COND := undefined;
        end case;
    return;
end COND;
```

Note that the use of an unspecified number of formal parameters in a procedure is not allowed in our notation and is done here only to clarify the semantics of COND. The use of COND is illustrated below:

(COND ((ATOM (QUOTE A))   10)
   (T   NIL))   yields 10 since (QUOTE
                 A) evaluates to an atom

(COND ((EQ (QUOTE A) (QUOTE B)) QUOTE C))
   (T   (QUOTE A))   ) yields A since the atoms A
                 and B differ

(COND ((EQ 10 (ADD1 9)) NIL) (T 0)) yields NIL since (ADD1
                 9) equals 10

Conditional expressions can appear as expressions within conditionals, and they can appear as the predicates in conditionals, provided that the corresponding expressions are themselves predicates.

It is relatively easy to define functions in LISP. The LISP system provides a procedure named DEFINE that is used, and DEFINE takes a single list as its argument. The list given to DEFINE consists of any number of sublists, and each sublist has exactly two elements: the name of a function to be defined and the function definition. The form of a call to DEFINE is:

(DEFINE (QUOTE   ((fn1 fd1) (fn2 fd2) . . . (fnn fdn))))

where fni is the i'th function name to be defined, and fdi is the i'th function definition. For clarity, the individual function definitions generally start on different lines of code, and the entire expression appears this way:

```
(DEFINE (QUOTE   (
         (fn1      fd1)
         (fn2      fd2)
          •
          •
         (fnn      fdn)
     )   ) )
```

Each fni is an atomic symbol that is the name of the function; each fdi is a function definition called a *lambda expression*. (See Church [1941] for the underlying formalism.) Lambda expressions convey to the LISP system the same information that appears in the procedure definitions of most programming languages; namely, the names of the formal parameters and the statements that make up the procedure body. Lambda expressions appear this way:

(LAMBDA   (formal _ parameters)   expression)

where 'expression' is any valid LISP expression. This can best be illustrated with the well known function FACTORIAL:

```
(DEFINE   (QUOTE   (
0         1        2

   (FACTORIAL   (LAMBDA   (N)
   3            4         5 5'

      (COND
      6
```

```
(      (EQ N 0)   1   )
7      8        8'     7'

(T     (TIMES N    (FACTORIAL   (DIFFERENCE N 1)  )    )     )
9      10         11           12              12' 11' 10' 9'
       )  )  )  )  )  )
       6' 4' 3' 2' 1' 0'
```

The parentheses have been numbered in order to simplify reference to the definition. In the above definition, DEFINE has a single actual parameter, a list, delimited by the #2 parentheses. The list can have any number of two-element sublists, but, in the above example, there is a single sublist delimited by the #3 parentheses. The sublist has two elements: the atomic symbol 'FACTORIAL', which is the name of the function being defined, and a lambda expression delimited by the #4 parentheses; the lambda expression has three parts: the word 'LAMBDA', the list of formal parameters delimited by #5 parentheses, and an expression. The expression is a conditional expression and is delimited by the #6 parentheses. The conditional has two parts: the predicate (EQ N 0) followed by the expression 1 and the predicate T followed by the expression (TIMES N (FACTORIAL (DIFFERENCE N 1))). Since the symbol 'N' appears in the list of formal parameters following the word 'LAMBDA', its value is determined by the value of the actual parameter when the procedure is invoked. Within the COND statement, if the value of variable N is equal to zero, then the value of the conditional is 1, which is the value returned by the function FACTORIAL. If the value of N is not zero, then the second predicate T is evaluated; its value is **true**. (The reason that the symbol 'T' in the conditional evaluates to **true** and therefore can be used in this way is that in most LISP systems, the atom 'T' is initialized to **true**; similarly, NIL is initialized to **false** (*nil*).) In this case the value of FACTORIAL would be (TIMES N (FACTORIAL (DIFFERENCE N 1))), which invokes the procedure recursively with new actual parameter $N-1$. This expression causes $N-1$ to be evaluated, the result of that evaluation to be passed to FACTORIAL, and the result produced by FACTORIAL to be multiplied by N. The final product is the value returned by FACTORIAL. The syntax may be awkward and the final form difficult to read, but the definition is indeed the factorial function.

We can summarize the procedure definition facility of LISP this way. The definition:

(DEFINE (QUOTE((name (LAMBDA (formal_parameters) expression)))))

in LISP notation is equivalent to:

procedure name(formal _ parameters);
name : = expression;
return;
end name;

in algorithmic notation. We are now ready to look at various procedure definitions expressed in LISP notation and to study recursion as a mechanism for working with data structures.

Exercise 8.11. Give the LISP definition for Ackermann's function.

8.7.1 Preliminary procedures

We will assume throughout the following discussion that circular or recursive structures are not created. That is, the only structures that we will allow are those that can be expressed in list or dot notation or created using CONS. This is not a severe restriction, and it does prevent the procedures being defined from getting into an infinite loop. (Recursive structures can be created, if the programmer manipulates the CAR and CDR fields of cells using the RPLACA and RPLACD primitives. See McCarthy et al, 1969. Our assumption simply disallows the use of these primitives.)

One useful predicate on pairs of list structures is the test for equality. The function EQ tests for equality of atoms, and the predicates ATOM and NULL test whether or not their arguments are atomic or the empty list, respectively. Using these functions, one can write a procedure EQUAL that tests whether or not two structures are identical. The predicate EQUAL is defined as follows:

```
(DEFINE (QUOTE (
  ( EQUAL (LAMBDA (X Y) (COND
    ( (ATOM X) (COND ( (ATOM Y) (EQ X Y) )
                     (  T      NIL) )
    ( (ATOM Y) NIL)
    ( (EQUAL   (CAR X) (CAR Y) ) (EQUAL (CDR X) (CDR Y) ) )
    (  T       NIL)  ) ) ) ) )
```

which can be written in algorithmic notation this way:

```
procedure EQUAL (X,Y);
case
    ( ATOM(X) ):
        begin
            case
                ( ATOM(Y) ):                EQUAL := EQ(X,Y);
```

```
              (true):                    EQUAL := NIL;
          end case
        end;
      ( ATOM(Y) ):                       EQUAL := NIL;
      ( EQUAL(CAR(X),CAR(Y) ) ):         EQUAL := EQUAL(CDR(X),CDR(Y) );
      ( true):                           EQUAL := NIL;
  end case;
  return,
  end EQUAL;
```

Note that the same general principle is used here that was used in the procedure SEARCH given in the previous section. In this procedure, if both actual parameters are atomic, then the predicate EQ is used. If either X is atomic and Y is not atomic, or vice versa, then EQUAL returns NIL. Otherwise, if the left halves of the structure are EQUAL, then EQUAL returns the value obtained after testing the right halves of the structure for EQUALity. (On many LISP systems, EQUAL is also used for comparing numeric values for equality. For those systems, EQUAL agrees with the above definition for non-atomic values, and EQUAL must be used when comparing numeric atoms.)

A second useful predicate determines whether or not a given structure is a member of a list; that is, let L be the list (e1 e2 e3 . . . en), and let S be a non-null list structure. The question, 'is S identically one of the elements e1 through en?' is answered by the predicate MEMBER:

```
(DEFINE (QUOTE (
    (MEMBER (LAMBDA (S L) (COND
      ( (NULL L) NIL )
      ( (EQUAL (CAR L) S)    T )
      (     T      (MEMBER S (CDR L) ) ) ) ) ) ) ) ) )
```

This procedure first tests whether or not L is empty and if so returns NIL. If L is not empty then MEMBER checks whether or not S EQUALs the first member of the list. If it does, then MEMBER returns T; otherwise, MEMBER returns the value obtained by applying itself recursively to the remainder of the list. (Recall that if L is a list, then (CAR L) is the first element of the list, and (CDR L) is the list formed by removing the first element.)

Exercise 8.12. In LISP, write the procedure SEARCH described in the previous section.

One procedure that is sometimes useful is to apply a function to each element of a list and create a new list of the values returned by the applications of that function; that is: suppose L = (e1 e2 . . . en) is a list, then (MAPLIST L FN) returns the list ((FN e1) (FN e2) . . . (FN en)). The procedure MAPLIST is defined below:

```
(DEFINE (QUOTE (
   ( MAPLIST (LAMBDA (L FN) (COND
      ( (NULL L) NIL )
      (    T      (CONS (FN (CAR L) ) (MAPLIST (CDR L) FN) ) )
                                       ) ) ) ) ) )
```

The procedure first checks whether L is empty and if so returns NIL; otherwise, it 'CONSes' FN of the first element with MAPLIST applied to the remainder of the list. In general, this is how lists are created using CONS.

A similar procedure can be written that applies a predicate to each element of a list. A new list is created having all those elements of the original list for which the predicate returns T. The procedure DELETE is defined as follows:

```
(DEFINE (QUOTE (
   ( DELETE (LAMBDA (L PR) (COND
      ( (NULL L) NIL )
      ( (PR (CAR L) ) (CONS (CAR L) (DELETE (CDR L) PR) ) )
      (    T      (DELETE (CDR L) PR) ) )   ) ) ) ) )
```

8.7.2 Sets in LISP

A list having no repeated elements can be thought of as a set. The procedure MAKESET given below can be used to create a set by removing duplicate elements in a list. The procedures UNION, INTERSECTION, and SETDIF (set difference) can then be easily written.

```
(DEFINE (QUOTE (
   ( MAKESET (LAMBDA (L) (COND
      ( (NULL L) NIL )
      ( (MEMBER (CAR L) (CDR L) ) (MAKESET (CDR L) ) )
      (    T      (CONS (CAR L) (MAKESET (CDR L) ) ) )
         ) ) )
   ( UNION (LAMBDA (L M) (COND
      ( (NULL L) M )
      ( (NULL M) L )
      ( (MEMBER (CAR L) M) (UNION (CDR L) M) )
      (    T      (CONS (CAR L) (UNION (CDR L) M ) ) )
         ) ) )
   ( INTERSECTION (LAMBDA (L M) See Exercise 8.14.) )
   (SETDIF (LAMBDA (L M) See Exercise 8.15.) ) ) ) )
```

In this example, all four functions are defined using a single DEFINE statement.

Exercise 8.13. Define a function for appending one list onto a second list. That is, if L = (el e2. . .en) and M = (f1 f2. . .fm), then (APPEND L M) returns the list (el e2. . .en f1 f2. . .fm).

Exercise 8.14. Write the function INTERSECTION, and rewrite the function UNION using APPEND and MAKESET.

Exercise 8.15. Define the function SETDIF that has two formal parameters L and M. SETDIF assumes L and M are sets and returns the set L with all elements that are also in M removed.

8.7.3 Tables in LISP

In LISP, tables are called *association lists, property lists,* or *pair lists,* and the attributes and values are often called indicators and values. One technique for implementing property lists is to use a list whose first element is the first indicator and whose second element is the first value, and alternate between indicator and value. This is how several versions of LISP maintain the property lists of atoms as we will describe later. An alternate way is to use a list of dotted pairs where the CAR of each pair is the indicator, and the CDR of each pair is its value. We will first show how the second technique can be implemented.

The first procedure to be defined, PAIRLIS, has three arguments. The first and second arguments are lists, and the third argument is an already existing list of pairs of the desired type. PAIRLIS creates a list of pairs of corresponding elements in the first two lists, and appends the third list to that list of pairs. As an example, if ATL (attribute list) is the list (at1 at2 . . . atn), VL (value list) is the list (v1, v2 . . . vk) and PL (pair list) is the list (p1 p2 . . . pm), then (PAIRLIS ATL VL PL) would return the list ((at1.v1) (at2.v2) . . . (ati.vi) p1 p2 . . . pm), where i is the smaller of m and k. The procedure is defined as follows:

```
(DEFINE (QUOTE (
    ( PAIRLIS (LAMBDA (ATL VL PL) (COND
        ( (NULL ATL) PL )
        ( (NULL VL) PL )
        (   T      (CONS (CONS (CAR ATL) (CAR VL) )
                         (PAIRLIS (CDR ATL) (CDR VL) PL) ) )
                         ) ) ) ) ) )
```

The second procedure ASSOC has two arguments, a pair list and an indicator. ASSOC either returns the first pair whose CAR EQUALs the given indicator, or it returns NIL. ASSOC is defined this way:

```
(DEFINE (QUOTE (
        ( ASSOC (LAMBDA (PL IND) (COND
        ( (NULL PL) NIL )
        (   T      (COND
                        ( (EQUAL  IND  (CAR  (CAR  PL) ) )  (CAR
                        PL) )
                        (    T      (ASSOC (CDR PL) IND) ) ) )
                                   ) ) ) ) ) )
```

The procedure SUB2 is similar to ASSOC but returns either the value of an indicator, if one is found or the indicator itself, if a value is not found. Furthermore, SUB2 assumes that indicators are atoms. The definition of SUB2 follows:

```
(DEFINE (QUOTE (
        ( SUB2 (LAMBDA (PL IND) (COND
        ( (NULL PL) IND )
        ( (EQ (CAR (CAR PL) ) IND)   (CDR (CAR PL) ) )
        (   T      (SUB2 (CDR PL) IND) ) ) ) ) ) ) )
```

The third table handling procedure is called SUBLIS. Let ST be an arbitrary structure and let PL be a list of pairs. The procedure SUBLIS searches through the structure ST and replaces each atom, say AT, that it finds in ST by the value (SUB2 PL AT). Thus if an atom has a value in PL then that value is substituted in the structure; otherwise the structure is unchanged. The function SUBLIS is defined this way:

```
(DEFINE (QUOTE (
        (SUBLIS (LAMBDA (PL ST) (COND
        ( (ATOM ST) (SUB2 PL ST) )
        (     T      (CONS (SUBLIS PL (CAR ST) )
                     (SUBLIS PL (CDR ST) ) ) ) ) ) ) ) ) )
```

Using this procedure, one can think of the atoms in a structure as being variables and the pair list PL as holding the values of the variables. The procedure SUBLIS substitutes the corresponding value for each variable. The pair list holds the bindings of variables to be substituted in the structure.

8.7.4 Property lists and structures in LISP

As a final example, we will discuss the property list facility of LISP and show one way that arbitrary graph structures can be embedded in the LISP language.

The LISP system maintains a structure called a *property list* for each symbolic atom. A property list is a table that holds a set of indicators and their corresponding values. Typical properties of atoms are their print names, their definitions as functions, and their values as constants. As an example, when a function is defined by the DEFINE function, the lambda expression for the function is placed on the property list of the function name under the special indicator EXPR. Other indicators are use for subroutines, function subroutines, constant values and so forth.

The property list of an atom is a list consisting of the number −1 followed by pairs of entries. The first element following the '−1' is an indicator, and the following entry is its value. Indicators and values alternate thereafter. The property list for the atom FACTORIAL would appear as shown in Figure 8.13, if the DEFINE statement for FACTORIAL given earlier were executed:

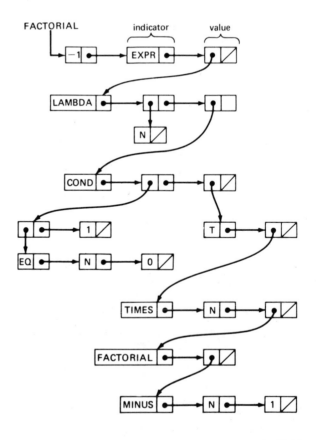

Figure 8.13. The internal representation of the procedure FACTORIAL.

The importance of the property list facility is that the programmer can insert arbitrary indicator-value pairs on the property lists of atoms, using the system functions DEFLIST and GET. The procedure DEFLIST has two arguments, a list of lists and an indicator. Each list on the list of lists must have two elements, an atom, and an expression. DEFLIST places the corresponding expression on the property list of each of the atoms under the given indicator. As an example,

(DEFLIST   (QUOTE (
                (DOG SPOT)
                (CAT FELIX)
                (MOUSE MICKEY) (QUOTE NAME))))

would place SPOT on the property list of DOG under indicator NAME; FELIX on the property list of CAT under the indicator NAME; and MICKEY on the property list of MOUSE under the indicator NAME. As a second example, the statement (DEFINE (QUOTE L)) is equivalent to (DEFLIST (QUOTE L) (QUOTE EXPR)).

The function GET has two arguments, an atom and an indicator. The value returned by GET is the value of that indicator, if one exists; otherwise GET returns NIL. In the above example, the value of (GET (QUOTE DOG) (QUOTE NAME)) would be SPOT, while the value of (GET (QUOTE DOG) (QUOTE EXPR)) would be NIL. Using these functions, we will describe how graph structures can be created and manipulated. A more comprehensive discussion of graph structures is given in Chapter 4.

A *directed graph* is an abstract set of objects called *nodes*, together with a set of pairs of nodes called *directed edges*. The edge (n1, n2) would originate at node n1 and terminate at node n2. We will assume that graphs, nodes, and edges will be labelled as shown in a typical graph below. For each graph, L, we call the set of nodes the *node set,* and, for each node, we define two sets: the *set of*

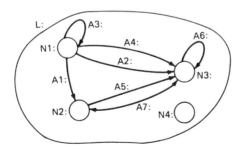

outward edges (SOG) and the *set of inward edges* (SIG). Outward edges are directed away from the node, and inward edges point toward the node. This new notation is used here because it was used by the GRASPE language, which we describe in this section. SOG and SIG correspond to the arc-set-out and arc-set-in of Chapter 4. In the illustrated graph, L is the label of the graph, N1, N2, N3, and N4 are the labels of the nodes, and A1 thru A7 are the labels of the edges. The set (N1, N2, N3, N4) is the node set, and for node N3, (A2, A4, A5, A6) is the set of inward edges, and (A6, A7) is the set of outward edges.

One way to implement structures of this general type is as follows. If L is the label of a graph, then the node set of L is placed on the property list of the atom L. We will use the indicator NS to stand for the node set. The structure for the illustrated graph is shown below. For each node on the graph, we place on the

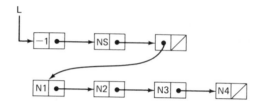

property set of the node label its *set of inward pairs* (SIP), dotted with its *set of outward pairs* (SOP). The graph name will be the indicator. The set of inward pairs of node N is a set of dotted pairs, where each pair consists of a node label dotted with an arc label. One dotted pair occurs for each arc that terminates at node N. The node label is the label of the node where the arc begins, and the arc label is the label of the connecting arc. A similar definition is made for the set of outward pairs. This is illustrated below. For the above graph, the set of outward pairs for node N1 is ((N2.A1) (N3.A2) (N1.A3) (N3.A4)), and the set of inward pairs for node N1 is ((N1.A3)). As is evident, the set of outward pairs is represented as a list of dotted pairs whose CARs are the destination nodes and

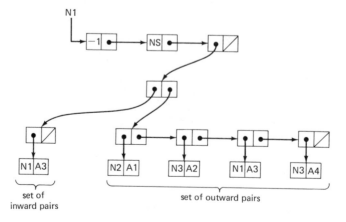

whose CDRs are the arc labels. Similarly, the set of inward pairs is represented as a list of dotted pairs whose CARs are the source nodes and whose CDRs are the arc labels. There is no special structure for the arcs, but from the sets of inward and outward pairs, we can easily obtain the sets of inward and outward arcs, the set of adjacent nodes, and so forth.

It is not difficult to see that all the information contained in the graph is represented in the structure. What remains to be done is to describe the procedures for 1) building such structures, 2) modifying them, and 3) extracting pertinent information from them. In the paragraphs that follow, we will give some of the necessary procedures and assign several others as exercises. For a complete system that uses these structures, see Pratt and Friedman (1971).

The procedure NODESET has a graph label as its argument and either returns the node set of the graph, if one exists or NIL (**false**) otherwise. The functions SOP (*Set of Outward Pairs*) and SIP (*Set of Inward Pairs*) have two arguments, a node label and a graph label. Each function either returns the required set, if it exists or NIL, if it does not. For the graph illustrated earlier, (NODESET (QUOTE L)) returns the value (N1 N2 N3 N4), (SIP (QUOTE N1) (QUOTE L)) returns ((N1.A3)), and (SOP (QUOTE N1) (QUOTE L)) returns ((N2.A1) (N3.A2) (N1.A3) (N3.A4)). These functions are defined as follows:

```
(DEFINE (QUOTE (
        ( NODESET (LAMBDA (L) (GET L (QUOTE NS) ) ) )
        (SOP (LAMBDA (N L) (CDR (GET N L) ) ) )
        (SIP (LAMBDA (N L) (CAR (GET N L) ) ) )       ) ) )
```

Given the sets of inward and outward pairs, it is very easy to obtain the sets of inward and outward edges and the sets of nodes adjacent to the given node, both inwardly adjacent, outwardly adjacent, or either. For outward and inward edges, we simply need the CDRs of the dotted pairs on the sets of outward and inward pairs, and, for outward and inward nodes, we need the CARs of the dotted pairs of outward and inward pairs. For the set of adjacent nodes, we take the union of the two sets described above. Using the following notation:

SON set of outward nodes
SIN set of inward nodes
SOG set of outward edges
SIG set of inward edges
SAN set of adjacent nodes = SON union SIN
SAG set of adjacent edges = SOG union SIG

we can define the functions as follows:
```
(DEFINE (QUOTE (
    (SON (LAMBDA (N L) (MAKESET (MAPLIST(SOP N L)
        (QUOTE CAR) ) ) ) )
    (SIN (LAMBDA (N L) (MAKESET (MAPLIST(SIP N L)
        (QUOTE CAR) ) ) ) )
    (SOG (LAMBDA (N L) (MAKESET (MAPLIST (SOP N L)
        (QUOTE CDR) ) ) ) )
    (SIG (LAMBDA (N L) (MAKESET (MAPLIST (SIP N L)
        (QUOTE CDR) ) ) ) )
    (SAN (LAMBDA (N L) (UNION (SON N L) (SIN N L) ) ) )
    (SAG (LAMBDA (N L) (UNION (SOG N L) (SIG N L) ) ) ) ) ) ) )
```

Recall that MAPLIST applies its function argument to each element of a list and returns the list of values so derived. For function SON, MAPLIST is applied to the set of outward pairs with function CAR. Hence it returns a list of nodes with possible duplicates. MAKESET simply deletes the duplication and returns the resulting set; the functions SIN, SOG, and SIG work the same way. The functions SAN and SAG take the unions of the other two sets.

The entire set of procedures for manipulating graphs as represented here are given in Figure 8.14. Functions whose names begin with 'C' create the structures: CEGR (create graph), CISN (create isolated node), COP (create outward pair), and so forth. Functions whose names begin with 'D' destroy structures: DOG (delete outward edge, DEGR (delete graph), etc. The following sequence of LISP statements creates the graph shown earlier:

```
(CEGR (QUOTE L))
(CISN (QUOTE N1) (QUOTE L) )
(CISN (QUOTE N2) (QUOTE L) )
(CISN (QUOTE N3) (QUOTE L) )
(CISN (QUOTE N4) (QUOTE L) )
(COP (QUOTE N1) (QUOTE A1) (QUOTE N2) (QUOTE L) )
(COP (QUOTE N1) (QUOTE A2) (QUOTE N3) (QUOTE L) )
(COP (QUOTE N1) (QUOTE A3) (QUOTE N1) (QUOTE L) )
(COP (QUOTE N1) (QUOTE A4) (QUOTE N3) (QUOTE L) )
(CIP (QUOTE N3) (QUOTE A5) (QUOTE N2) (QUOTE L) )
(CIP (QUOTE N3) (QUOTE A6) (QUOTE N3) (QUOTE L) )
(CAP (QUOTE N2) (QUOTE A7) (QUOTE N3) (QUOTE L) )
```

Because of the tediousness of repeatedly typing the word "QUOTE" for data entry as shown above, many LISP systems called EVALQUOTE LISP automatically insert the "QUOTE." When using EVALQUOTE LISP, the input consists of pairs consisting of a function name and a list of arguments. The above data would appear as shown below for EVALQUOTE LISP.

CEGR (L)
CISN (N1 L)
CISN (N2 L)
CISN (N3 L)
CISN (N4 L)
COP (N1 A1 N2 L)
COP (N1 A2 N3 L)
COP (N1 A3 N1 L)
COP (N1 A4 N3 L)
CIP (N3 A5 N2 L)
CIP (N3 A6 N3 L)
CIP (N2 A7 N3 L)

Notice also that function definitions must also be modified for EVALQUOTE LISP. Figure 8.14 shows the appearance of data for use with an EVALQUOTE LISP system.

```
DEFINE ( (
    (SOP (LAMBDA (N L) (CDR (GET N L) ) ) )
    (SOG (LAMBDA (N L) (MAKESET (MAPCAR (SOP N L) (QUOTE CDR) ) ) ) )
    (SOGX (LAMBDA (N M L) (FUNC (SOP N L) (QUOTE CAR) (QUOTE CDR) ) ) )
    (SON (LAMBDA (N L) (MAKESET (MAPCAR(SOP N L) (QUOTE CAR) ) ) ) )
    (SONX (LAMBDA (N A L) (FUNC A (SOP N L) (QUOTE CDR) (QUOTE CAR) ) ) )
    (SIP (LAMBDA (N L) (CAR (GET N L) ) ) )
    (SIG (LAMBDA (N L) (MAKESET (MAPCAR (SIP N L) (QUOTE CDR) ) ) ) )
    (SIGX (LAMBDA (N M L) (FUNC M(SIP N L) (QUOTE CAR) (QUOTE CDR) ) ) )
    (SIN (LAMBDA (N L) (MAKESET (MAPCAR(SIP N L) (QUOTE CAR) ) ) ) )
    (SINX (LAMBDA (N A L) (FUNC A(SIP N L) (QUOTE CDR) (QUOTE CAR) ) ) )
    (SAP (LAMBDA (N L) (UNION(SOP N L) (SIP N L) ) ) )
    (SAG (LAMBDA (N L) (UNION(SOG N L) (SIG N L) ) ) )
    (SAGX (LAMBDA (N M L) (UNION (SOGX N M L) (SIGX N M L) ) ) )
    (SAN (LAMBDA (N L) (UNION(SON N L) (SIN N L) ) ) )
    (SANX (LAMBDA (N A L) (UNION(SONX N A L) (SINX N A L) ) ) )
    (FUNC (LAMBDA (X PRS FA FB) (COND( (NULL PRS)NIL)( (EQUAL (FA(CAR PRS) )X)
        (CONS (FB (CAR PRS) ) (FUNC X(CDR PRS)FA FB) ) )
        (T (FUNC X(CDR PRS)FA FB) ) ) ) )
    (DOP(LAMBDA (N A M L) (AND (PUTPROP N L(CONS (SIP N L) (SETDIF (SOP N L)
        (LIST(CONS M A) ) ) ) ) (PUTPROP M L (CONS (SETDIF (SIP M L) (LIST
        (CONS N A) ) ) (SOP M L) ) ) ) ) ) )
```

Figure 8.14. A listing of GRASPE, a complete set of graph processing functions. This listing shows GRASPE for an EVALQUOTE LISP. The functions UNION, SETDIF, MAKESET, and MEMBER must be added.

```
(DOG(LAMBDA (N L) (NOT(MAPC(SOP N L) (FUNCTION(LAMBDA(P) (DOP N(CDR P)
    (CAR P)L) ) ) ) ) ) )
(DOGX(LAMBDA(N M L) (NOT (MAPC(SOGX N M L) (FUNCTION(LAMBDA(A)
    (DOP N A M L) ) ) ) ) ) )
(DIP(LAMBDA(N A M L) (DOP M A N L) ) )
(DIG(LAMBDA (N L) (NOT(MAPC(SIP N L) (FUNCTION(LAMBDA(P) (DIP N(CDR P)
    (CAR P) L) ) ) ) ) ) )
(DIGX(LAMBDA(N M L) (DOGX M N L) ) )
(DAP (LAMBDA(N A M L) (AND(DOP N A M L) (DIP N A M L) ) ) )
(DAG (LAMBDA(N L) (AND(DOG N L) (DIG N L) ) ) )
(DAGX(LAMBDA(N M L) (AND(DOGX N M L) (DIGX N M L) ) ) )
(DISN(LAMBDA(N L) (OR(SOP N L) (SIP N L) (AND(PUTPROP N L NIL)
    (PUTPROP L(QUOTE NS) (SETDIF (NODESET L) (LIST N) ) ) ) ) ) )
(DEGR(LAMBDA(L) (OR(NODESET L) (REMPROP L(QUOTE NS) )T) ) )
(CEGR(LAMBDA(L) (OR(NODESET L) (PUTPROP L (QUOTE NS)NIL) ) ) )
(CISN (LAMBDA(N L) (OR(GET N L) (AND(PUTPROP N L(QUOTE (NIL.NIL) ) )
    (PUTPROP L(QUOTE NS)
    (UNION(LIST N) (NODESET L) ) ) ) ) ) )
(COP (LAMBDA(N A M L) (AND(CISN N L) (CISN M L)
    (PUTPROP N L(CONS(SIP N L) (UNION(SOP N L) (LIST(CONS M A) ) ) )
    (PUTPROP M L(CONS(UNION(SIP M L) (LIST(CONS N A) ) )
    (SOP M L) ) ) ) ) )
(CIP(LAMBDA(N A M L) (COP M A N L) ) )
(CAP(LAMBDA(N A M L) (AND(COP N A M L) (CIP N A M L) ) ) )
(PUTPROP(LAMBDA(AT IND VAL) (AND(DEFLIST(LIST(LIST AT VAL) )IND) ) ) )
(NODESET(LAMBDA(L) (GET L(QUOTE NS) ) ) )
(MAPLIST(LAMBDA(X FN) (COND( (NULL X)NIL) (T(CONS(FN X) (MAPLIST(CDR X)
    FN) ) ) ) ) )
(MAPCAR(LAMBDA(X FN) (COND( (NULL X)NIL) (T(CONS(FN(CAR X) ) (MAPCAR
    (CDR X)FN) ) ) ) ) )
) )
```

Figure 8.14. (continued)

8.7.5 Comments about the efficiency of these techniques

It should by now be evident that LISP is a very flexible and concise language for creating and manipulating structures. It has taken very little code to develop rather complex structures, and, in general, LISP system implementations are not large either. However, the procedures developed recursively, such as described in Figure 8.14 for graph processing, are often very inefficient. Consider for example the function UNION: UNION has two arguments, two sets to be included; UNION picks off the first element of one of the sets and looks to see if it is in the other set; this is done using MEMBER. MEMBER does a linear search of the second set. If two sets having 100 elements each are to be UNIONed together, then 100 linear searches of 100 elements would be made, and the execution time would be proportional to the product of the lengths of the sets.

Contrast this with a hash table implementation of sets. The search time is essentially constant. Furthermore, the number of searches has to be only as large as the number of elements in the smaller of the two sets. This suggests tht if set-theoretic operations are to be done frequently, then a language in which hashed tables are supported should be used.

As anyone who uses LISP knows, most implementations of LISP provide facilities that enable reasonably efficient, non-recursive functions to be coded. The PROG feature can be used to create program loops for searching list structures, and RPLACA and RPLACD enable the CAR and CDR fields of cells to be directly modified, enabling rapid insertions and deletions of cells in lists. It is therefore not necessary to reconstruct an entire list when an element is to be added or deleted, as was done, for example, by UNION. In fact, a combination of recursion and iteration enable efficient yet concise implementations to be easily developed in LISP. (An efficient implementation of the graph processing procedures described here has already been coded in LISP.)

Since there are no declarations in LISP, it is necessary for the LISP system to determine the types of data to be processed (for addition, subtraction, etc.) before the operation can be performed. This dynamic type-checking also takes time and reduces the efficiency of arithmetic operations. (This problem is shared with all languages that dynamically determine datatypes, including SNOBOL4.)

8.8 SUMMARY

Recursion is a powerful tool, for both defining functions and for implementing them in programming languages; however, recursive procedures are often inefficient, particularly when they rebuild entire structures rather than simply inserting or deleting elements. Although powerful, recursion is a tool which must be used with care. When it comes to the ease of using recursion for manipulating data structures, LISP is probably the best language available, and because of its popularity, many dialects are available, often incorporating facilities that overcome the disadvantages just mentioned.

Projects

Project 8.1. Experiments performed while using LISP for a variety of applications have shown that approximately 80% of all CDRs that are dotted pairs are in the adjacent cell in memory. This suggests that memory can be saved by having a flag in the CAR field of each cell that has the value 1 if the CDR is a dotted pair that is in an adjacent cell, and the value 0, if the CDR is not a dotted pair or not in the adjacent cell. If the flag has value 1, then the CDR field of the given cell is not present, and the adjacent cell contains the dotted pair represented in the same way. If the flag has value 0, then the CDR must be inspected to determine if it is a pointer to a dotted pair or a value. This is illustrated below:

The LISP structure (AB(CDEH)(F.G) as it may appear in memory.

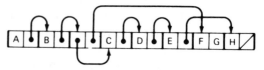

The same structure using the suggested representation.

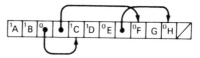

Describe memory management routines for such a system. Can you find a linear time memory compaction algorithm for this system?

Project 8.2 A *context-free grammar* consists of the following four parts:
1. A set N of symbols called non-terminal symbols.
2. A set T, disjoint from N, called terminal symbols.
3. An element S from the set N called the start symbol (or sentence variable).
4. A finite set of pairs called productions, whose first elements are symbols in N, and whose second elements are strings of symbols in S or T.

For example, G = ((S,R) , (0,1), S, ((S,0S1), (S,0R1), (R,1R0), (R,10))) designates a grammar, where S and R are non-terminal symbols, 0 and 1 are terminal symbols, S is the start symbol, and (S,0S1), (S,0R1), (R,1R0), and (R,10) are the productions.

A string $\bar{x}' = x_1 x_2 x_3 \ldots x_{i-1} y_1 y_2 \ldots y_{m-1} y_m x_{i+1} x_{i+2} \ldots x_n$ is directly derivable from the string $\bar{x} = x_1 x_2 x_3 \ldots x_{n-1} x_n$ in G in case $(x_i, y_1 y_2 y_3 \ldots y_m)$ is a production in G. For example, 00010111 is directly derivable from 000R111 in the above grammar, since (R,10) is a production. A string $\bar{y}$ is derivable from a string $\bar{x}$ in case there is a sequence of strings $\bar{x}_1, \bar{x}_2, \ldots \bar{x}_k$, where $\bar{x} = \bar{x}_1$, $\bar{y} = \bar{x}_k$, and $\bar{x}_j$ is directly derivable from $\bar{x}_{j-1}$ for j from 2 to k. The string 00001110001111 is derivable from 00S11 in the grammar G given above since:

000S111	is directly derivable from	00S11
0000R1111	is directly derivable from	000S111
00001R01111	is directly derivable from	0000R1111
000011R001111	is directly derivable from	00001R01111
00001110001111	is directly derivable from	000011R001111.

A string is in the language generated by G in case it can be derived from the sentence variable.

Design and code a procedure for determining whether a given string is derivable within a given grammar. The input to your procedure should be a grammar given in the form used in the above example, followed by the subject string. Output should either be a message NOT DERIVABLE in case the string is not derivable in the given grammar, or a sequence of strings, starting with the start symbol, and ending with the subject string, where each string is directly derivable from the previous string.

REFERENCES AND ADDITIONAL READINGS

Books

Allen, J.R. (1978) *Anatomy of LISP*. New York: McGraw-Hill Book Company.

Berkeley, E.C., and Bobrow, D.G. (Eds.) (1966) *The Programming Language LISP: Its Operation and Applications*. Cambridge, Massachusetts: The M.I.T. Press.

Church, A. (1941) The Calculi of Lambda-Conversion. Princeton, N.J.: Princeton University Press.

Friedman, D.P. (1974) *The Little LISPer*. Palo Alto, California: Science Research Associates, Inc.

Maurer, W.D. (1972) *The Programmer's Introduction to LISP*. New York: American Elsevier Inc.

McCarthy, J.; Abrahams, P.W.; Edwards, D.J.; Hart, T.P.; and Levin, M.I. (1962) *LISP 1.5 Programming Language*. Cambridge, Massachusetts: The M.I.T. Press. (Second Edition copyright 1969.)

Rogers, H. Jr. (1967) *Theory of Recursive Functions and Effective Computability*. New York: McGraw-Hill Book Company.

Siklóssy, L. (1976) *Let's Talk LISP*. Englewood Cliffs, New Jersey: Prentice-Hall, Inc.

Winston, P.H. (1977) *Artificial Intelligence*. Reading, Massachusetts: Addison-Wesley Publishing Co., Inc.

Articles and Technical Reports

Bobrow, D.G., and Murphy, D.L. A note on the efficiency of a LISP computation in a paged machine. *CACM* Vol. 11, No. 8, Aug. 1968, 558.

Bobrow, D.G., and Murphy, D.L. Structure of a LISP system using two-level storage. *CACM* Vol. 10, No. 3, Mar. 1967, 155-159.

Cheney, C.J. A nonrecursive list compacting algorithm. *CACM* Vol. 13, No. 11, Nov. 1970, 677-678.

Clark, D.W. A fast algorithm for copying list structures. *CACM* Vol. 21, No. 5 May 1978, 351-357.

Clark, D.W., and Green, C. An empirical study of list structures in LISP. *CACM* Vol. 20, No. 2, Feb. 1977, 78-87.

Fisher, D.A. Copying cyclic list structures in linear time using bounded workspace. *CACM* Vol. 18, No. 5, May 1975, 251-252.

Friedman, D.P.; Dickson, D.C.; Fraser, J.J.; and Pratt, T.W. GRASPE 1.5. A graph processor and its applications. 1969. Department of Computer Science, The University of Houston.

Lindstrom, G. Copying list structures using bounded workspace. *CACM* Vol. 17, No. 4, April 1974, 198-202.

McCarthy, J. Recursive functions of symbolic expressions and their computation by machine. *CACM* Vol. 3, No. 4, Apr. 1960, 184-195.

Naur, P. (Editor); Backus, J.W.; Bauer, F.L.; Green, J.; Katz, C.; McCarthy, J.; Perlis, A.J.; Rutishauser, H.; Samelson, B., Vauquois, B.; Wegstein, J.H.; Wijngaarden, A. van; and Woodger, M. Revised Report on the algorithmic langauge ALGOL 60. *CACM* Vol. 6, No. 1, Jan. 1963, 1-17.

Pratt, T.W., and Friedman, D.P. A language extension for graph processing and its formal semantics. *CACM* Vol. 14, No. 7, July 1971, 460-467.

Robson, J.M. A bounded storage algorithm for copying cyclic structures. *CACM* Vol. 20, No. 6, June 1977, 431-433.

9
Some Systems That Use
Interesting Data
Structures

OVERVIEW

In this chapter, we describe three examples of software systems where structures play an important part. The systems described are: IMS, a hierarchical database system; ESP³, a high-level graphics system; and GROPE, a graph processing system. For each system, we discuss the purpose of the system, the user interface language, and the data structures used in its implementation.

9.1 INTRODUCTION

Although we have given a number of examples to illustrate the concepts presented in this text, most of them have been small or incomplete. In this chapter, we describe three interesting and different software systems where data structures play an important part. The first system described is IMS (Information Management System), a database system that runs on the IBM 360/370 series computers. IMS is a hierarchical system and uses tree structures to store the data. The second system described is ESP³ (Extended SNOBOL Picture Pattern Processor), a high-level graphics language; The ESP³ system uses multi-linked structures to represent pictures. The third system is GROPE (Graph Operations Extension), a graph processing system implemented as a set of FORTRAN routines on CDC 6600 and IBM 360 computers. GROPE uses a variety of data structures including, lists, sets, nodes, arcs, and graphs. Although the three systems were developed by different people for different purposes, they share a common goal of providing a group of users with a special purpose, high-level, easy to use system, where the data structures and basic algorithms are provided. We will now examine each of these systems in some detail.

410

9.2 IMS: A HIERARCHICAL DATABASE SYSTEM

A *database* is a collection of data stored on a secondary storage device and used in an application system; for example, a hospital might keep a database containing information concerning patients, employees, supplies, and accounting. Most databases are relational structures; that is, there are relationships linking the basic entities together. In the hospital example, some of the employees may be doctors; for each doctor, there will be a group of patients who are current patients of that doctor, and a group of patients who are previous patients of that doctor. Also, for each patient, there will be a group of doctors who have cared for that patient.

A hospital administrator receiving a complaint from a patient may wish to find out who all the doctors are who have cared for that patient. The administrator must *query* the database to find the answer to his question. Thus a database system must consist of a structure for storing the data and a retrieval system, including a query language. In this section, we will discuss the structure and implementation of IMS, a hierarchical database system. We will also describe briefly the IMS query language. The design of a query language is beyond the scope of this book.

9.2.1 The IMS structure

The information in IMS databases has a natural hierarchic structure. For example, for each patient in the hospital database, name, age, height, weight, address, phone number, current allergies, current ailments, and past history of illnesses could be important. In an IMS system, the data for one patient might have the structure shown below. Each patient has a patient number which uniquely identifies him or her and a record containing personal data, such as age, height, weight, address, and so on; each patient can have several different current allergies, each of which is identified by an allergy number, and several different current ailments, each of which is identified by an ailment number.

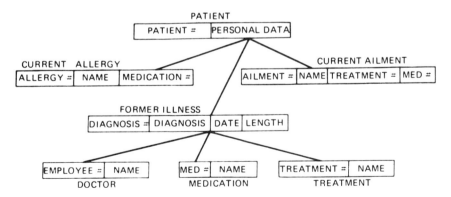

Finally, each former illness is included in the structure, along with each doctor who cared for the patient during that illness, each medication given, and each treatment required.

The blocks in the tree structure shown above represent IMS *segment prototypes,* and the tree structure shows the hierarchical relationship among the segment prototypes. The block labeled PATIENT is a prototype for all PATIENT *segments.* Each segment will be a fixed length block containing a set of fixed length *field occurrences;* thus each PATIENT segment will contain two fixed length fields: PATIENT NUMBER and PATIENT DATA. (In reality, the PERSONAL DATA field would probably be partitioned into the many smaller fields it represents; we have merged them for simplicity.)

Associated with each PATIENT segment will be a set of CURRENT ALLERGY segments, a set of CURRENT AILMENT segments, and a set of a FORMER ILLNESS segments. Associated with each FORMER ILLNESS segment will be a set of DOCTOR segments, a set of MEDICATION segments, and a set of TREATMENT segments. Figure 9.1 shows such a structure for a sample patient, Jane Doe.

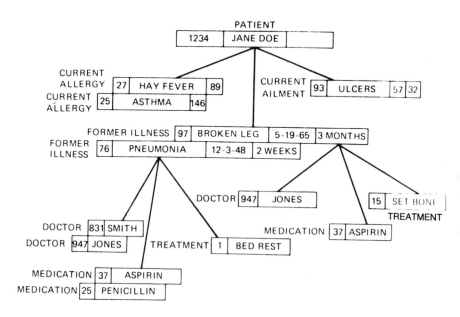

Figure 9.1. The structure of a patient segment for a sample patient, Jane Doe, in a hypothetical IMS system.

Jane is identified in the database by her PATIENT NUMBER of 1234. She currently has two allergies, hayfever and asthma, represented by CURRENT ALLERGY segments, and one current ailment, ulcers, represented by a CURRENT AILMENT segment. She has had two former illnesses that required hospitalization, pneumonia in 1948 and a broken leg in 1965. For the pneumonia occurrence, she was cared for by Doctors Smith and Jones, given aspirin and penicillin, and treated with bed rest. For the broken leg, she was given aspirin, and the bone was set. From looking at the structure, we might suspect that aspirin is a favorite remedy of Dr. Jones, but we would have to look at more patients to be sure.

The data structure for each patient has a tree-like organization. The root node is a PATIENT segment; the PATIENT segment is the *parent* segment of three child segments, some of which have child segments of their own. Note that the branches in Figure 9.1 are not necessarily meant to be pointers but merely show the hierarchic structure. We will examine several different implementations of the structure after briefly describing the IMS query language.

9.2.2 The IMS query language

The IMS system permits the definition of a structure, insertion and deletion of segments, and retrieval of information from the structure. We will be concerned with only the insertion, deletion, and retrieval aspects. The following operations are allowed:

	Operation	Use
GU	GET UNIQUE	direct retrieval
GN	GET NEXT	sequential retrieval
GNP	GET NEXT WITHIN PARENT	sequential retrieval under current parent
GHU	GET HOLD UNIQUE	direct retrieval with DLET/REPL option
GHN	GET HOLD NEXT	sequential retrieval with DLET/REPL option
GHNP	GET HOLD NEXT WITHIN PARENT	sequential retrieval under current parent with DLET/REPL option
ISRT	INSERT	add a new segment

| DLET | DELETE | delete a segment |
| REPL | REPLACE | replace a segment |

We will use the simplified syntax suggested by Date (1975) to illustrate the use of some of these commands.

The GET UNIQUE (GU) command causes a forward scan starting at the beginning of the database. The segment retrieved will be the first segment that satisfies all the conditions specified in the command. For example, the command:

> GU PATIENT (PATIENT # = 1234)
>   CURRENT ALLERGY (MEDICATION # = 146)

would retrieve Jane's 'asthma segment'.
The command:

> GU PATIENT (PATIENT # = 1234)
>   FORMER ILLNESS (DIAGNOSIS # = 97)
>   DOCTOR

would retrieve a segment representing Dr. Jones.

The GET NEXT (GN) command starts scanning at the current position in the database and retrieves the next segment that satisfies the specified conditions. The current position is the segment last accessed by any retrieval or insertion operation. Thus to access all of Jane's doctors in the database of Figure 9.1, we could use a set of commands containing a loop as follows:

> GU PATIENT (PATIENT # = 1234)
>   ILLNESS
>   DOCTOR
> LOOP GN DOCTOR
>   GO TO LOOP

To retrieve all the doctors for just one illness, the GET NEXT WITHIN PARENT command can be used.

Once information is retrieved using a GU or GN command, it can be printed or further manipulated by the user. The commands for working with the retrieved data are beyond the scope of this discussion. Likewise, when a user wishes to insert new data into a database, he or she must first build the segment to be inserted, also using commands not described here. Once built, the new segment can be inserted in the database using the IMS INSERT command.

The INSERT (ISRT) command allows insertion of a new segment anywhere in the database. For example, to insert a new medication under one of Jane's illnesses, an IMS User must build the new segment in the I/O area and then issue the command:

ISRT PATIENT (PATIENT # = 1234)
FORMER ILLNESS (NAME = PNEUMONIA)
MEDICATION

The insert command finds the parent of the segment to be inserted and then enters the new segment in the correct place.

9.2.3 Implementations

The IMS system can use any of four different storage and access methods. We will describe two of these implementation techniques: a simple sequential implementation and a more complex linked and hashed implementation.

Sequential implementation

In the sequential implementation, the hierarchical sequence is represented entirely by physical contiguity. Each segment is immediately followed by its successor in the hierarchical sequence. The sequential implementation of part of the hospital database, including the structure of Figure 9.1, is shown below. Notice that with this representation, insertion and deletion would be difficult. Thus for sequentially implemented IMS databases, only the "get" operations (GU, GN, and GNP) are allowed. In order to insert or delete segments, the user must create a whole new database.

PATIENT	CURRENT ALLERGY	CURRENT ALLERGY	CURRENT AILMENT
123	27 HAY FEVER	25 ASTHMA	93 ULCERS
JANE DOE	89	146	57 32

FORMER ILLNESS	DOCTOR	DOCTOR	MEDI- CATION	MEDI- CATION	TREATMENT
76 PNEUMONIA	947	831	37	25	1
12-3-48 2 WEEKS	JONES	SMITH	ASPIRIN	PENICILLIN	BED REST

FORMER ILLNESS	DOCTOR	MEDI- CATION	TREATMENT	PATIENT
97 BROKEN LEG	947	37	15	1235
5-19-65 3 MO	JONES	ASPIRIN	SET BONE	JOHN DEER

Linked and hashed implementation

A more complex implementation, which is also more powerful than the sequential implementation, uses both hashing and linking techniques. Two blocks of storage are provided for the database: the root segment area and the overflow area. Root segments each have a sequence field. The value in the sequence field is used as a hash key, and the hash function produces an address of a record in the root segment area. When inserting a root segment into the database, the IMS routine will store the new segment in the record whose address was produced by the hash funtion if that record has enough space. If the record does not have enough space, the routine will store the new segment in the next available record in the root segment area or, if the root segment area is full, in the next available record in the overflow area. All root segments that hash to one record are kept on a linked list ordered by sequence number and with header in the record accessed by the hash function.

This concept is illustrated below for four PATIENT segments which all hash to the same record in the root segment area. There are 100 records in the root segment area, each capable of holding two segments; the hash function is $f(x) =$ remainder $(x/100) + 1$. Patient 1234 is the first segment that hashes to address 35, and it is stored there; patient 334 is the second segment that hashes to address 35, and it is also stored in the segment beginning at address 35; patient 734 is the third segment to hash to address 35. The record at address 35 is now full, and the

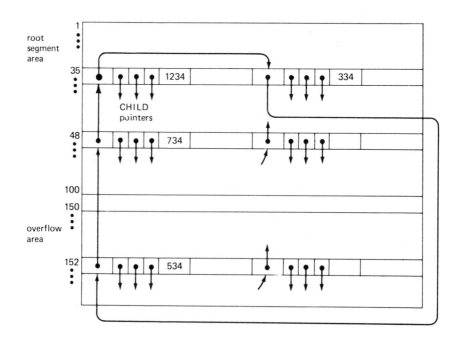

new segment is stored in the next available record in the root segment area at address 48. Finally, patient 534 hashes to address 35 when the root segment area is completely full and is stored in the overflow area at address 152. In the final configuration shown, the four patient segments that hashed to address 35 are all linked together in a circular list ordered by field PATIENT NUMBER.

A segment that is not a root segment is stored in the next available location in the overflow area, connected to its parent segment or previously stored sibling by a pointer. This scheme is shown below for the structure of Figure 9.1. Each node has zero or more CHILD pointers, which point to its children, and zero or one NEXT pointers, which point to its next sibling. The system must maintain a prototype of each segment type, so that it knows the structure of each segment pointed to by a CHILD pointer.

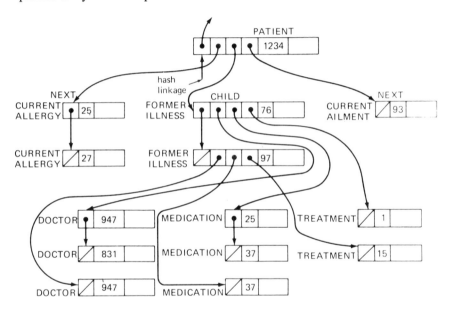

The linked and hashed implementation provides direct access to root segments and allows insertion and deletion of any segments; thus it is more powerful and more efficient than the sequential implementation. The sequential implementation has the advantage that the database can be stored on and accessed from a magnetic tape. The linked and hashed access requires more space and the direct access capabilities of disk I/O.

9.3 ESP³: A GRAPHICS SYSTEM

ESP³ (Extended SNOBOL Picture Pattern Processor) is a high-level graphics language which allows users to create complex two-dimensional line drawings and search them using a SNOBOL-like picture pattern facility. The data structures used by the graphics portion of the language will be described in this chapter.

9.3.1 The ESP³ language

Data types in the ESP³ language include the POINT, an ordered pair of numbers representing a point in two-space, and the PICTURE, a data structure representing a two-dimensional line drawing. A PICTURE is constructed as a result of evaluating a picture expression. A picture expression consists of a set of picture components joined together by the composition operator "¢." The components of a picture expression may be other pictures, or they may be chosen from the set of built-in, geometric primitives: LINE, CIRCLE, ARC, FIGURE, FUNCTION, CURVE, RECTANGLE, SQUARE, and TRIANGLE. During evaluation of a picture expression, each component of the expression may be assigned to a variable. This is done using the dynamic assignment operator ":". These concepts are illustrated in the following ESP³ assignment statement. (The '+' indicates a continuation line.)

```
SNOWMAN = BODY : DRAW('CIRCLE','BOT=(3,2);RADIUS=2;')
+    ¢ HEAD : DRAW('CIRCLE','BOT=POINT(BODY,"TOP");
+                 RADIUS=1;')
+    ¢ LEFTARM : DRAW('LINE','START=POINT(BODY,"LEFT");
+                 ANGLE=180;LENGTH=1;')
+    ¢ RIGHTARM : DRAW('LINE','START=POINT(BODY,'RIGHT');
+                 ANGLE=0;LENGTH=1;')
```

This statement instructs the system to create a line drawing consisting of: a circle of radius 2 (inches) with bottom point at the point (3,2); a circle of radius 1 with bottom point at the top point of the first circle; a horizontal line of length 1 with start point at the left point of the first circle, extending to the left; and a second horizontal line of length 1 with start point at the right point of the first circle, extending to the right. The first circle is assigned to the identifier BODY, the second circle to the identifier HEAD, the lines to the identifiers LEFTARM and RIGHTARM, respectively, and the whole picture to the identifier SNOWMAN. Evaluation of the picture expression causes the construction of a data structure that will be described in the next section. The statement:

PLOT = SNOWMAN

will then cause the following picture to be drawn. (The point labels in the picture are not printed by ESP³.)

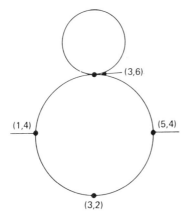

Another important aspect of the ESP³ system is its ability to translate, rotate, or scale any ESP³ picture. The ESP³ statement:

```
FLIPPED_SNOWMAN = TURNPIC(SNOWMAN,'ANGLE=180;
+              ABOUT=POINT(SNOWMAN,"TOP");')
```

causes the system to construct a data structure representing the picture derived from rotating the SNOWMAN picture 180 degrees counterclockwise about its top point. The statement:

```
MOVED_FLIPPED_MAN = TRANSPIC(FLIPPED_SNOWMAN,
+          'POINT(FLIPPED_SNOWMAN,"BOT")=>(8,2)')
```

causes the system to construct a data structure representing the picture derived from moving the FLIPPED_SNOWMAN picture in such a way that the bottom point of the resultant picture is at the point (8,2). Finally, the statement:

```
SNOWPIC = SNOWMAN ¢ MOVED_FLIPPED_MAN
```

causes the system to construct a data structure representing the following picture.

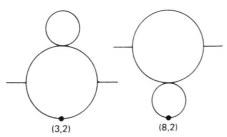

9.3.2 The picture data structure

The data structure for an ESP³ picture was designed:

1. for simplicity;
2. to minimize storage requirements;

and 3. to lend itself to transformations, plotting, or any calculations that might be performed on a picture.

The following design was used.

An instance of a primitive is represented by a (sequential) table or block with fields containing the name of the primitive and a minimal, canonical set of features needed to represent and manipulate that primitive. For example, the center and radius are one minimal set of features that can be used to represent a circle; the canonical set of features used by ESP³ to represent a circle are the top point and the radius. In addition to the minimal canonical features, each primitive has a field containing its LTOP (left topmost) point, which was used in the pattern recognition portion of the system. For a circle, the LTOP point corresponds to the top of the circle. In the SNOWMAN example, the circle called BODY would be represented by the table:

PRIM	'CIRCLE'
RADIUS	2
LTOP	(3,6)

and the line called LEFTARM would be represented by the table:

PRIM	'LINE'
START	(1,4)
END	(0,4)
LTOP	(0,4)

A picture that has only primitive components consists of a header pointing to a singly linked list of tables representing primitives. The header is of the form:

FIRSTCOMP	LASTCOMP	REFTABLE	MATCHFORM

where FIRSTCOMP and LASTCOMP contain pointers to the first and last primitives in the picture. REFTABLE contains a pointer to a table of special user-defined names associated with the picture and will not be covered in this text. MATCHFORM is used in the pattern recognition portion of the system and will also not be covered. Each table representing a primitive has an extra field, the FLINK field, that contains the forward link or pointer to the next primitive. The data structure for the SNOWMAN picture is shown below.

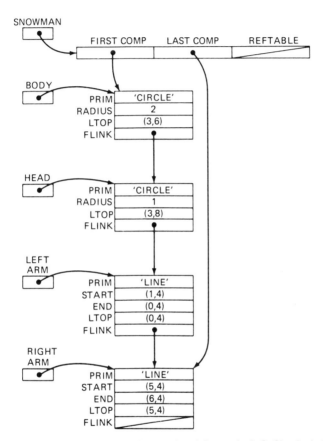

Redrawn from Data Structures for Picture Processing: A Survey by L.G. Shapiro in *Computer Graphics and Image Processing* **11**, 1979. Academic Press, New York.

Picture components that are pictures, but not primitives, are represented by tables which contain a pointer to the picture, an indication of which transformation (if any) is to be applied to the picture, and the parameters of the transformation. For example, the rotated snowman FLIPPED_SNOWMAN is a picture consisting of the single table:

PICTURE	● ────────	→ to SNOWMAN
TRANSF	'ROTE'	
ABOUT	(3,8)	
ANGLE	180	

and the translated, rotated snowman, MOVED_FLIPPED_MAN, consists of the table:

PICTURE	● ────────	→ to FLIPPED_SNOWMAN
TRANSF	'TRAN'	
DX	5	
DY	−6	

In the table for FLIPPED_SNOWMAN, 'ROTE' indicates the rotation: (3,8) is the point to rotate about, and 180 is the angle of the rotation. In the table for MOVED_FLIPPED_MAN, 'TRAN' indicates translation, and the 5 and 6 indicate the number of inches to move in the X and Y directions, respectively.

The picture SNOWPIC, which is composed of the pictures SNOWMAN and MOVED_FLIPPED_MAN, is represented by the data structure of Figure 9.2. Note that the primitives in SNOWMAN are represented only once in storage. The original picture SNOWMAN, the rotated snowman, FLIPPED_SNOWMAN, and the translated rotated snowman, MOVED_FLIPPED_MAN, all share one copy of the primitives. Thus the criterion to minimize storage has been met, as has the criterion for simplicity. A transformation can easily be added to the data structure by creating a new picture consisting of one component that points to the old picture and specifies the transformation to be applied and its parameters. We will now describe the algorithm for plotting a picture from its data structure.

9.3.3 Plotting a picture

In order to plot a picture, routines must be called to plot all the primitives with all transformations applied. For instance, in order to plot the picture FLIPPED_SNOWMAN, we must apply the rotation transformation to each primitive of SNOWMAN and then plot the resulting rotated, primitives. We will assume the existence of a set of device dependent plotting routines which actually cause the physical plotting to take place. In particular the statement:

call LINE (START, END)

causes a straight line to be plotted from point START to point END, and the statement:

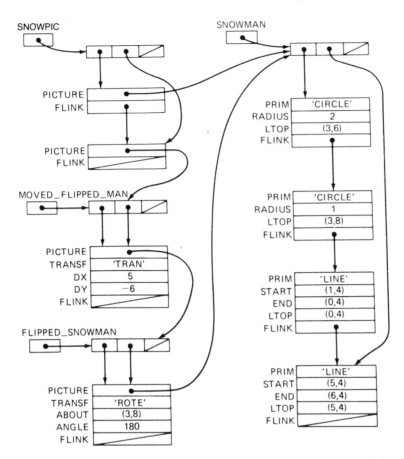

Figure 9.2. The data structure for the entire picture SNOWPIC. The structure includes the structures for the pictures SNOWMAN, FLIPPED_SNOWMAN, and MOVED_FLIPPED_MAN, and the transformations involved. Redrawn from Data Structures for Picture Processing: A Survey by L.G. Shapiro in *Computer Graphics and Image Processing* **11**, 1979. Academic Press, New York.

call CIRCLE(RADIUS, LTOP)

causes a circle to be plotted with its top point at point LTOP and with radius RADIUS.

The plotting algorithm involves a traversal of the data structure. Processing a picture node means processing each of its first-level components. Processing a non-primitive component means placing in a stack the transformation information from that component, processing the picture node pointed to by that component, and then removing from the stack the transformation information for that component. Processing a primitive component means applying all transformations currently on the stack to the primitive and calling a device dependent plotting routine to plot the transformed primitive. The procedure PLOT given below implements the traversal algorithm.

In this procedure, separate templates are given for primitive components representing circles, primitive components representing lines, non-primitive components with no transformation, non-primitive components with translation transformation, non-primitive components with rotation transformation, and non-primitive components with scale transformation. The procedure is written this way, because the original ESP³ system was implemented this way in SNOBOL4. In some other languages (PASCAL, for example), it is necessary to use one type of structure for all picture components. This is due to the fact that PASCAL requires a pointer to be declared as a pointer to a particular type of structure, and one pointer could not sometimes point to a primitive component and sometimes to a non-primitive component. We have assumed in this algorithm that a single pointer can point to any structure and that the function DATATYPE with argument POINTER returns the template name of the structure to which POINTER is pointing in the form of a character string. Note that there are statements in the algorithm where the template name of a structure pointed to by a pointer is not explicitly known. Since making the template names known in every statement would require awkward changes to the SNOBOL algorithm, the algorithm was left in its original form, using SNOBOL4 pointer conventions instead of our own.

The algorithm uses a sequential stack ASTACK that holds pointers to components containing transformations. Thus adding a transformation to the stack is implemented by pushing a pointer onto the stack and removing a transformation is implemented by popping a pointer. We will use the procedures PUSH and POP and the predicate FULL for sequential stacks given in Chapter 2. Calls to these procedures are of the form:

> **call** PUSH(STACK, VAL)
> **call** POP(STACK)
> **if** (FULL(STACK)) **then** . . . **endif**

where STACK has the structure defined by:

> **template** 1 STACK,
>   2 HEADER,
>   3 TOPEL   INTEGER,
>   3 MAXELS   INTEGER,
>   2 ELEMENTS(●MAXELS)   DATATYPE;

TOPEL is the element number of the top stack element, and MAXELS is the maximum number of elements the stack can hold. DATATYPE stands for the data type of the stack elements. (See Chapter 2 for precise definitions.) A sequential linear list was chosen to implement the stack in this algorithm. The list is used as a stack when pushing and popping have to be done. Applying all the stacked transformations to a primitive is achieved by sequentially traversing the list from the top to the bottom, accessing the transformation pointed to by each element, and applying the appropriate formula, depending on type of transformation and parameters.

procedure PLOT(APIC);
comment Traverse the picture APIC and call the device dependent plot routines to plot the primitives;

template	1	POINT,	
		2 XVAL	REAL,
		2 YVAL	REAL;
template	1	PICTURE,	
		2 FIRSTCOMP	COMPONENTPTR,
		2 LASTCOMP	COMPONENTPTR,
		2 REFTABLE	POINTER,
		2 MATCHFORM	POINTER;
template	1	CIRCLEPRIM,	
		2 FLINK	COMPONENTPTR,
		2 PRIM	STRING,
		2 LTOP	POINT,
		2 RADIUS	REAL;
template	1	LINEPRIM,	
		2 FLINK	COMPONENTPTR,
		2 PRIM	STRING,
		2 LTOP	POINT,
		2 START	POINT,
		2 END	POINT;
template	1	PICTURECOMP,	
		2 FLINK	COMPONENTPTR,
		2 PICTURE	POINTER **to** PICTURE;
template	1	TRANCOMP,	
		2 FLINK	COMPONENTPTR,
		2 PICTURE	POINTER **to** PICTURE,
		2 TRANSF	STRING,
		2 DX	REAL,
		2 DY	REAL;
template	1	ROTECOMP,	
		2 FLINK	COMPONENTPTR,
		2 PICTURE	POINTER **to** PICTURE,
		2 TRANSF	STRING,
		2 ABOUT	POINT,
		2 ANGLE	REAL;

```
template      1      SCALCOMP,
                     2 FLINK               COMPONENTPTR,
                     2 PICTURE             POINTER to PICTURE,
                     2 TRANSF              STRING,
                     2 ABOUT               POINT,
                     2 FACTOR              REAL;
template      1      STACK,
                     2 HEADER,
                        3 TOPEL            INTEGER,
                        3 MAXELS           INTEGER,
                     2 ELEMENTS(●MAXELS)   COMPONENTPTR;
template      COMPONENTPTR POINTER to (CIRCLEPRIM, LINEPRIM,
                     PICTURECOMP, TRANCOMP, ROTECOMP,
                     SCALCOMP);
declare APIC PICTURE;
declare COMPPTR COMPONENTPTR;
declare ASTACK STACK;
if (APIC = null) then return endif;
COMPPTR := [APIC].FIRSTCOMP;
while (COMPPTR ≠ null) do
     begin
         case
             (DATATYPE([COMPPTR]) = 'PICTURECOMP'):
                 call PLOT([COMPPTR].PICTURE);
             (DATATYPE([COMPPTR]) = 'TRANCOMP'
               or DATATYPE([COMPPTR]) = 'ROTECOMP'
               or DATATYPE([COMPPTR]) = 'SCALCOMP'):
                 begin
                     if (FULL(ASTACK) ) then call ERROR endif;
                     call PUSH(ASTACK, COMPPTR);
                     call PLOT([COMPPTR].PICTURE);
                     call POP(ASTACK)
                 end;
             (DATATYPE ([COMPPTR]) = 'CIRCLEPRIM'):
                 begin
                     NEWRAD := APPLY_STACK_TO_REAL
                                 (ASTACK, [COMPPTR].RADIUS);
                     NEWTOP := APPLY_STACK_TO_POINT
                                 (ASTACK,[COMPPTR].LTOP);
                     call CIRCLE(NEWRAD, NEWTOP)
                 end;
             (DATATYPE([COMPPTR] = 'LINEPRIM'):
                 begin
                     NEWSTART := APPLY_STACK_TO_POINT
                                 (ASTACK, [COMPPTR].START);
```

```
        NEWEND := APPLY_STACK_TO_POINT
                (ASTACK, [COMPPTR].END);
        call LINE(NEWSTART, NEWEND)
        end;
      end case;
      COMPPTR := [COMPPTR].FLINK
    end;
end PLOT;


procedure APPLY_STACK_TO_POINT(ASTACK,APOINT)
comment The templates in PLOT are omitted here for brevity;
comment Apply all applicable transformations on the stack ASTACK to the point
        APOINT and return the resultant point;
declare STACKPTR INTEGER;
declare ASTACK STACK;
declare ACOMP COMPONENTPTR;
declare (APOINT, NEWPOINT, APPLY_STACK_TO_POINT) POINT;
NEWPOINT := APOINT;
STACKPTR := ASTACK.HEADER.TOPEL;
while (STACKPTR > 0) do
    begin
        ACOMP := ASTACK.ELEMENTS(STACKPTR);
        case
            (DATATYPE ([ACOMP]) = 'TRANCOMP'):
                begin
                    [NEWPOINT].XVAL := [NEWPOINT].XVAL
                                    + [ACOMP].DX;
                    [NEWPOINT].YVAL := [NEWPOINT].YVAL
                                    + [ACOMP].DY
                end;
            (DATATYPE ([ACOMP]) = 'ROTECOMP'):
                begin
                    NEWX := [NEWPOINT].XVAL;
                    NEWY := [NEWPOINT].YVAL;
                    ASIN := SIN([ACOMP].ANGLE);
                    ACOS := COS([ACOMP].ANGLE);
                    ABOUTX := [[ACOMP].ABOUT].XVAL;
                    ABOUTY := [[ACOMP].ABOUT].YVAL;
                    [NEWPOINT].XVAL := (NEWX - ABOUTX) * ACOS
                                    - (NEWY - ABOUTY) * ASIN + ABOUTX;
                    [NEWPOINT].YVAL := (NEWX - ABOUTX) * ASIN
                                    + (NEWY - ABOUTY) * ACOS + ABOUTY
                end;
```

```
              (DATATYPE ([ACOMP]) = 'SCALCOMP'):
                begin
                  NEWX := [NEWPOINT].XVAL;
                  NEWY := [NEWPOINT].YVAL;
                  ABOUTX := [[ACOMP].ABOUT].XVAL;
                  ABOUTY := [[ACOMP].ABOUT].YVAL;
                  FACTOR := [ACOMP].FACTOR;
                  [NEWPOINT].XVAL := (NEWX − ABOUTX)
                              * FACTOR + ABOUTX;
                  [NEWPOINT].YVAL := (NEWY − ABOUTY)
                              * FACTOR + ABOUTY
                end;
              end case;
              STACKPTR := STACKPTR − 1
        end;
    APPLY_STACK_TO_POINT := NEWPOINT;
    return;
    end APPLY_STACK_TO_POINT;


procedure APPLY_STACK_TO_REAL(ASTACK,AREAL)
comment The templates in PLOT are omitted here for brevity;
comment Apply all applicable transformations in the stack to the real value AREAL and
        return the resultant value;
declare STACKPTR INTEGER;
declare ACOMP COMPONENTPTR;
declare ASTACK STACK;
declare (AREAL, NEWREAL, APPLY_STACK_TO_REAL) REAL;
NEWREAL := AREAL;
STACKPTR := ASTACK.HEADER.TOPEL;
while (STACKPTR > 0) do
    begin
      ACOMP := ASTACK.ELEMENTS(STACKPTR);
      if (DATATYPE([ACOMP]) = 'SCALCOMP')
      then NEWREAL := NEWREAL * [ACOMP].FACTOR endif;
      STACKPRT := STACKPTR − 1
    end
APPLY_STACK_TO_REAL := NEWREAL;
return;
end APPLY_STACK_TO_REAL;
```

Exercise 9.1. Trace through the execution of the PLOT procedure for the picture
SNOWPIC.

9.4 GROPE: A GRAPH PROCESSING SYSTEM

GROPE (*GR*aph *OP*erations *E*xtension) is a graph processing system implemented as a collection of FORTRAN routines. The GROPE system allows a user to create and manipulate a variety of data structures including atoms, ordered pairs, lists, nodes, arcs, and graphs. In this section, we will describe the relationships among GROPE structures, the operations on these structures, and their implementation.

There are numerous applications areas where relationships can be conveniently expressed in graph notation. (See Chapter 4.) Figures 9.3-9.6 show several graph structures and the relationships they represent; these include a PERT network (Figure 9.3), a transition network used for sentence recognition (Figure 9.4), a semantic network (Figure 9.5), and a graph representing pictorial relationships (Figure 9.6).

When graph structures are used to represent complex relationships, the nodes and arcs of the graph, as well as the graphs themselves, generally represent temporal, spatial, or physical quantities. As a result, in order to create an adequately general structure, it is useful to be able to assign values to arcs, nodes, and graphs. These values are used to quantify the relationships expressed by the graphs. For example, in Figure 9.3, the values shown on the arcs are the activity numbers. The mean time required for completion of activities (shown in the table) could also be represented in the graph structure.

In GROPE, each entity (graph, arc, node, list, etc.) can be assigned two different values: an *object* and a *value*. In Figure 9.3, the objects of the arcs could be the activity numbers, and the values of the arcs could be the mean time for completion of the activities. Objects and values are similar in that almost any GROPE entity can be an object or value: however, most GROPE entities are required to have an object, whereas values are usually optional.

9.4.1 GROPE entities

There are 15 different types of entities in GROPE; we will briefly describe each of these entities.

quoted integer	Small integers where range depends on the particular implementation.
atom	Integers, real numbers, double precision real numbers, function atoms (whose values are the entry point addresses of functions), and literal atoms (character strings). The data that an atom represents is called the *image* of the atom.
pair	An ordered pair, consisting of a GROPE object and a GROPE value (see below).

Activity Number	Start Node	End Node	Mean	Activity Time Standard Deviation
1	1	2	13.0	3.00
2	1	3	5.5	1.18
3	3	2	7.0	1.00
4	3	4	16.5	2.50
5	3	6	5.2	0.84
6	6	5	6.0	1.00
7	6	7	10.3	1.67
8	4	9	3.2	0.50
9	5	4	20.0	3.32
10	5	8	4.0	0.71
11	7	8	3.2	0.84
12	8	9	16.5	1.18
13	2	4	14.7	1.34

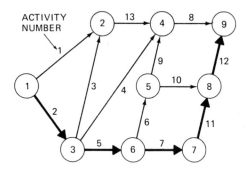

Figure 9.3. A simple PERT network. The edge labels are activity numbers, and the dark edges are the expected critical path. (from Pritsker and Kiviat [17], pp. 199-200. Reprinted by permission of Prentice-Hall, Inc., Englewood Cliffs, New Jersey.)

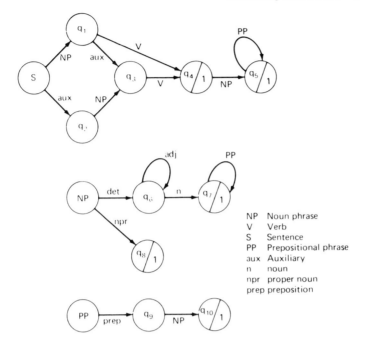

Figure 9.4. A simple transition network. S is the start state, q_4, q_5, q_7, q_8, q_{10} are the final states. (from Woods [20], p. 592).

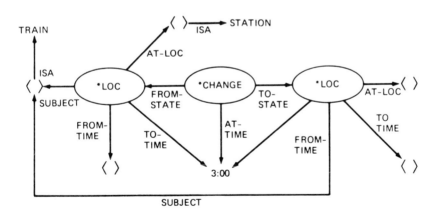

Figure 9.5. A portion of a semantic network. (Redrawn from Rumelhart and Norman [22], p. 457. Reproduced with permission).

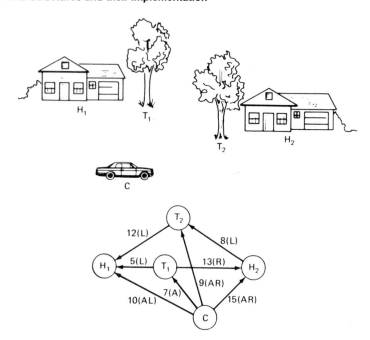

Figure 9.6. The graph representation for pictorial relationships. (after Pavlidis [24], p. 217).
Key: A=above, L=left, R=right,
H=house, T=tree, C=car.

arc	An ordered four-tuple, consisting of a from-node (the source of the arc), a to-node (the destination of the arc), an object, and a value.
node	An ordered seven-tuple, consisting of a graph (in which the node resides), a set of inward arcs, a set of outward arcs, an object, a value, a current-arc-in, and a current-arc-out. (The current-arc-in and current-arc-out are designated arcs in the set of inward and outward arcs. These are the last arcs⁻ crossed by readers traversing the graph.)
graph	A three-tuple consisting of a node set, an object, and a value.
list	A three-tuple consisting of a linear list of GROPE entities, an object, and a value.
pset	A linear list of pairs. (Short for *property set*.) A pset has no object or value.
rseto	A linear list associated with a node that contains all outward arcs attached out of the node. Rseto's have no object or value.
rseti	A linear list associated with a node that contains all inward arcs attached in to that node. Rseti's have no object or value.

nset	A set associated with each GROPE entity that contains all nodes that share the given entity as an object. An nset has no object or value.
ndset	A set associated with each graph that contains all nodes currently attached to that graph. A ndset has no object or value.
grset	A set associated with the GROPE system that contains all graphs currently related to GROPE.
reader cell	A three-tuple consisting of two GROPE entities and a value. The two entities are a set being read and an element of the set being read. The value is the value of the element being read.
obset	The set of all GROPE objects.

9.4.2 GROPE objects and values

Of the 15 types of GROPE entities, six are designated as GROPE objects. They are:

atoms	pairs
arcs	nodes
graphs	lists

Only these data types can be designated as objects of other entities. All 15 GROPE data types can be used as values for GROPE entities.

9.4.3 Relationships and structures

It can be seen from the above definitions that each GROPE entity is related to one or more other GROPE entities. In this section, we will summarize the relationships among the various entities. Each arc has a to-node and from-node. If an arc is in the arc-set-out of its from-node, it is *attached-out*; if an arc is in the arc-set-in of its to-node, it is *attached-in*. If an arc is both attached-out and attached-in, it is *attached* or *complete;* if an arc is neither attached-out nor attached-in, it is *detached* or *isolated*. If a node is in the ndset of its graph, it is *related* to the graph; a node that is not in the ndset of its graph is *isolated*. If a node is in the nset of its object, it is *attached* to its object; otherwise it is *detached* from its object or *isolated*. If a graph is in the grset of GROPE, it is *related* to GROPE.

Each object in GROPE may have a property set. If an object has a property set, that property set is *affixed* to the object. An object may have a property set, an object, and a value; however, if several objects share the same property set, then they also must have the same value. A property set consists of a list of pairs. Each pair in a property set is *attached* to that property set; if a pair is not attached to any property set, it is *isolated*. Some of these concepts are illustrated pictorially with a three-node graph.

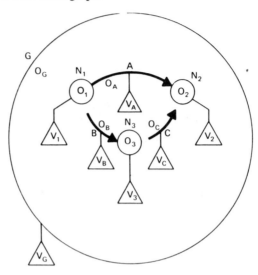

N1,N2,N3-nodes	A,B,C arcs
O_1—object of N_1	O_A object of A
O_2—object of N_2	O_B object of B
O_3—object of N_3	O_C object of C
V_1—value of N_1	V_A value of A
V_2—value of N_2	V_B value of B
V_3—value of N_3	V_C value of C

G—graph
O_G—object of G
V_G—value of G

The graph G consists of nodes N1, N2, and N3, arcs A, B, and C, and their associated objects and values. Arc A is attached to both its from-node N1 and its to-node N2; arc B is detached from its from-node N1 and attached to its to-node N3; arc C is an isolated arc. The arc-set-out of node N1 and the arc-set-in of node N2 both consist of arc A; the arc-set-in of node N3 consists of arc B. The arc-set-in of node N1, the arc-set-out of node N2, and the arc-set-out of node N3 are all empty sets. It is not apparent from the picture whether the nodes are related to G or attached to their objects, or whether G is related to GROPE. These conditions are the result of the application of GROPE operators (to be discussed).

GROPE operations can be divided into six types: functions that create GROPE structures, functions that modify GROPE structures, functions that traverse GROPE structures, functions that return existing GROPE entities, predicates, and mapping functions. We will describe several example operations from each class.

9.4.4 GROPE functions and predicates

Functions that create GROPE entities

Since there are several types of GROPE atoms, the function to create them has to be flexible. The function ATOM(BITS, NUM) returns (a descriptor to) an atom whose type is specified by the value of the argument NUM. The form of BITS depends on the type of atom; For instance, if NUM>0, a literal atom is created. In this case, BITS is a word, or vector array, containing the character string, and NUM is its dimension in words. If NUM = 0, an integer atom is created. In this case, BITS must be a fullword integer. If NUM = −3, a function atom is created. Here, BITS is an external entry point address. In any case, if an atom already exists for the (BITS, NUM) pair, that atom is returned; otherwise a new atom is created.

Arcs can be attached-out of their from-nodes, attached-in to their to-nodes, attached to both, or isolated; thus GROPE includes four arc creation functions. CRARC(NF, OBJ, NT) [create arc] creates and returns an arc with from-node NF, to-node NT, object OBJ, and value 0. The arc created by CRARC is attached to its to-node and from-node. CRARCO(NF, OBJ, NT) [create arc out] creates an arc that is attached-out of its from-node but not attached-in to its to-node; CRISR(NF, OBJ, NT) [create isolated arc] creates and returns an isolated arc.

Functions that modify GROPE structures

For each type of GROPE structure, there is a set of functions to modify it. For example, QUEUE(E,L) adds element E to the end of list L, STACK(E,L) adds element E to the beginning of list L, and POP(L) removes and returns the first element of list L; thus a list can be treated as a stack or queue or both by using the appropriate operations. Other examples include the function ANODE(OBJ, G), which adds a node with object OBJ having no attached arc to graph G; HANG(OBJ, VAL), which makes VAL the value of object OBJ, and UNHANG(OBJ) which removes any value from object OBJ. DETRCO(RC) detaches arc RC from its from-node, DETRCI(RC) detaches arc RC from its to-node, ATTRCO(RC) attaches arc RC to its from-node, and ATTRCI(RC) attaches arc RC to its to-node. In general, for each relationship, a function is provided for establishing and terminating that relationship.

Functions that traverse GROPE structures

Readers are GROPE structures that are used for searching through other GROPE structures. Readers can be used to traverse lists, property sets, arc-sets-in, arc-sets-out, nsets, ndsets, readers, the obset, the grset, graphs, or nodes. A reader consists of a linear list (actually a tree structure) of reader cells that point to various elements in the GROPE structures being traversed. An example of a reader moving operation is TO(RDR), which moves the reader RDR forward one element in the structure being traversed and returns the new element being scanned or the value zero, if RDR cannot move. If RDR is traversing a linear structure, then it moves from beginning to end (circularly, if necessary); if RDR is a graph reader scanning node N, then it is moved across the first arc in the arc-set-out of N following the *current-arc-out* of N (the last arc in the arc-set-out that was crossed), and the arc just crossed becomes the current-arc-out.

Functions that return existing GROPE entities

A user of the GROPE system often has to retrieve either a structure or an attribute of a structure. The system provides routines to return each type of structure or attribute that might be requested; for example, FRNODE(RC) returns the from-node of arc RC, GRAPH(N) returns the graph of node N, and LENGTH(LS) returns the length of the linear structure LS. Similar functions are provided for returning values of pairs, ndsets of graphs, nsets of objects, the obset of GROPE, and so on. We will see that the GROPE data structure makes these functions very easy to implement.

Predicates

GROPE also provides a set of functions that tests a condition pertaining to a structure and returns the structure if the condition is true, and 0 if the condition is false. These include such predicates as, ISARC(VAL), which returns VAL, if VAL is an arc and 0 if VAL is not an arc, and ISATBG(RDR), which returns RDR, if RDR is scanning the first element (the beginning) of a linear structure and otherwise returns 0. A third example is EQUAL(VAL1,VAL2), which returns VAL1, if VAL1 and VAL2 are equal or are element-wise, equal linear structures and 0 otherwise.

Mapping functions

In addition to the reader facilities, GROPE provides a collection of functions that apply a user-specified function to each successive element in a structure, until a prespecified condition is met. For example, MAPFT(LS, FUN, ARG2, ARG3, ARG4, ARG5) applies the function FUN to each successive element of linear structure LS with the additional arguments ARG2, ARG3, ARG4, and ARG5. If

LS consists of elements E1, E2, and E3, then the following three statements are executed:

> CALL FUN(E1, ARG2, ARG3, ARG4, ARG5)
> CALL FUN(E2, ARG2, ARG3, ARG4, ARG5)
> CALL FUN(E3, ARG2, ARG3, ARG4, ARG5).

The function LOFT(LS, FUN, ARG2, ARG3, ARG4, ARG5) applies FUN to each successive element of LS, and if FUN returns a valid GROPE entity, that entity is queued into a new list. After LOFT has processed each element of LS, the newly created list is returned. The function ANDFT(LS, FUN, ARG2, ARG3, ARG4, ARG5) applies FUN to each successive element of LS, until, for some element E, FUN(E, ARG2, ARG3, ARG4, ARG5) returns 0; when that happens, ANDFT terminates processing and returns 0. If FUN returns true for all elements in LS, then ANDFT returns LS.

9.4.5. Implementation of GROPE structures

In this section we describe the IBM 360/370 implementation of the GROPE system.

GROPE descriptors

A GROPE *descriptor* is a fullword value that designates a GROPE structure. A descriptor is divided into fields as follows:

G	KIR	KAR

The KIR field contains a five-bit flag that identifies the type of GROPE structure designated by the descriptor; the KAR field contains a pointer to the structure. The second bit of the G field is the garbage collector mark bit and is only used when the descriptor is part of a GROPE structure. The remaining bits of the G field are not used. The KIR field flag designations are:

flag	structure
1	quoted integer
2	atom
3	pair
4	arc
5	node
6	graph
7	list
8	property set

9	arc-set-out
10	arc-set-in
11	n-set
12	node set
13	graph set
14	reader cell
15	obset
0	no object (or value)

GROPE descriptors appear in several of the GROPE structures; in addition, a program variable may contain a GROPE descriptor, in which case the corresponding FORTRAN identifier designates a GROPE structure. For example, the statement:

$$A = ATOM\ ('TEST', 4)$$

assigns to A a descriptor that designates a literal atom consisting of the string 'TEST'. The statement:

$$G = CREGR(QUOTE(0))$$

creates a graph and assigns to G a descriptor for the new graph. (The object of the graph is the quoted integer 0.) In these examples, we say that A has data type "atom" and G has data type "graph."

Memory management

Memory for all GROPE structures is allocated dynamically from a single array provided by the user. The array is divided by the GROPE system into three heaps called SYSTEM SPACE, FULLWORD SPACE, and FREEWORD SPACE, and one stack used by the garbage collection routines. SYSTEM SPACE is used for system variables, obset buckets (see below), and an initial address list used by the garbage collector. FULLWORD SPACE is used for the images of atoms and, although allocated dynamically, memory in FULLWORD SPACE is not reclaimed once allocated. FREEWORD SPACE is used for all other GROPE structures and is allocated dynamically and reclaimed during garbage collection. Memory in FREEWORD SPACE is maintained as three lists of available space of one, two, and four words and is allocated as described in Chapter 7, Section 7.2.7.

GROPE cells

The basic unit from which GROPE structures are built is the *cell*. A cell is divided into fields as follows:

G	KIR	KAR	KSR	KDR

The G-KIR-KAR field usually forms a GROPE descriptor. The KSR field is used to contain either a pointer or a length; the KDR field generally contains a pointer to another structure.

In the remainder of this section, we will describe how some of the GROPE entities are implemented. We shall denote by '$<X>$' an entity of type X, by '$\{X\}$' a link used in forming a structure of type X, and by '[X]' a pointer to a structure of type X. For example, in a cell of the form:

VAL	LINK	SUBLIST
$<$ integer $>$	$\{$ cell $\}$	[list]

the VAL field contains an integer value, the LINK field contains a link to another cell, and the SUBLIST field contains a pointer to a list.

Quoted integers

Quoted integers are special atoms whose integer value falls between -2^{17} and $2^{17}-1$. Quoted integers are stored directly in their FORTRAN identifier (descriptor). A quoted integer has the form:

G	KIR	KAR
	1	$<$ integer $>$

where $<$integer$>$ indicates an 18-bit, 2's complement integer. G is set to '1'B in any descriptor stored in a FORTRAN identifier.

Atoms

There are five types of GROPE atoms: integer atoms, real atoms, double-precision real atoms, function atoms, and literal atoms. Their structures are indicated below:

Integer atoms, integers between -2^{17} and $2^{17}-1$:

G	KIR	KAR	KSR	KDR
	1	< integer >	{ nset }	[obset]

Here <integer> is an 18-bit, 2's complement integer stored directly in the KAR field of the atom.

Integer atoms, integers larger than $2^{17}-1$:

G	KIR	KAR	KSR	KDR
	0	{ integer }	{ nset }	[obset]

Here {integer} points to a fullword integer taken from fullword space.

Literal atoms having one or two characters:

G	KIR	KAR	KSR	KDR
	5	< image >	{ nset }	[obset]

Here <image> is one or two characters. If both characters are blank, the atom is the blank literal atom of length 1.

Literal atoms having N characters, $3 \leq N \leq 24$:

G	KIR	KAR	KSR	KDR
	N + 3	{ image }	{ nset }	[obset]

Here {image} points to [N/4] contiguous words in fullword space that contain the character string, padded on the right with blanks, if necessary.

Literal atoms having N characters, $25 \leq N \leq 40$:

G	KIR	KAR	KSR	KDR
	21 + N/4	{ image }	{ nset }	[obset]

Here {image} is a pointer to [N/4] contiguous words in fullword space that contain the character string.

Literal atoms having N characters, N>40:

G	KIR	KAR	KSR	KDR
	{ 31 }	{ image }	{ nset }	[obset]

Here {image} is a pointer to [N/4] contiguous words in fullword space. In this case, the first [N/4] words contain the character string, padded on the right with blanks, if necessary, and the last word contains 0 (an invalid 360 character), which is used to mark the end of the string.

Real atoms:

G	KIR	KAR	KSR	KDR
	2	{real}	{nset}	[obset]

Here {real} points to a single precision, floating point number in fullword space.

Double-precision real atoms:

G	KIR	KAR	KSR	KDR
	3	{ real }	{nset }	[obset]

Here {real} points to a double precision, floating point number in fullword space.

Function atoms:

G	KIR	KAR	KSR	KDR
	4	{entry}	{nset }	[obset]

Here {entry} is a pointer to the entry point of the function.

A FORTRAN GROPE program that creates several types of atoms and the data structures created by the program are shown below.

```
C     A PROGRAM TO CREATE ATOMS.
C
      DIMENSION ARRAY (500)
      EXTERNAL FUN
      CALL SETUP(ARRAY,500,.1,0)
      A1 = ATOM(500,0)
      A2 = ATOM(1234567,0)
      A3 = ATOM(3.141,−1)
      A4 = ATOM(3.1415926536,−2)
      A5 = ATOM(FUN,−3)
      A6 = ATOM('A      ',1)
      A7 = ATOM('THIS IS AN ATOM ',4)
      CALL EXIT
      END
```

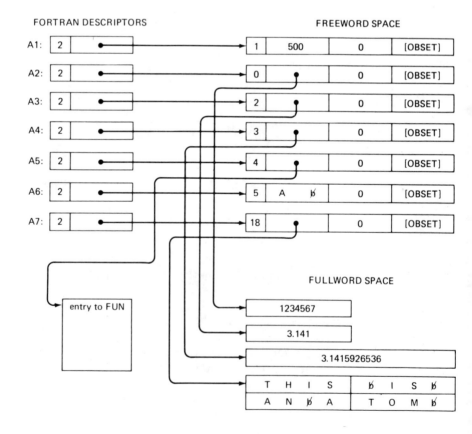

[OBSET] denotes a pointer linking the cell into the obset of GROPE.

Arcs

An arc requires two cells from freeword space and has the structure:

G	KIR	KAR	KSR	KDR
	FO	{object}	{frnode}	[rseto]
	FV	{ value}	{tonode}	[rseti]

The G-KIR-KAR field of the first cell is a descriptor for the object of the arc, and the G-KIR-KAR field of the second cell is a descriptor for the value of the arc. {FRNODE} and {TONODE} are pointers to the from-node and to-node of the arc, and [RSETO] and [RSETI] are link fields that link this arc into the RSETO and RSETI of the from-node and to-node, respectively.

Nodes

A node requires four cells from freeword space and has the structure:

G	KIR	KAR	KSR	KDR
	FO	{ object}	{ graph }	[nset]
	FV	{ value }	[ndset] .u	[ndset] .d
	4	{ curco}	< len.rseto >	{ end.rseto }
	4	{ curci }	< len.rseti >	{ end.rseti }

Here the G-KIR-KAR field of the first two cells are descriptors for the object and value of the node. The node set is doubly linked and [NDSET].u and [NDSET].d are the up and down (backward and forward) links, respectively. The KSR-KDR fields of the bottom two cells give the lengths of and pointers to the arc-set-out and arc-set-in of the node, respectively. They are the headers for the arc-set-out and arc-set-in.

Graphs

A graph uses two cells in freeword space and has the structure:

G	KIR	KAR	KSR	KDR
	FO	{object}	[grset] .u	[grset] .d
	FV	{value}	< len.ndset >	{end.ndset}

Again, the G-KIR-KAR fields are descriptors for the object and value of the graph. Figure 9.7 shows a simple GROPE graph and its storage structure.

Obset

The obset is the set of all GROPE atoms. A fraction of the user-provided memory is set aside for a collection of *obset-buckets*. The obset header is within the SYSTEM SPACE and points to the first cell that contains the obset buckets. The KIR fields of the bucket cells are unused, and the KAR, KSR, and KDR fields provide initial links to the atoms. When an atom is created, its image is used to provide a hash address to one of the obset buckets, and the atom is then added to the end of the list which originates at that bucket. The last atom on such a list has its KDR field 0, indicating end of list.

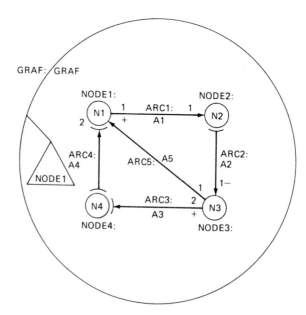

Figure 9.7. A simple GROPE graph and its memory representation.

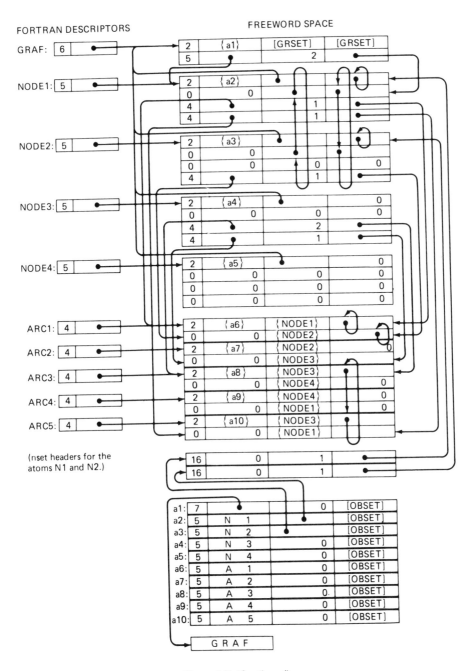

Figure 9.7. (Continued).

9.5 SUMMARY

We have presented three examples of real systems that provide special purpose software to a group of users. Each system contains complex data structures and basic procedures that allow the user to manipulate his data using relatively simple commands. It is always these two components, data structures and procedures for their manipulation, that form the basis of useful software systems.

REFERENCES AND ADDITIONAL READINGS

Books

Date, C.J. (1975) *An Introduction to Database Systems*. Reading, Massachusetts: Addison-Wesley Publishing Co., Inc.

Findler, N.V., Pfaltz, J.L., and Bernstein, H.J. (1972) *Four High-Level Extensions of FORTRAN IV: SLIP, AMPPL-II, TREETRAN, SYMBOLANG*. New York: Spartan Books.

Pritsker, A.A.B., and Kiviat, P.J. (1969) *Simulation with GASP II, A FORTRAN Based Simulation Language*. Englewood Cliffs, New Jersey: Prentice-Hall, Inc.

Tou, J.T. (Ed.) (1974) *Information Systems, COINS IV*. New York: Plenum Press.

Articles

Baron, R.J., Friedman, D.P., Shapiro, L.G., and Slocum, J. Graph Processing using GROPE/360. Technical Report 73-13, December 1973, Department of Computer Science, The University of Iowa.

Friedman, D.P. GROPE: A graph processing language and its formal definition. Technical Report No. 20, August 1973, Department of Computer Science, The University of Texas at Austin.

Nievergelt, J. Binary search trees and file organization. *Computing Surveys* Vol. 6, No. 3, Sept. 1974, 195-207.

Pavlidis, T. Grammatical and graph theoretic analysis of pictures. In Nake, F., and Rosenfeld, A. (Eds.) (1972) *Graphic Languages*. Amsterdam: North-Holland Publishing Company, 210-224.

Rich, H. SPITBOL GROPE: A collection of SPITBOL functions for working with graph and list structures. Technical Report 75-02, January 1975, Department of Computer Science, The University of Iowa.

Rumelhart, D.E., and Norman, D.A. Active semantic networks as a model of human memory. In *Advanced Papers of the Third International Joint Conference on Artificial Intelligence*. August, 1973, Menlo Park, California: Stanford Research Institute Publications Department, 450-457.

Shapiro, L.G. ESP³: A high-level graphics language. *Computer Graphics* Vol. 9, No. 1, Spring 1975, 70-75.

Shapiro, L.G., and Baron R.J. ESP[3]: A language for pattern description and a system for pattern recognition. *IEEE Trans. on Software Eng.* Vol. SE-3, No. 2, Mar. 1977, 169-183.

Slocum, J. The graph processing language GROPE. Technical Report NL-22, August 1974, Department of Computer Science, The University of Texas at Austin.

William, R. A survey of data structures for computer graphics systems. *Computing Surveys* Vol. 3, No. 1, Mar. 1971, 1-22.

Woods, W.A. Transition network grammar for natural language analysis. *CACM* Vol.13, No. 10, Oct. 1970, 591-606.

General References

Books

Aho, A.V., Hopcroft, J.E., and Ullman, J.D. (1976) *The Design and Analysis of Computer Algorithms*. Reading, Massachusetts: Addison-Wesley Publishing Co., Inc.

Aho, A.V., and Ullman, J.D. (1977) *Principles of Compiler Design*. Reading, Massachusetts: Addison-Wesley Publishing Co., Inc.

Bates, F., and Douglas, M.L. (1975) *Programming Language/One with Structured Programming*. Third Edition. Englewood Cliffs, New Jersey: Prentice-Hall, Inc.

Berkeley, E.C., and Bobrow, D.G. (Eds.) (1966) *The Programming Language LISP: Its Operation and Applications*. Cambridge, Massachusetts: The M.I.T. Press.

Berztiss, A.T. (1971) *Data Structures Theory and Practice*. New York: Academic Press, Inc.

Blatt, J.M. (1969) *Basic FORTRAN IV Programming*. Sydney, Australia: Computer Systems (Aust.) Pty. Ltd.

Brillinger, P.C., and Cohen, D.J. (1972) *Introduction to Data Structures and Non-Numeric Computation*. Englewood Cliffs, New Jersey: Prentice-Hall, Inc.

Cress, P., Dirksen, P., and Graham, J.W. (1970) *FORTRAN IV with WATFOR and WATFIV*. Englewood Cliffs, New Jersey: Prentice-Hall, Inc.

Davidson, M. (1973) *PL/I Programming with PL/C*. Boston: Houghton Mifflin Co.

Elson, M. (1975) *Data Structures*. Chicago, Illinois: Science Research Associates, Inc.

Elson, M. (1973) *Concepts of Programming Languages*. Chicago, Illinois: Science Research Associates, Inc.

Findler, N.V., Pfaltz, J.L., and Bernstein, H.J. (1972) *Four High-Level Extensions of FORTRAN IV: SLIP, AMPPL-II, TREETRAN, SYMBOLANG*. New York: Spartan Books.

Foster, J.M. (1967) *List Processing*. New York: American Elsevier Publishing Co., Inc.

Friedman, D.P. (1974) *The Little LISPer*. Palo Alto, California: Science Research Associates, Inc.

Genuys, F (1968) *Programming Languages*. New York: Academic Press.

Golden, J.T. (1965) *FORTRAN IV Programming and Computing*. Englewood Cliffs, New Jersey: Prentice-Hall, Inc.

Goodman, S.E., and Hedetniemi, S.T. (1977) *Introduction to the Design and Analysis of Algorithms*. New York: McGraw-Hill Book Co., Inc.

Gries, D. (1971) *Compiler Construction for Digital Computers*. New York: John Wiley & Sons, Inc.

Griswold, R.E. (1975) *String and List Processing in SNOBOL4: Techniques and Algorithms*. Englewood Cliffs, New Jersey: Prentice-Hall, Inc.

Griswold, R.E., and Griswold, M.T. (1973) *A SNOBOL4 Primer*. Englewood Cliffs, New Jersey: Prentice-Hall, Inc.

Griswold, R.E., Poage, J.F., and Polonsky, I.P. (1971) *The SNOBOL4 Programming Language,* Second edition. Englewood Cliffs, New Jersey: Prentice-Hall, Inc.

Harrison, M.C. (1973) *Data-Structures and Programming.* Glenview, Illinois: Scott, Foresman and Co.

Horowitz, E., and Sahni, S. (1976) *Fundamentals of Data Structures.* Woodland Hills, California: Computer Science Press, Inc.

Jensen, K., and Wirth N. (1976) *PASCAL User Manual and Report.* New York: Springer-Verlag.

Klinger, A., Fu, K.S., and Kunii, T.L. (1977) *Data Structures, Computer Graphics,* and *Pattern Recognition.* New York: Academic Press, Inc.

Knuth, D.E. (1973) *The Art of Computer Programming, Volume 1/Fundamental Algorithms,* Second Edition. Reading, Massachusetts: Addison-Wesley Publishing Co., Inc.

Lewis, T.G., and Smith, M.Z. (1976) *Applying Data Structures.* Boston, Massachusetts: Houghton Mifflin Co.

Mauer, H.A. (1977) *Data Structures and Programming Techniques.* Englewood Cliffs, New Jersey: Prentice-Hall, Inc.

Maurer, W.D. (1976) *The Programmer's Introduction to SNOBOL.* New York: Elsevier North-Holland, Inc.

Maurer, W.D. (1972) *The Programmer's Introduction to LISP.* New York: American Elsevier Inc.

McCarthy, J., Abrahams, P.W., Edwards, D.J., Hart, T.P., and Levin, M.I. (1969) *LISP 1.5 Programming Language, Second Edition.* Cambridge, Massachusetts: The M.I.T. Press.

Newell, A., Tonge, F., Feigenbaum, E.A., Green, B.F., Jr., and Mealy, G.H. (1964) *Information Processing Language-V Manual,* Second Edition. Englewood Cliffs, New Jersey: Prentice-Hall, Inc.

Pfaltz, J.L. (1977) *Computer Data Structures.* New York: McGraw-Hill Book Co., Inc.

Pratt, T.W. (1975) *Programming Languages: Design and Implementation.* Englewood Cliffs, New Jersey: Prentice-Hall, Inc.

Rosen, S. (1967) *Programming Systems and Languages.* New York: McGraw-Hill Book Co., Inc.

Rosenkrantz, D.J., and Stearns, R.E. (1976) *Compiler Design Theory.* Reading, Massachusetts: Addison-Wesley Publishing Co., Inc.

Sammet, J.E. (1969) *Programming Languages: History and Fundamentals.* Englewood Cliffs, New Jersey: Prentice-Hall, Inc.

Siklóssy, L. (1976) *Let's Talk LISP.* Englewood Cliffs, New Jersey: Prentice-Hall, Inc.

Stone, H.S. (1972) *Introduction to Computer Organization and Data Structures.* New York: McGraw-Hill Book Co., Inc.

Tou, J.T. (Ed.) (1974) *Information Systems, COINS IV.* New York: Plenum Press.

Waite, W.M. (1973) *Implementing Software for Non-Numeric Applications.* Englewood Cliffs, New Jersey: Prentice-Hall, Inc.

van Wijngaarden, A.; Mailloux, B.J.; Peck, J.E.L.; Meertens, L.G.L.T.; and Fisker, R.G. (1976) *Revised Report on the Algorithmic Language ALGOL 68.* New York: Springer-Verlag.

Wirth, N. (1976) *Algorithms + Data Structures = Programs.* Englewood Cliffs, New Jersey: Prentice-Hall, Inc.

Articles

Bobrow, D.G., and Raphael, B. A comparison of list-processing languages. *CACM* Vol. 7, No. 4, Apr. 1964, 231-240.

Clark, D.W. List structures: measurement, algorithms, and encodings. Technical Report, August 1976, Department of Computer Science, Carnegie-Mellon University.

Earley, J. Toward an understanding of data structures. *CACM* Vol. 14, No. 10, Oct. 1971, 617-627.

Gimpel, J.F. Blocks—A new datatype for SNOBOL4. *CACM* Vol. 15, No. 6, June 1972, 438-447.

Griswold, R.E., and Hanson, D.R. An overview of the SL5 programming language. Technical Report S5LD1b, October 1976, Department of Computer Science, The University of Arizona.

Guttag, J. Abstract data types and the development of data structures. *CACM* Vol. 20, No. 6, June 1977, 396-404.

Hallyburton, J.C., Jr. Advanced data structure manipulation facilities for the SNOBOL4 programming language. Technical Report S4D42, May 1974, Department of Computer Science, The University of Arizona.

Hansen, P.B. Concurrent programming concepts. *Computing Surveys* Vol. 5, No. 4, Dec. 1973, 223-245.

Hanson, D.R. The SL5 data structure facility. Technical Report S5LD6a, August 1976, Department of Computer Science, The University of Arizona.

Heller, J., and Shneiderman, B. A graph theoretic model of data structures. *SIGIR Forum,* Winter 1972, Vol. VII, No. 4, 36-44.

Kang, A.N.C.; Lee, R.C.T.; Chang, C.-L.; and Chang, S.-L. Storage reduction through minimal spanning trees and spanning forests. *IEEE Computers,* Vol. C-26, No. 5, May 1977, 425-434.

Muller, M.E., and Bank, W. An approach to multidimensional data array processing by computer. *CACM* Vol. 20, No. 2, Feb. 1977, 63-77.

Muntz, R.R., and Opdarbeck, H. Stack replacement algorithms for two-level directly addressable paged memories. *SIAM J. on Computing* Vol. 3, No. 1, Mar. 1974, 11-22.

Newell, A. and Shaw, J.C. Programming the logic theory machine. *Proc. WJCC,* 1957, 230-240.

Othmer, B.A. Programming language data structures: a comparative study. Technical Report No. 30, March 1974, The Department of Computer Science, Rutgers University.

Sammet, J.E. An annotated descriptor based bibliography on the use of computers for non-numerical mathematics. *Computing Rev.* Vol. 7, No. 4, July-Aug. 1966, B1-B31.

Shneiderman, B., and Scheuermann, P. Structured data structures. *CACM* Vol. 17, No. 10, Oct. 1974, 566-574.

Tou, J.T., and Wegner, P. (Eds.) Proceedings of a symposium on data structures in programming languages. *SIGPLAN Notices* Vol. 6, No. 2, Feb. 1971.

Weizenbaum, J. Knotted list structures. *CACM* Vol. 5, No. 3, Mar. 1962, 161-165.

Wise, D.S. Referencing lists by an edge. *CACM* Vol. 19, No. 6, June 1976, 338-342.

Author Index

Procedure Index

General Index

459